Demon Diary

Volume 3

ALSO AVAILABLE FROM  TOKYOPOP®

DEMON DIARY

Art by Kara
Story by Lee Yun Hee

VOLUME 3

Los Angeles • Tokyo • London

Translator - Lauren Na
English Adaption - Kelly Sue DeConnick
Contributing Editor - Robert Buscemi
Retouch & Lettering - Jesse Fernley
Cover Layout - Aaron Suhr

Editor - Marco Pavia
Managing Editor - Jill Freshney
Production Coordinator - Antonio DePietro
Production Manager - Jennifer Miller
Art Director - Matt Alford
Editorial Director - Jeremy Ross
VP of Production - Ron Klamert
President & C.O.O. - John Parker
Publisher & C.E.O. - Stuart Levy

Email: editor@TOKYOPOP.com
Come visit us online at www.TOKYOPOP.com

A TOKYOPOP® Manga

TOKYOPOP Inc.
5900 Wilshire Blvd., Suite 2000
Los Angeles, CA 90036

DEMON DIARY VOLUME 3

MAWAN-ILGI 1 ©2000 by KARA. All rights reserved.
First published in KOREA in 2000 by SIGONGSA Co., Ltd.
English translation rights arranged by SIGONGSA Co., Ltd.

English text ©2003 by TOKYOPOP Inc.

ISBN: 1-59182-156-8

First TOKYOPOP® printing: September 2003

10 9 8 7
Printed in Canada

THE STORY SO FAR

GODS AND DEMONS WAGE A NEVER-ENDING BATTLE, WITH THE MORTAL REALM AS THEIR BATTLEFIELD. ENTER RAENEF, THE BLACK SHEEP OF THE DEMON COURT, CLUELESS ABOUT HIS MAGICAL POWERS, AND APPARENT HEIR TO DEMON ROYALTY. THE WISE AND NOBLE ECLIPSE IS ASSIGNED TO HELP RAENEF CLAIM HIS BIRTHRIGHT AS A DEMON LORD.

IN A JOURNEY TO DISCOVER WHO HE REALLY IS, YOUNG RAENEF DECIDES TO LEAVE ECLIPSE UNTIL HE CAN RETURN A TRUE DEMON LORD. HE SPARES THE LIFE OF THE ENEMY HUMAN KNIGHT ERUTIS AND TAKES ON CHRIS, A BOY RAISED BY A PRIEST OF RASED...AND FORMS THE BEGINNING OF AN UNLIKELY ALLIANCE THAT MAY BE PIVOTAL TO CHANGING THE ROLE OF GODS AND DEMONS.

BUT IS RAENEF TRULY A DEMON LORD? CAN HE RESTORE HARMONY BETWEEN GODS AND DEMONS?

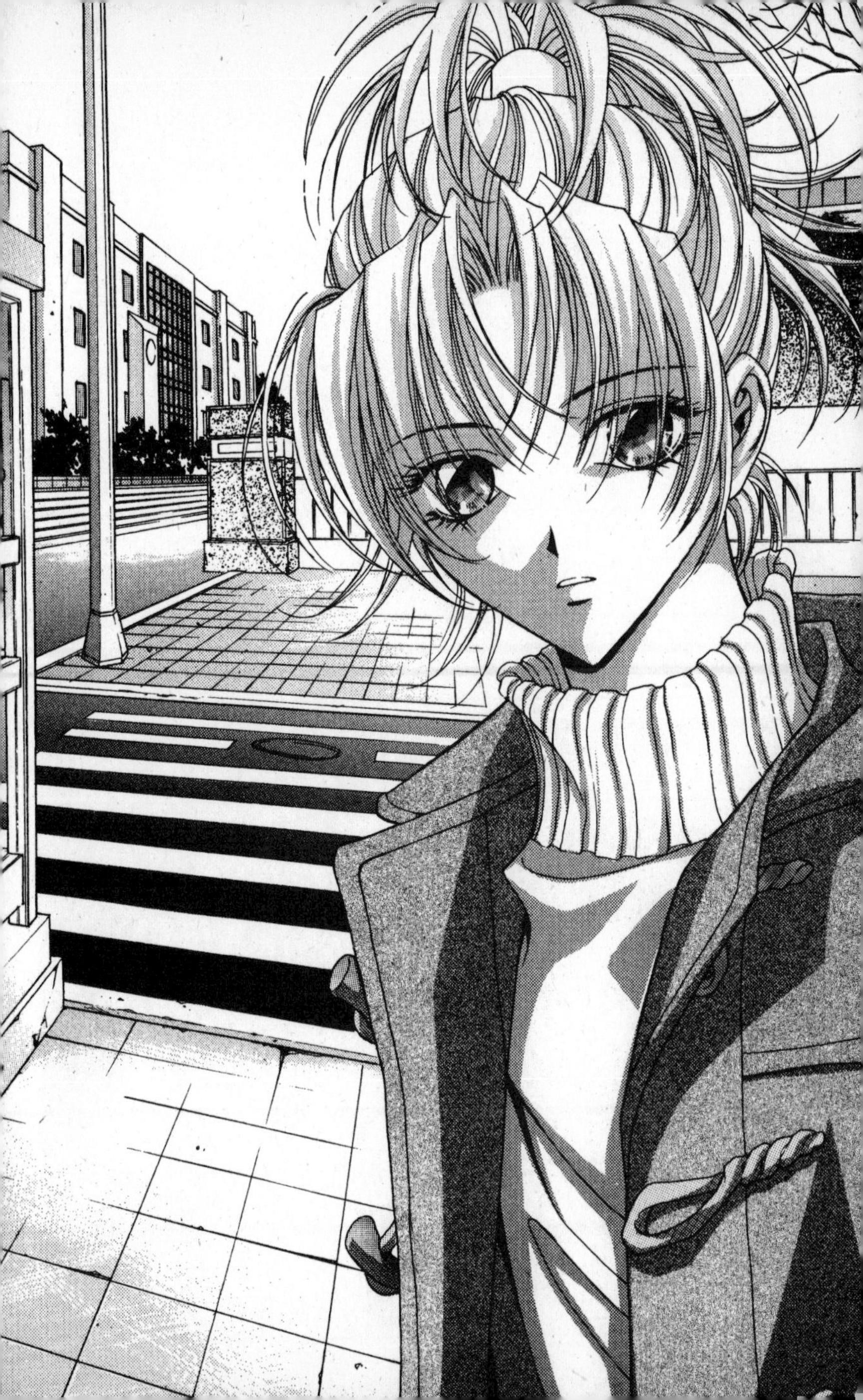

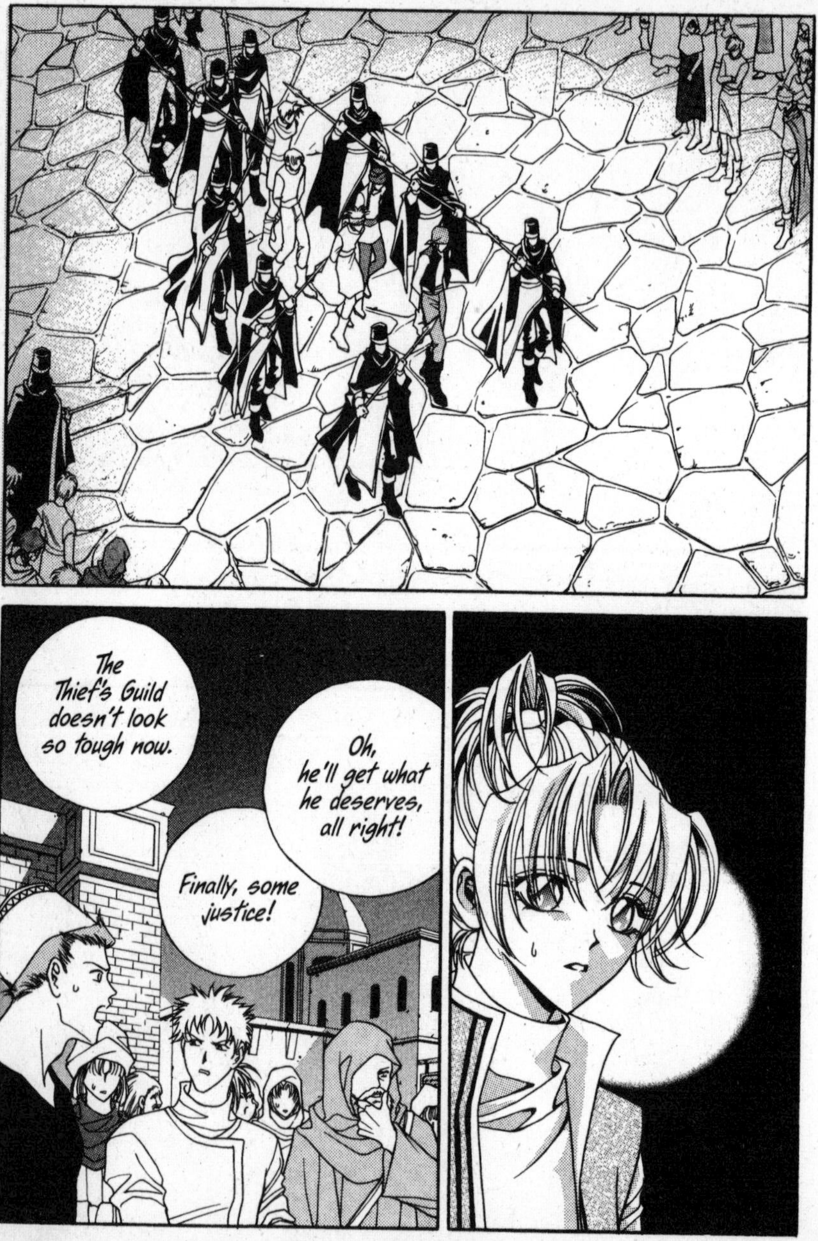
The Thief's Guild doesn't look so tough now.
Oh, he'll get what he deserves, all right!
Finally, some justice!

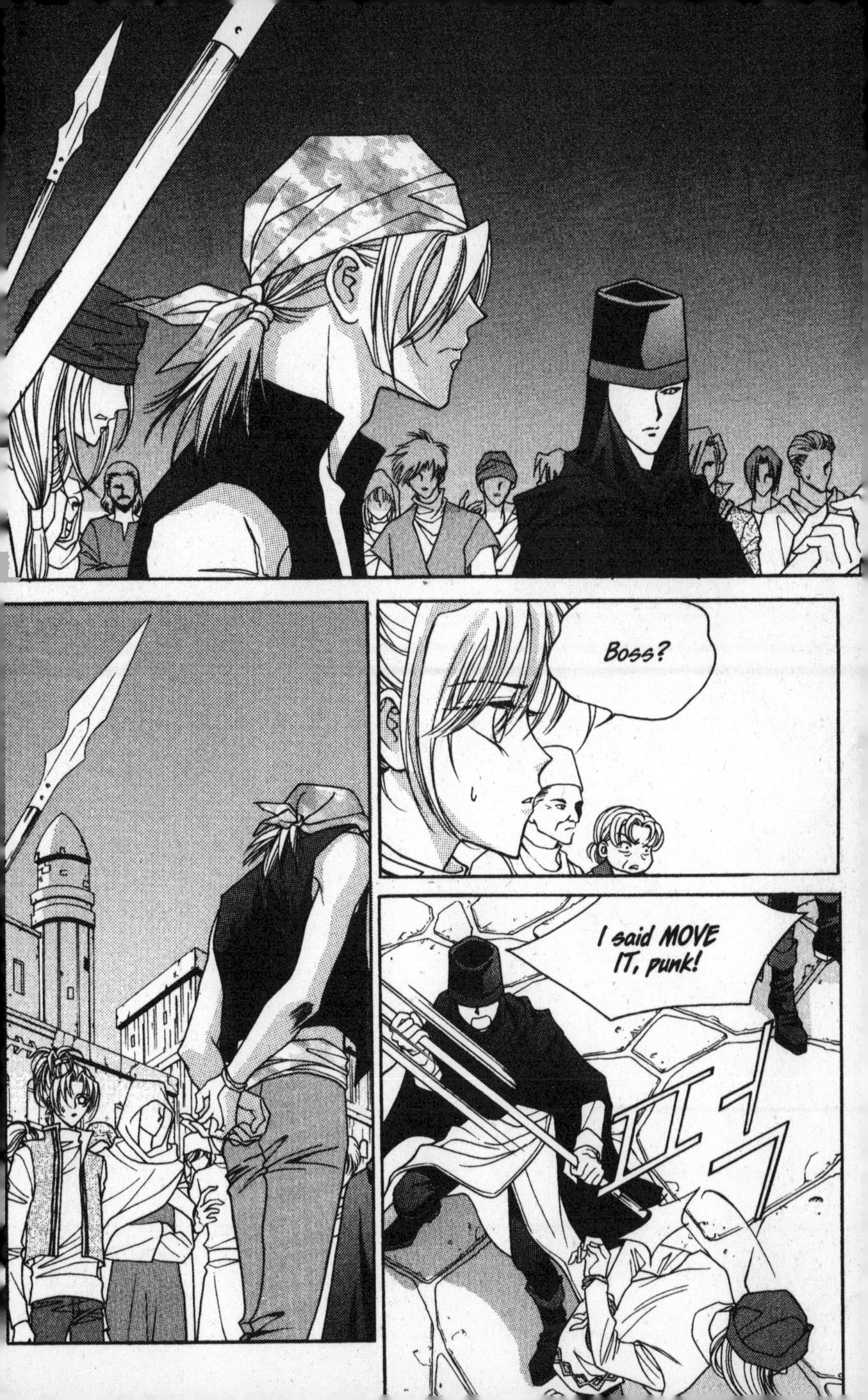

Boss?
I said MOVE IT, punk!

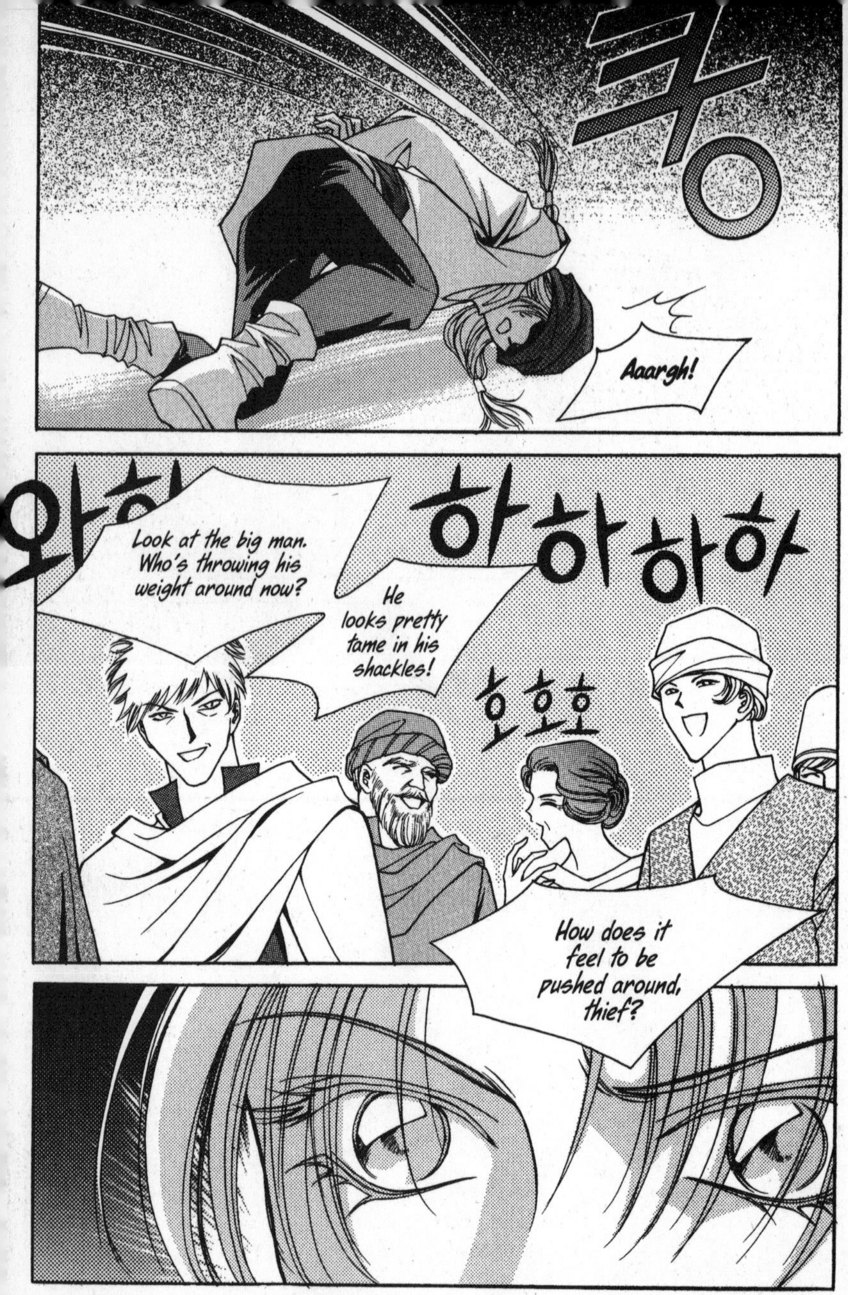

쿵
Aaargh!
와하
Look at the big man. Who's throwing his weight around now?
하하하하
He looks pretty tame in his shackles!
호호호
How does it feel to be pushed around, thief?

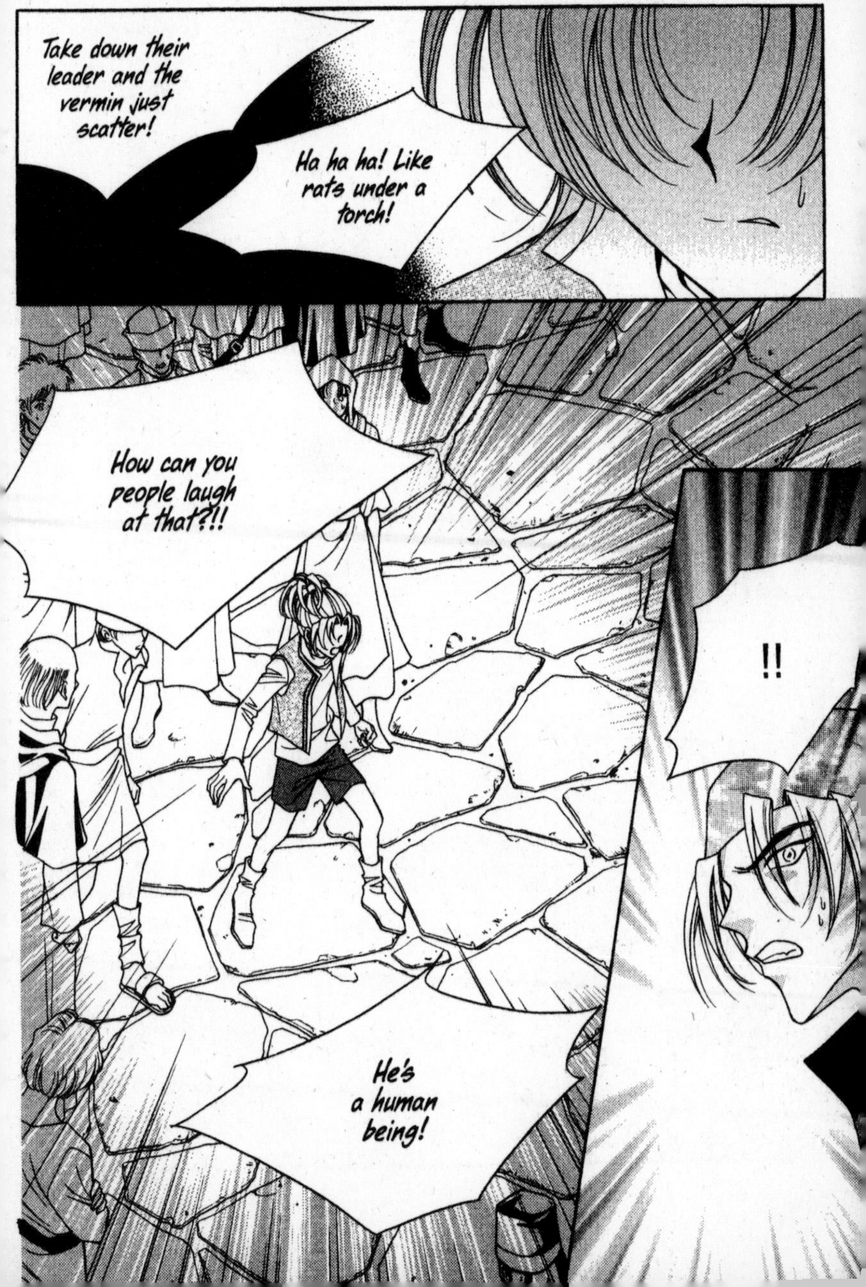
Take down their leader and the vermin just scatter!
Ha ha ha! Like rats under a torch!
How can you people laugh at that?!!
!!
He's a human being!

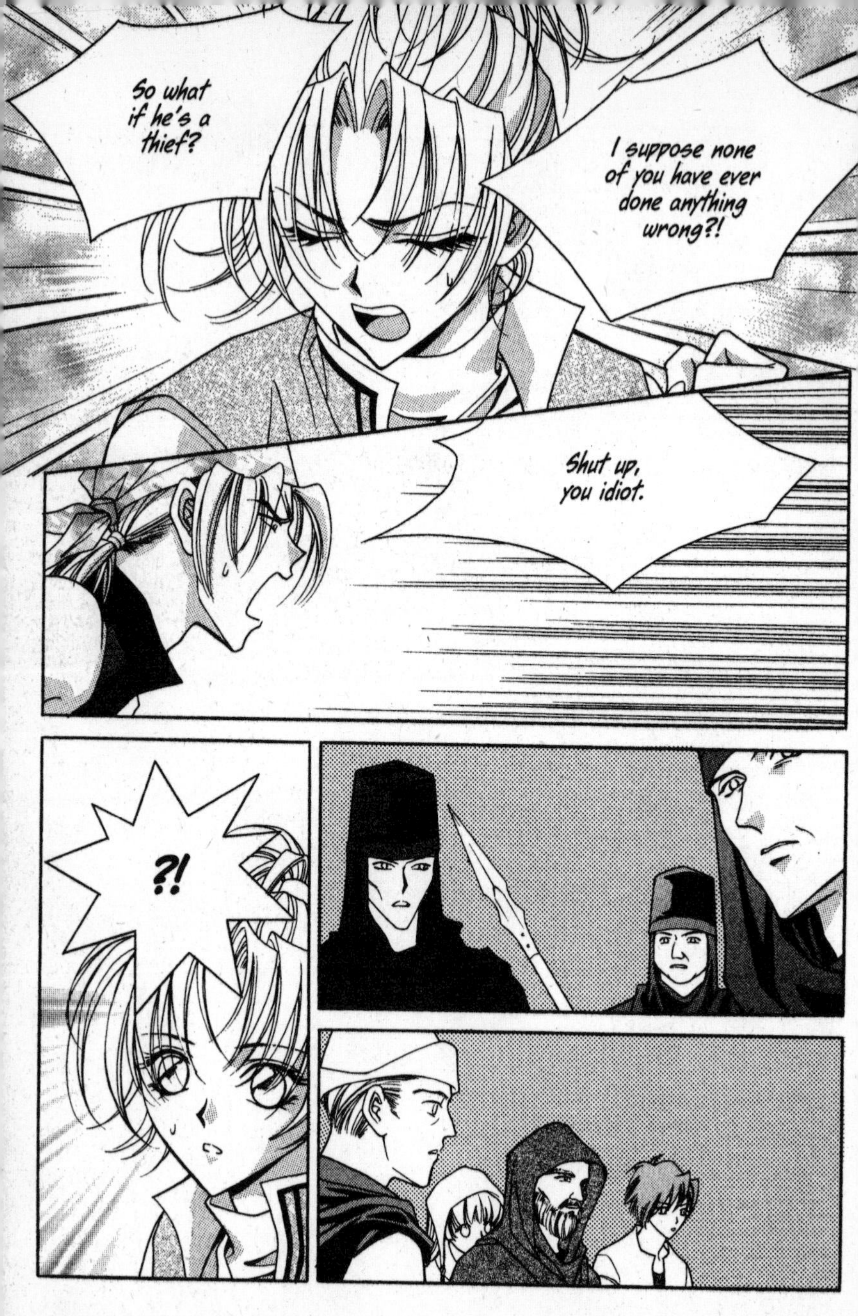

So what if he's a thief?
I suppose none of you have ever done anything wrong?!
Shut up, you idiot.
?!

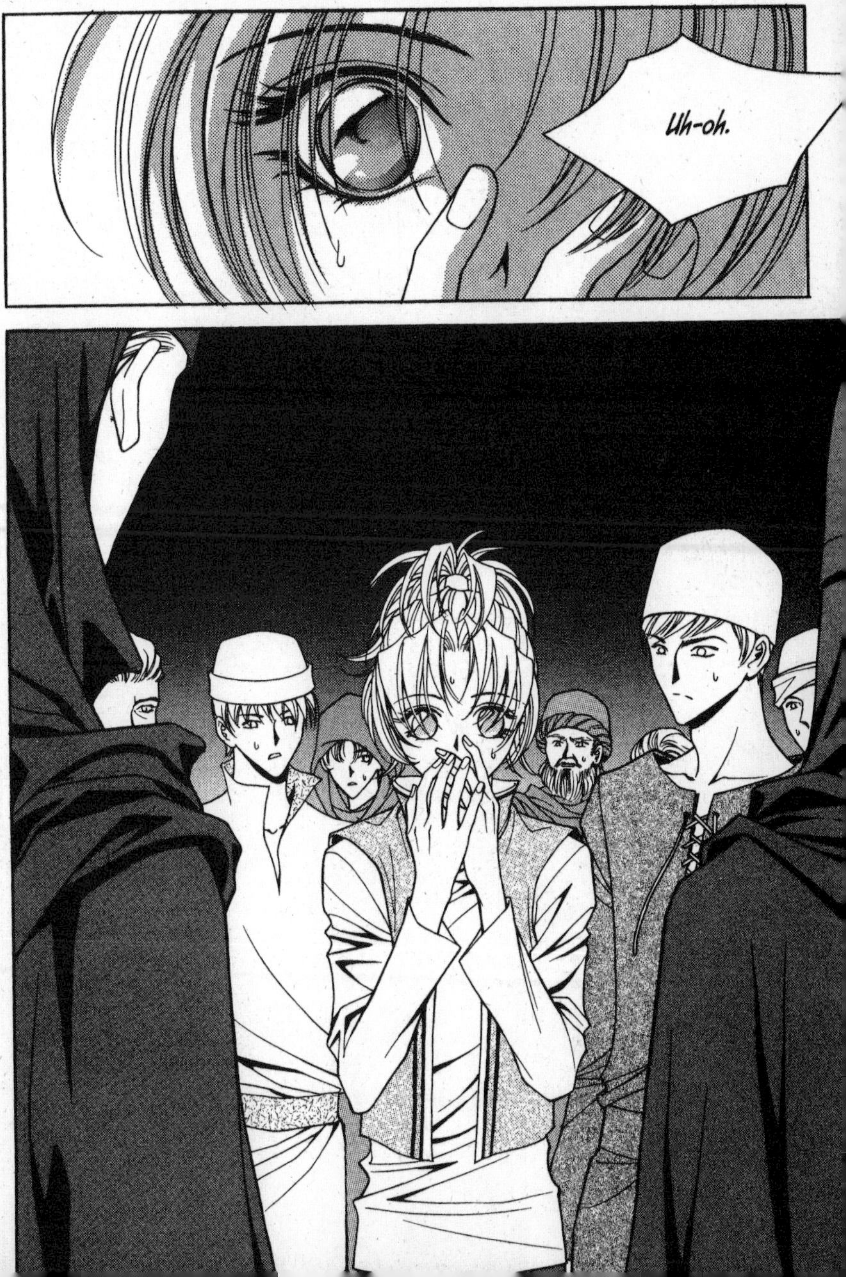
Uh-oh.

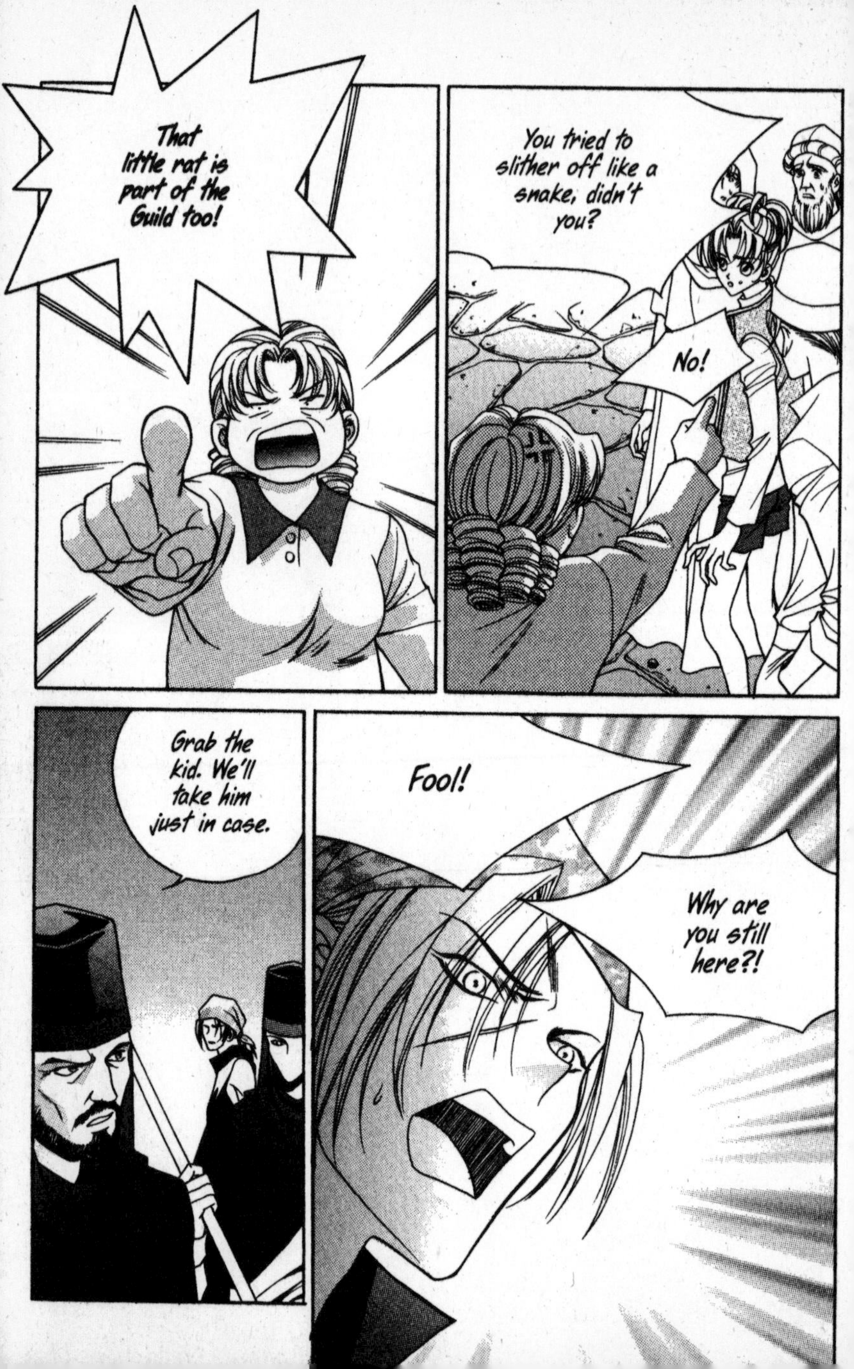
That little rat is part of the Guild too!
You tried to slither off like a snake, didn't you?
No!
Grab the kid. We'll take him just in case.
Fool!
Why are you still here?!

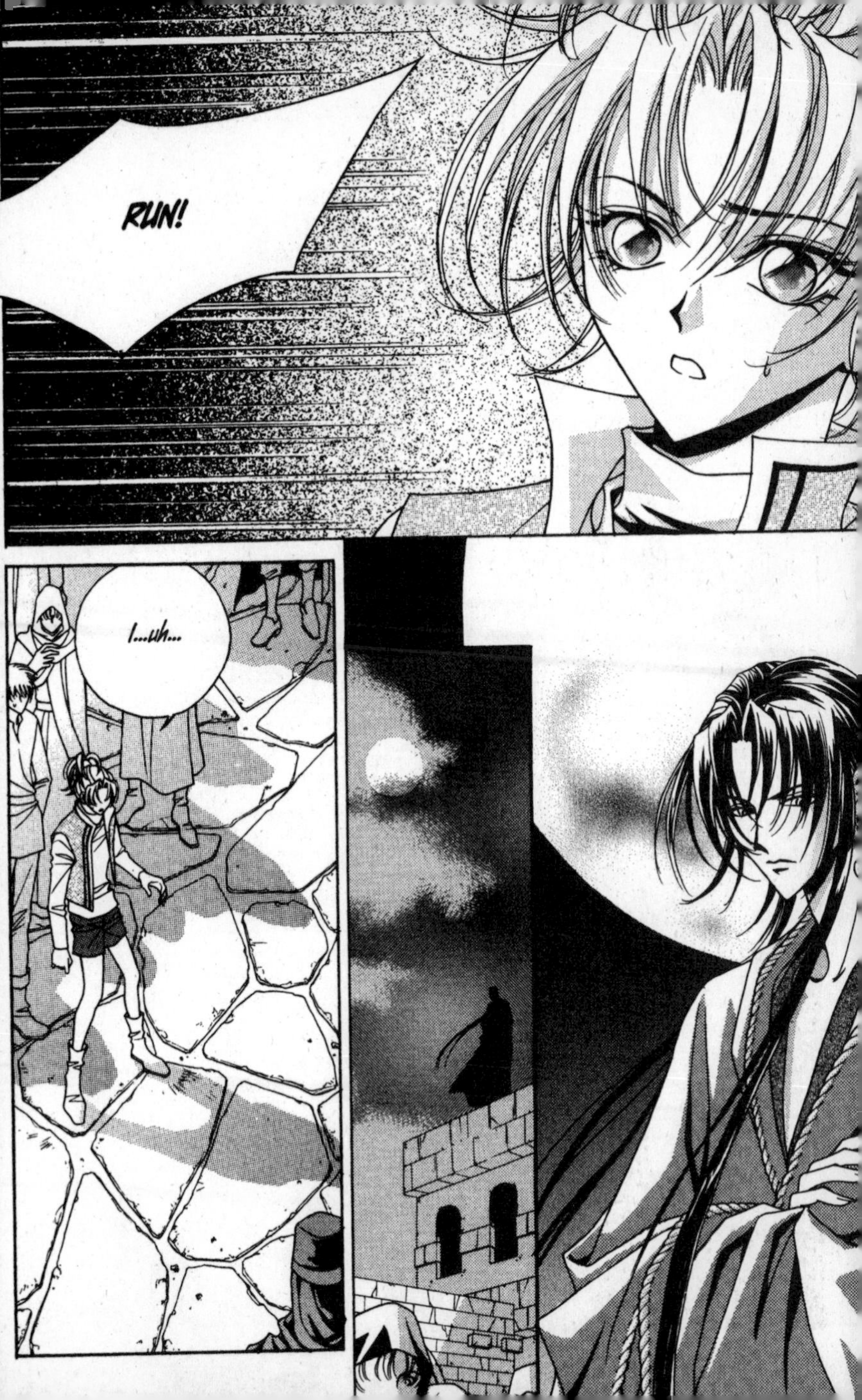
RUN!
I...uh...

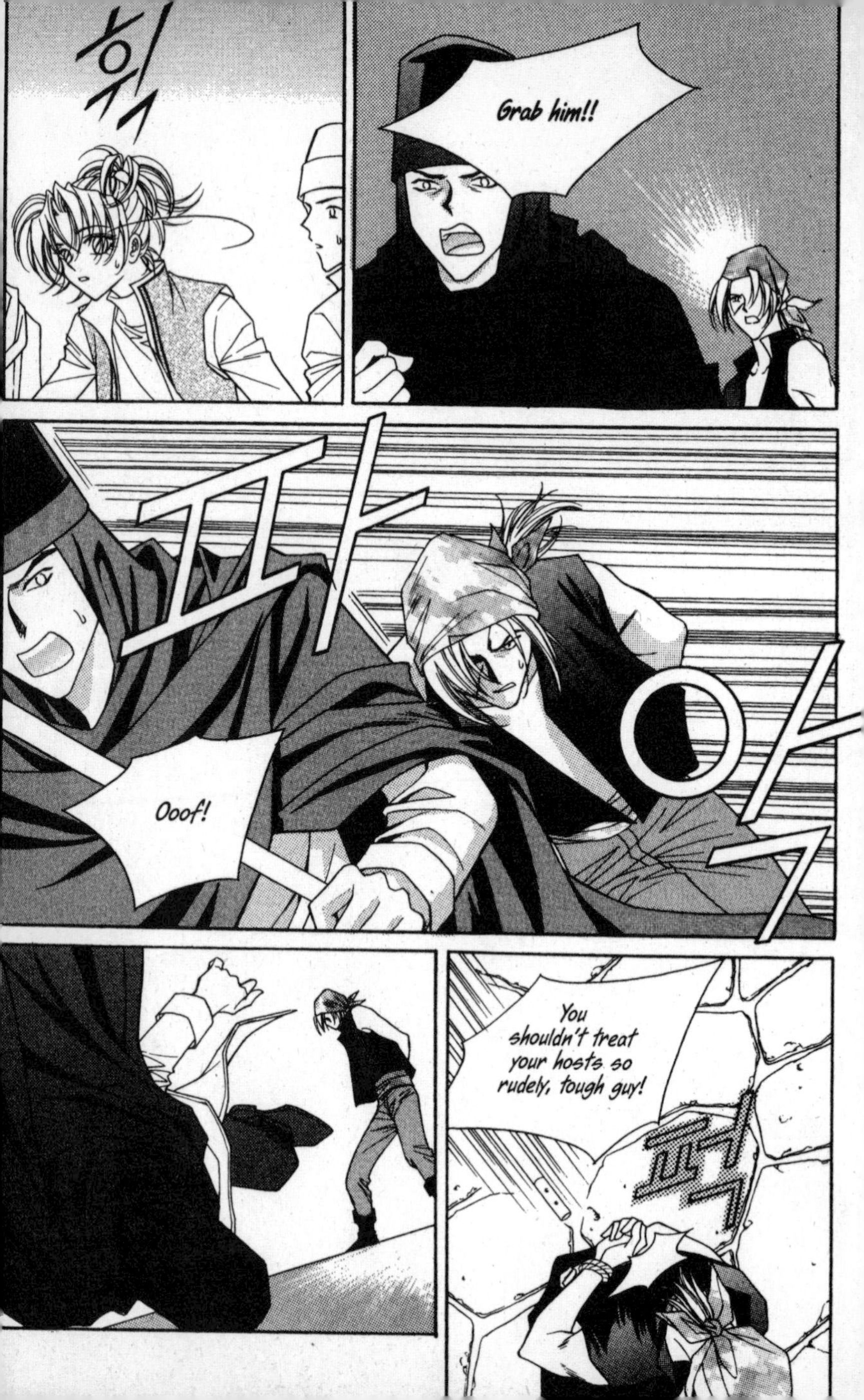
Grab him!!
Ooof!
파악
You shouldn't treat your hosts so rudely, tough guy!
퍽

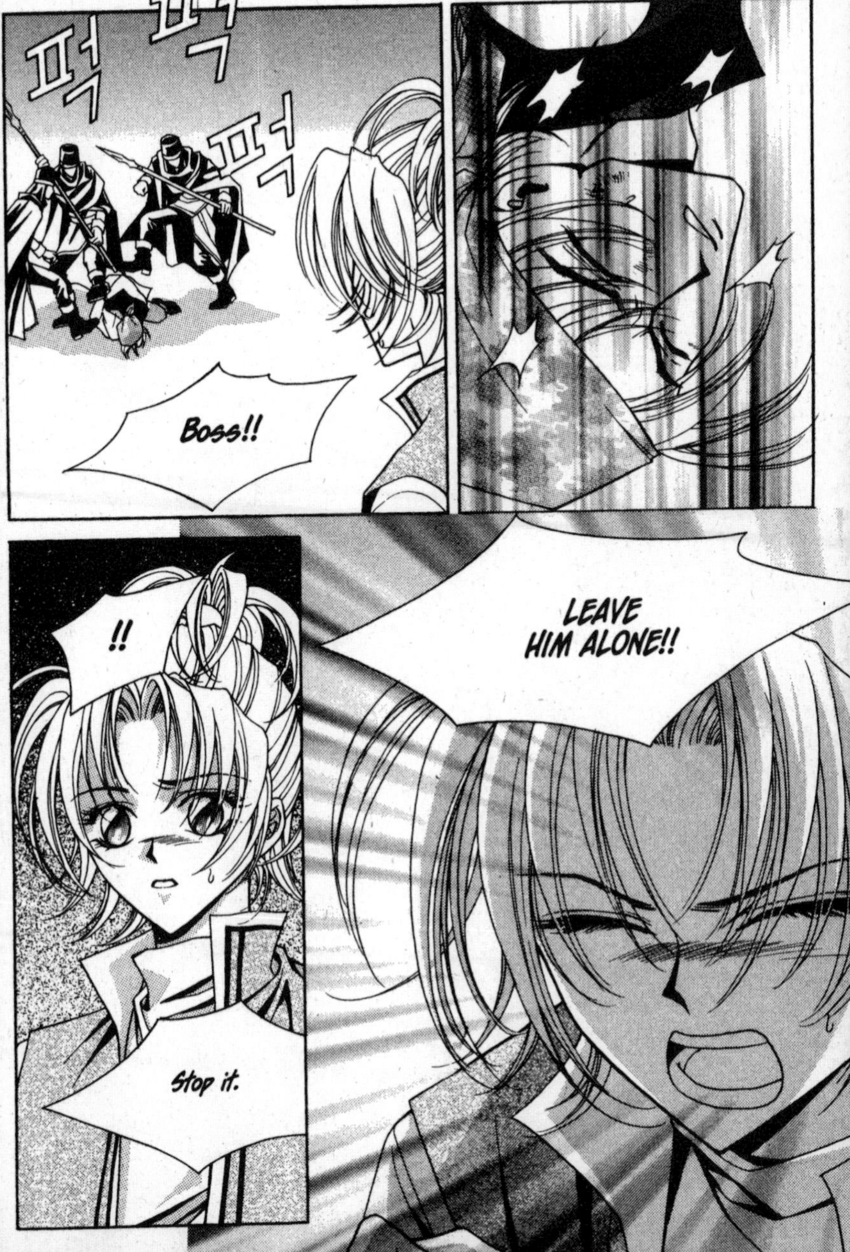
퍽
퍽
퍽
Boss!!
!!
Stop it.
LEAVE HIM ALONE!!

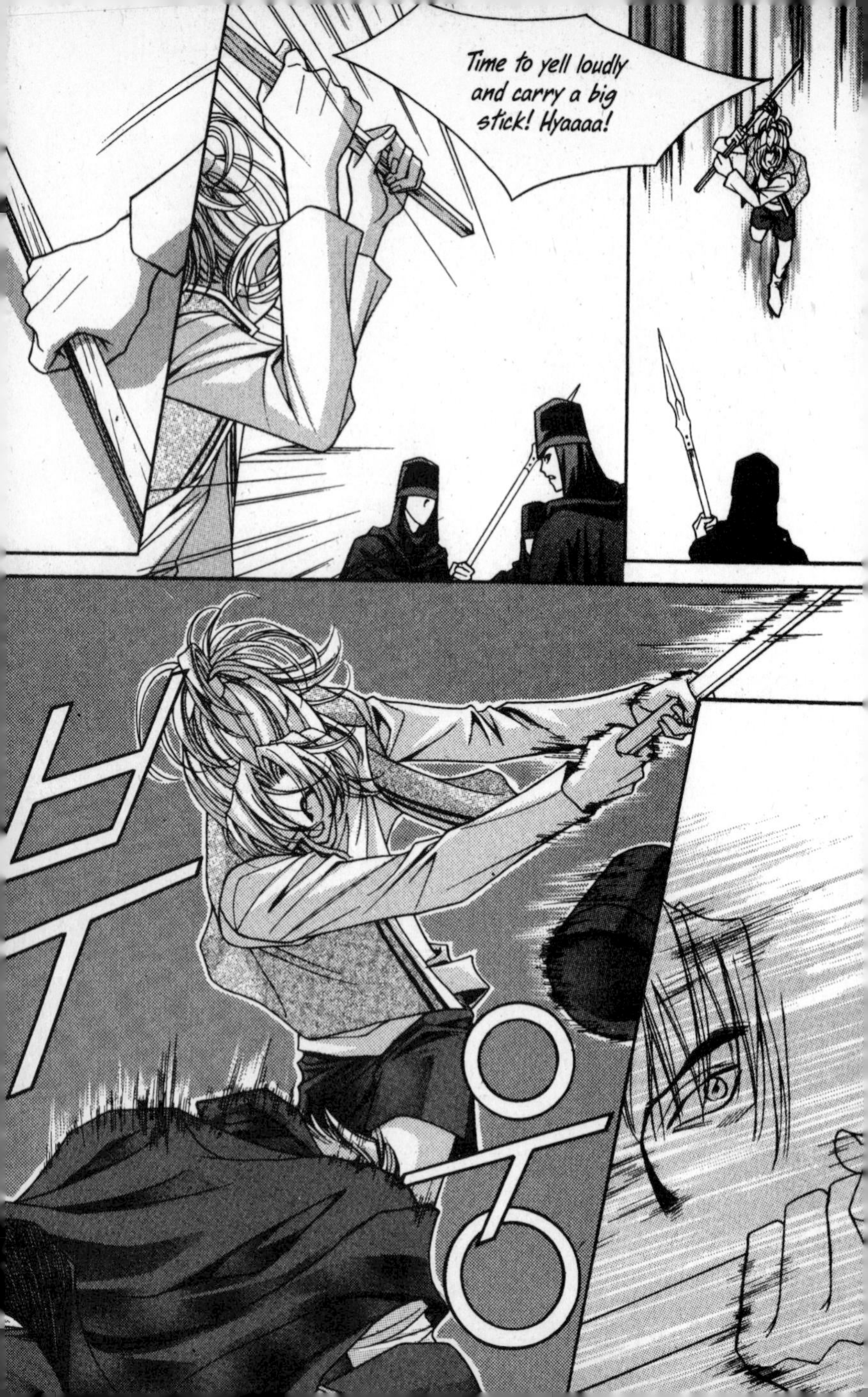
Time to yell loudly and carry a big stick! Hyaaaa!

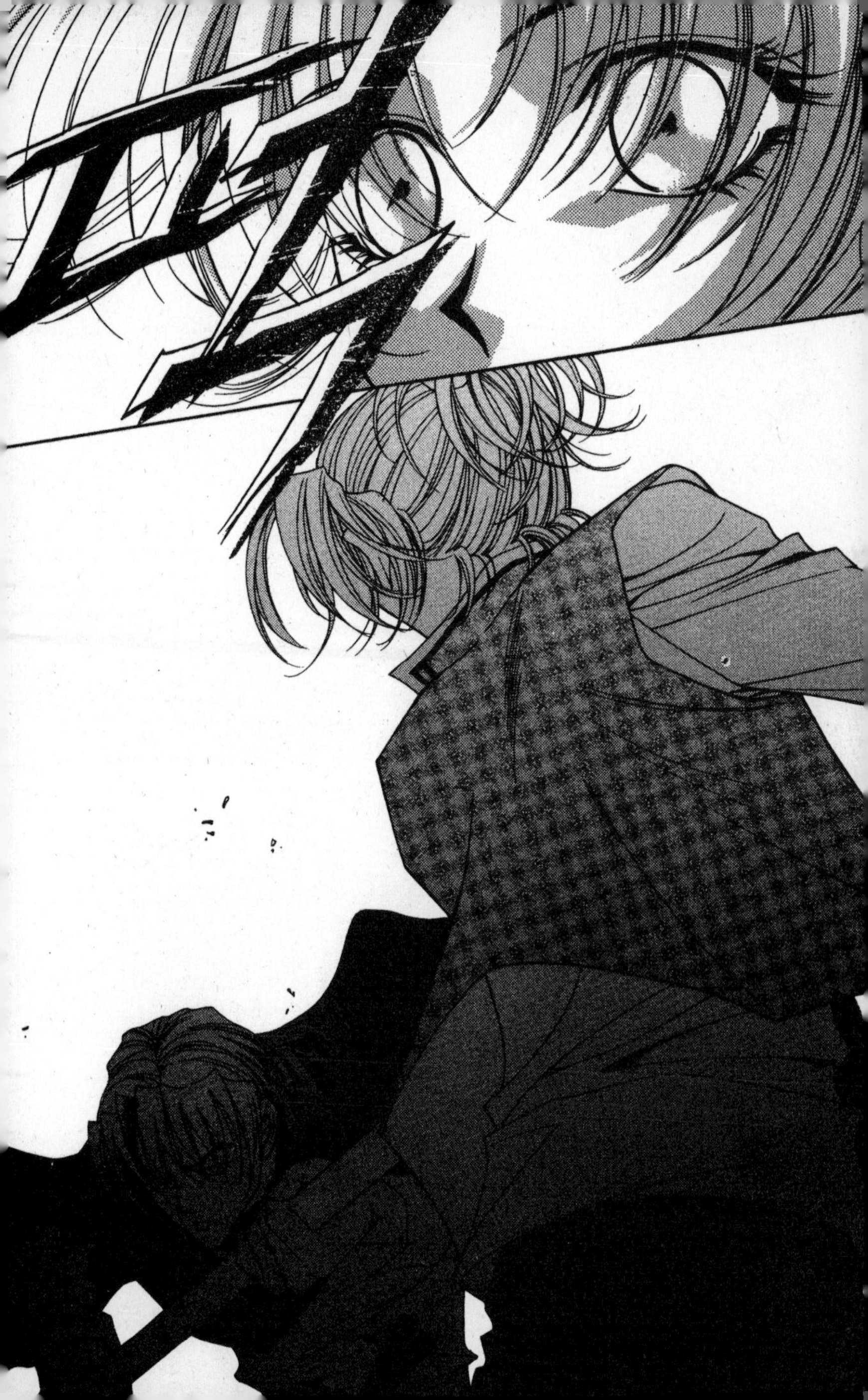

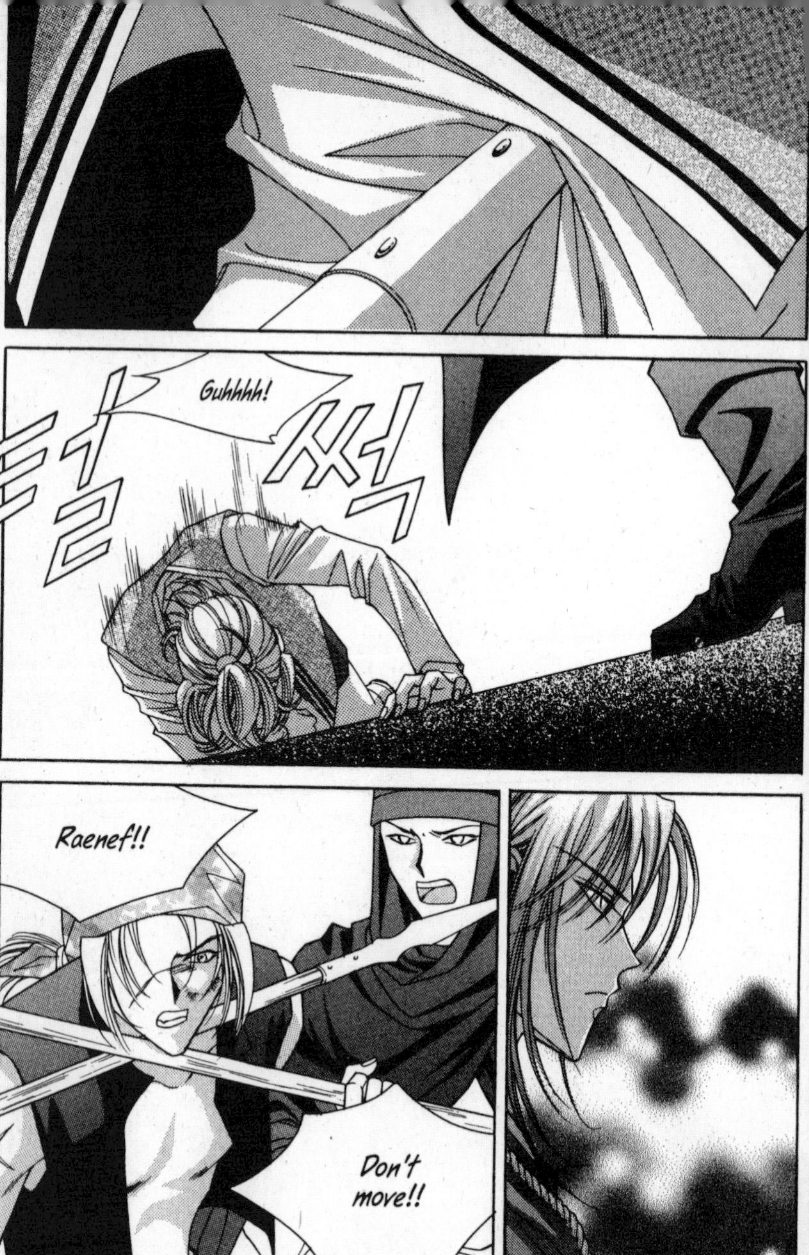
Guhhhh!
털
썩
Raenef!!
Don't move!!

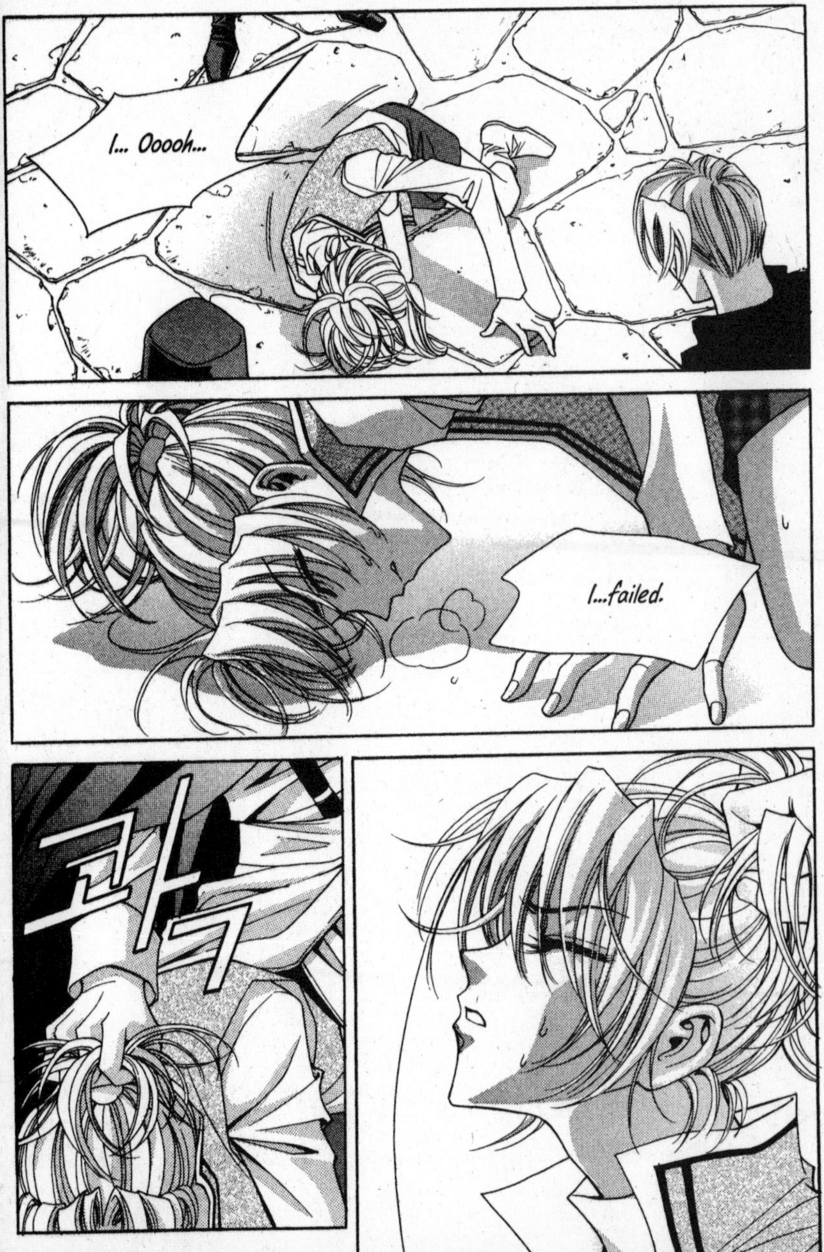
I... Ooooh...
I...failed.

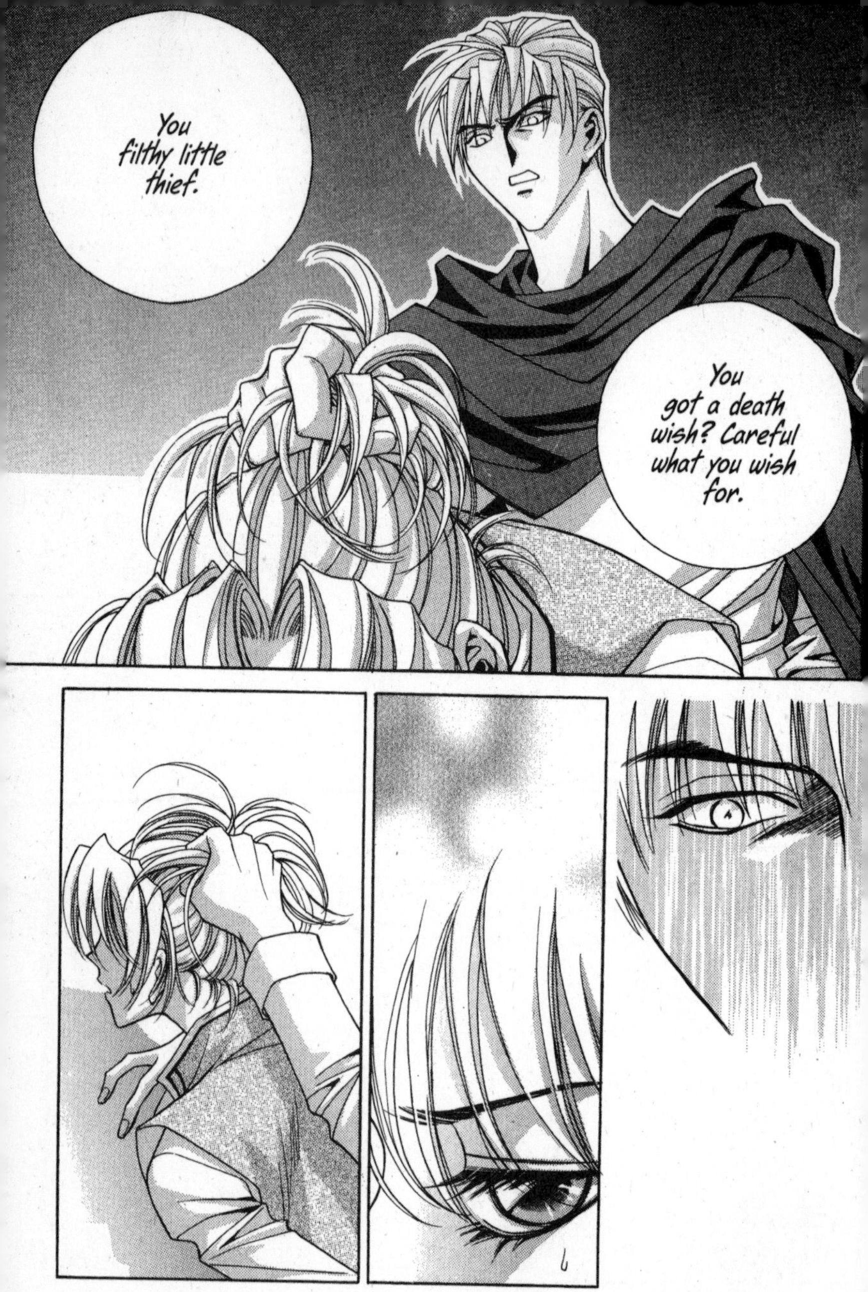
You filthy little thief.
You got a death wish? Careful what you wish for.

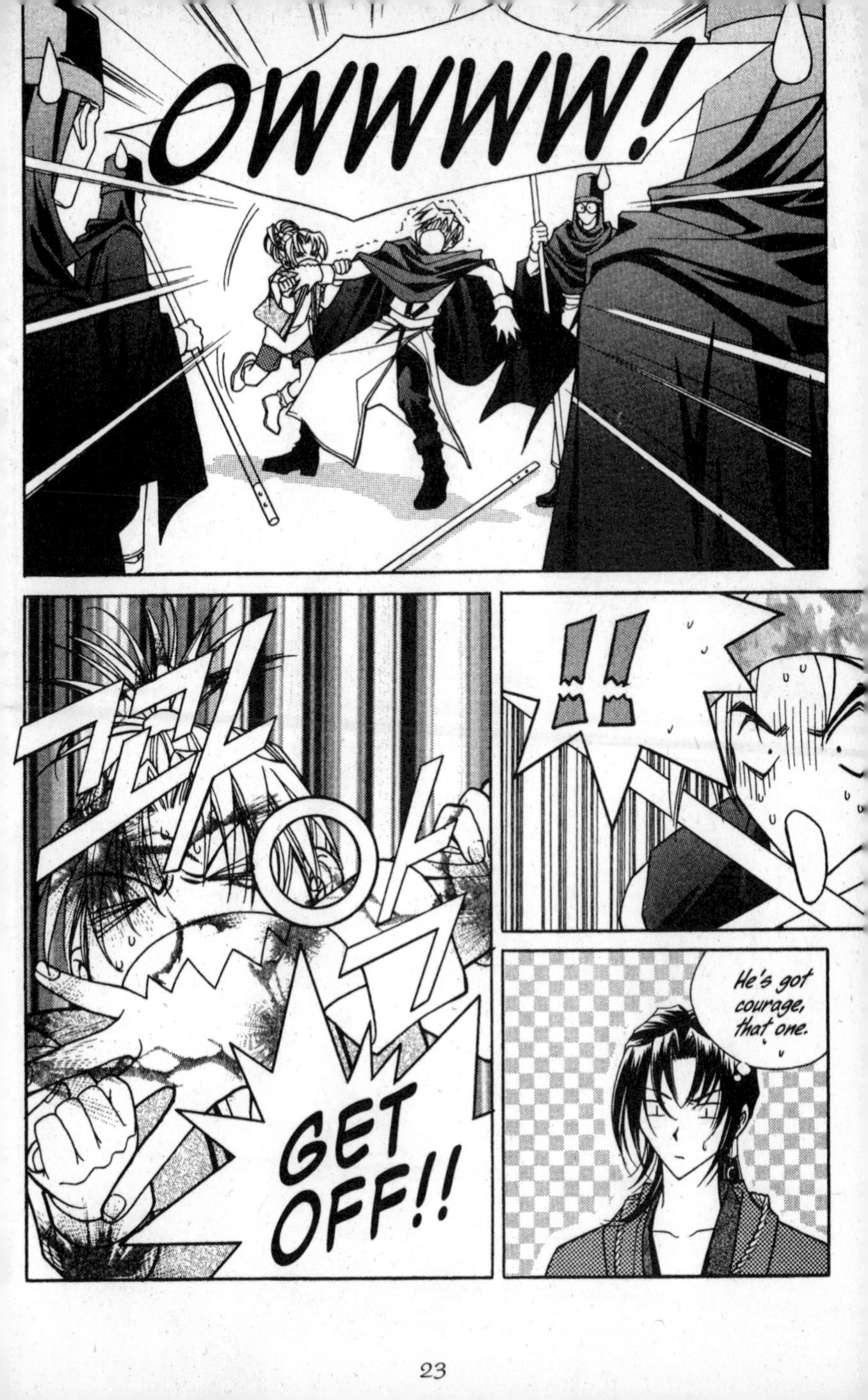
OWWWW!
GET OFF!!
!!
He's got courage, that one.

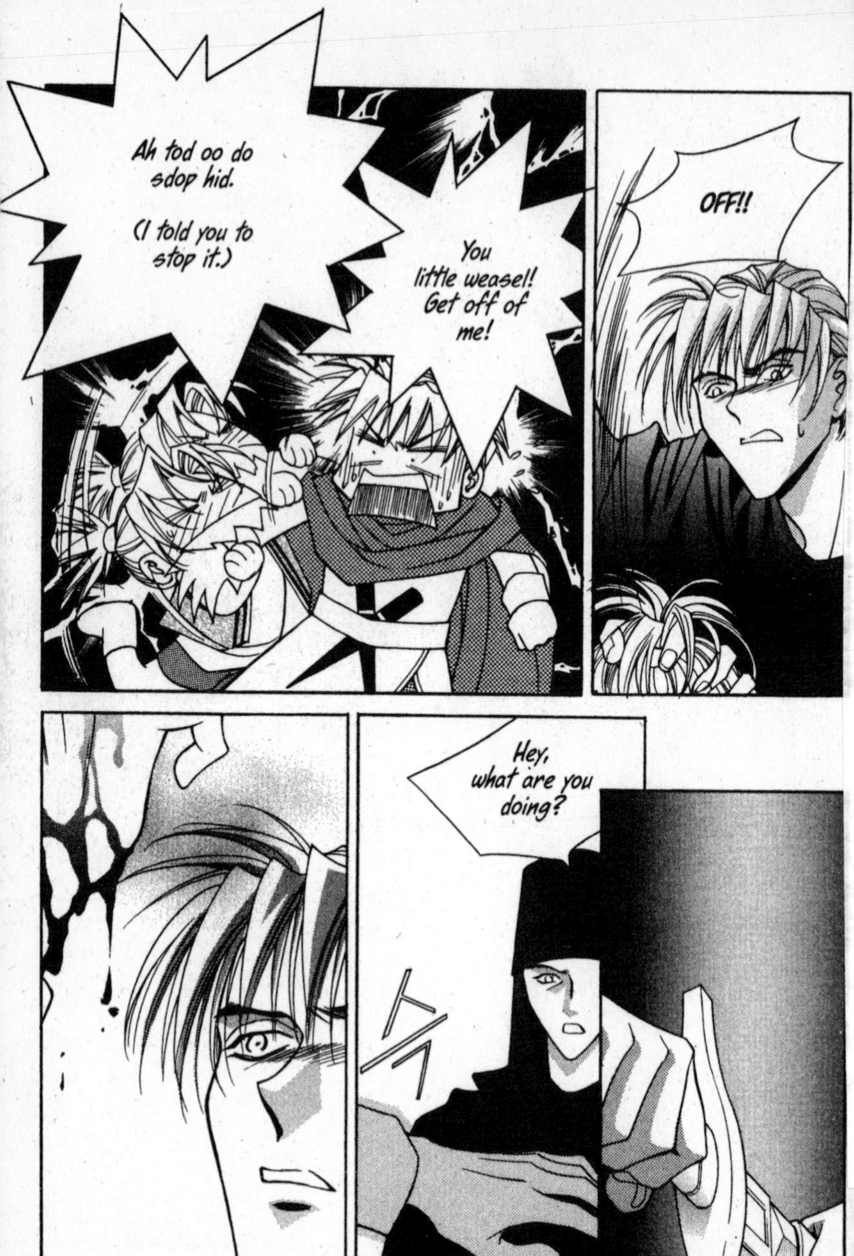
Ah tod oo do sdop hid.
(I told you to stop it.)
You little weasel! Get off of me!
OFF!!
Hey, what are you doing?

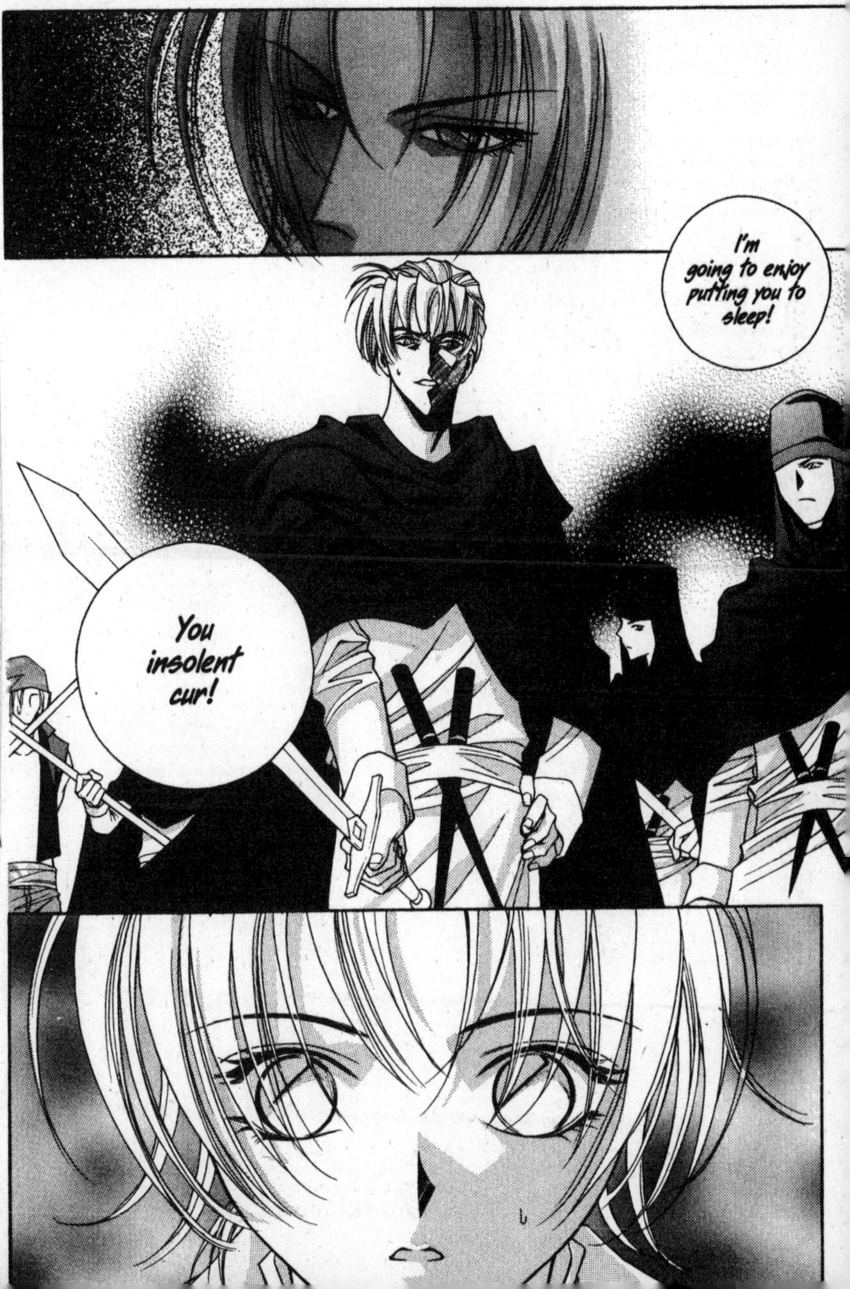
I'm going to enjoy putting you to sleep!
You insolent cur!

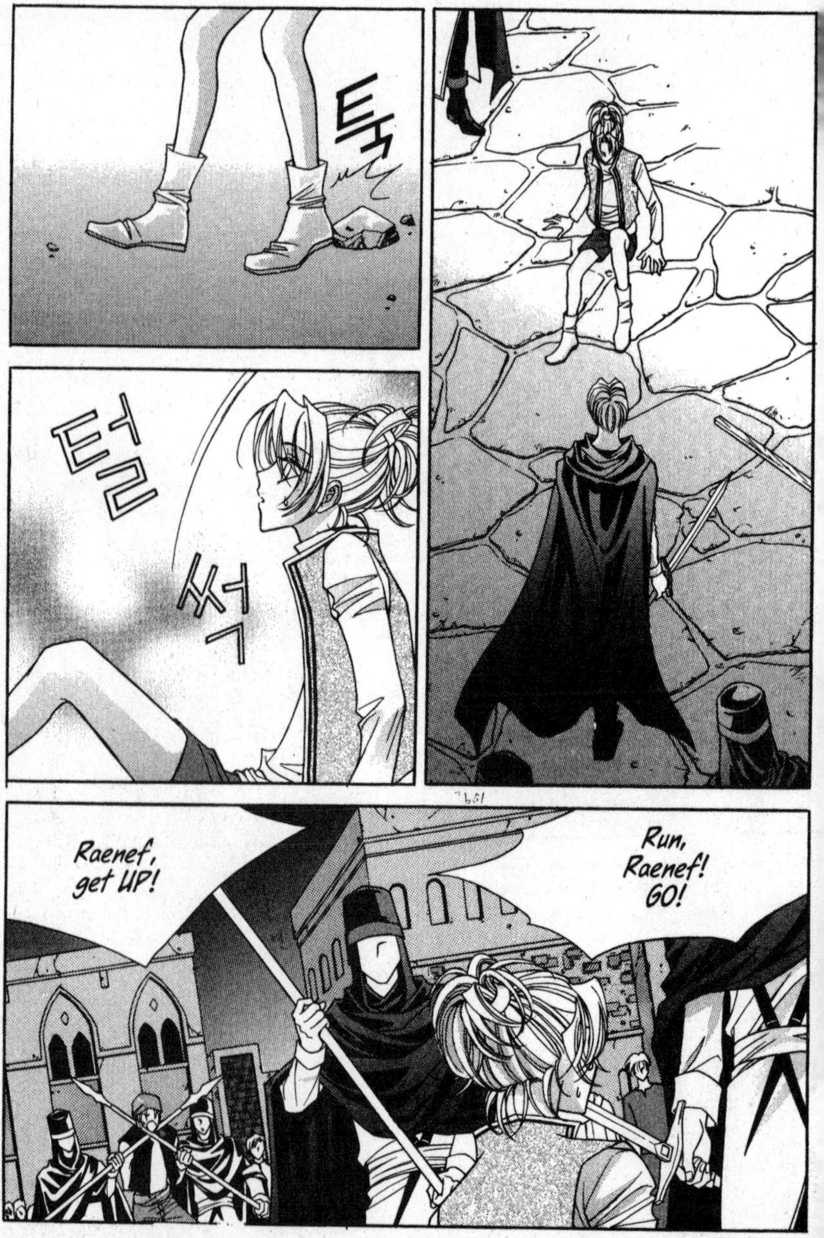
툭
털
썩
Raenef, get UP!
Run, Raenef! GO!

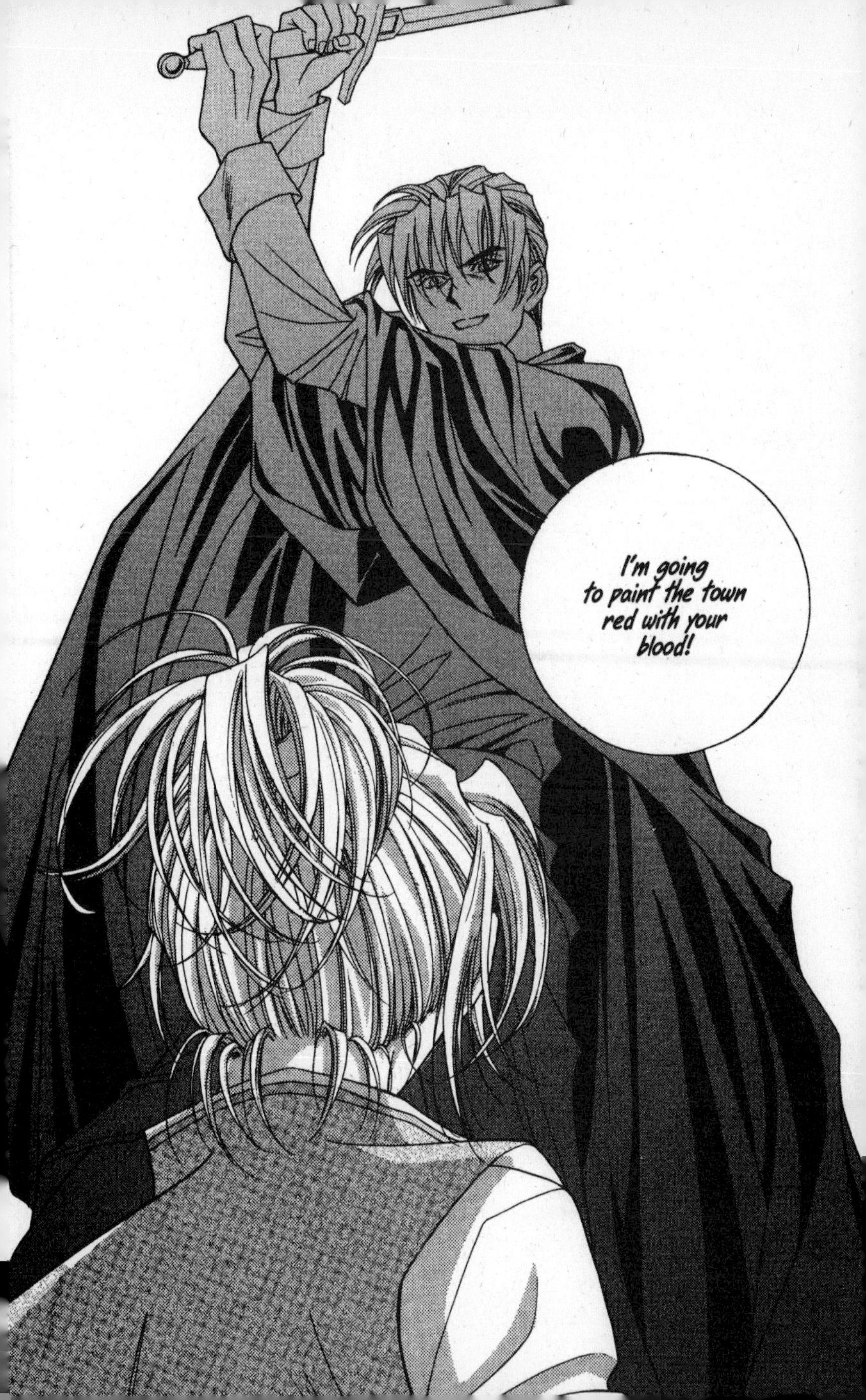
I'm going to paint the town red with your blood!

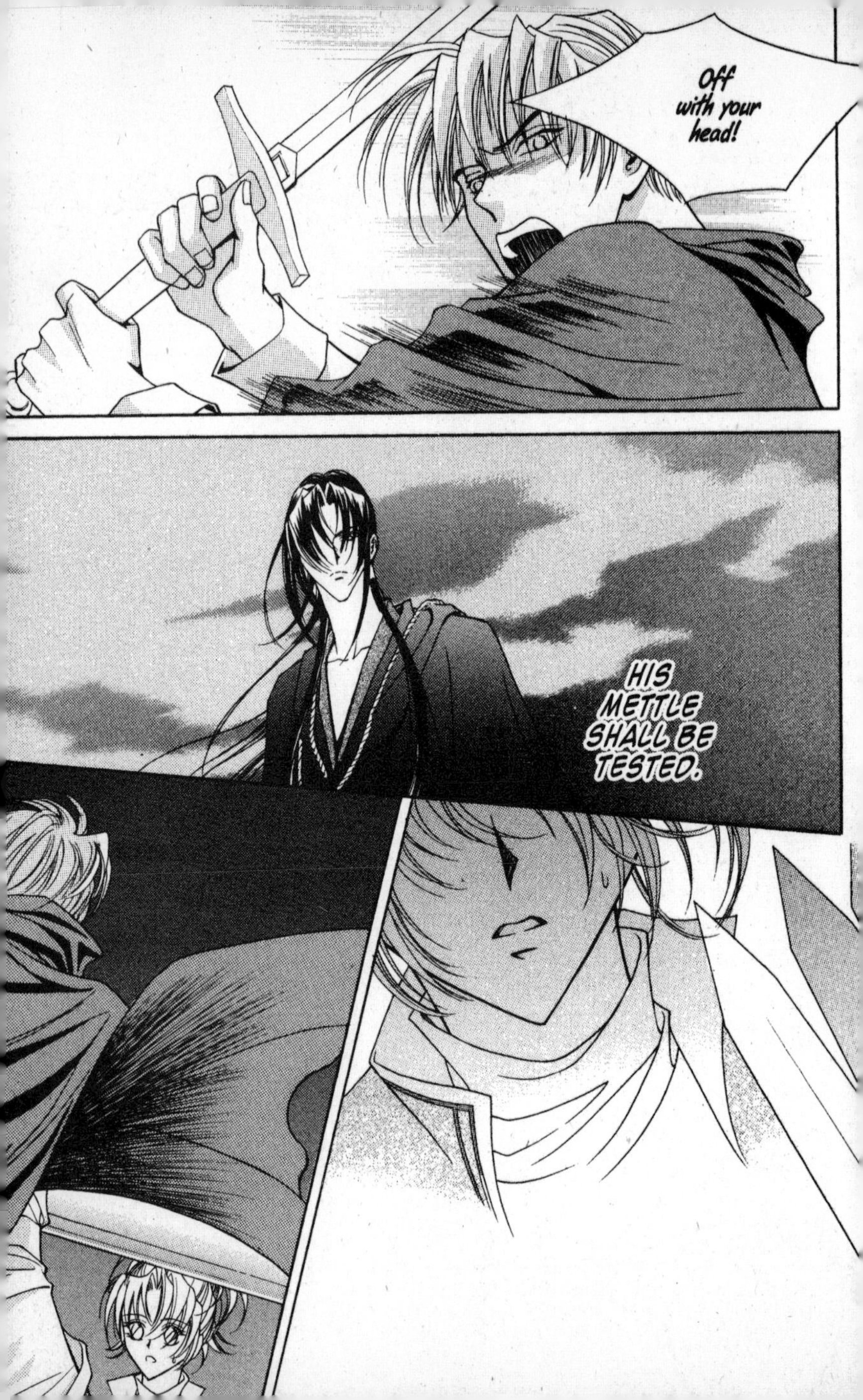
Off with your head!
HIS METTLE SHALL BE TESTED.

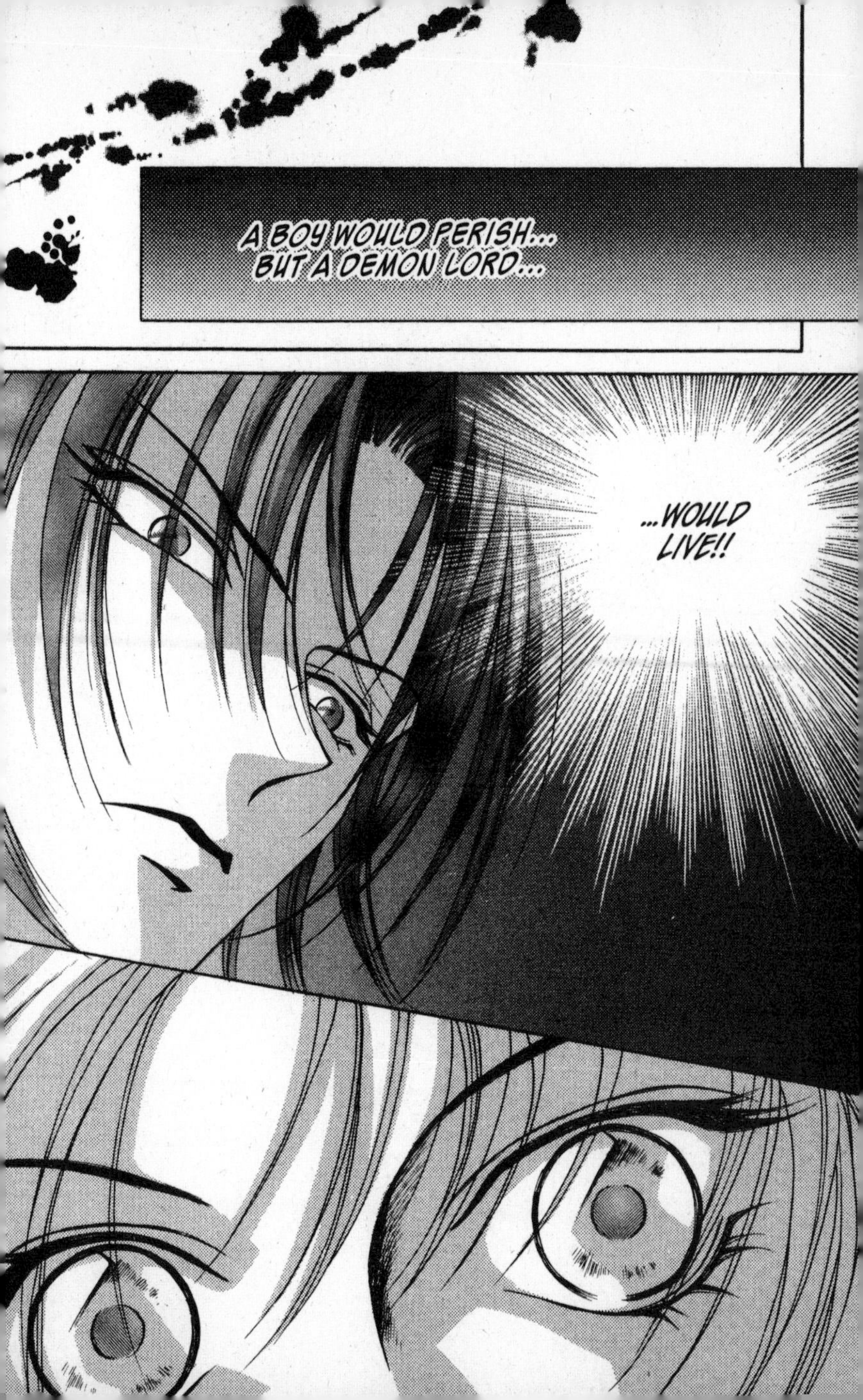
A BOY WOULD PERISH...
BUT A DEMON LORD...
...WOULD LIVE!!

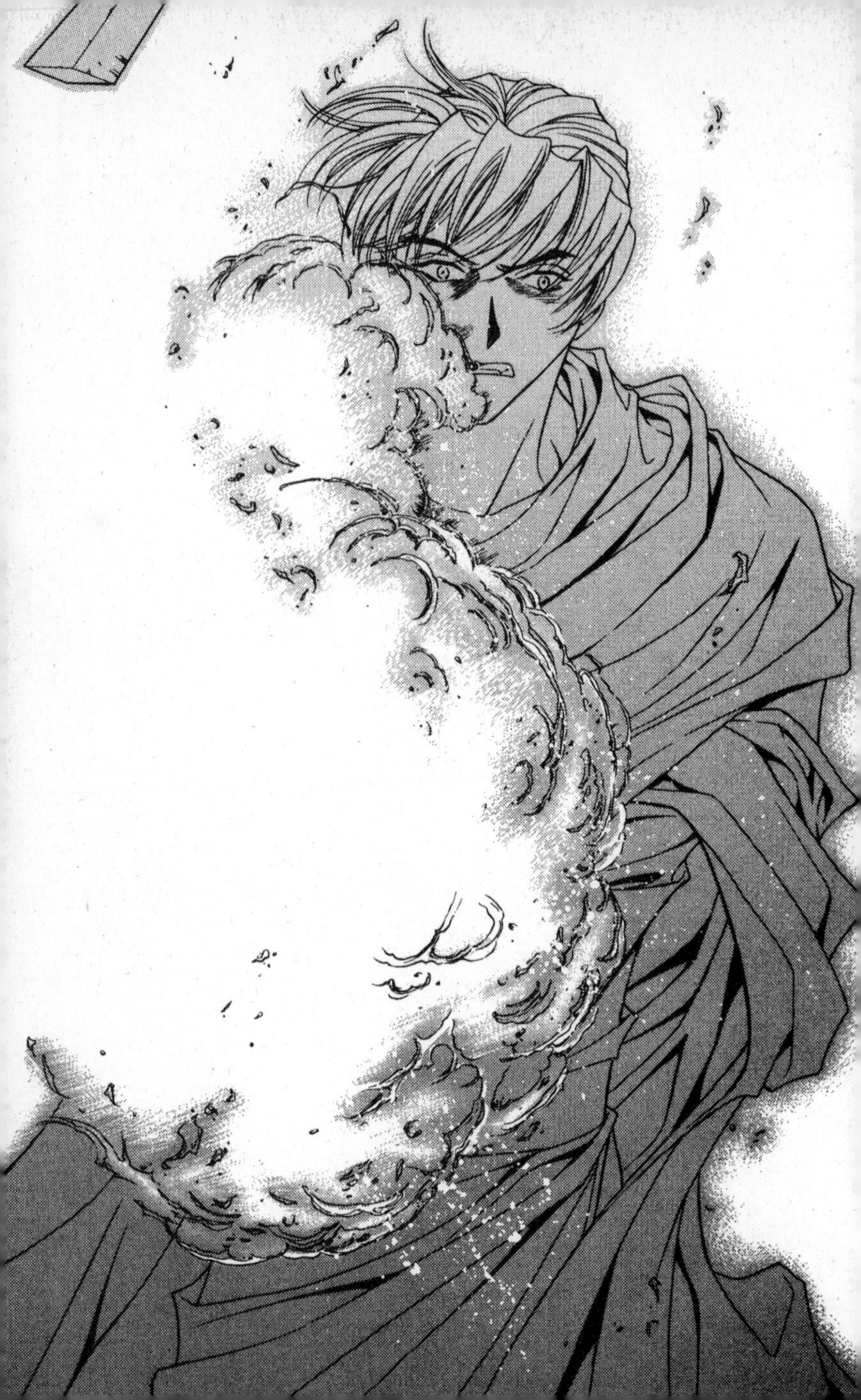

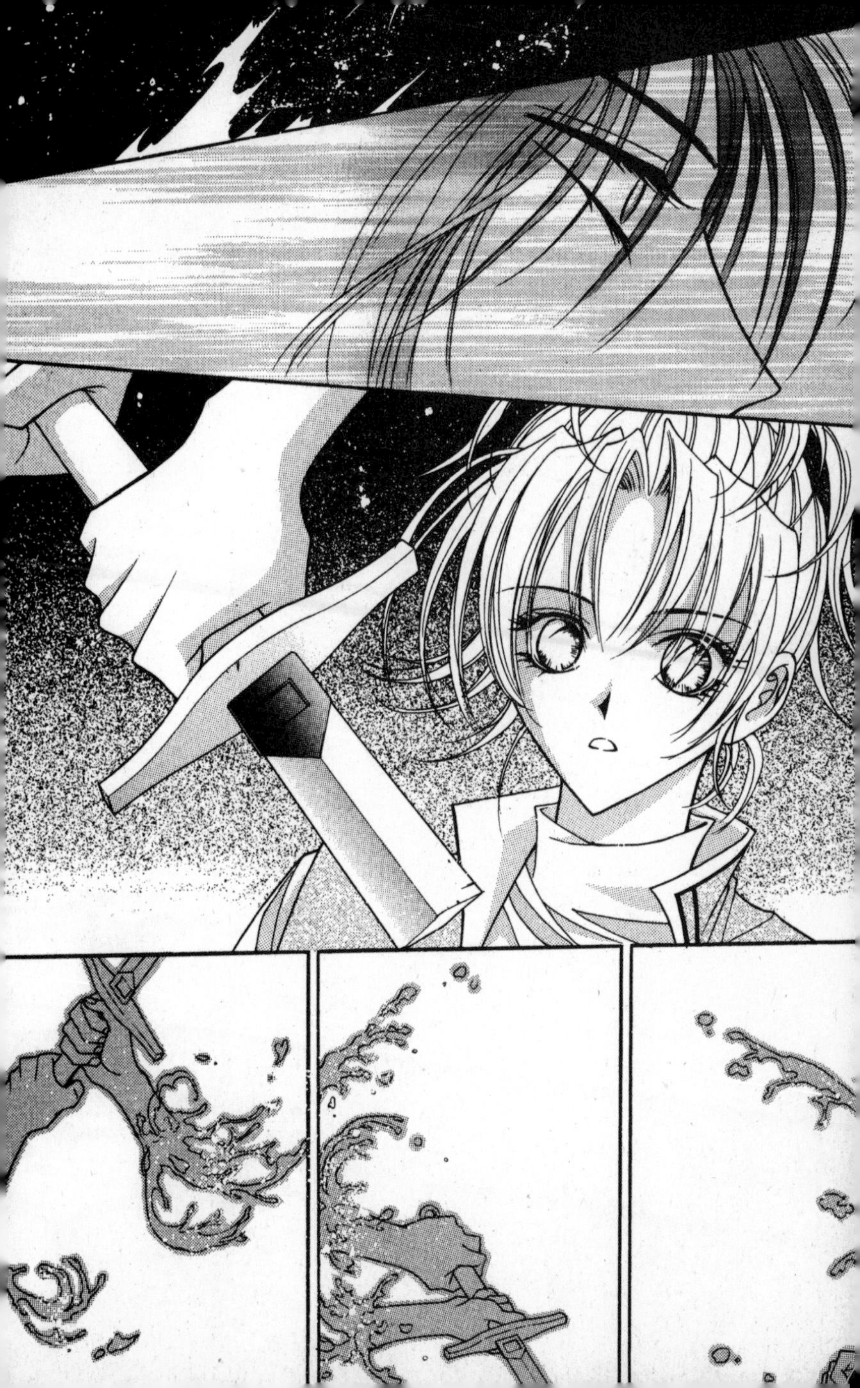

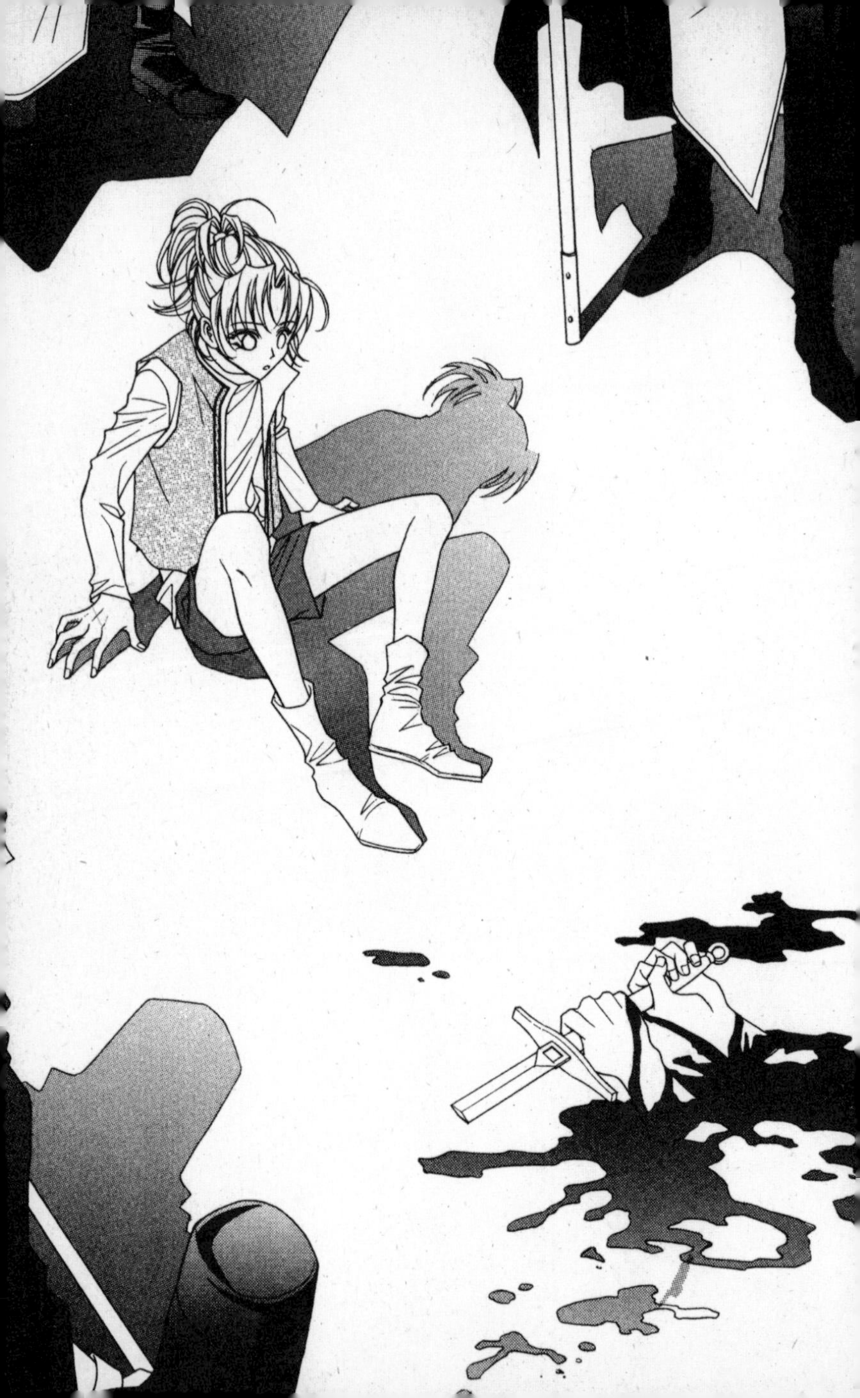

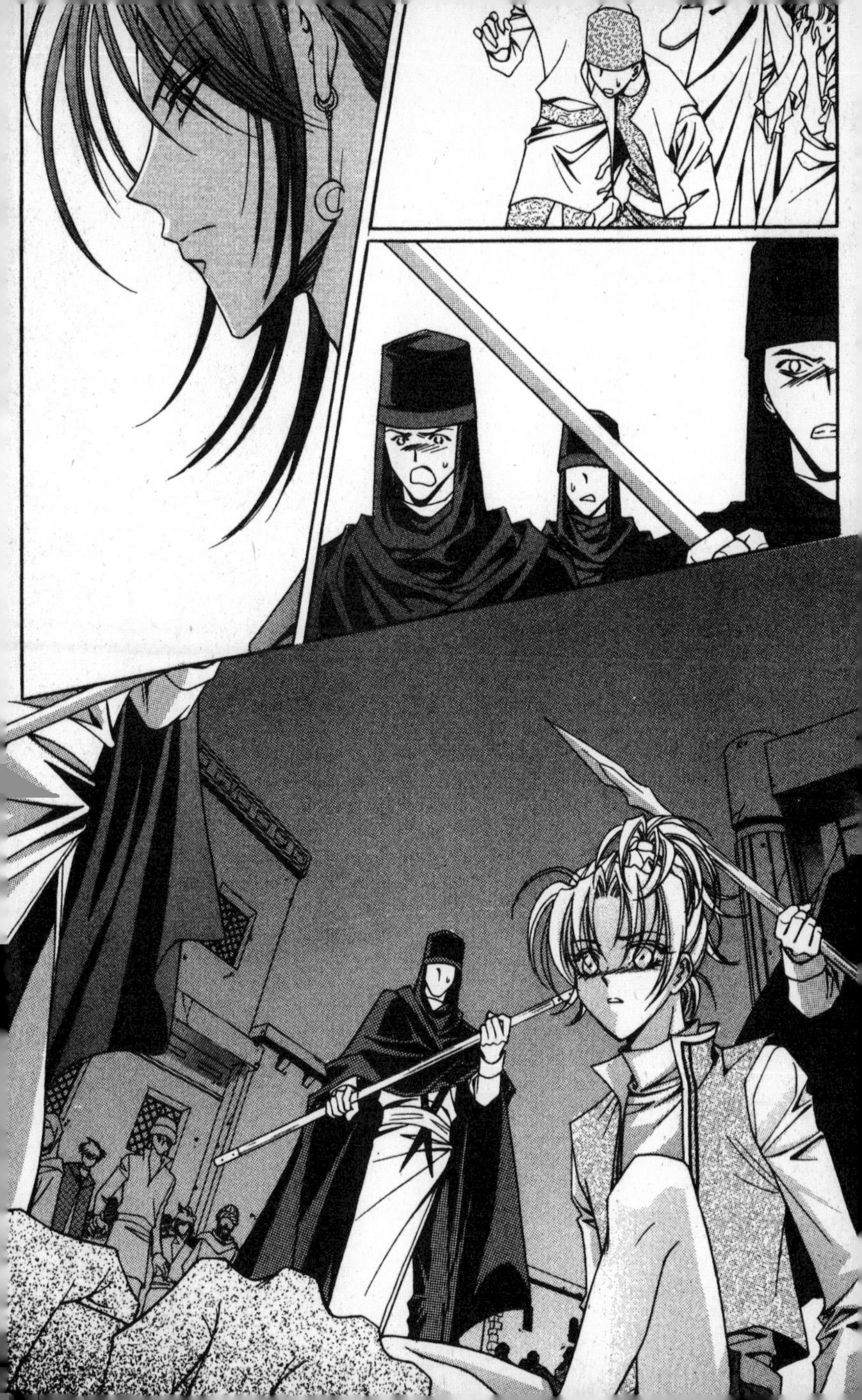

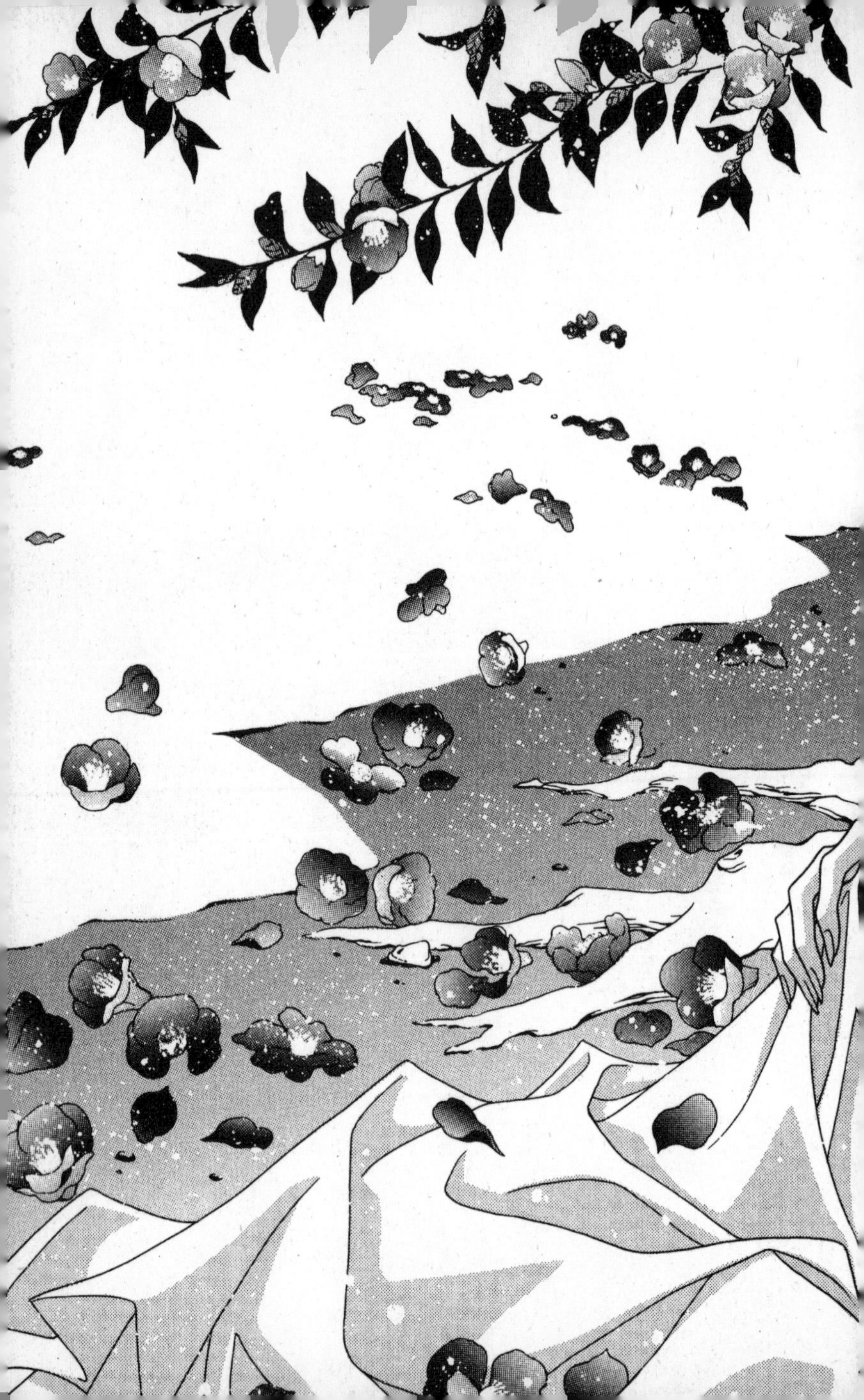

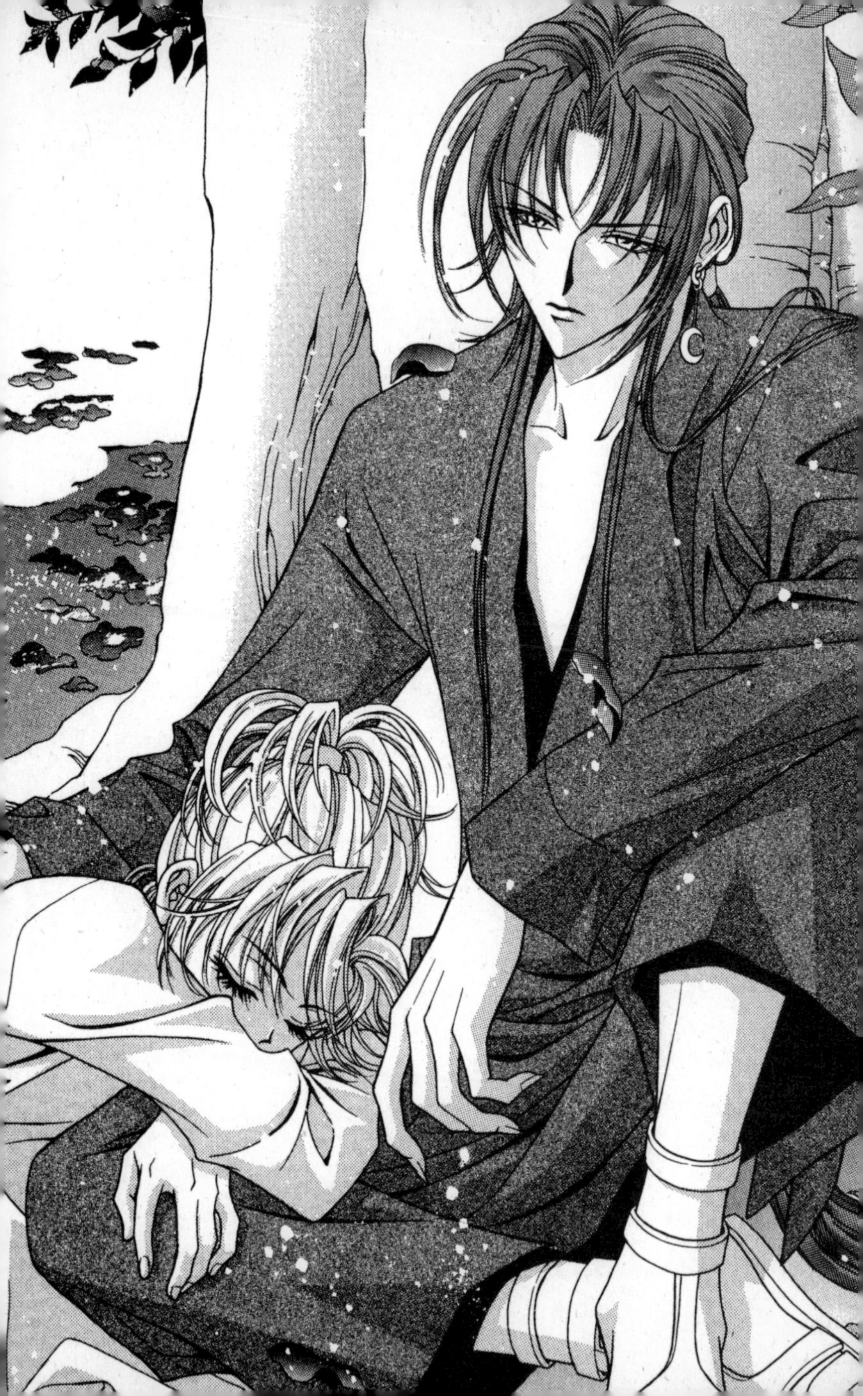

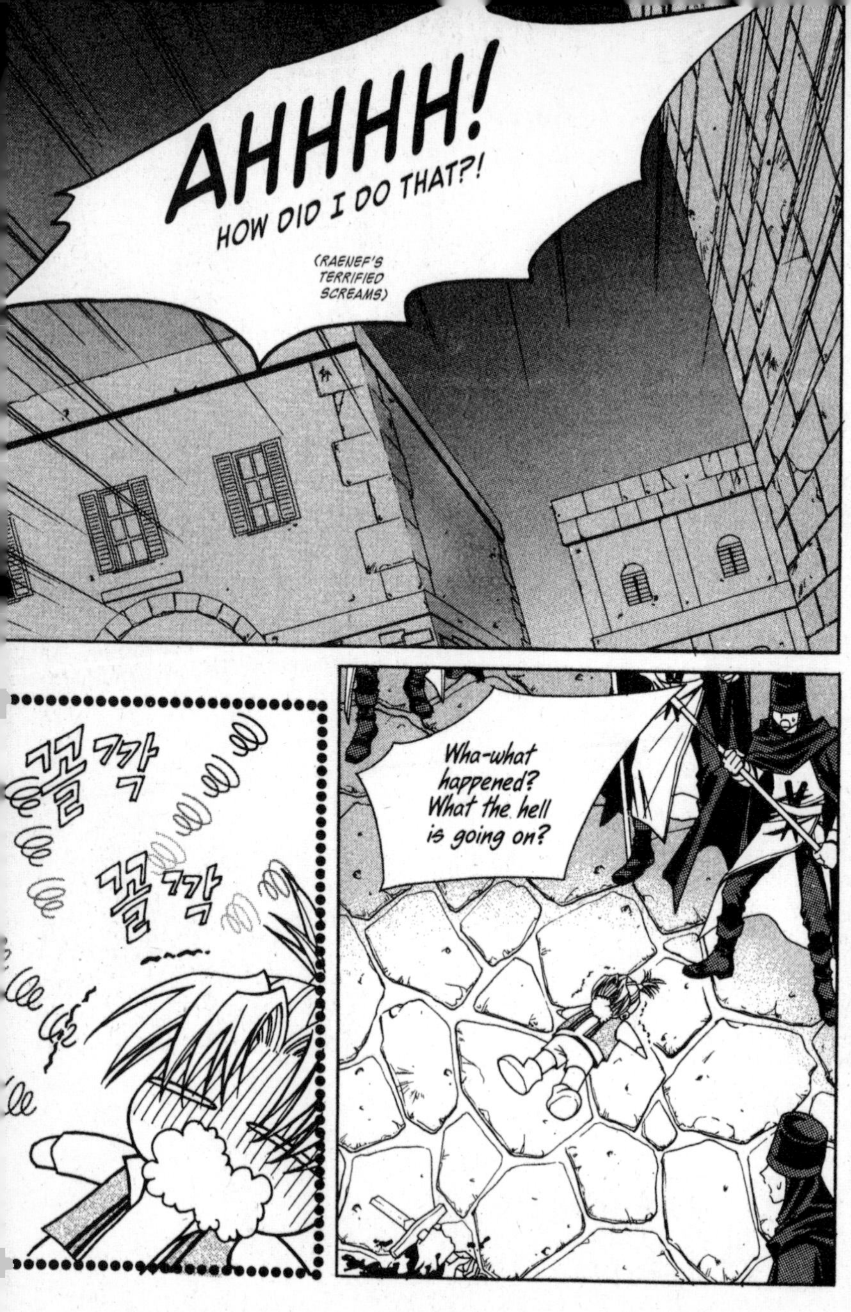
AHHHH!
HOW DID I DO THAT?!
(RAENEF'S TERRIFIED SCREAMS)
꼴깍
꼴깍
Wha-what happened? What the hell is going on?

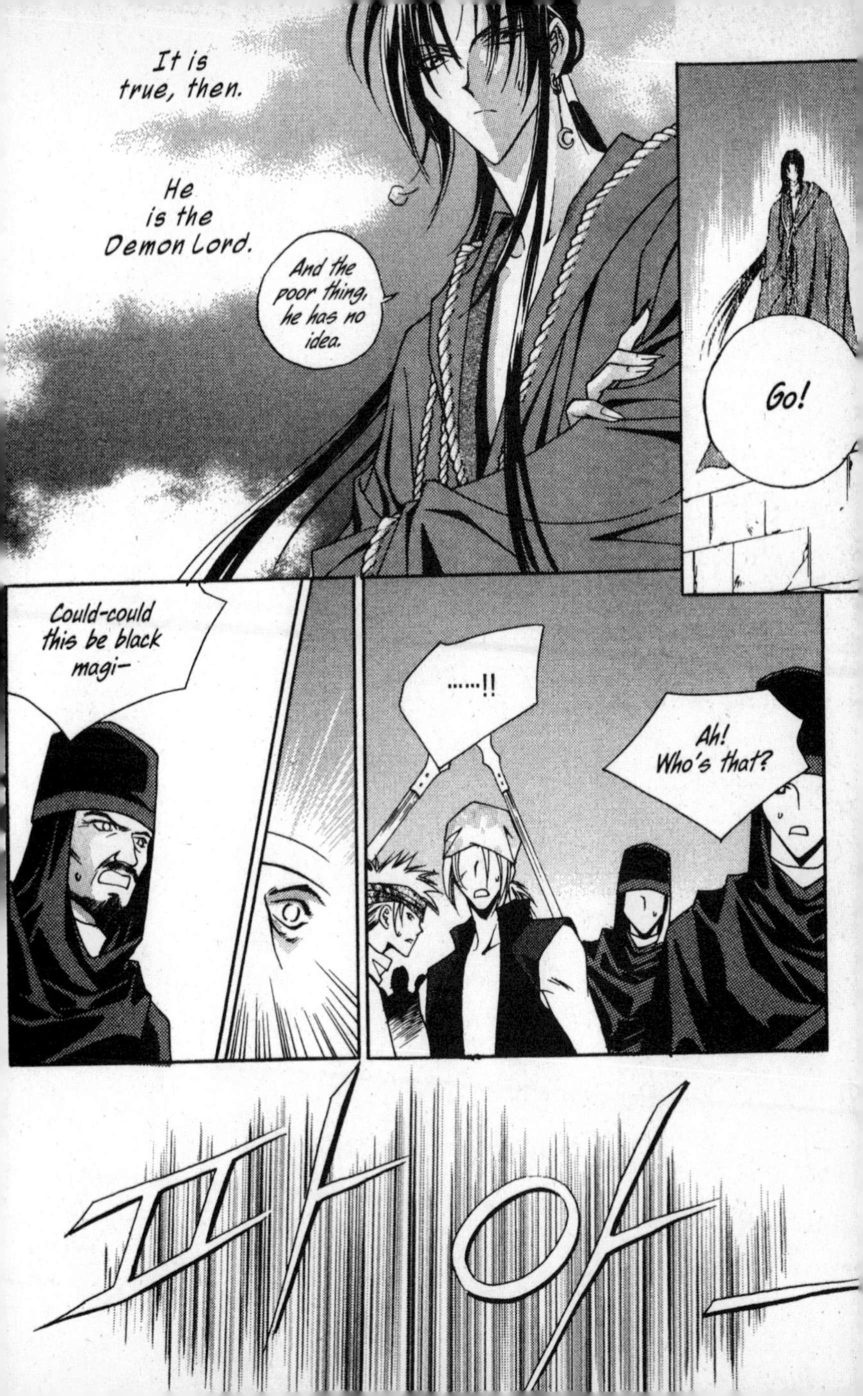
It is true, then.
He is the Demon Lord.
And the poor thing, he has no idea.
Go!
Could-could this be black magi-
......!!
Ah! Who's that?

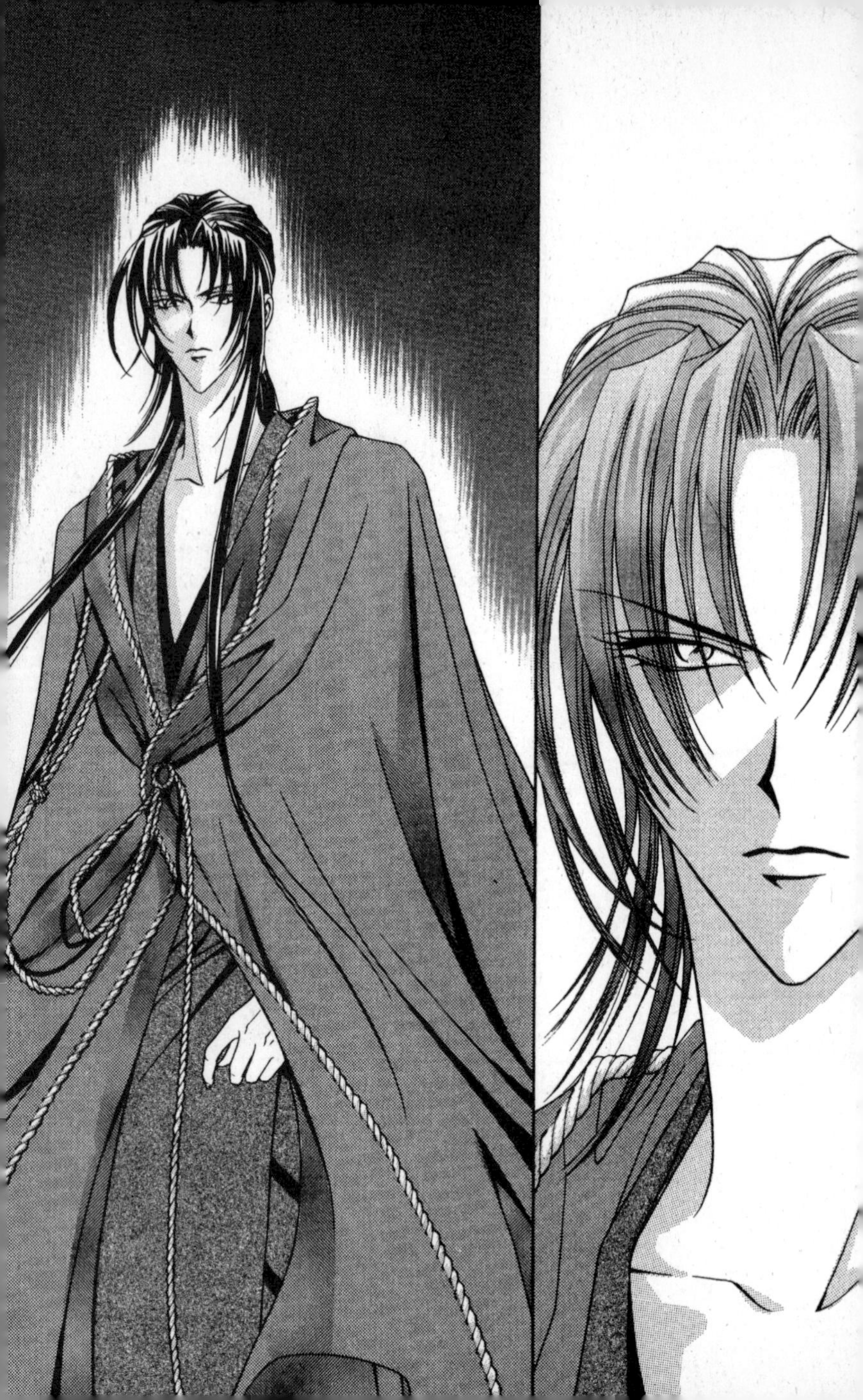

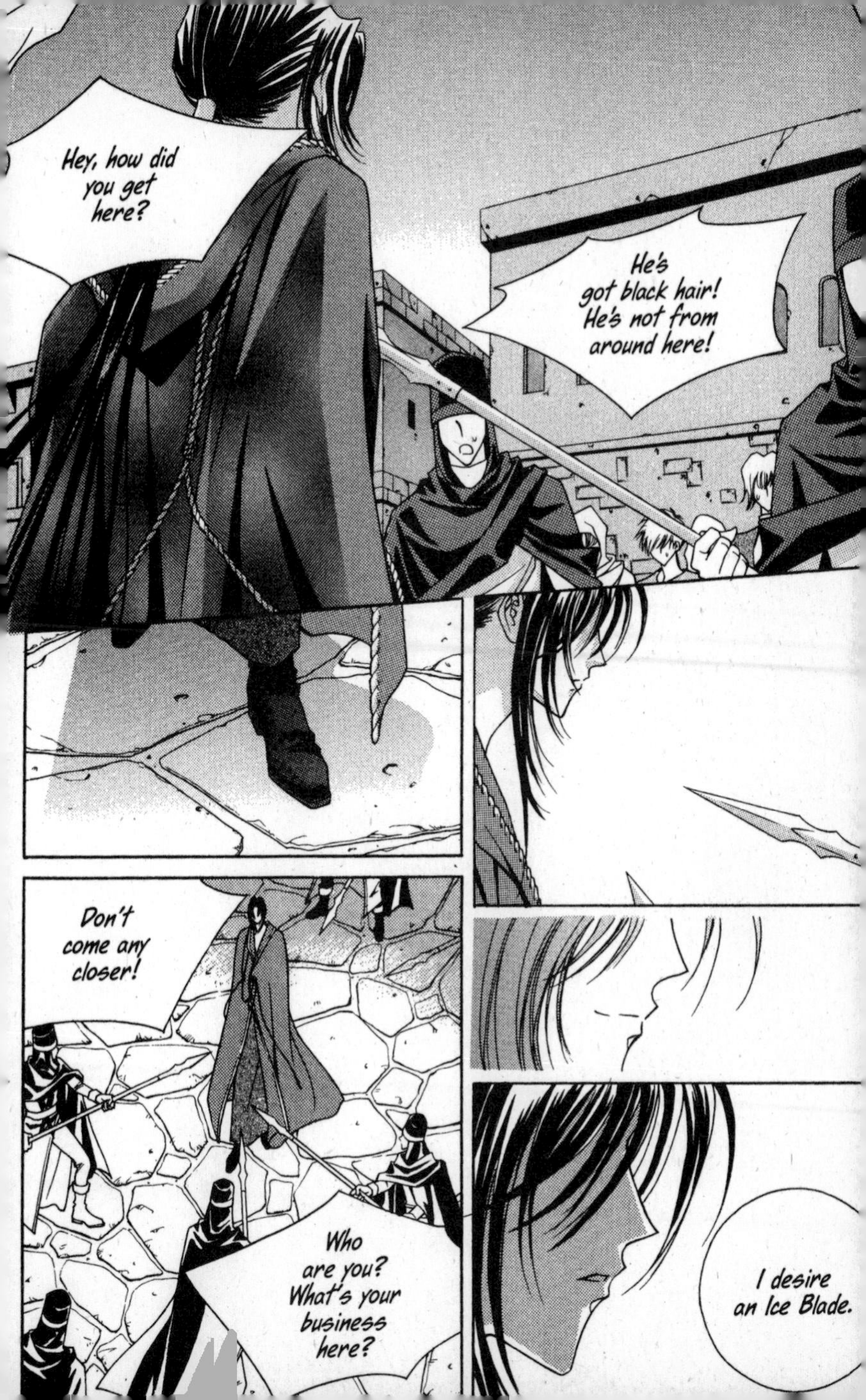
Hey, how did you get here?
He's got black hair! He's not from around here!
Don't come any closer!
Who are you? What's your business here?
I desire an Ice Blade.

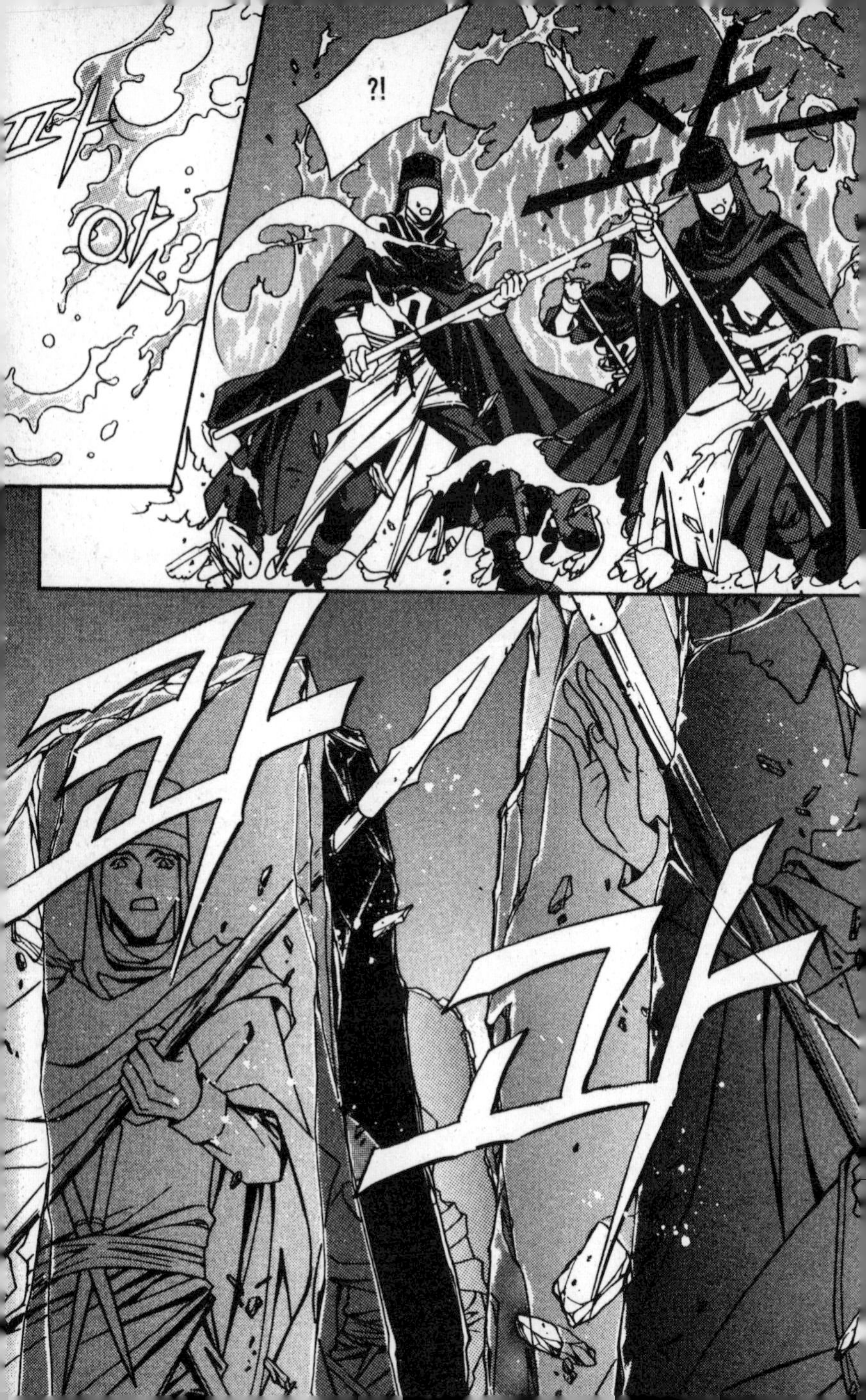
?!

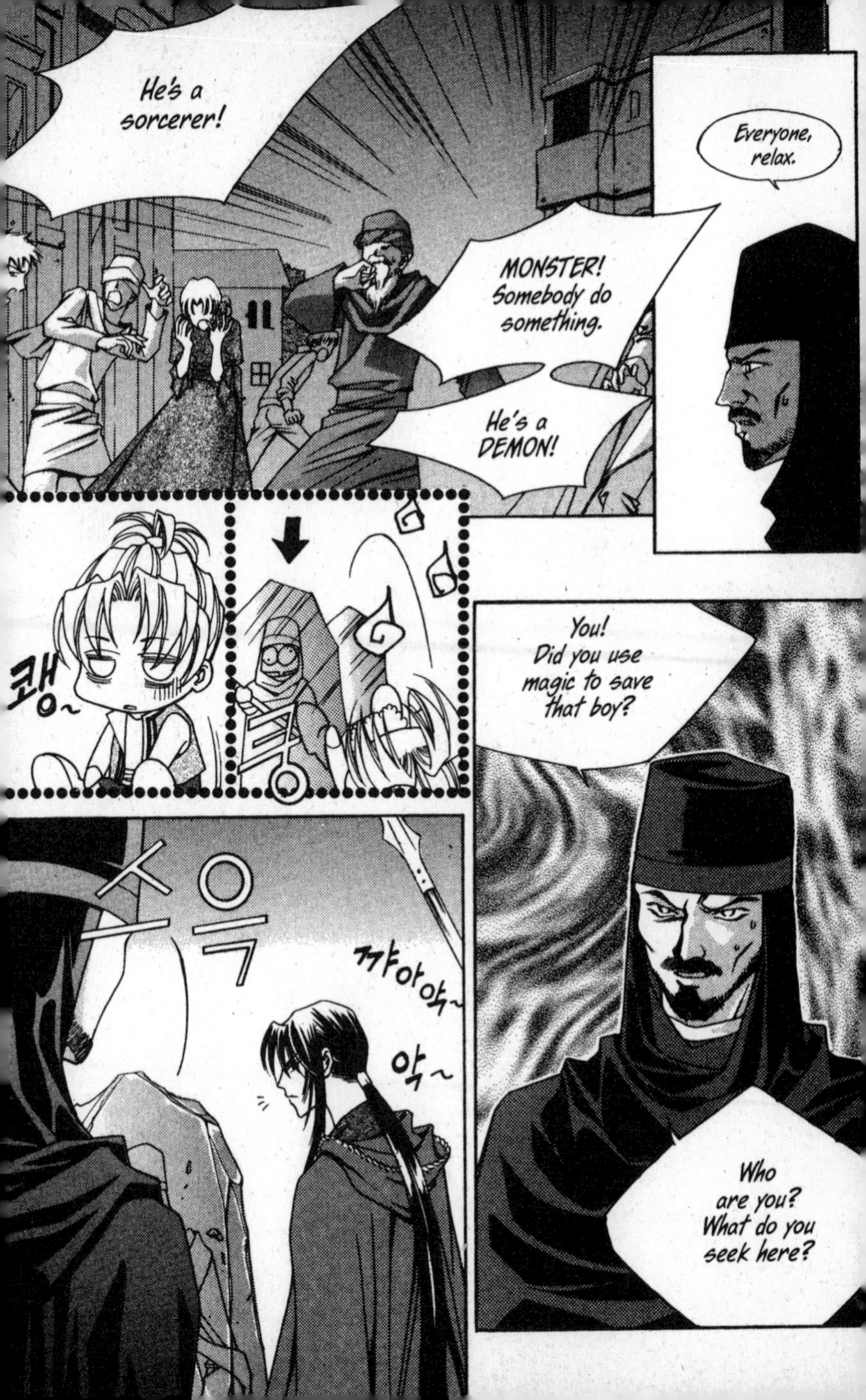
He's a sorcerer!
MONSTER! Somebody do something.
He's a DEMON!
Everyone, relax.
쾡~
쿵
스윽
꺄아악~
악~
You! Did you use magic to save that boy?
Who are you? What do you seek here?

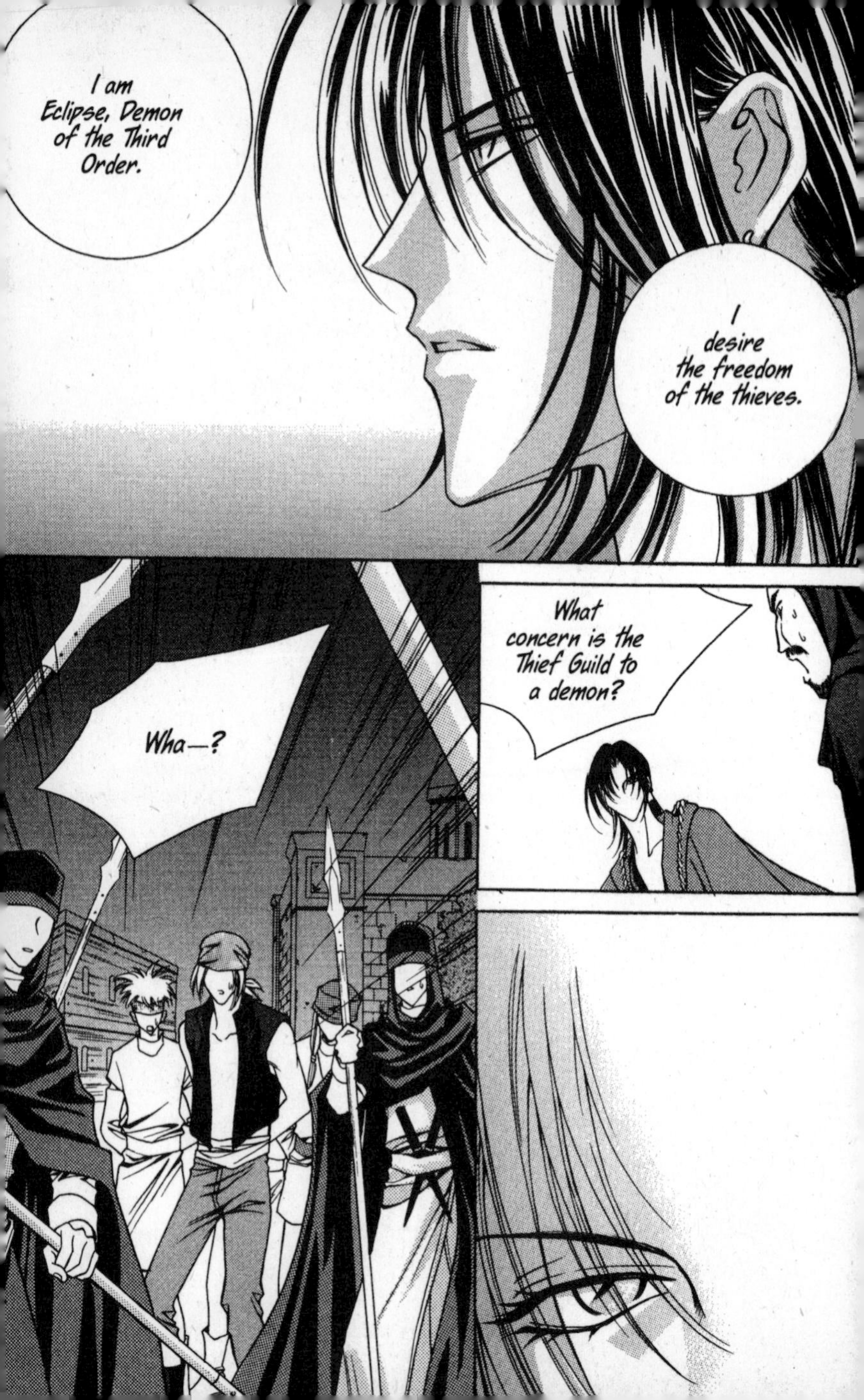
I am Eclipse, Demon of the Third Order.
I desire the freedom of the thieves.
Wha—?
What concern is the Thief Guild to a demon?

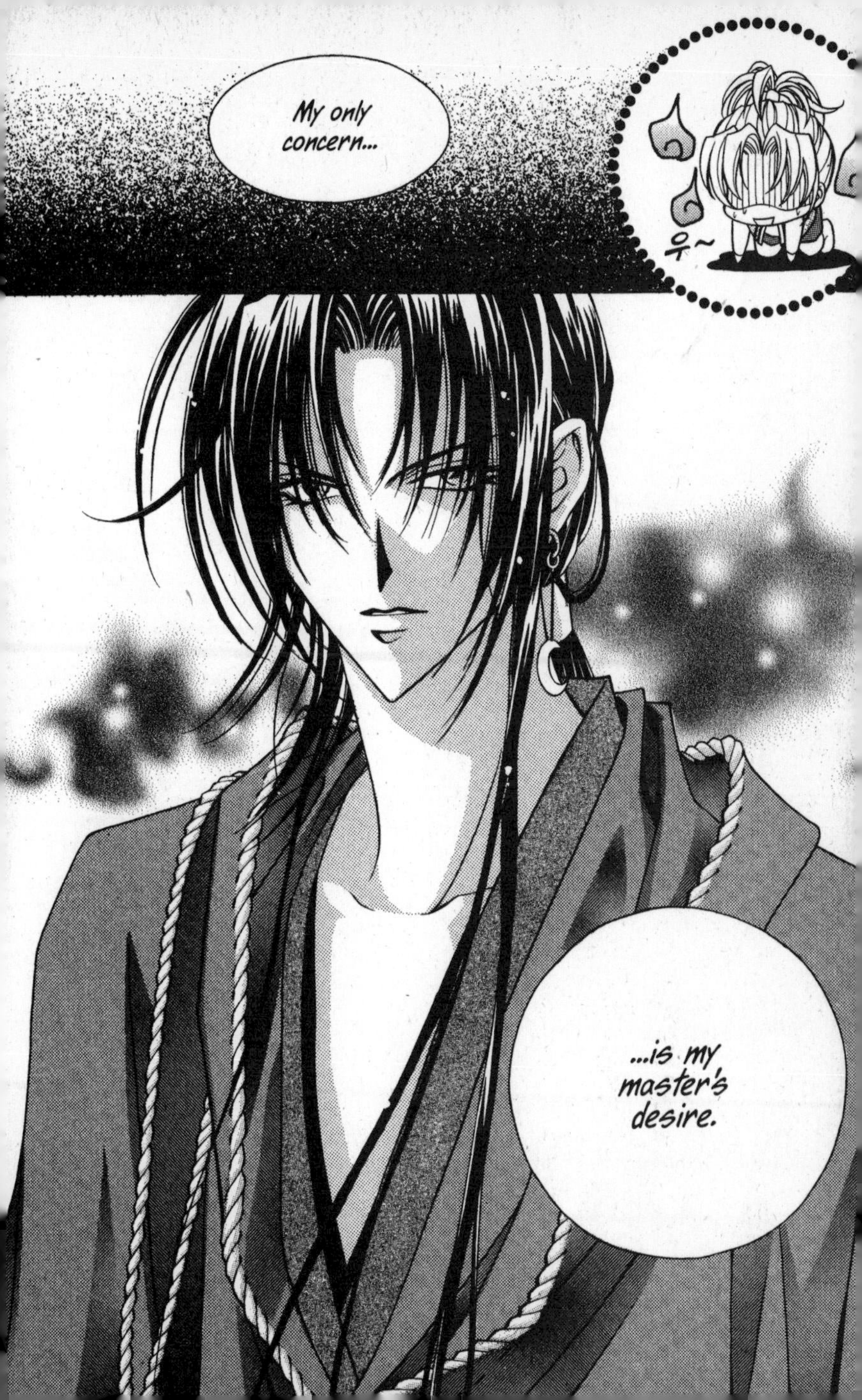
My only concern...
우~
...is my master's desire.

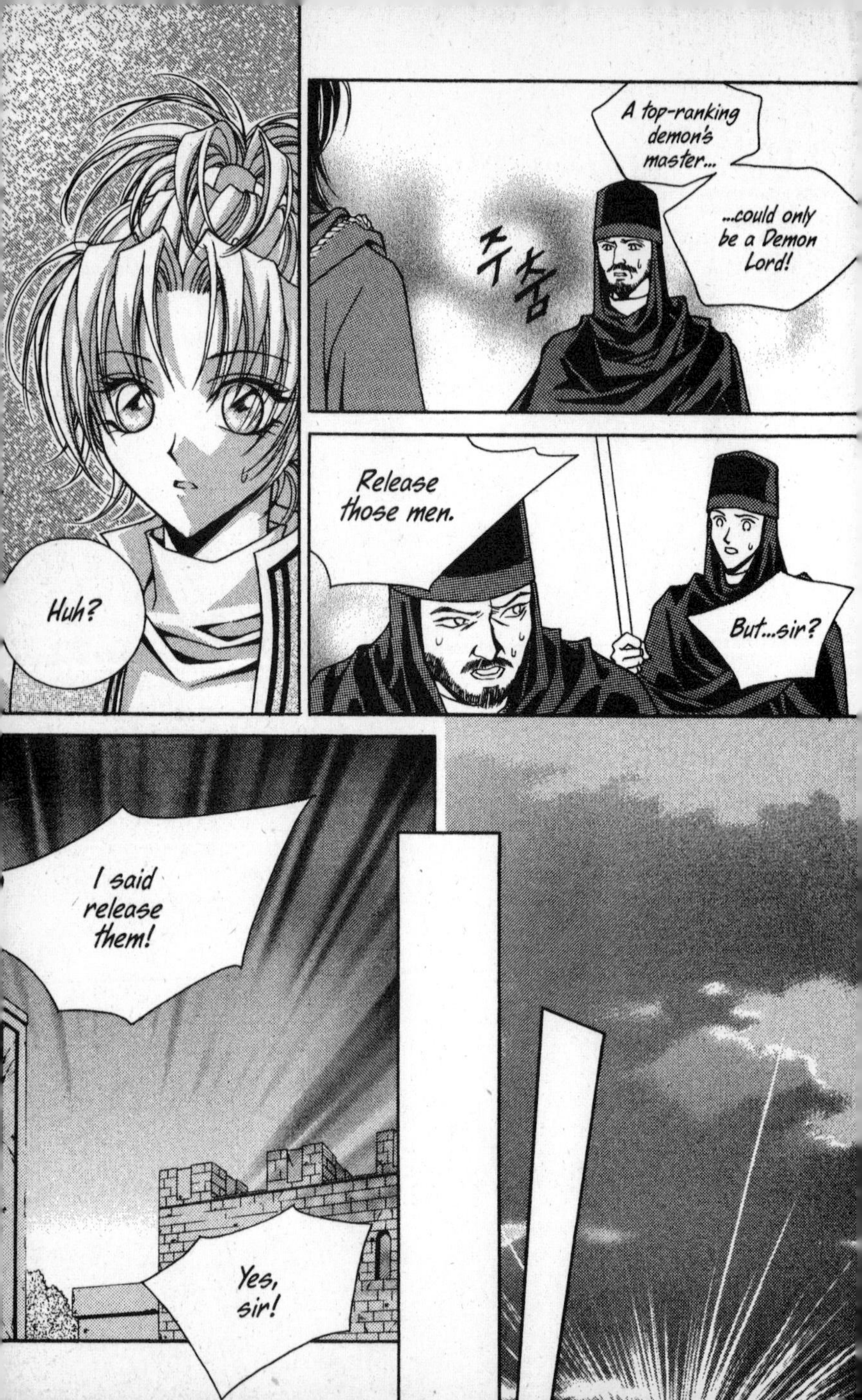
Huh?
A top-ranking demon's master...
...could only be a Demon Lord!
주춤
Release those men.
But...sir?
I said release them!
Yes, sir!

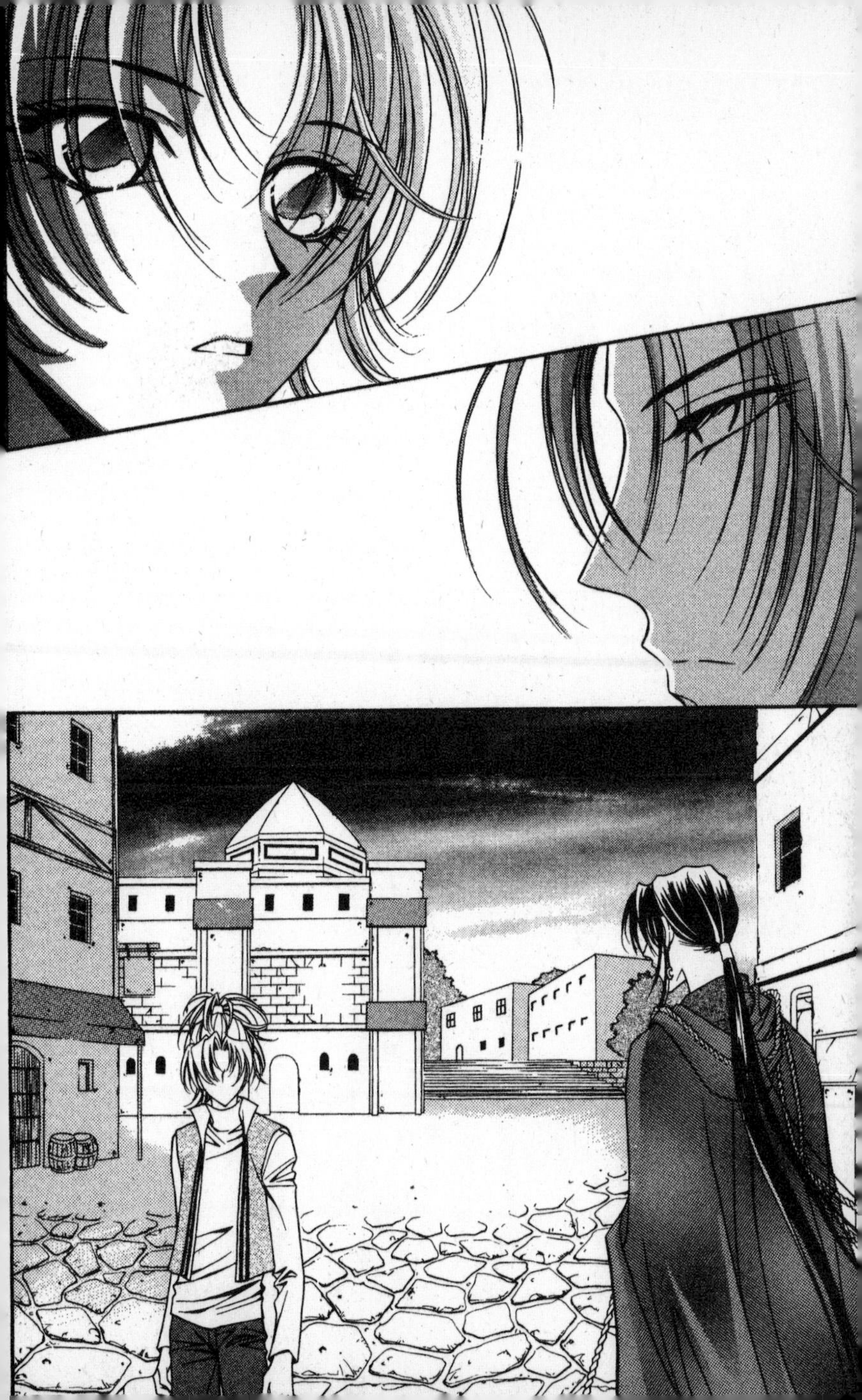

Mister... um...
Are you really a demon?
I always thought demons would be scarier.
Don't call me mister.
Please, my name is Eclipse.
I hate being called "Mister."
Eclipse.
Eclipse.
Eclipse.
It's all right, Sire.
Better memorize it.
Huh? What did you just call me?

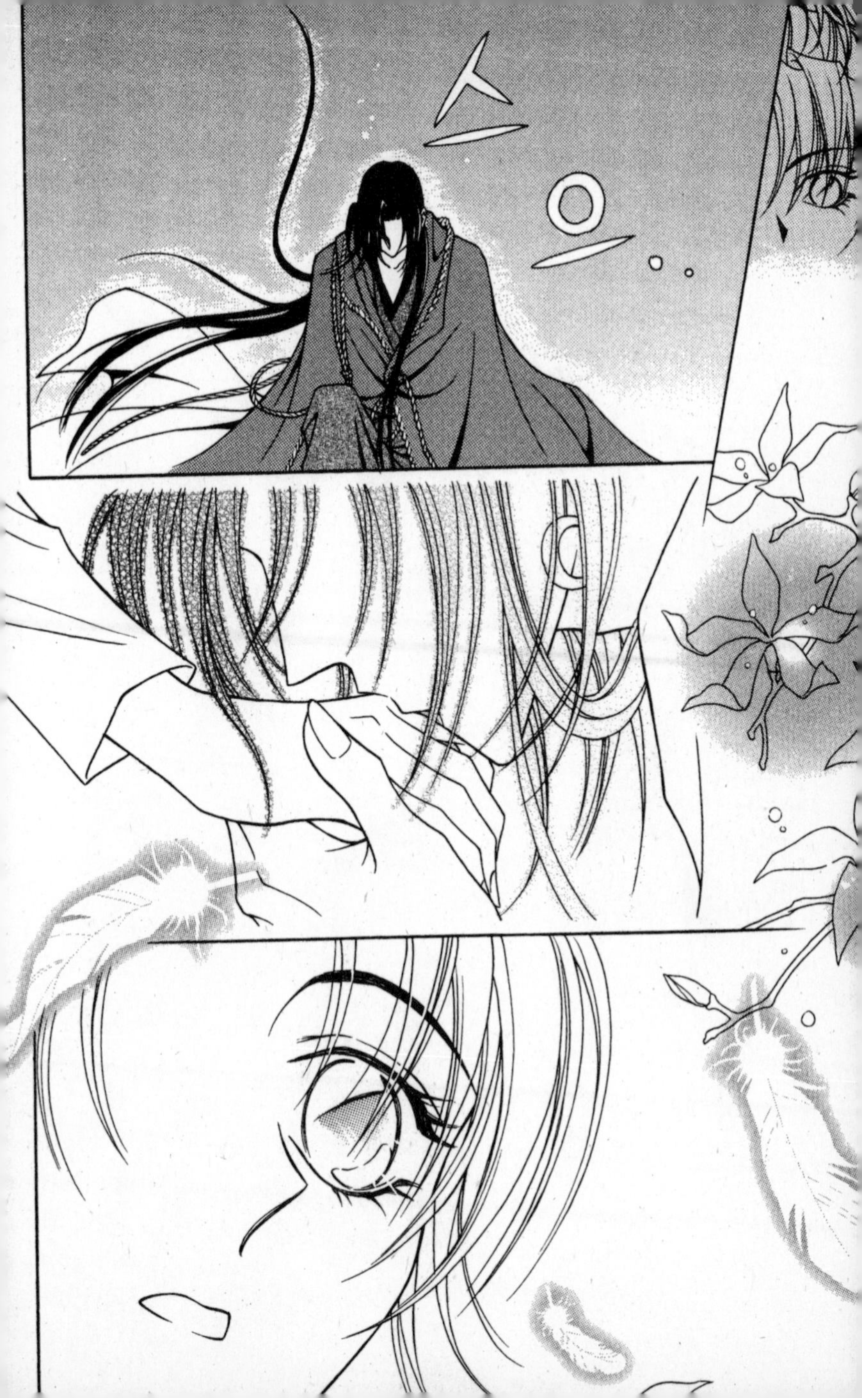

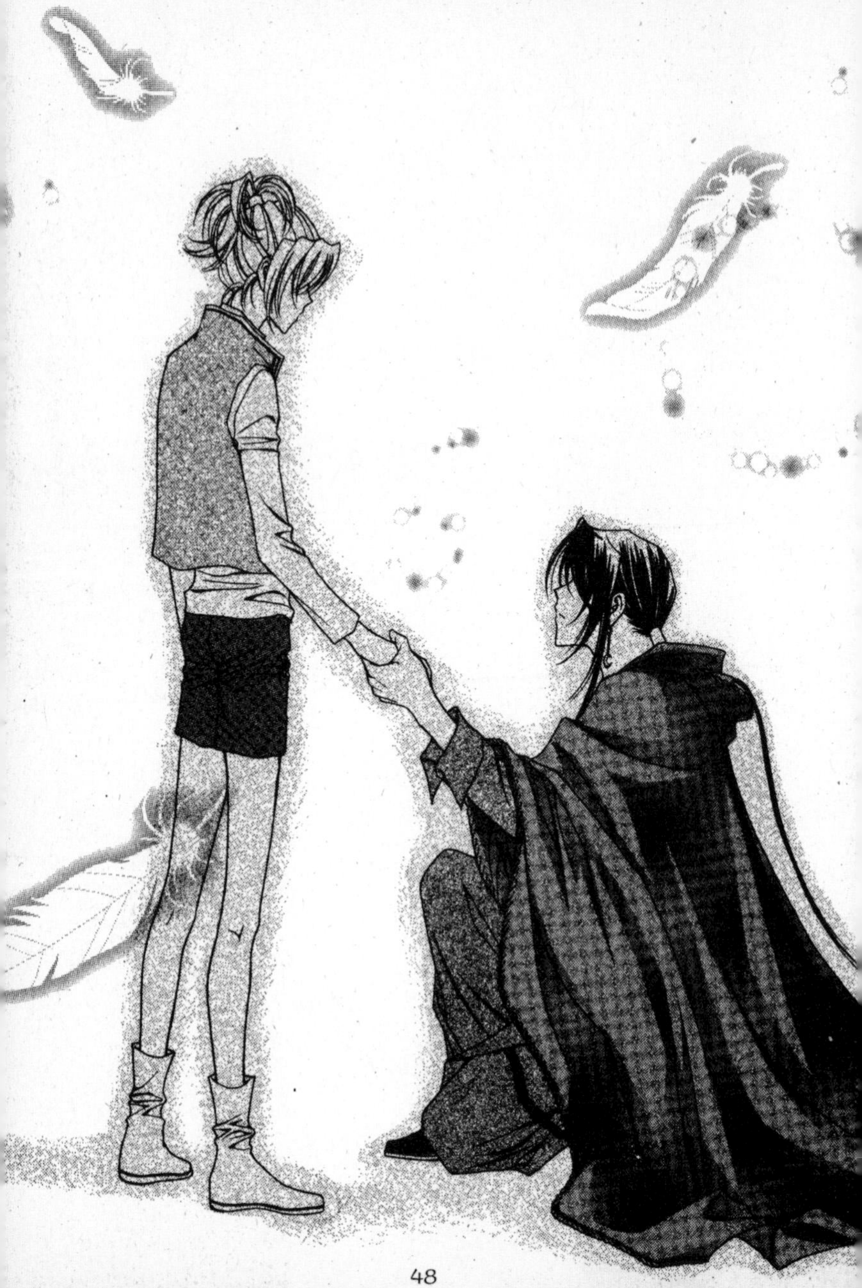

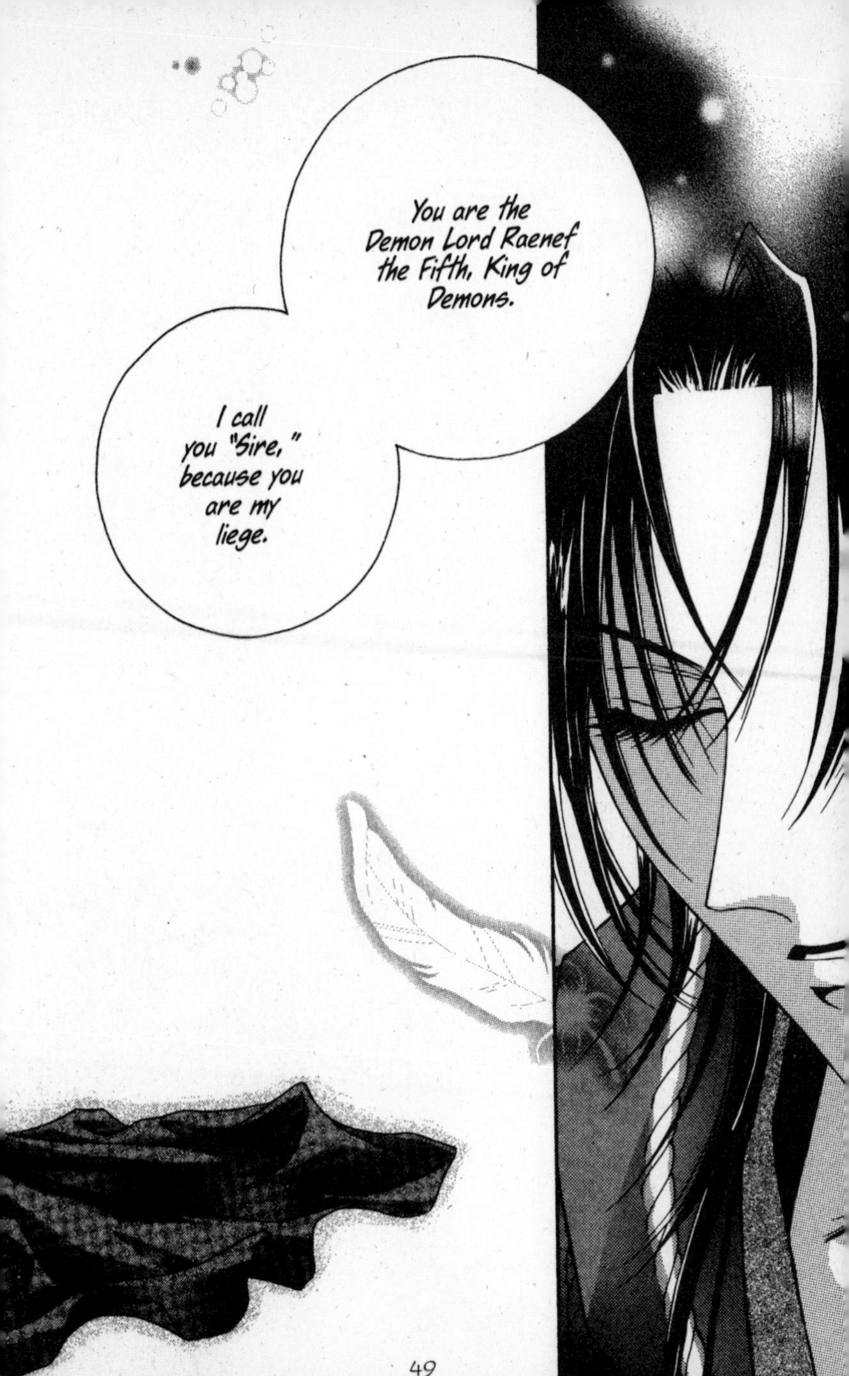
You are the Demon Lord Raenef the Fifth, King of Demons.
I call you "Sire," because you are my liege.

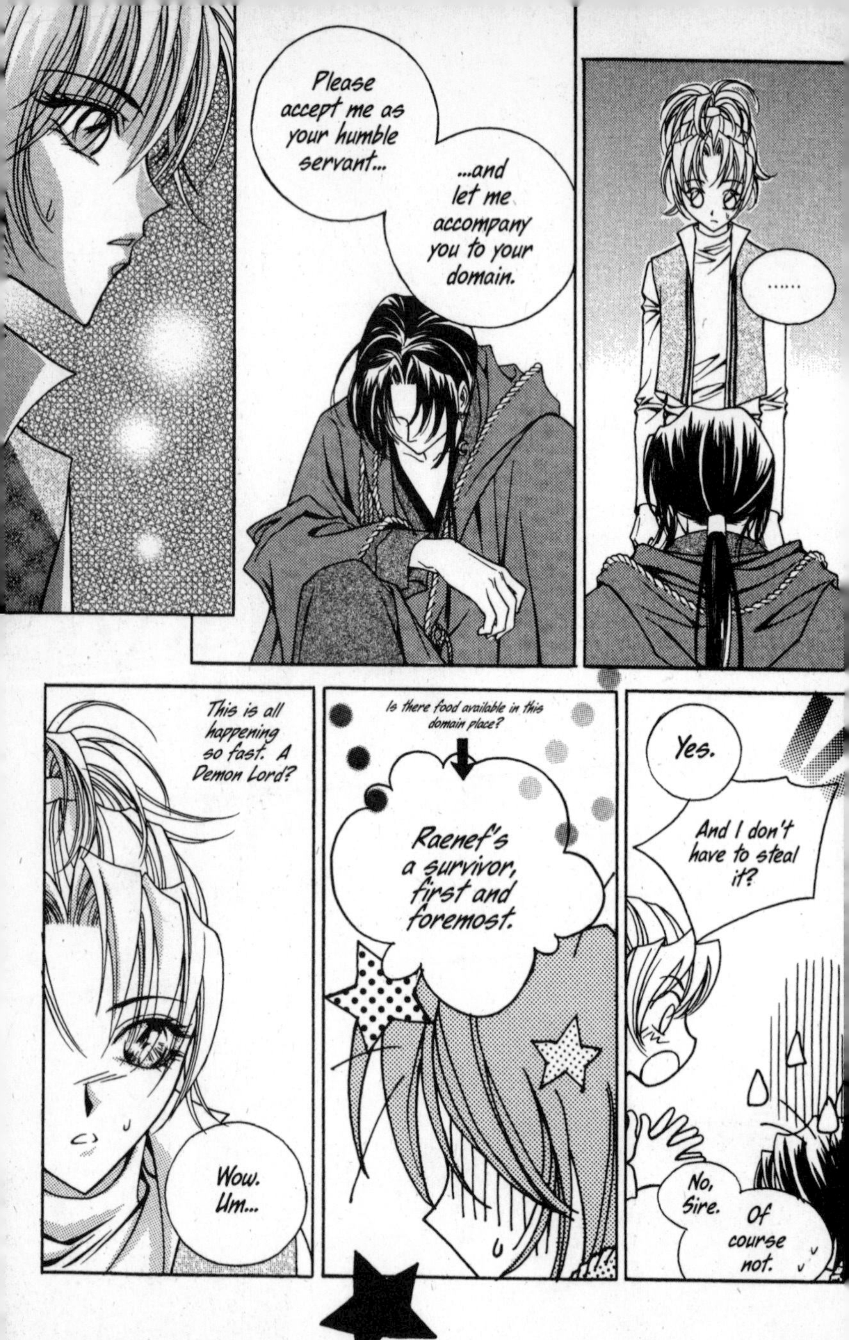
Please accept me as your humble servant...
...and let me accompany you to your domain.
......
This is all happening so fast. A Demon Lord?
Wow. Um...
Is there food available in this domain place?
Raenef's a survivor, first and foremost.
Yes.
And I don't have to steal it?
No, Sire.
Of course not.

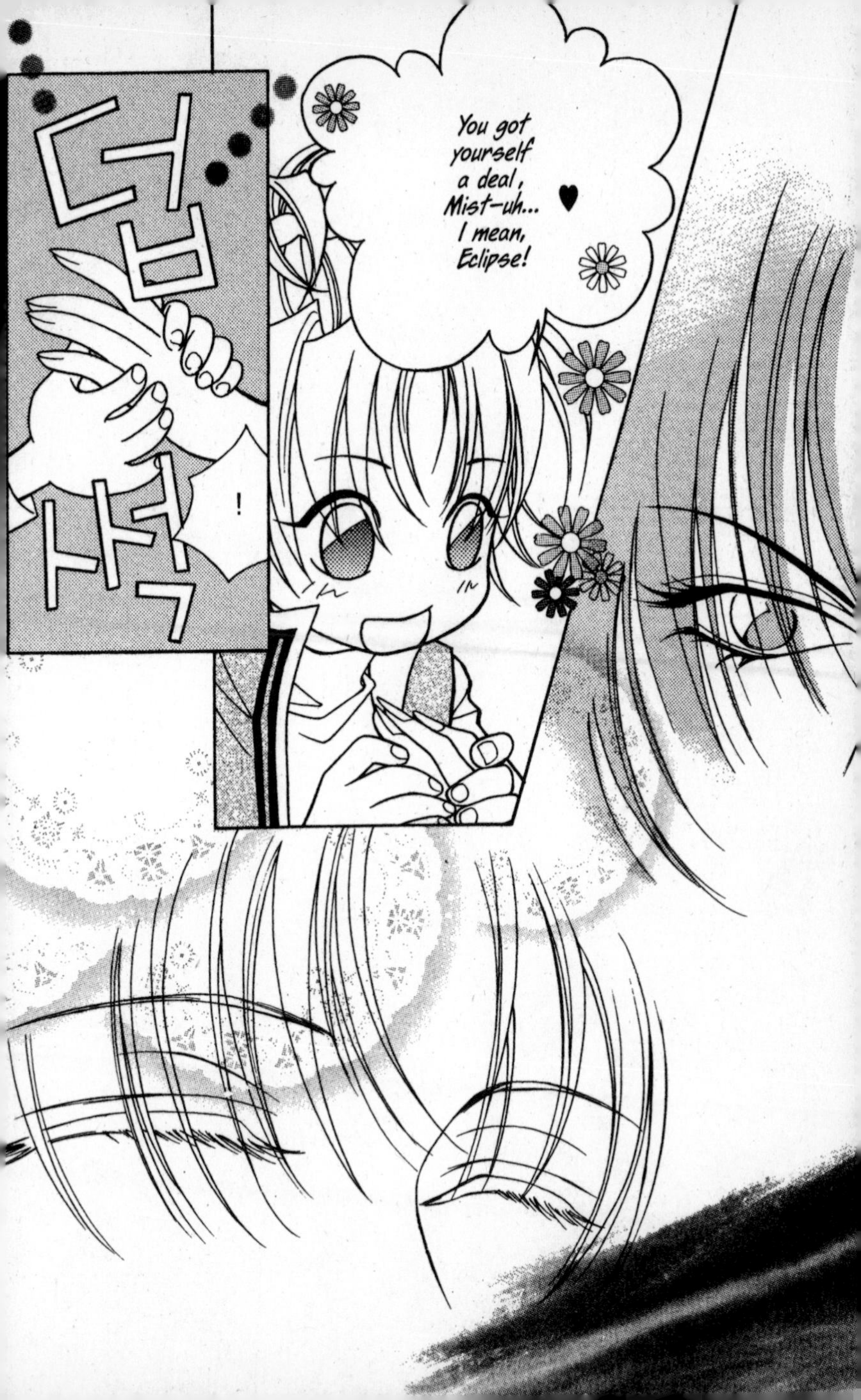

You got yourself a deal, Mist-uh... I mean, Eclipse!
!

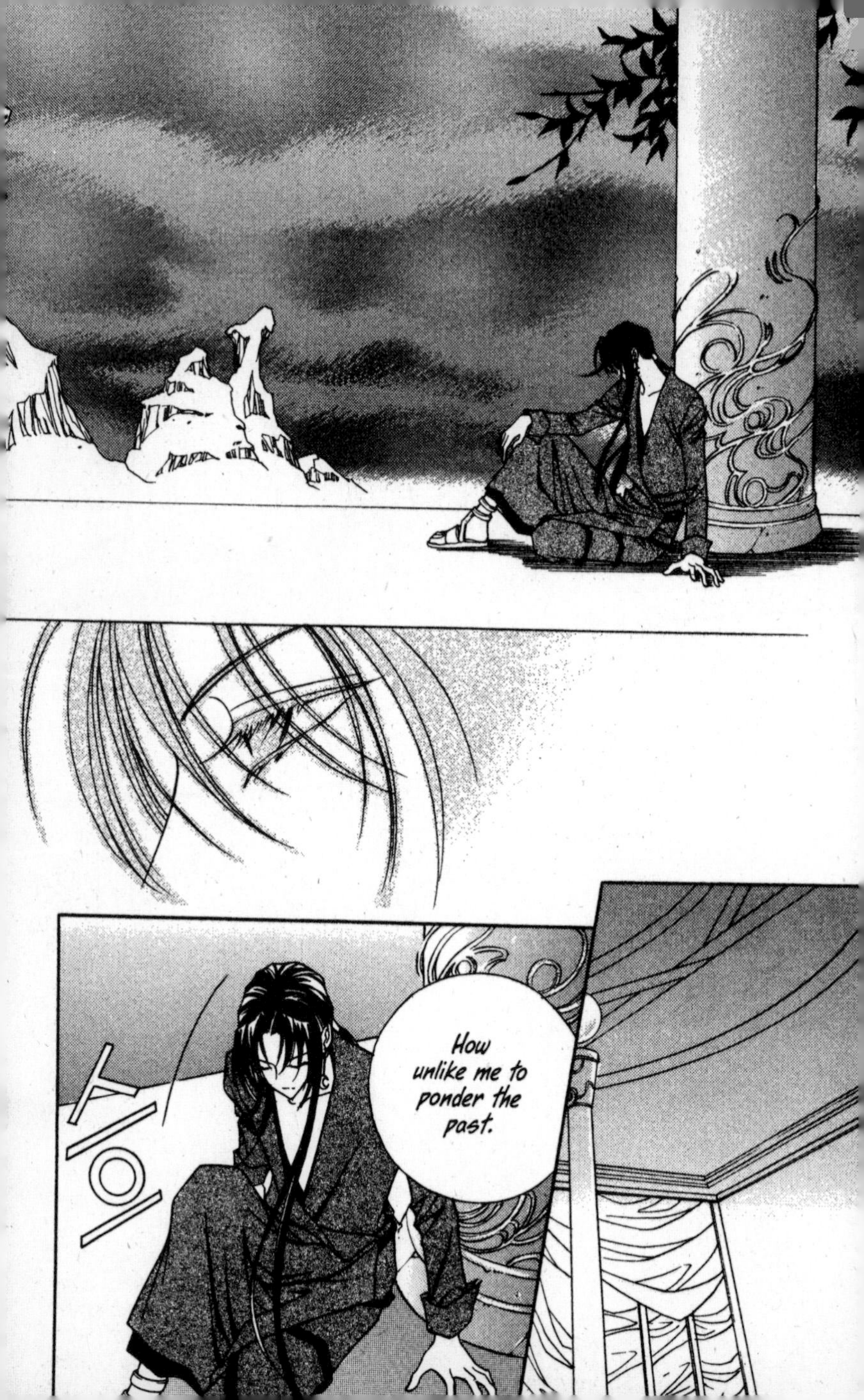
How unlike me to ponder the past.

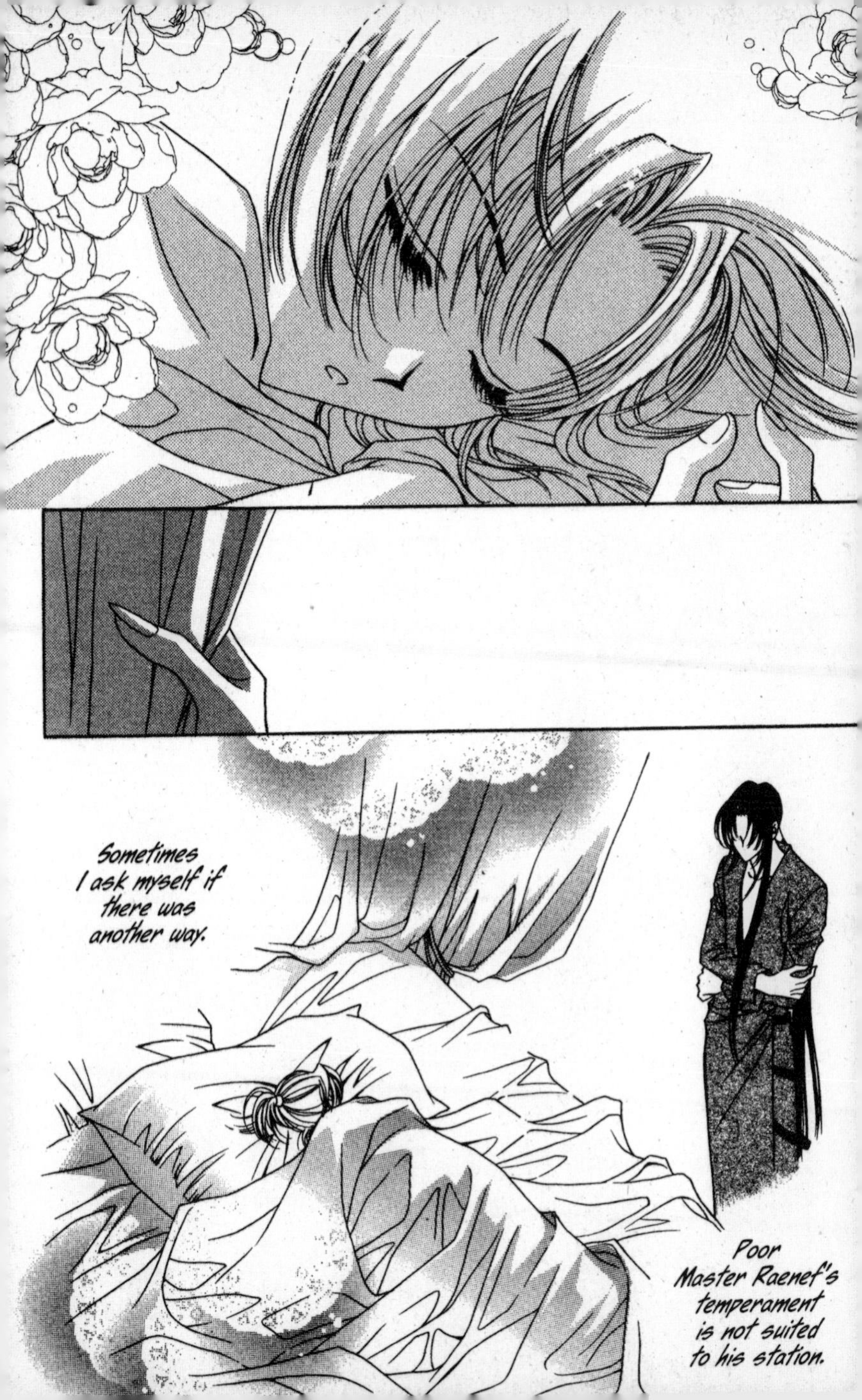
Sometimes I ask myself if there was another way.
Poor Master Raenef's temperament is not suited to his station.

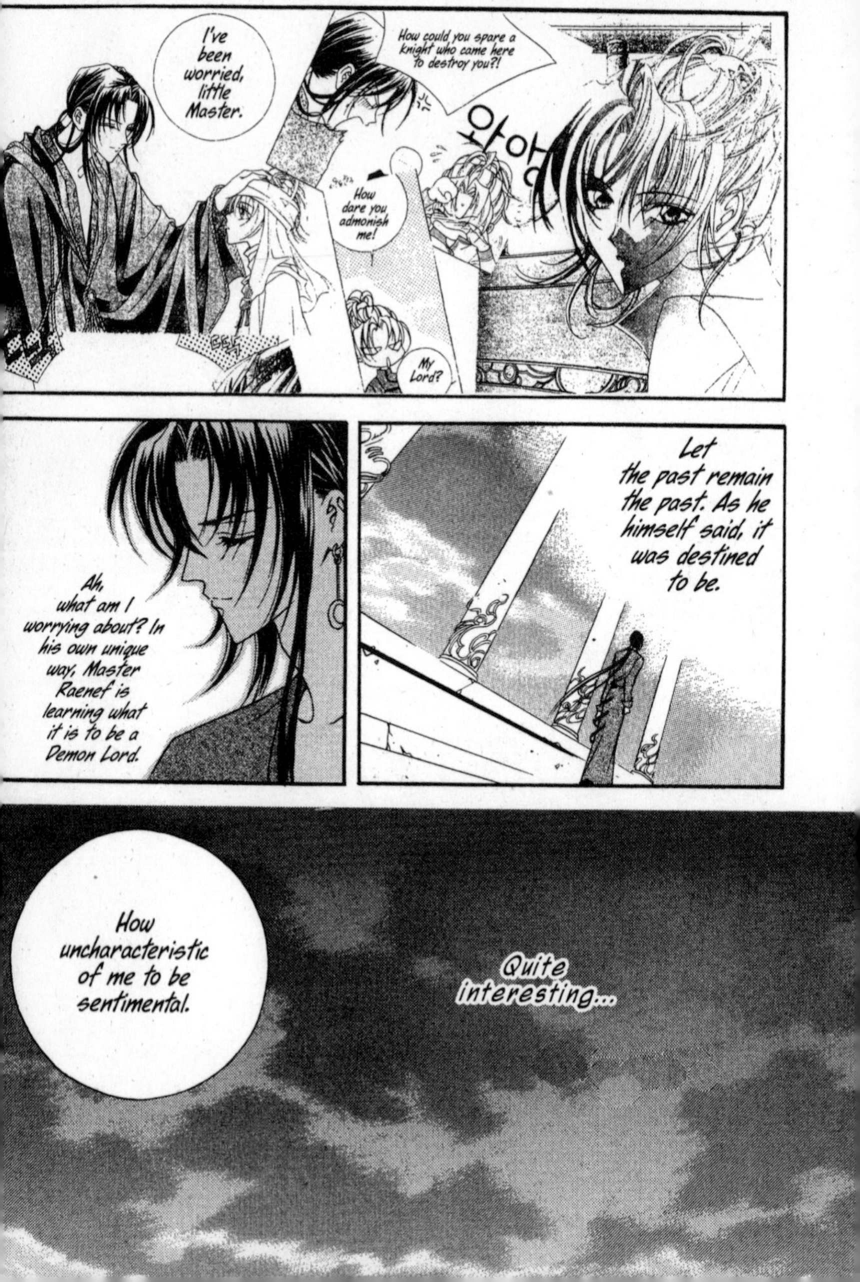
I've been worried, little Master.
How could you spare a knight who came here to destroy you?!
How dare you admonish me!
My Lord?
Ah, what am I worrying about? In his own unique way, Master Raenef is learning what it is to be a Demon Lord.
Let the past remain the past. As he himself said, it was destined to be.
How uncharacteristic of me to be sentimental.
Quite interesting...

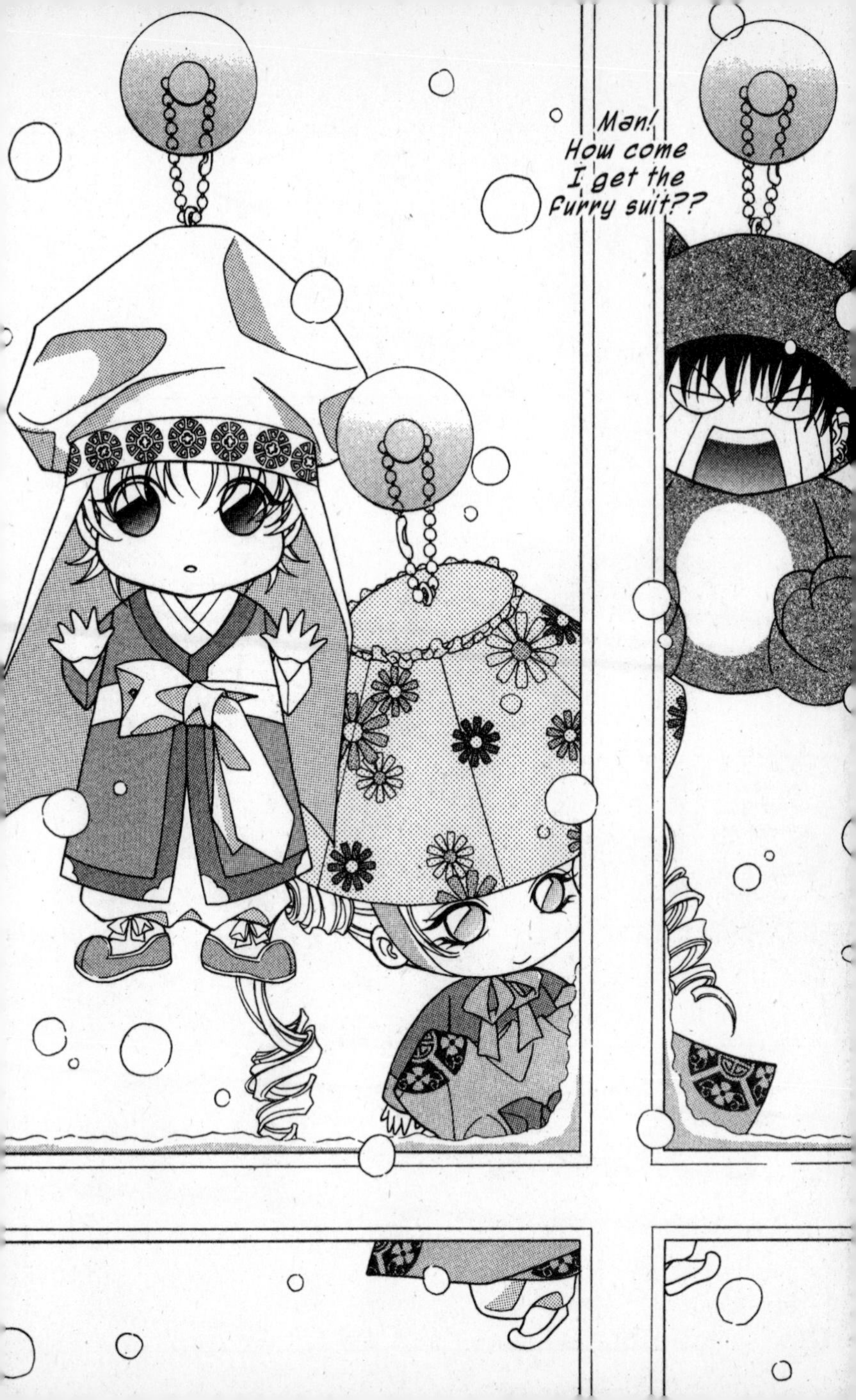
Man! How come I get the furry suit??

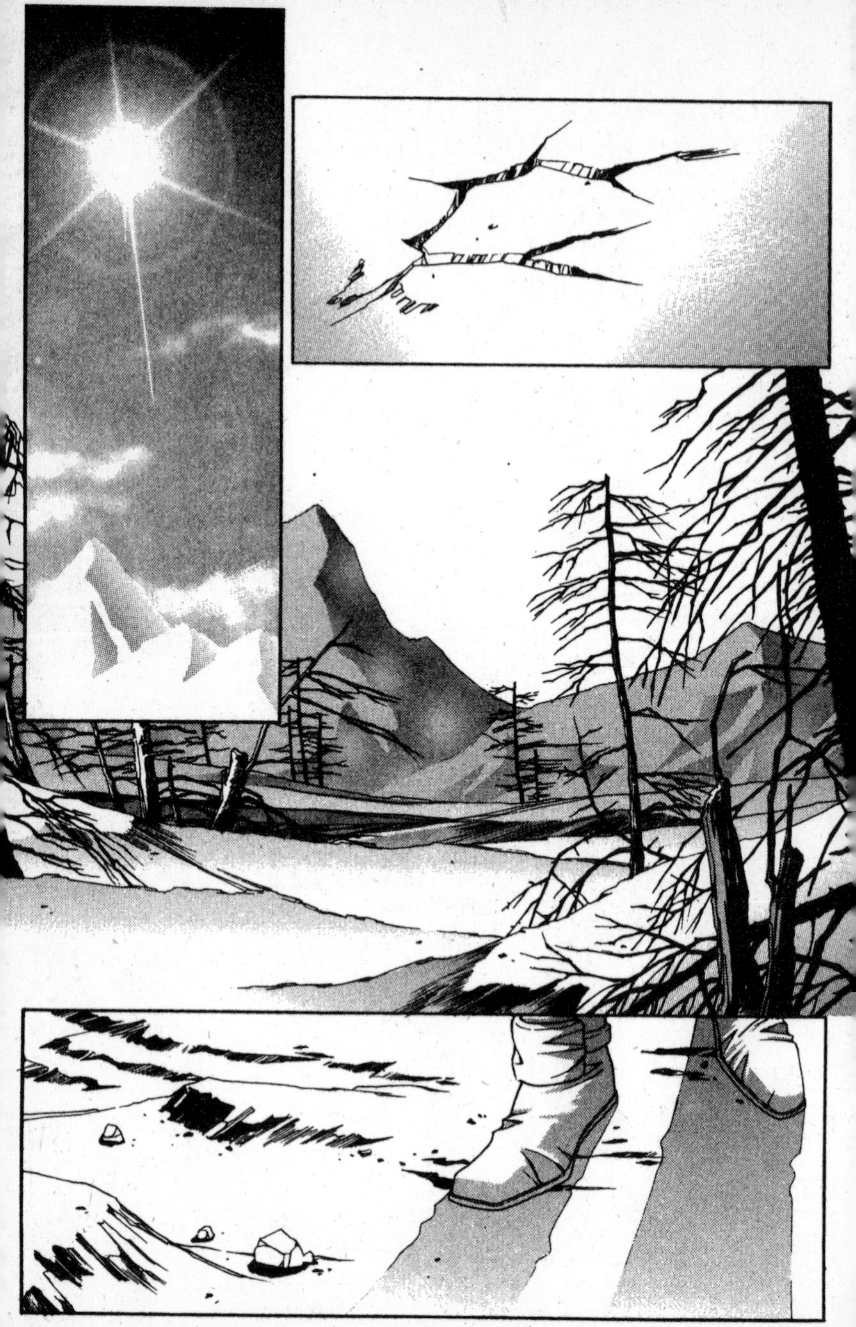

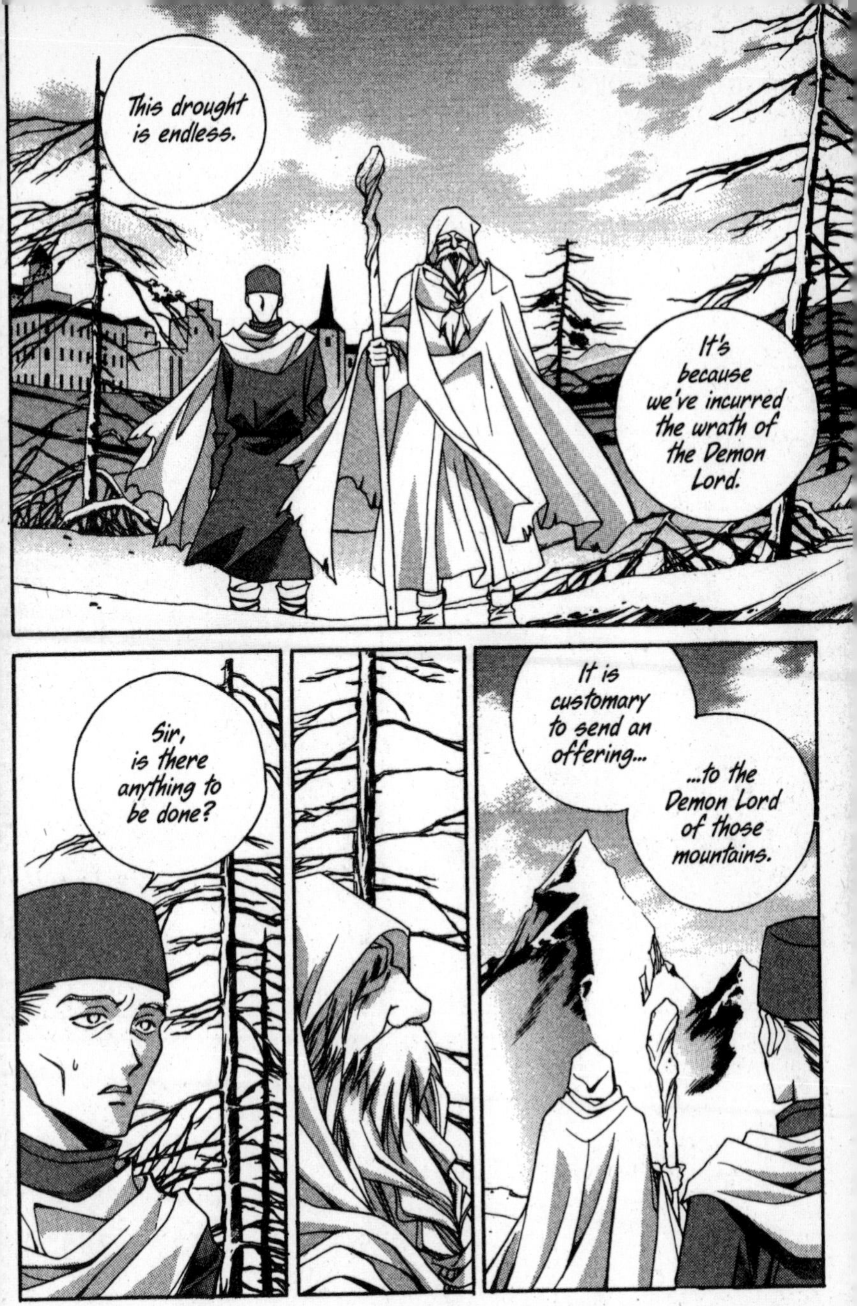
This drought is endless.
It's because we've incurred the wrath of the Demon Lord.
Sir, is there anything to be done?
It is customary to send an offering...
...to the Demon Lord of those mountains.

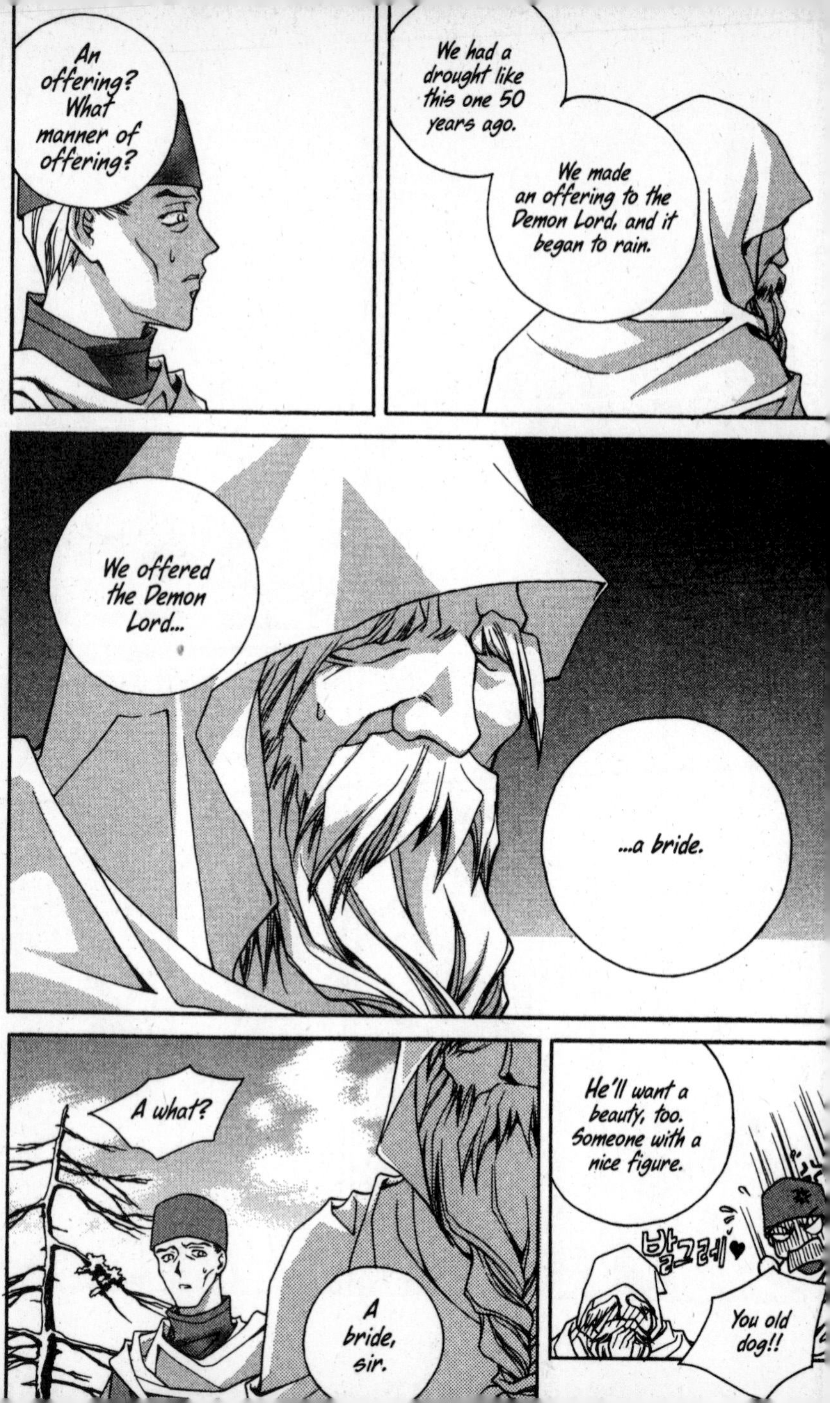
An offering? What manner of offering?
We had a drought like this one 50 years ago.
We made an offering to the Demon Lord, and it began to rain.
We offered the Demon Lord...
...a bride.
A what?
A bride, sir.
He'll want a beauty, too. Someone with a nice figure.
발그레♥
You old dog!!

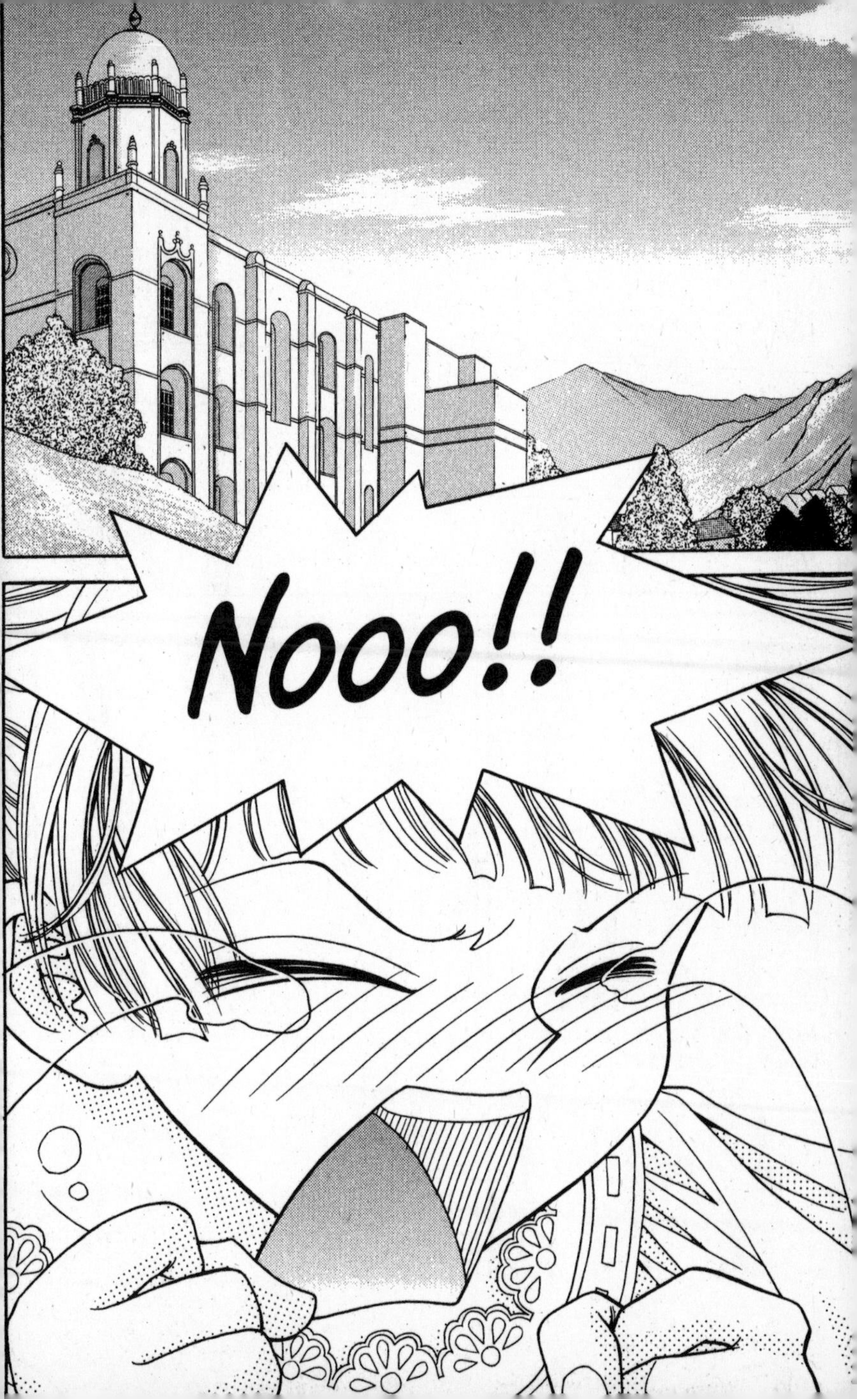
Nooo!!

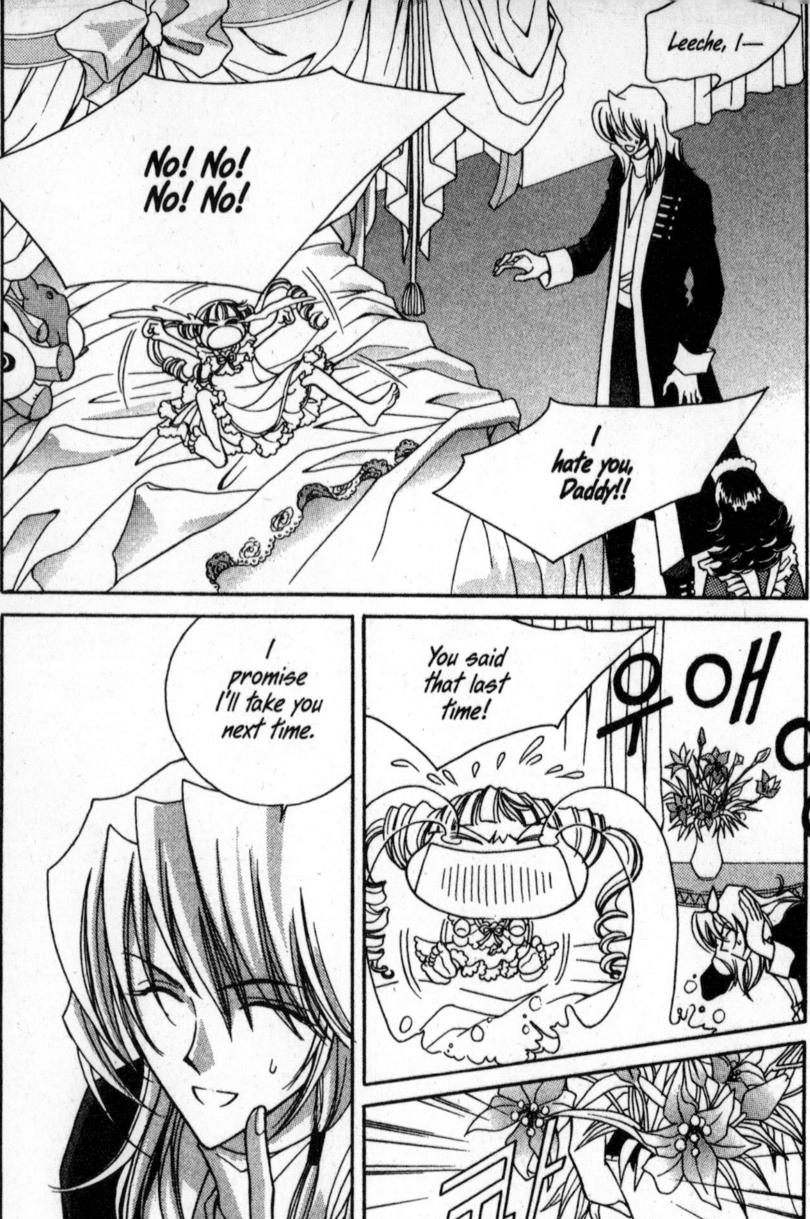
Leeche, I—
No! No! No! No!
I hate you, Daddy!!
I promise I'll take you next time.
You said that last time!
OH

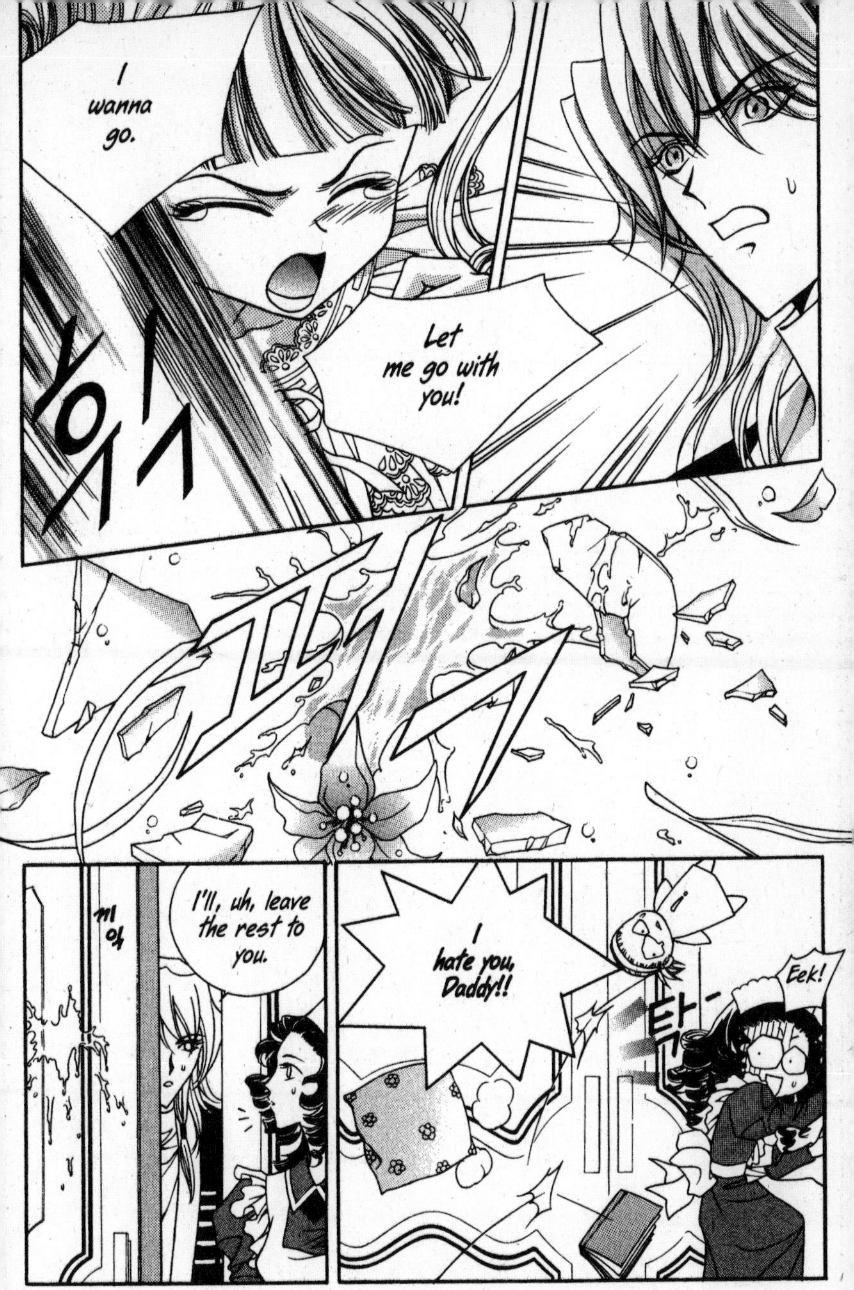
I wanna go.
Let me go with you!
I'll, uh, leave the rest to you.
I hate you, Daddy!!
탁-
Eek!

I fear I've spoiled her.
It's hard rearing a daughter alone.
Sire, the offering to the Demon Lord has arrived.
Oh, yes. I'll be right there.
Little brat!
I know she's the Lord's daughter, but her tantrums are too much!
Personally, I feel sorry for her.
Poor baby. Her mother was killed by demons, so her father's a little over-protective.

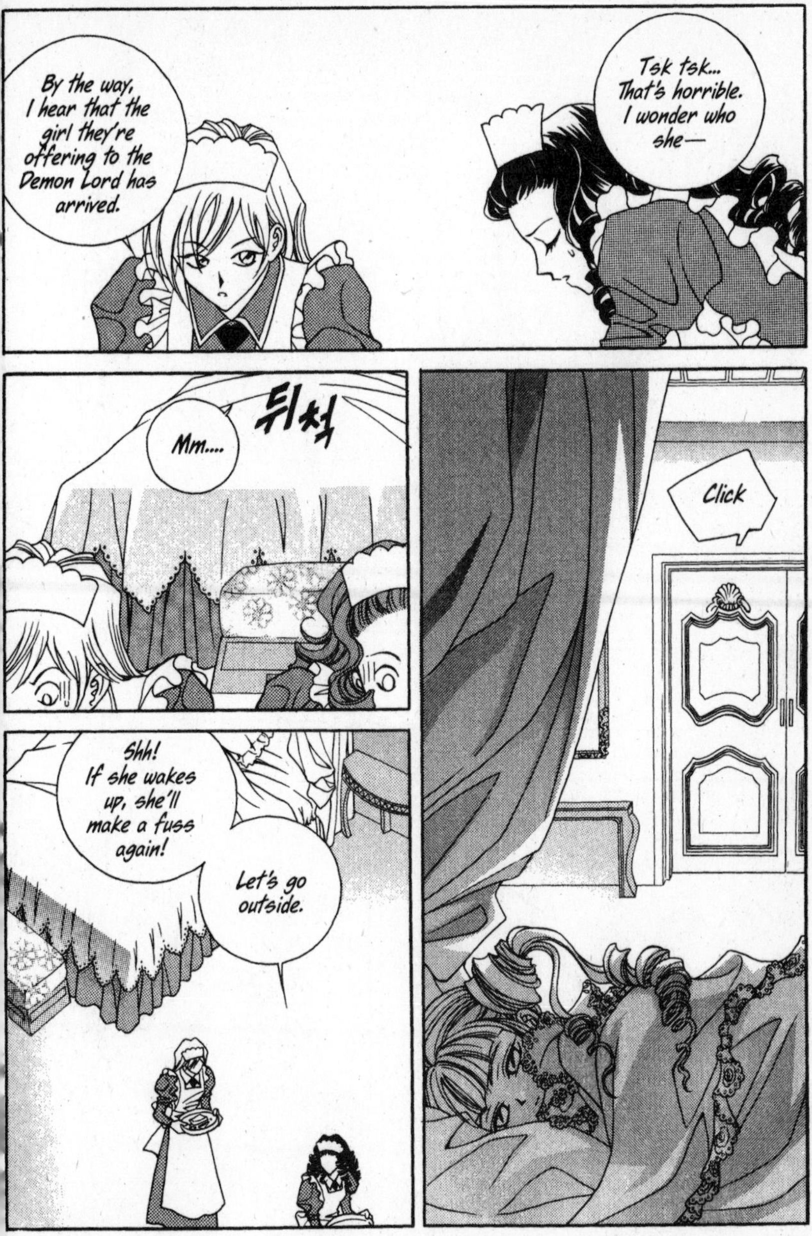
By the way, I hear that the girl they're offering to the Demon Lord has arrived.
Tsk tsk... That's horrible. I wonder who she—
Mm....
뒤척
Shh! If she wakes up, she'll make a fuss again!
Let's go outside.
Click

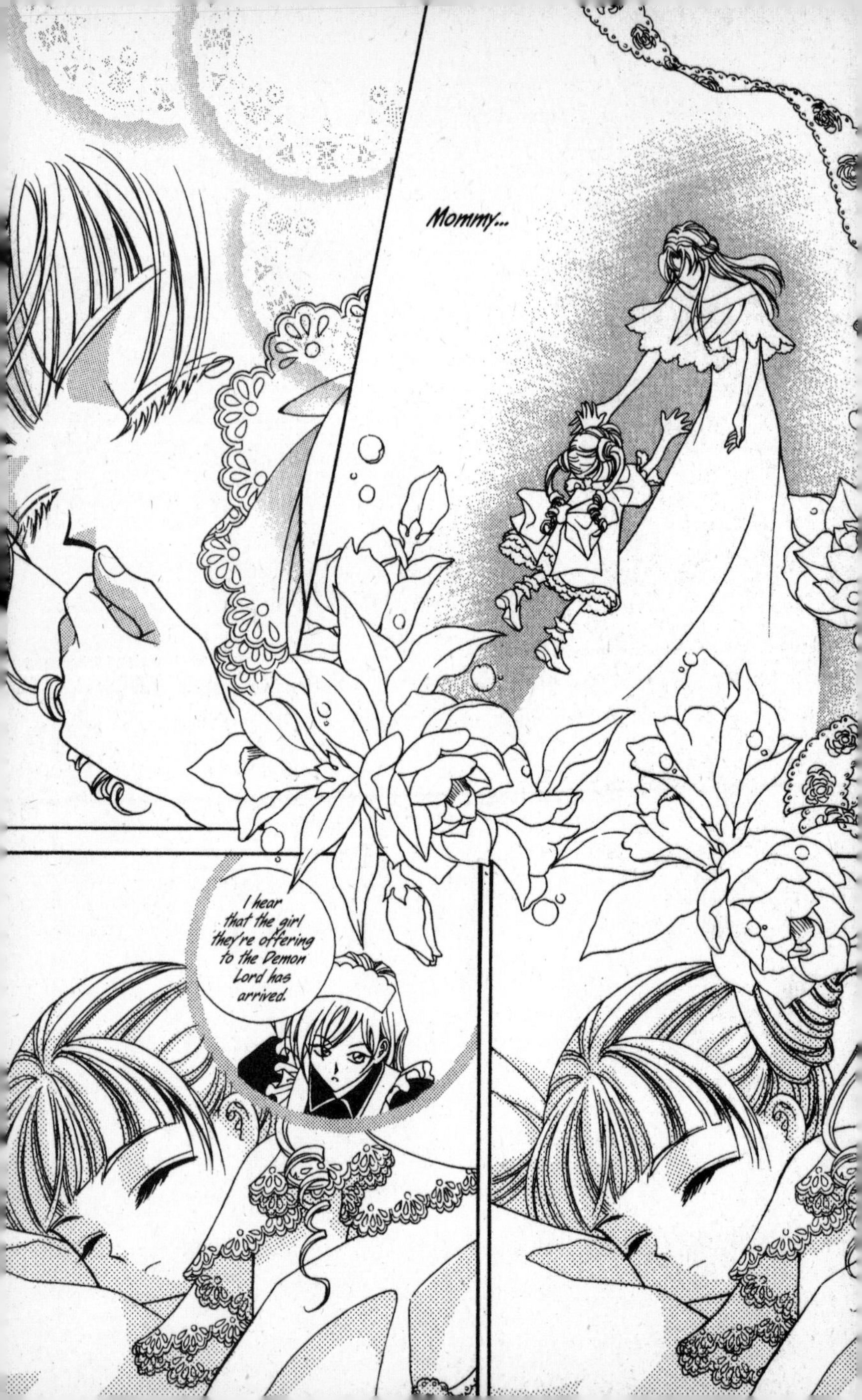
Mommy...
I hear that the girl they're offering to the Demon Lord has arrived.

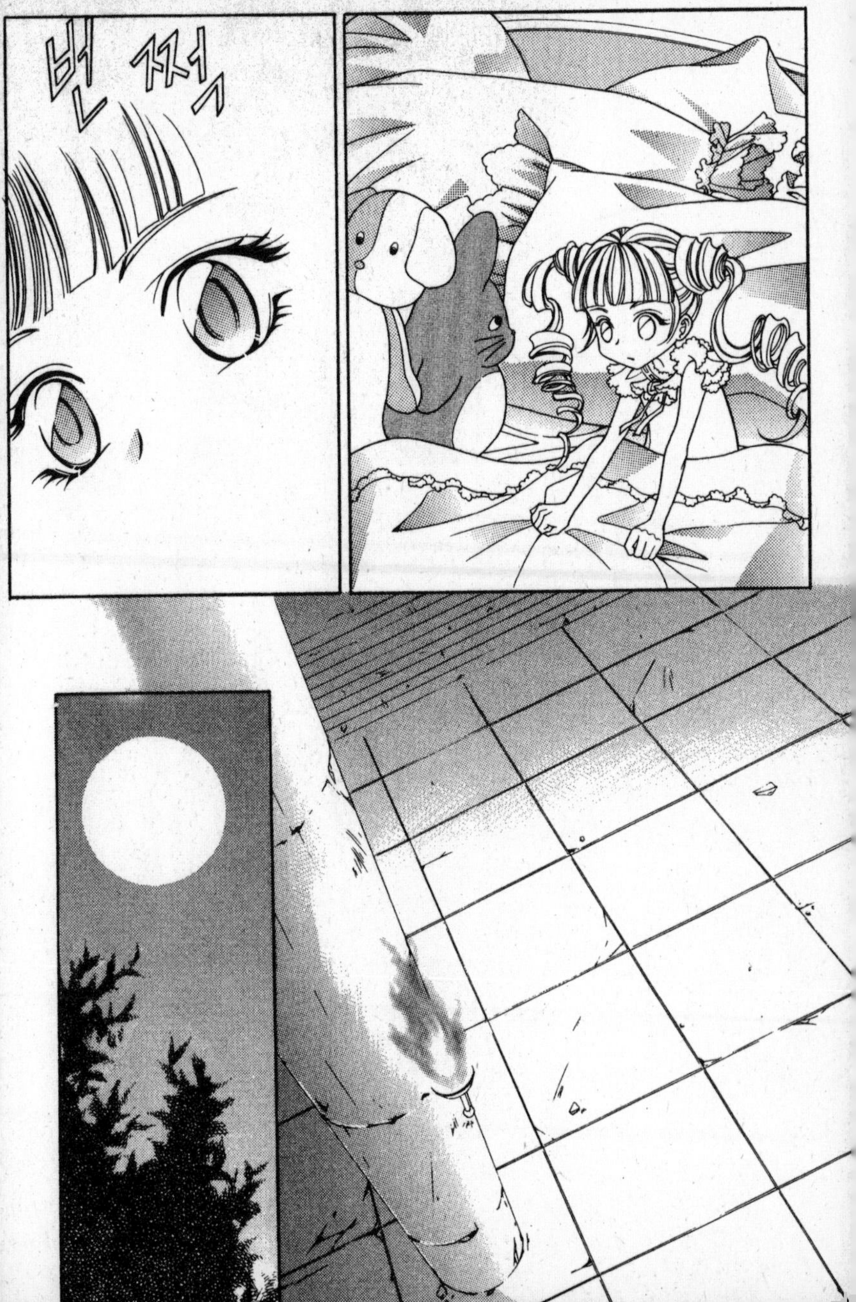
번쩍

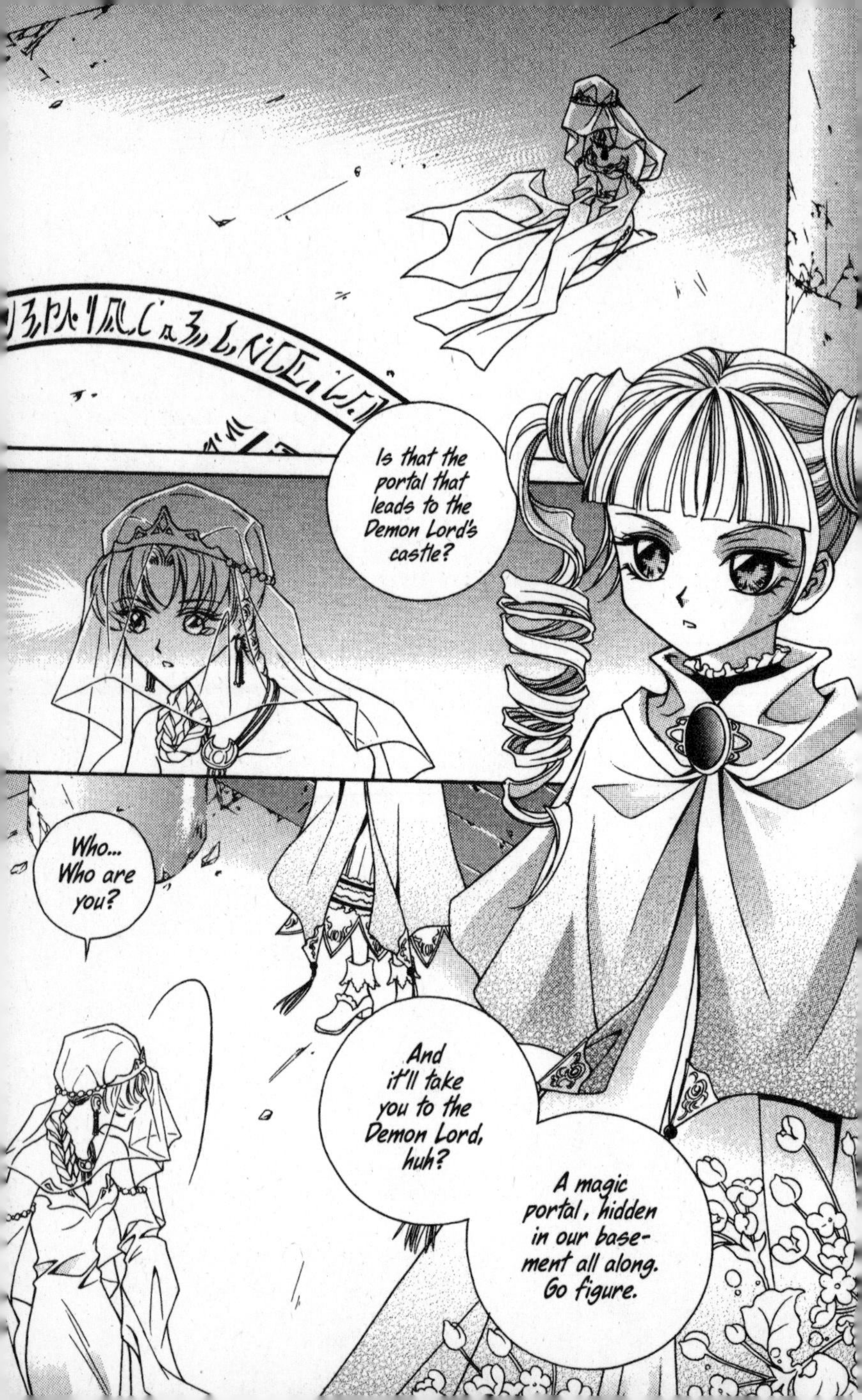
Is that the portal that leads to the Demon Lord's castle?
Who... Who are you?
And it'll take you to the Demon Lord, huh?
A magic portal, hidden in our base-ment all along. Go figure.

A child? How did you get here, little girl?
It's dangerous here. Go home.
Hey! I said run along!
털썩

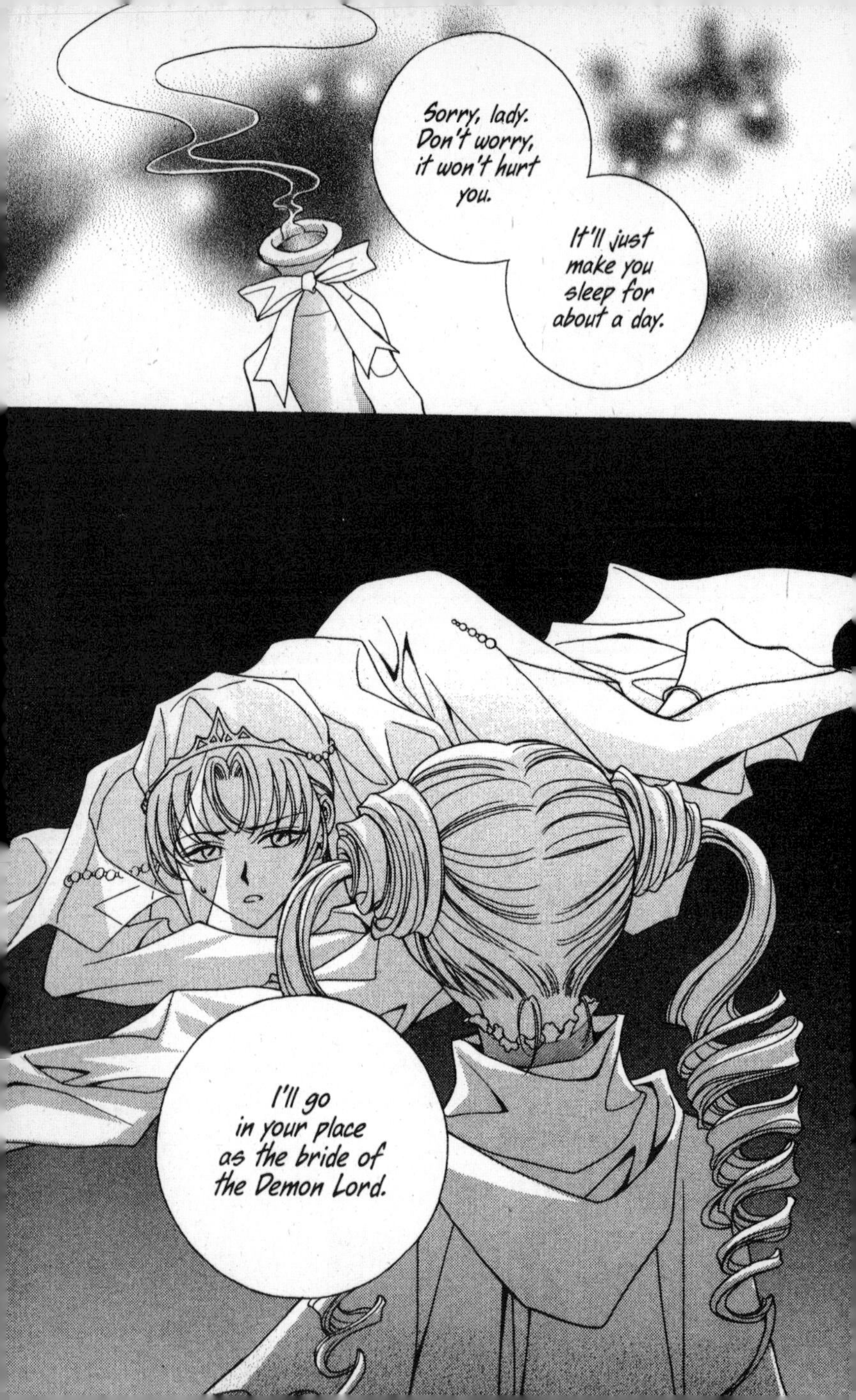
Sorry, lady. Don't worry, it won't hurt you.
It'll just make you sleep for about a day.
I'll go in your place as the bride of the Demon Lord.

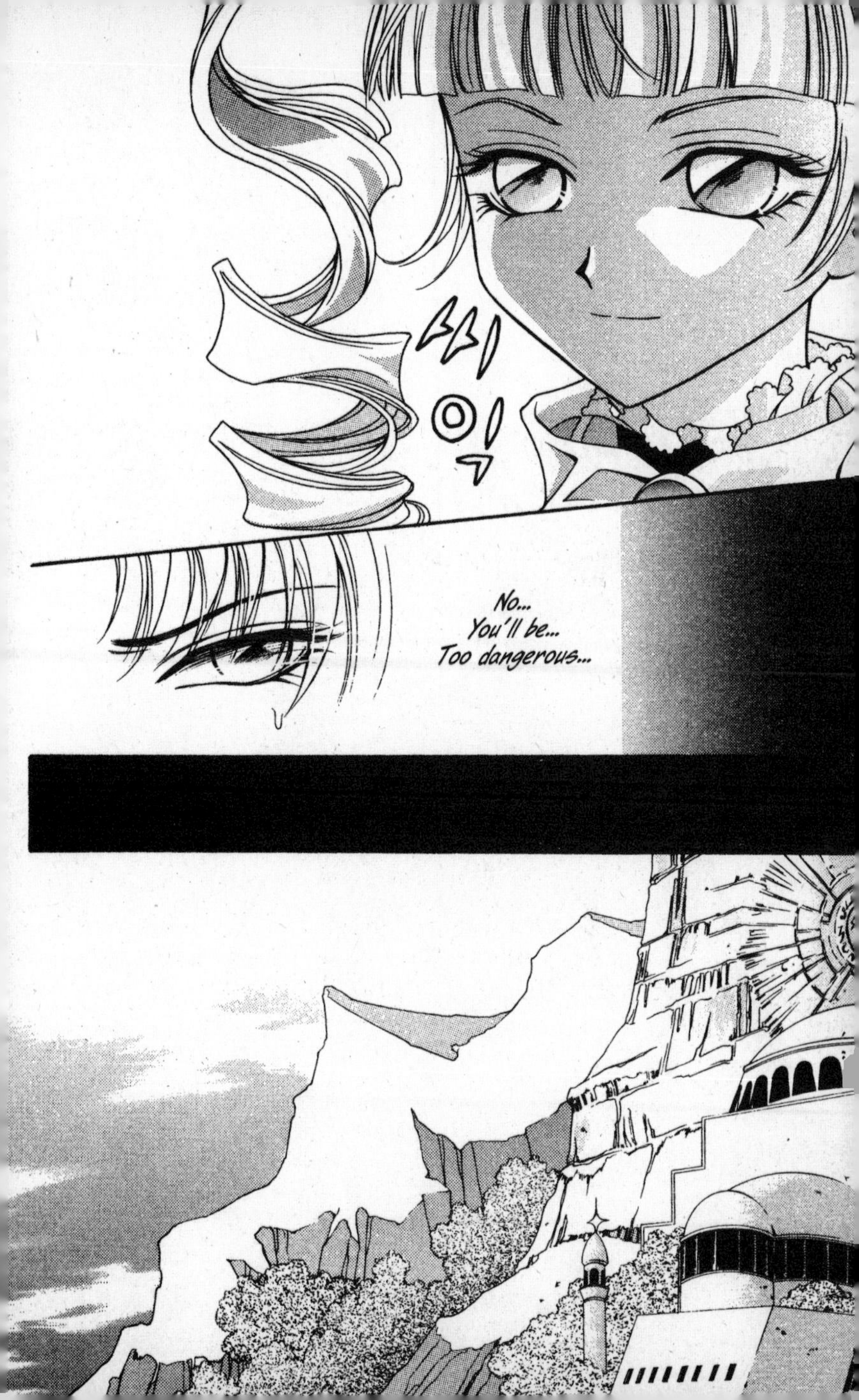
No... You'll be... Too dangerous...

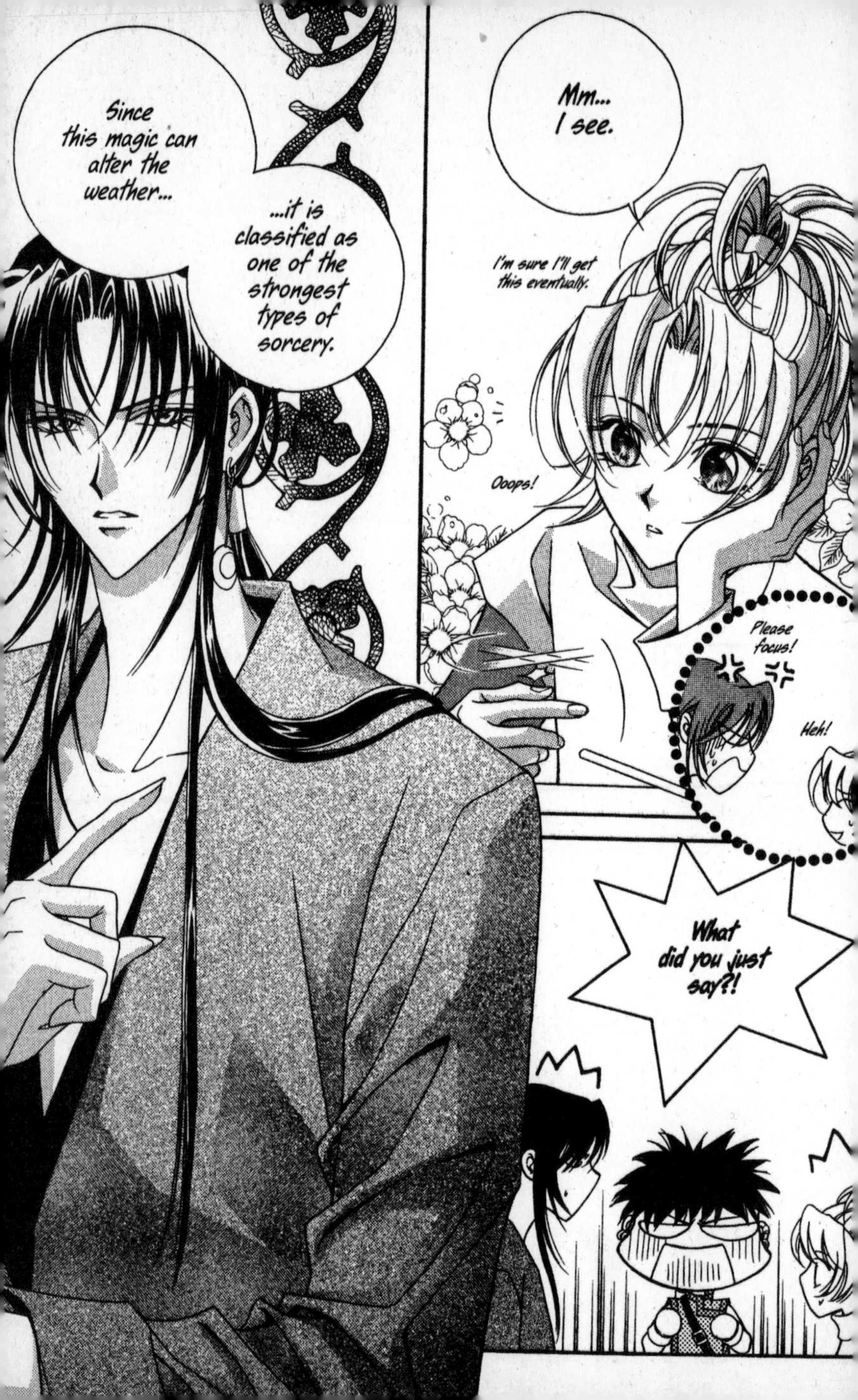
Since this magic can alter the weather...
...it is classified as one of the strongest types of sorcery.
Mm... I see.
I'm sure I'll get this eventually.
Ooops!
Please focus!
Heh!
What did you just say?!

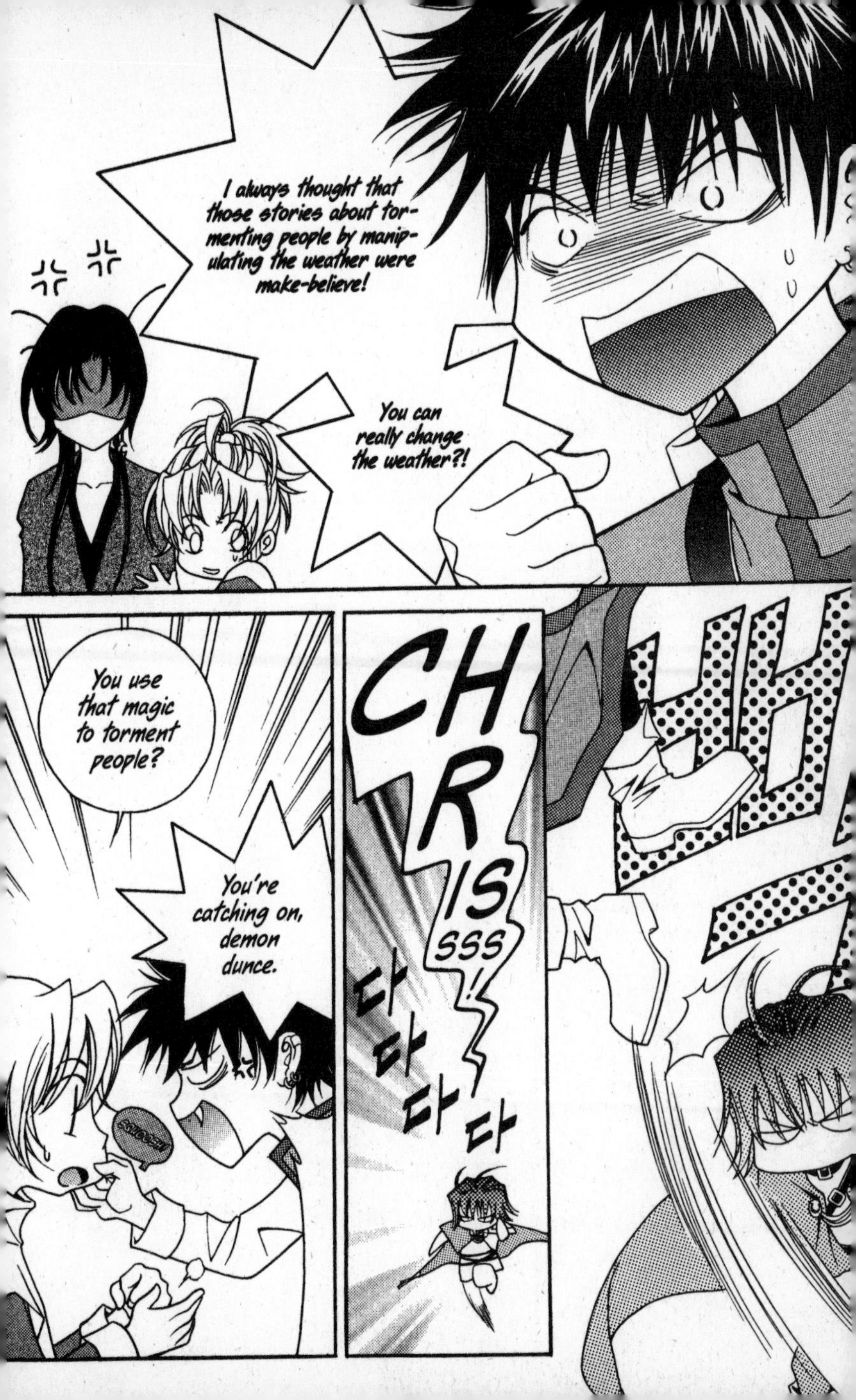
I always thought that those stories about tormenting people by manipulating the weather were make-believe!
You can really change the weather?!
You use that magic to torment people?
You're catching on, demon dunce.
CHRIS
SSS!
다
다
다
다

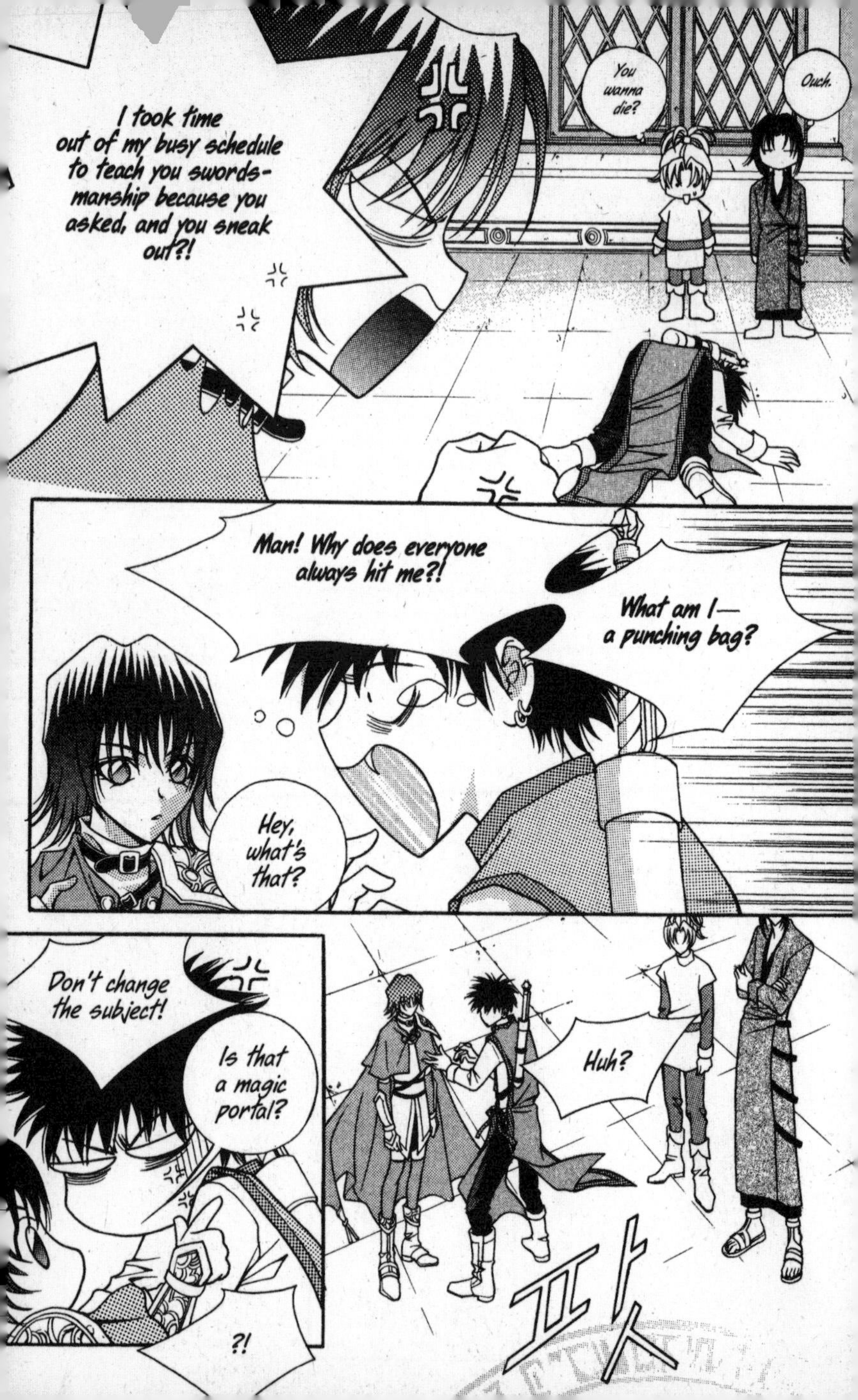
I took time out of my busy schedule to teach you swords-manship because you asked, and you sneak out?!
You wanna die?
Ouch.
Man! Why does everyone always hit me?!
What am I— a punching bag?
Hey, what's that?
Don't change the subject!
Is that a magic portal?
?!
Huh?

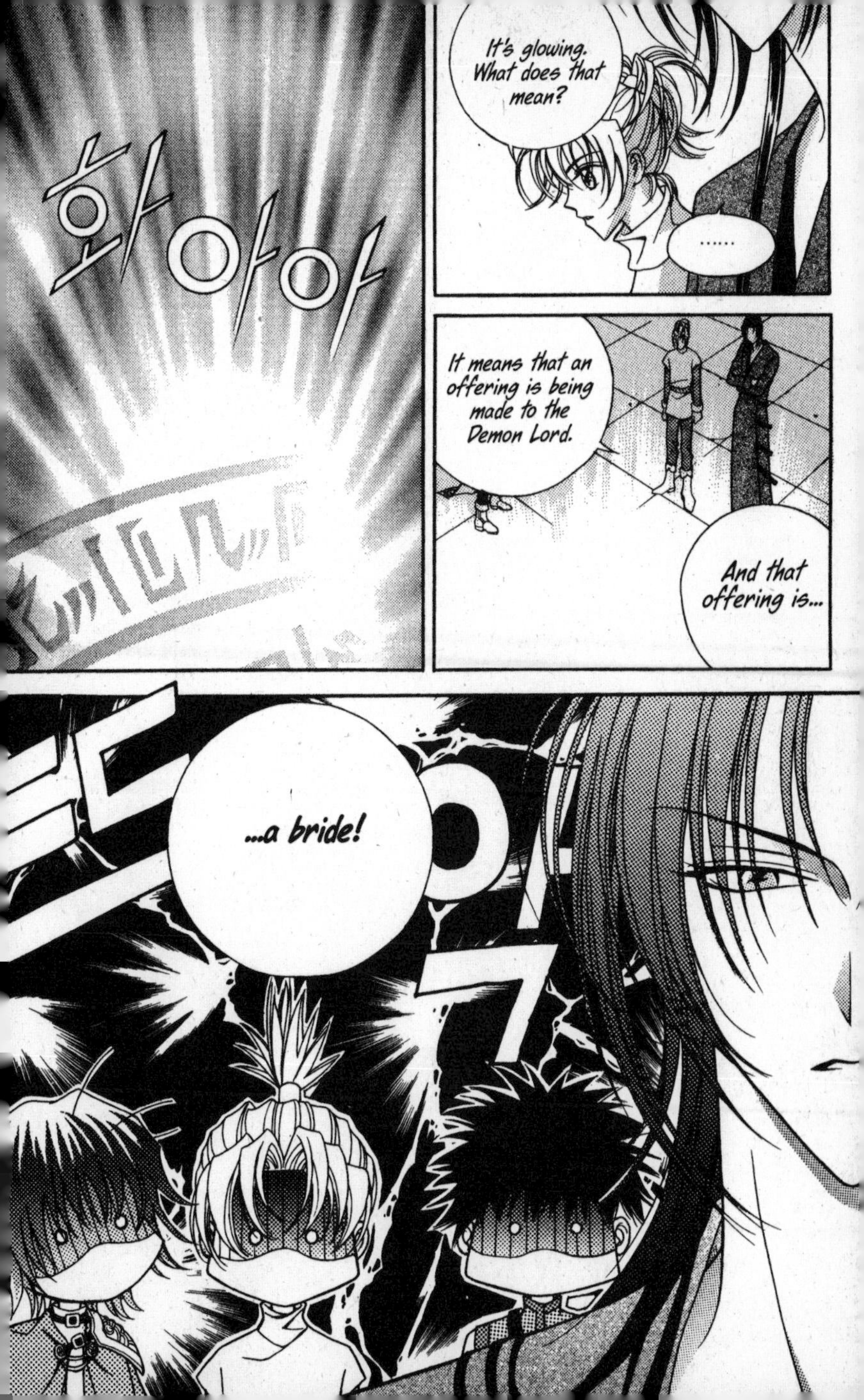
화아아
It's glowing. What does that mean?
......
It means that an offering is being made to the Demon Lord.
And that offering is...
...a bride!

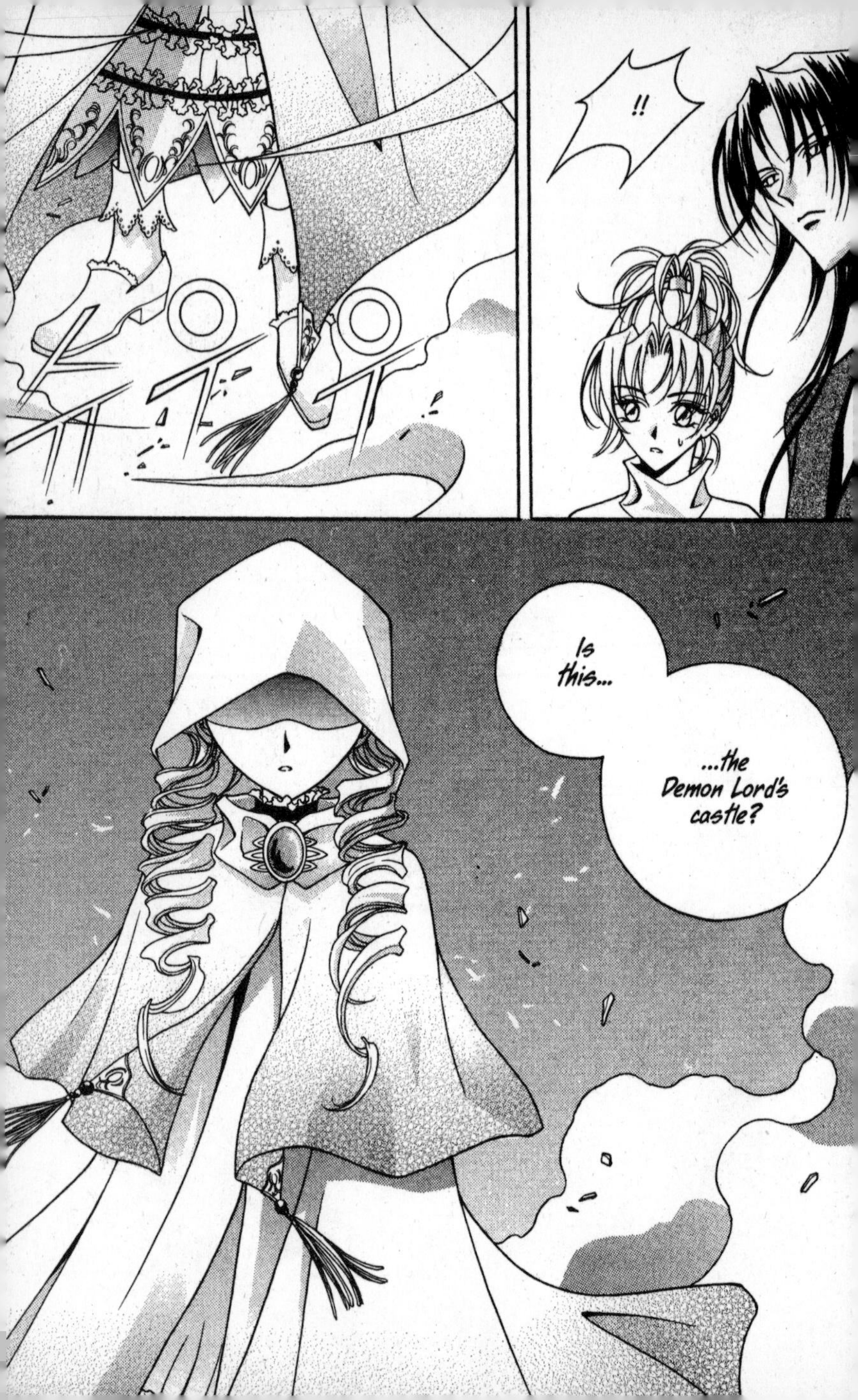
!!
Is this...
...the Demon Lord's castle?

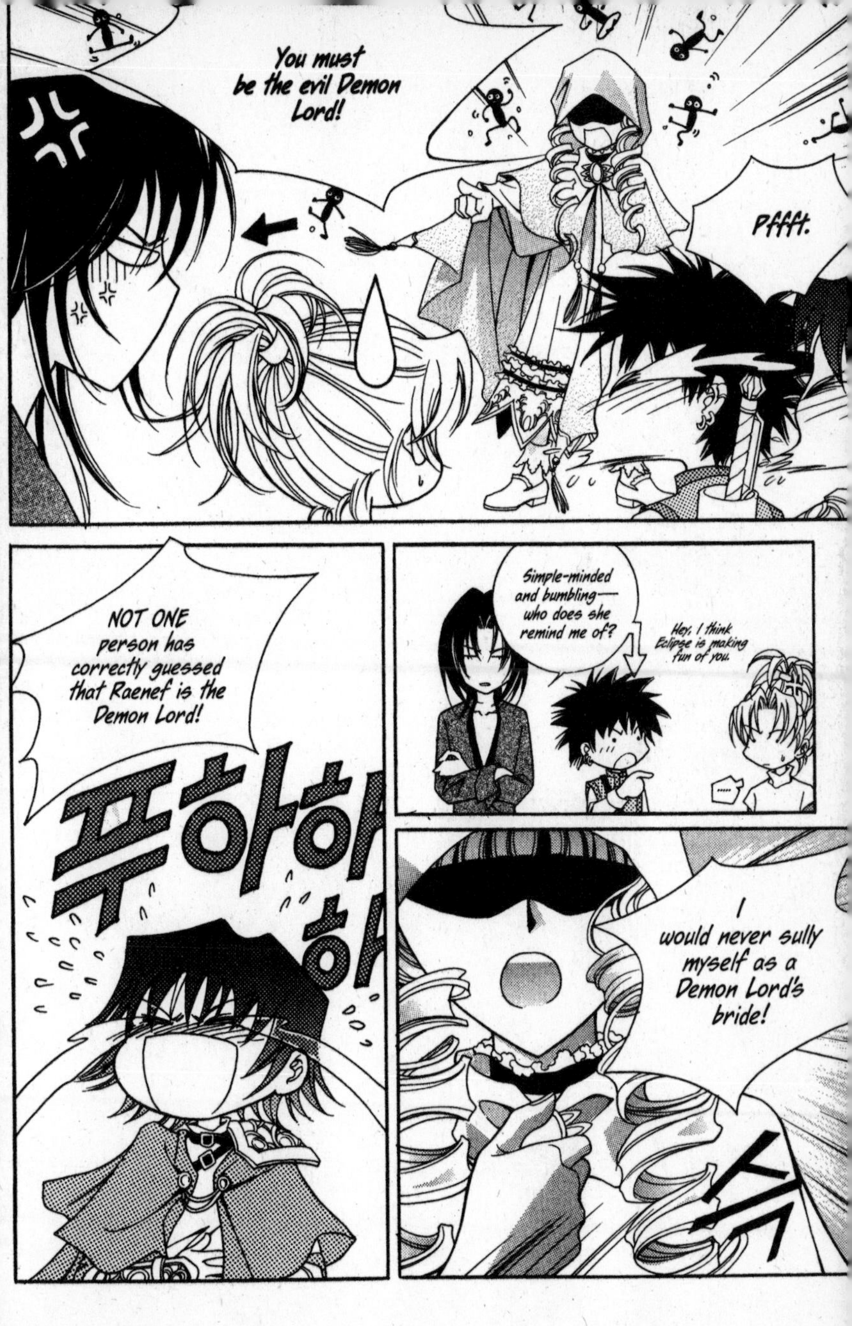
You must be the evil Demon Lord!
Pffft.
NOT ONE person has correctly guessed that Raenef is the Demon Lord!
푸하하
Simple-minded and bumbling—who does she remind me of?
Hey, I think Eclipse is making fun of you.
......
I would never sully myself as a Demon Lord's bride!

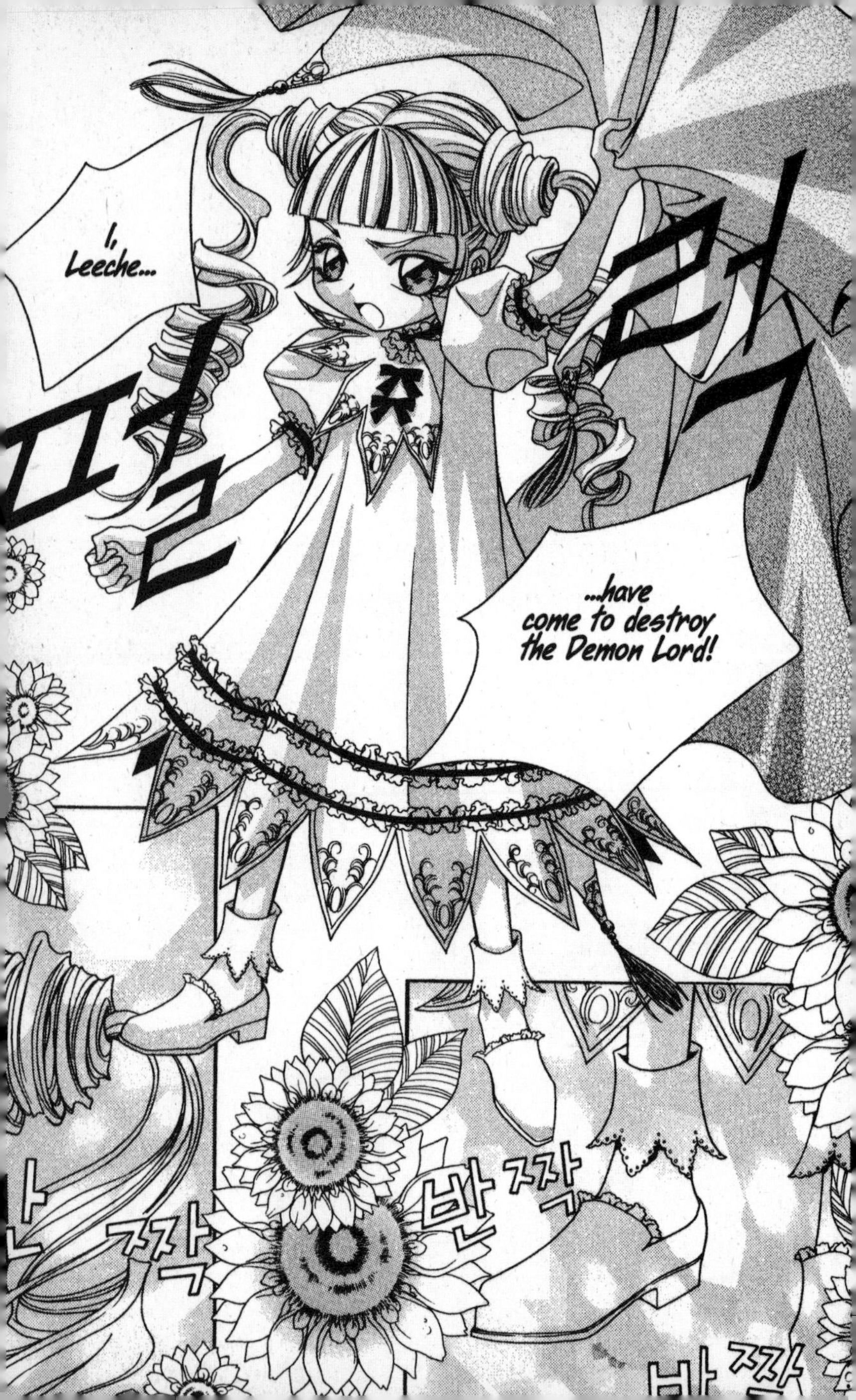
I, Leeche...
...have come to destroy the Demon Lord!
반짝

Why are they looking at me like that?

She's a little kid.

Not much of an offering.

There has never been an offering returned, so our only option is to keep her awhile.

Another ward to feed. What are you gonna do?

......

77

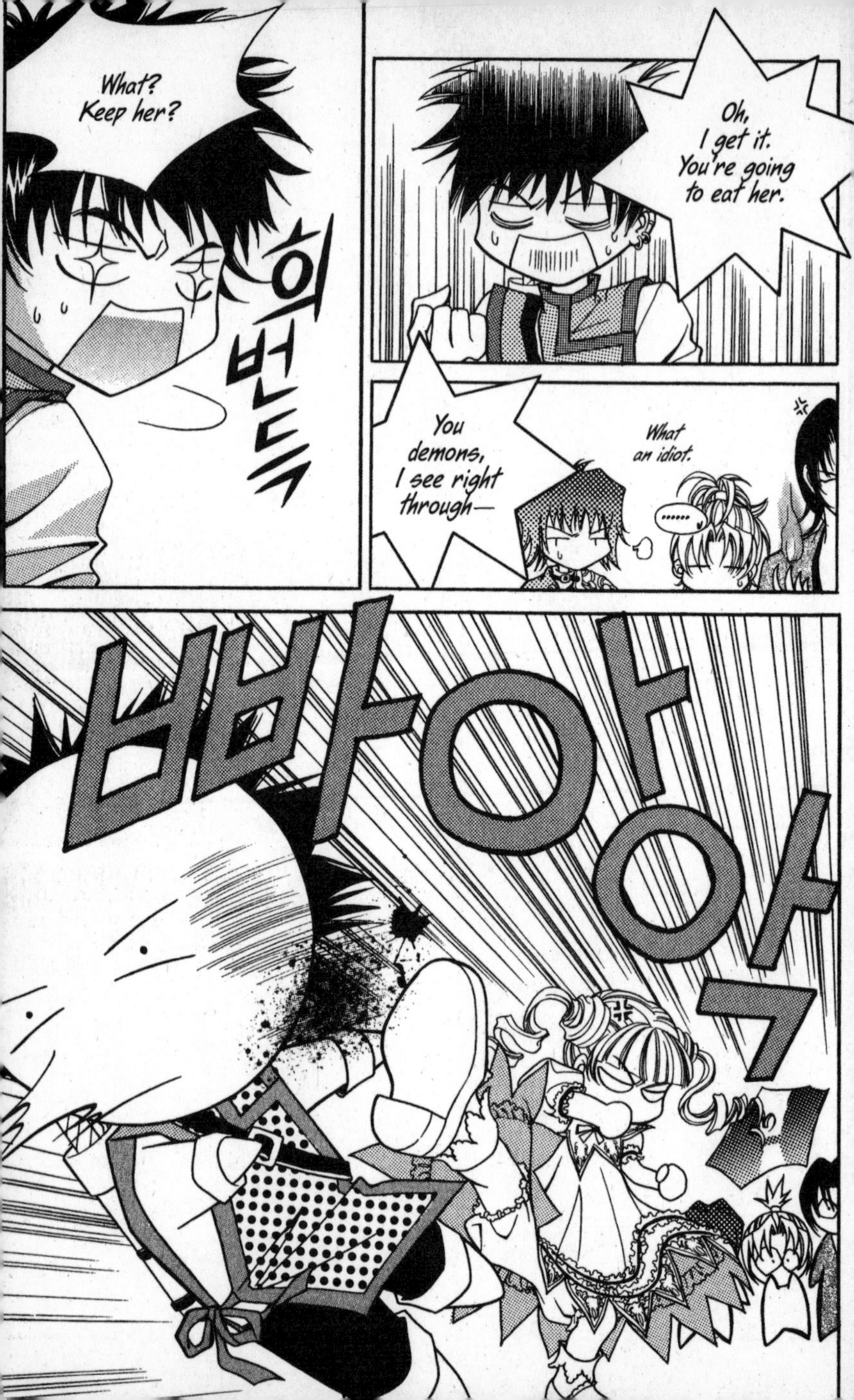
What? Keep her?
히번득
Oh, I get it. You're going to eat her.
You demons, I see right through—
What an idiot.
......
빠아아ㄱ

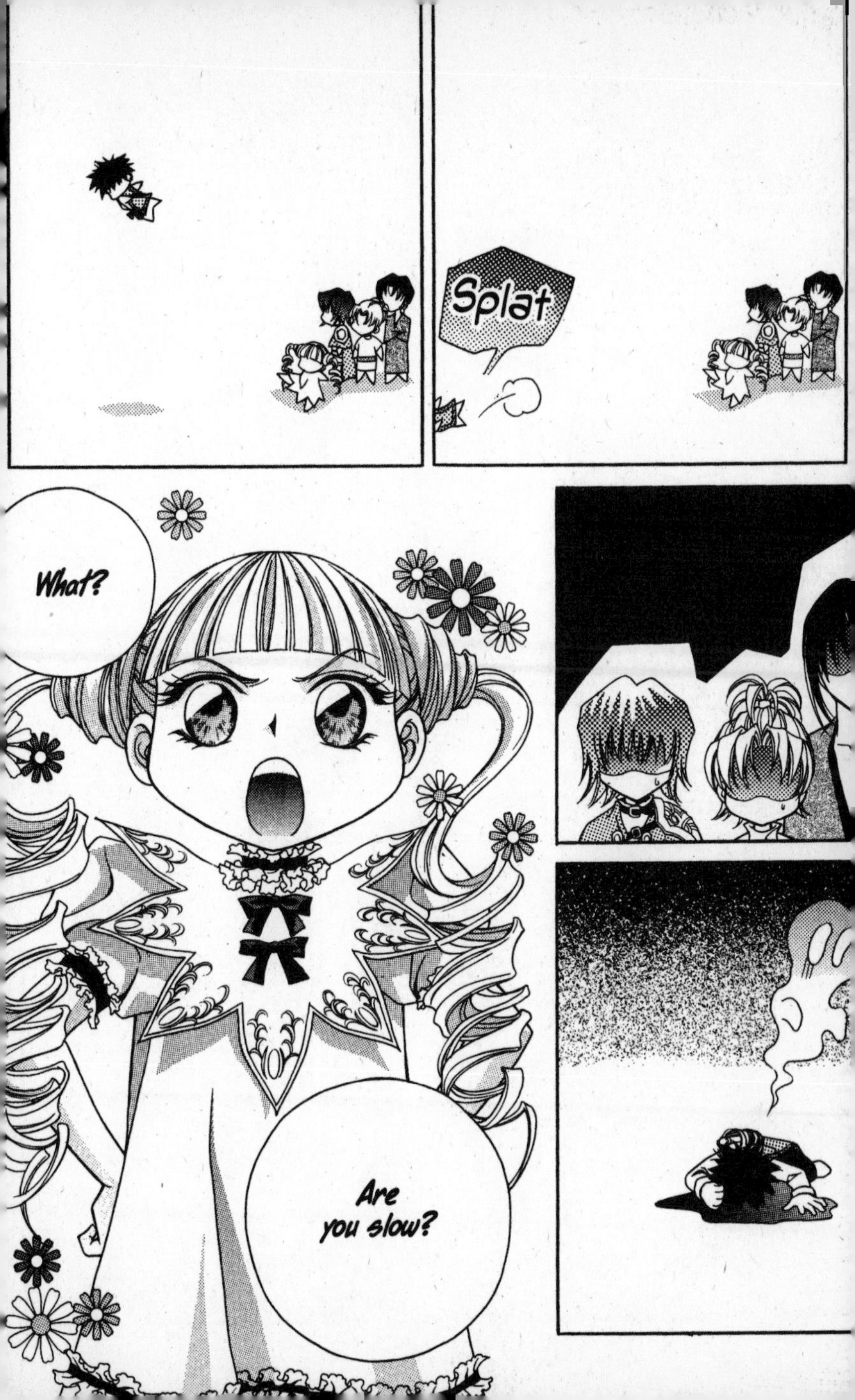
Splat
What?
Are you slow?

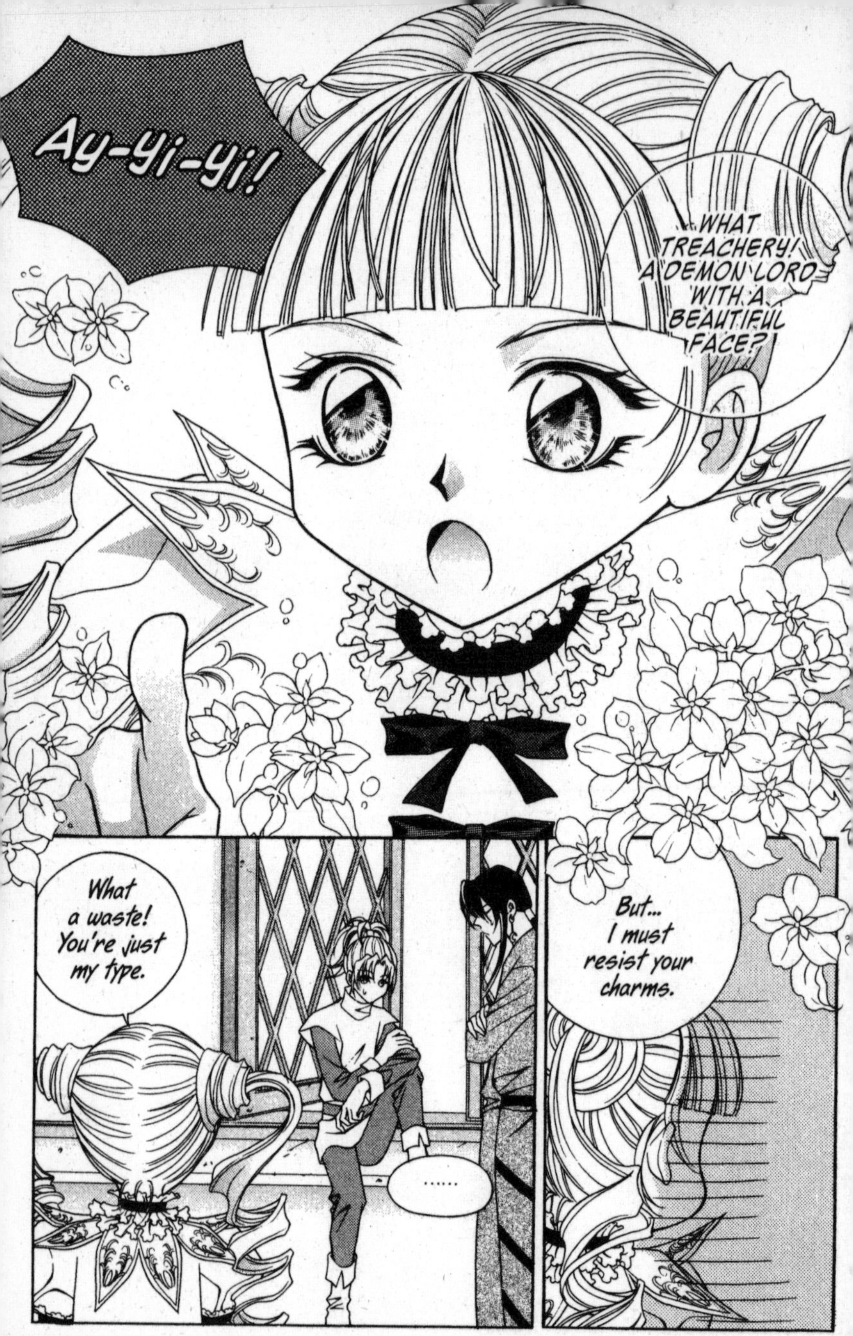
Ay-yi-yi!
WHAT TREACHERY! A DEMON LORD WITH A BEAUTIFUL FACE?
What a waste! You're just my type.
......
But... I must resist your charms.

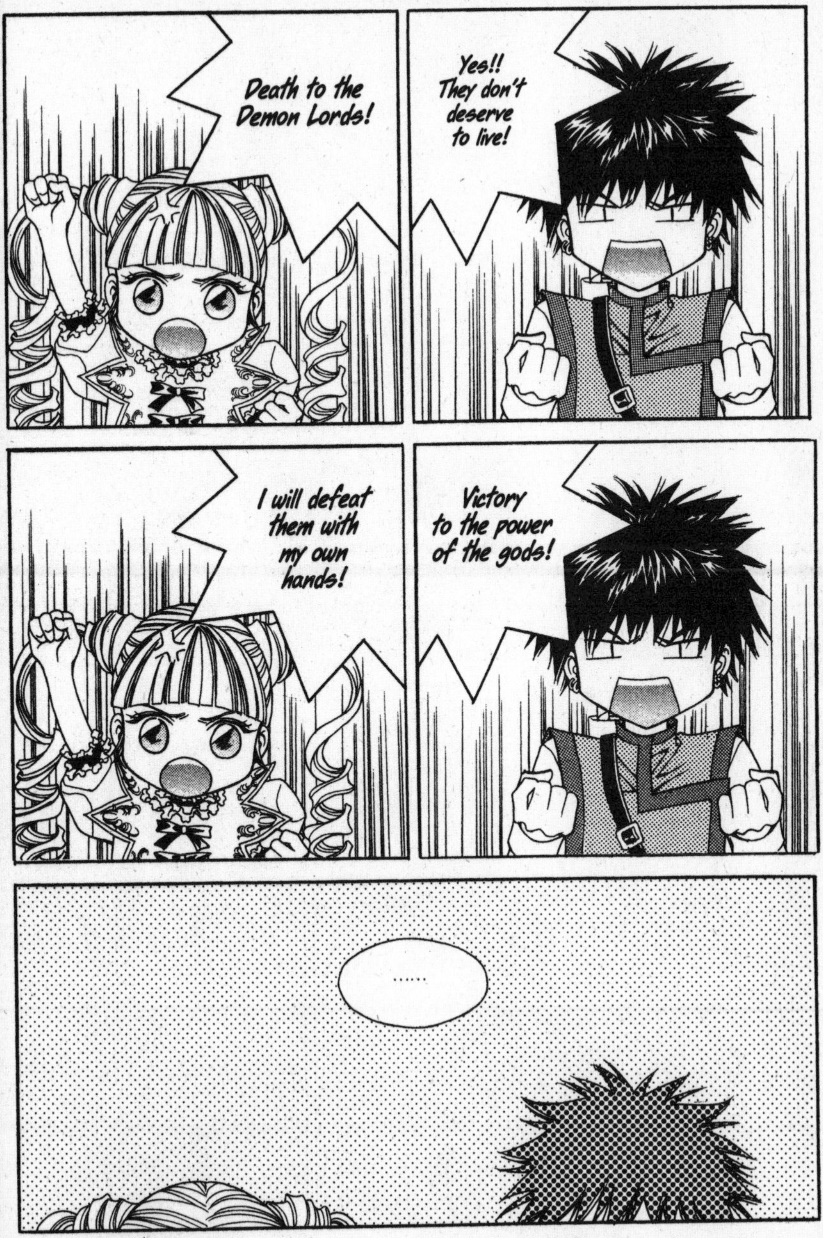
Death to the Demon Lords!
Yes!! They don't deserve to live!
I will defeat them with my own hands!
Victory to the power of the gods!
......

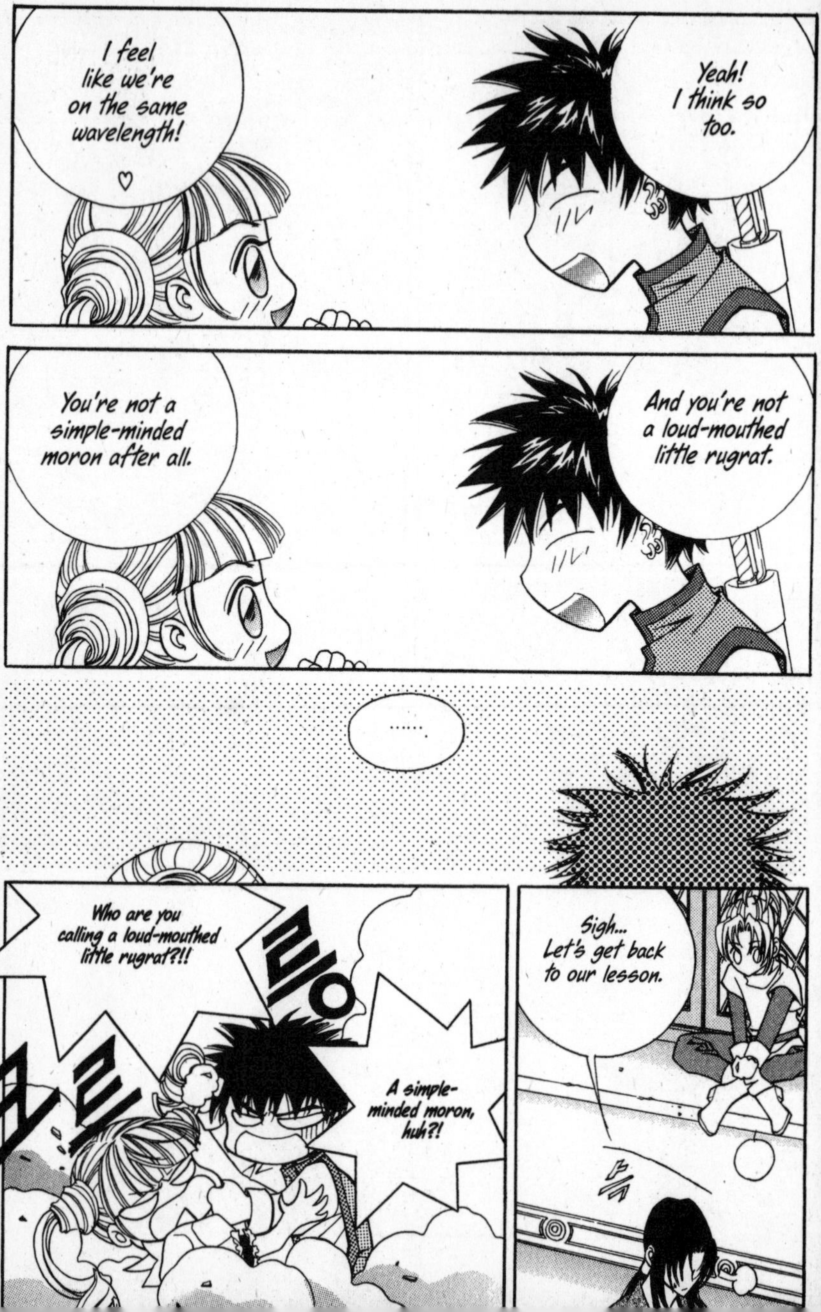
I feel like we're on the same wavelength! ♡
Yeah! I think so too.
You're not a simple-minded moron after all.
And you're not a loud-mouthed little rugrat.
....
Who are you calling a loud-mouthed little rugrat?!!
A simple-minded moron, huh?!
Sigh... Let's get back to our lesson.

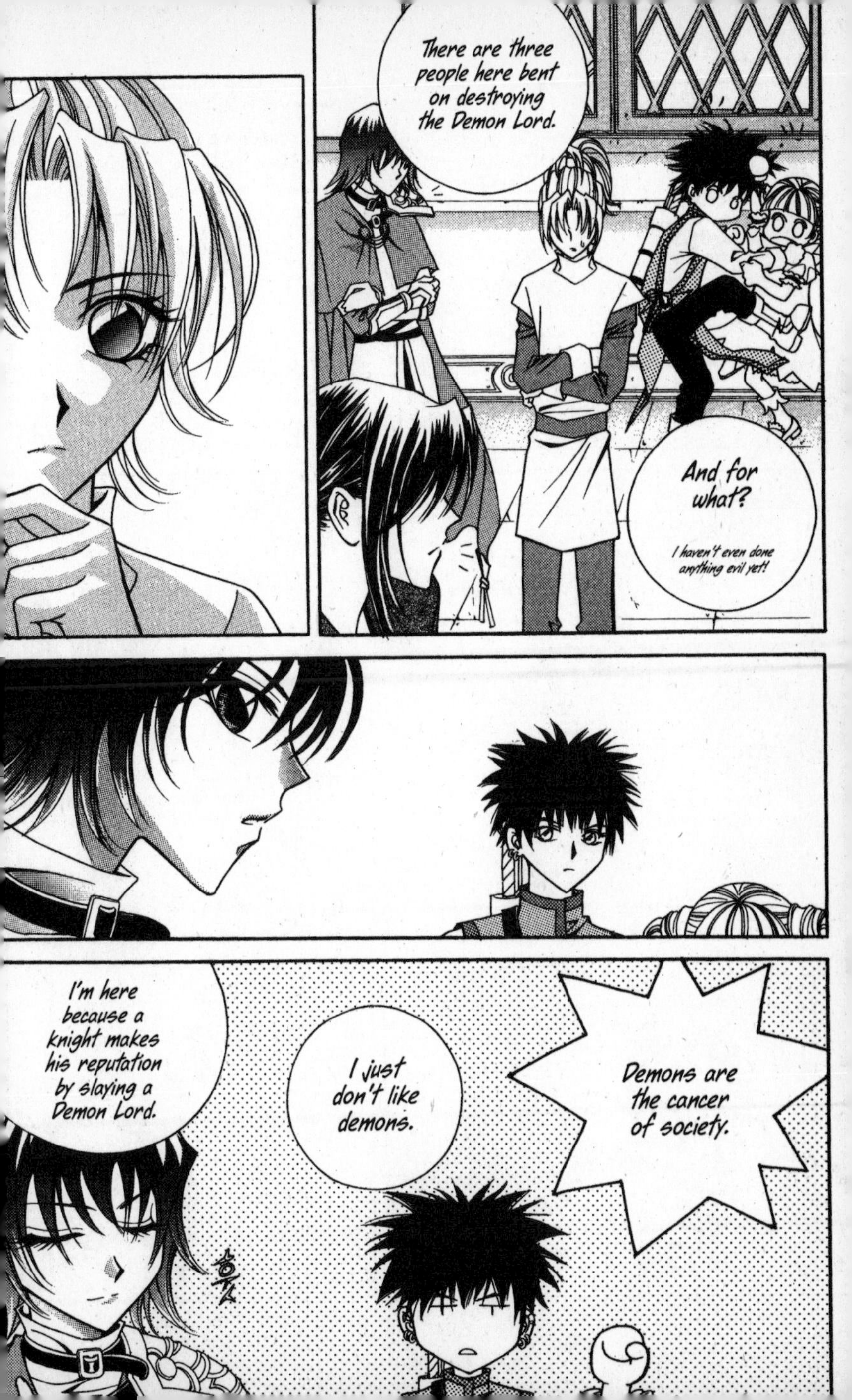
There are three people here bent on destroying the Demon Lord.
And for what?
I haven't even done anything evil yet!
I'm here because a knight makes his reputation by slaying a Demon Lord.
I just don't like demons.
Demons are the cancer of society.

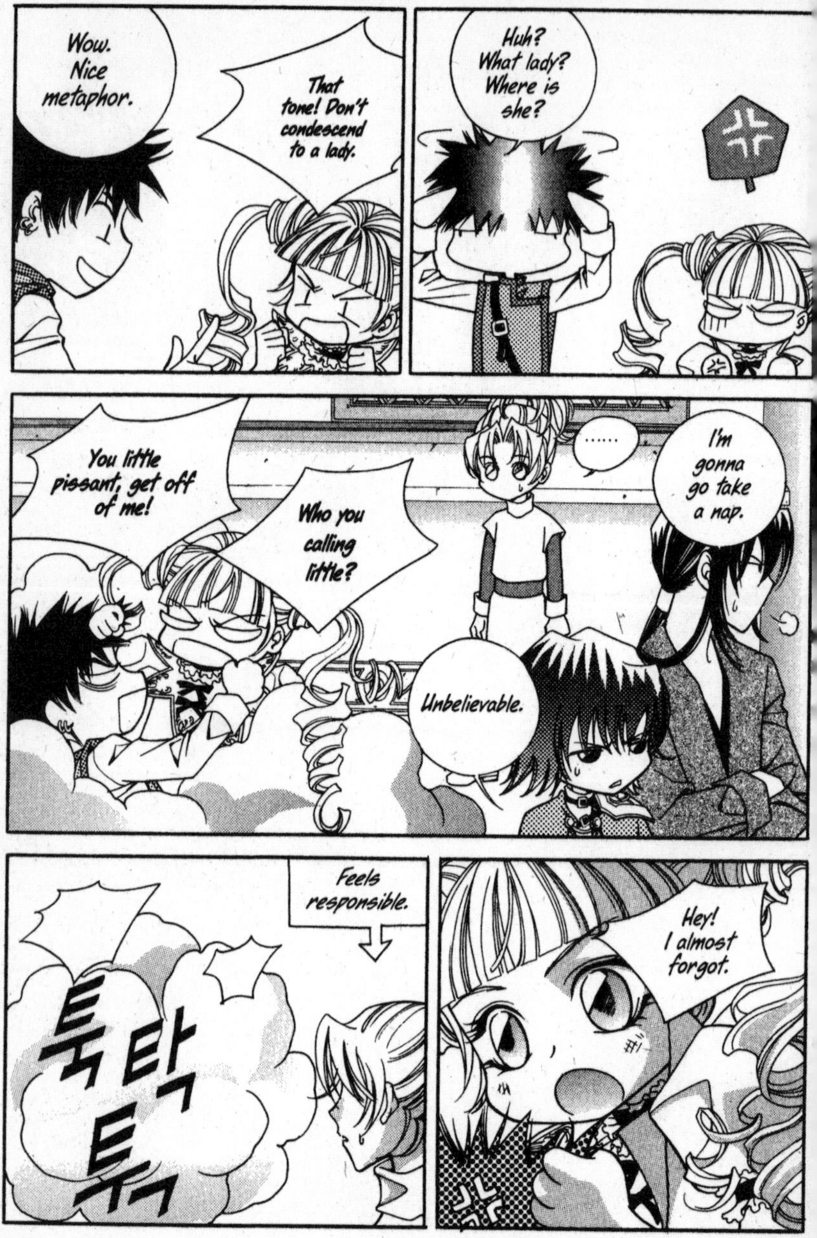
Wow. Nice metaphor.
That tone! Don't condescend to a lady.
Huh? What lady? Where is she?
You little pissant, get off of me!
Who you calling little?
......
I'm gonna go take a nap.
Unbelievable.
Feels responsible.
툭 탁 투
Hey! I almost forgot.

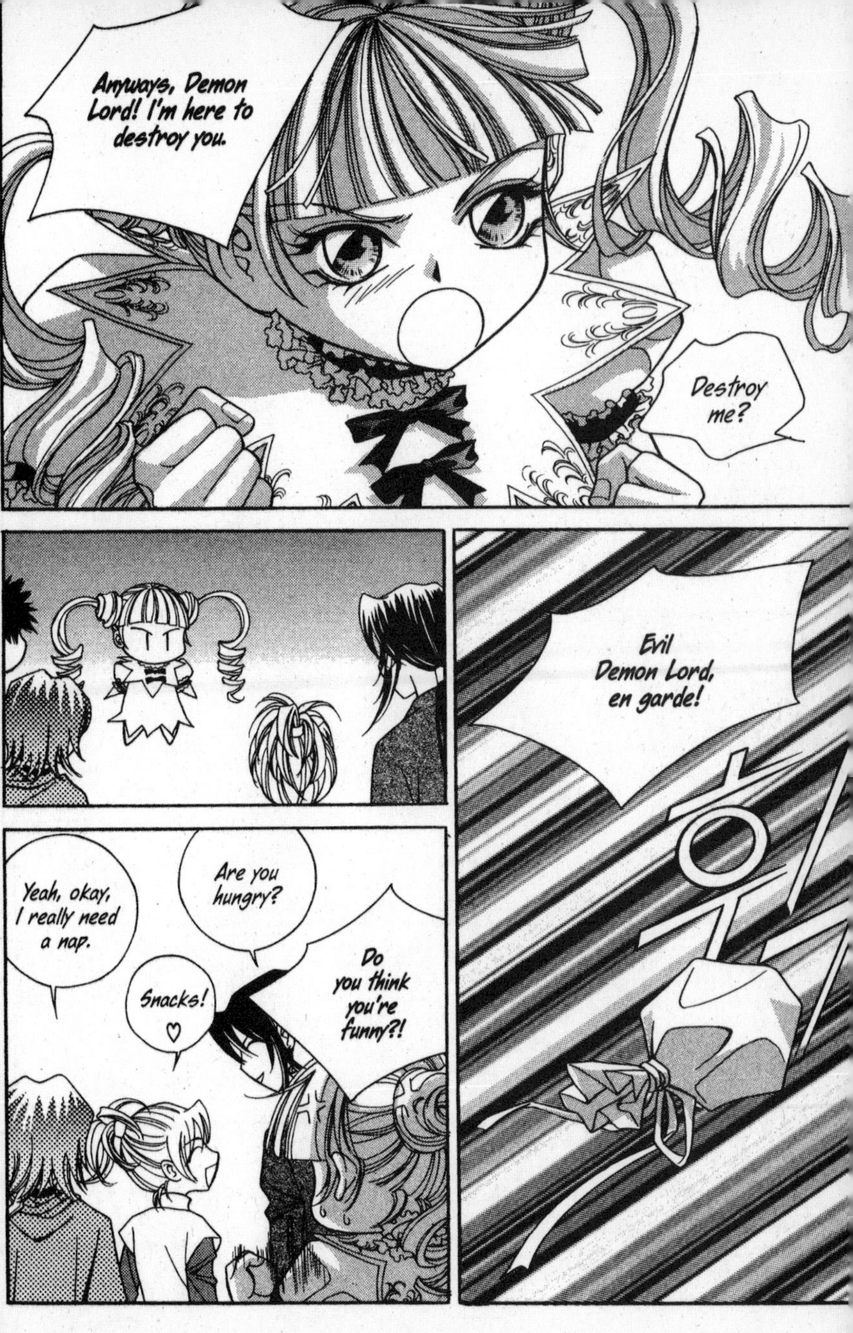
Anyways, Demon Lord! I'm here to destroy you.
Destroy me?
Yeah, okay, I really need a nap.
Are you hungry?
Snacks! ♡
Do you think you're funny?!
Evil Demon Lord, en garde!

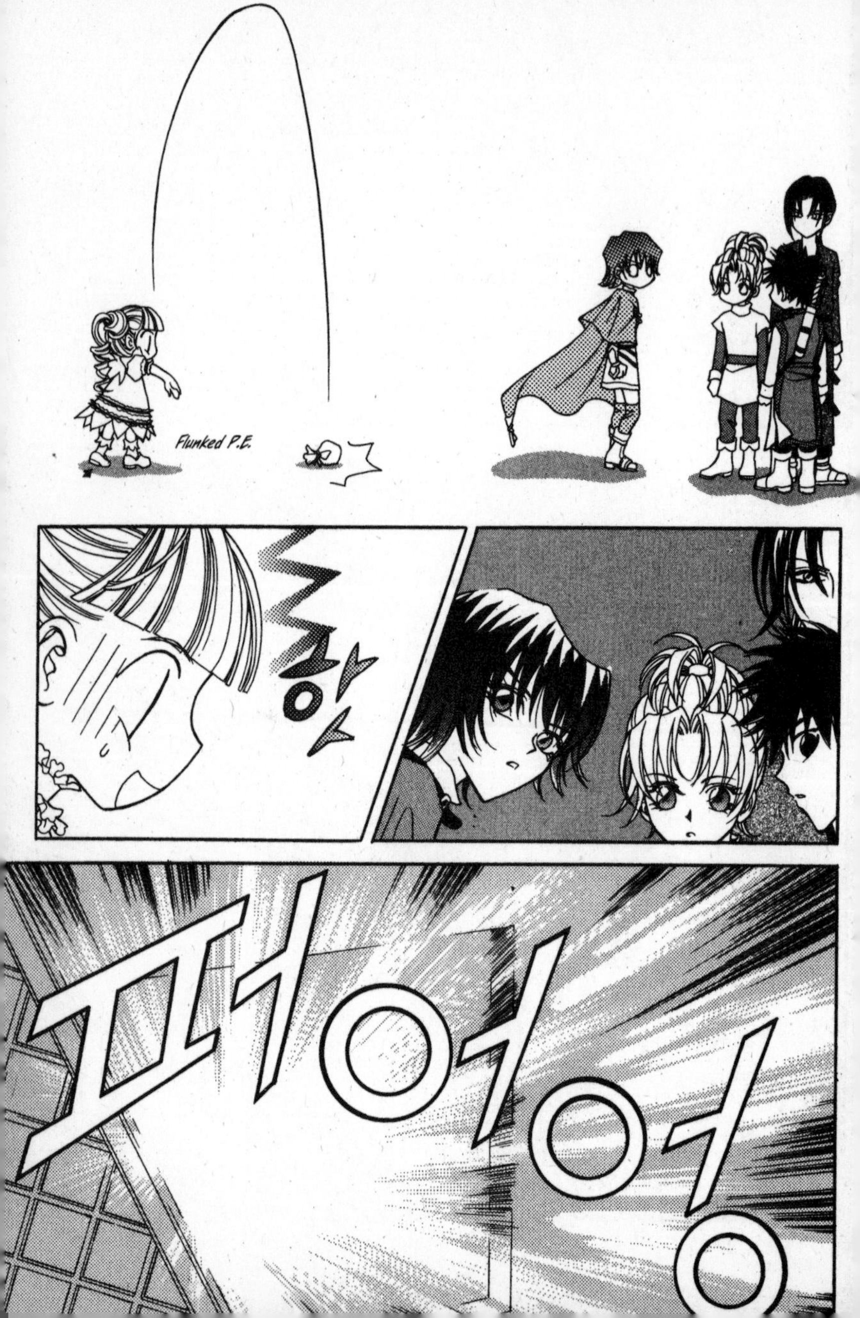
Flunked P.E.

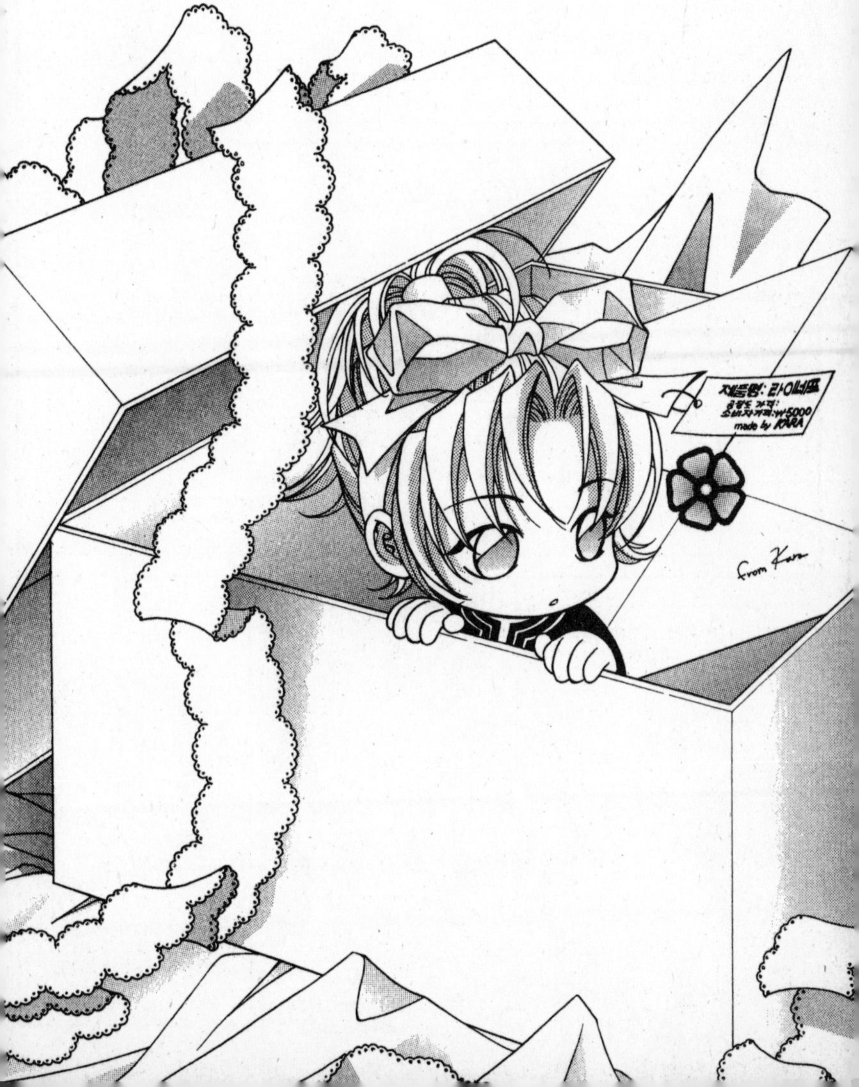
made by KARA
from Kara

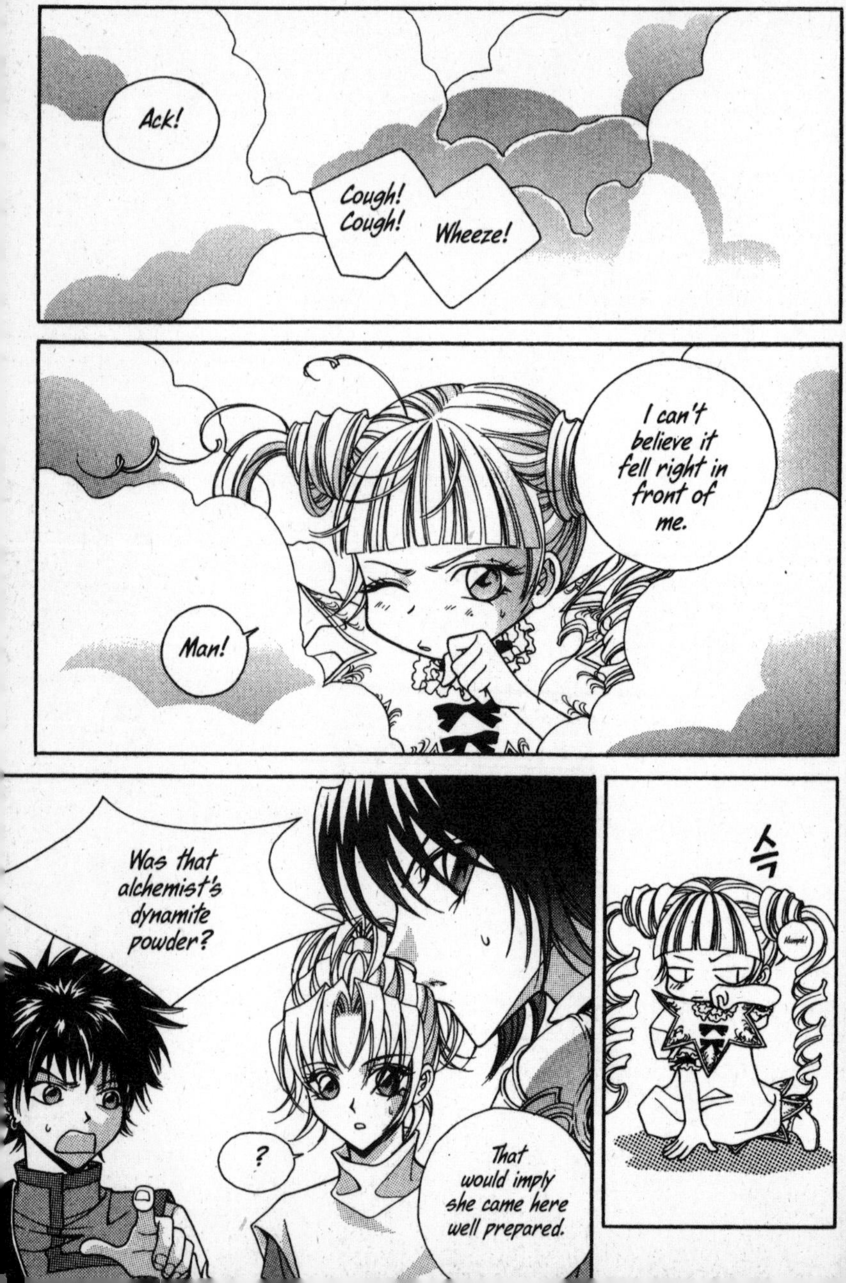
Ack!
Cough! Cough!
Wheeze!
I can't believe it fell right in front of me.
Man!
Was that alchemist's dynamite powder?
?
That would imply she came here well prepared.
Humph!

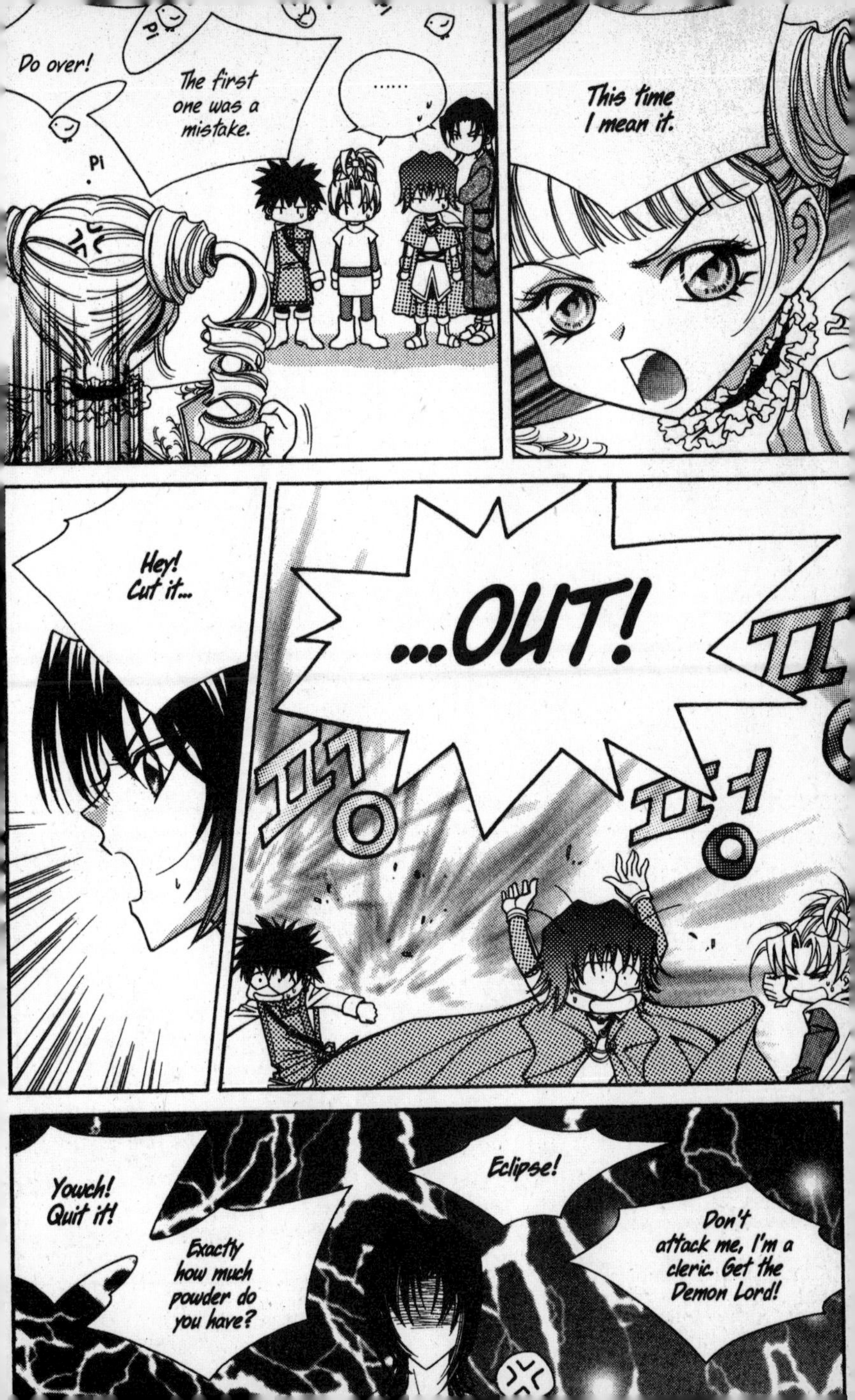
Pi
Do over!
The first one was a mistake.
......
Pi
This time I mean it.
Hey! Cut it...
...OUT!
Youch! Quit it!
Exactly how much powder do you have?
Eclipse!
Don't attack me, I'm a cleric. Get the Demon Lord!

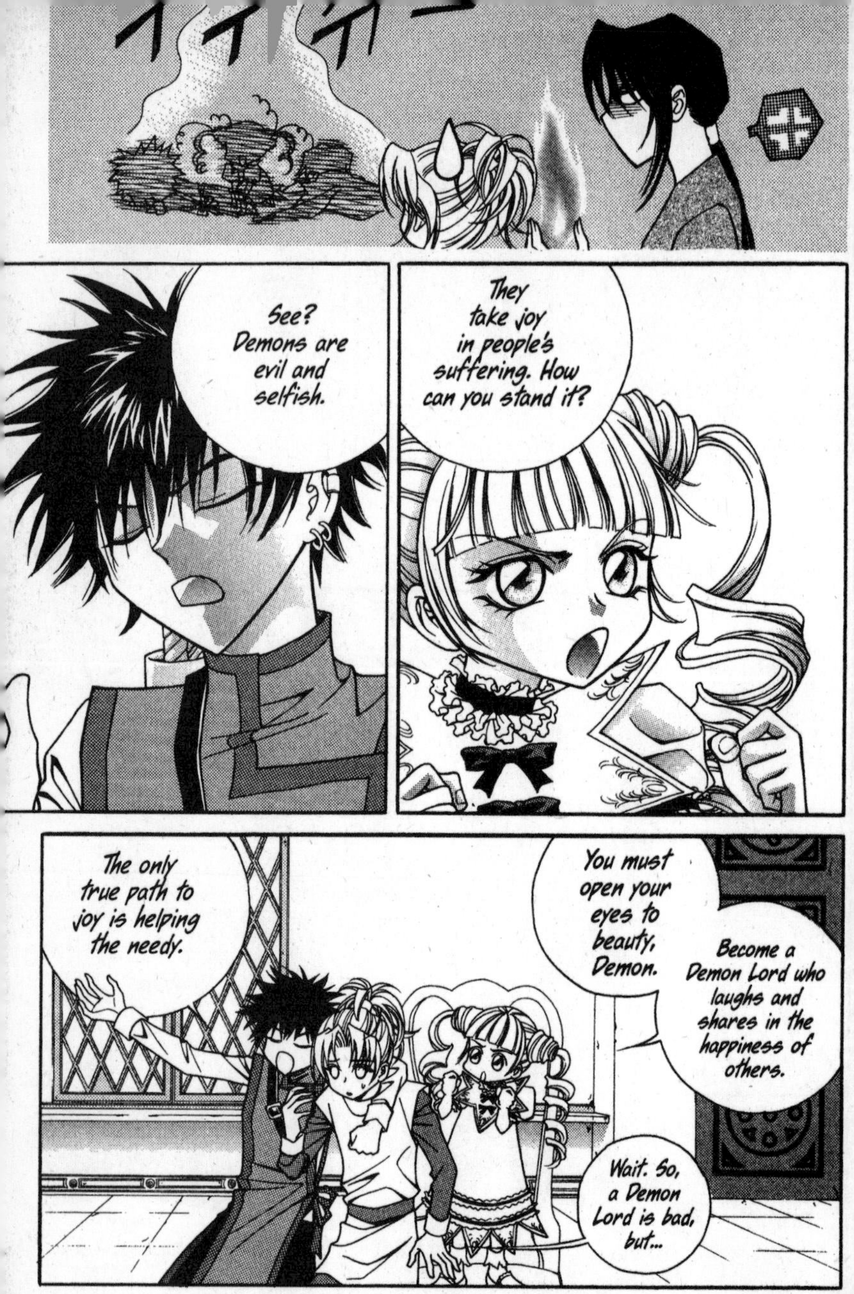
See? Demons are evil and selfish.
They take joy in people's suffering. How can you stand it?
The only true path to joy is helping the needy.
You must open your eyes to beauty, Demon.
Become a Demon Lord who laughs and shares in the happiness of others.
Wait. So, a Demon Lord is bad, but...

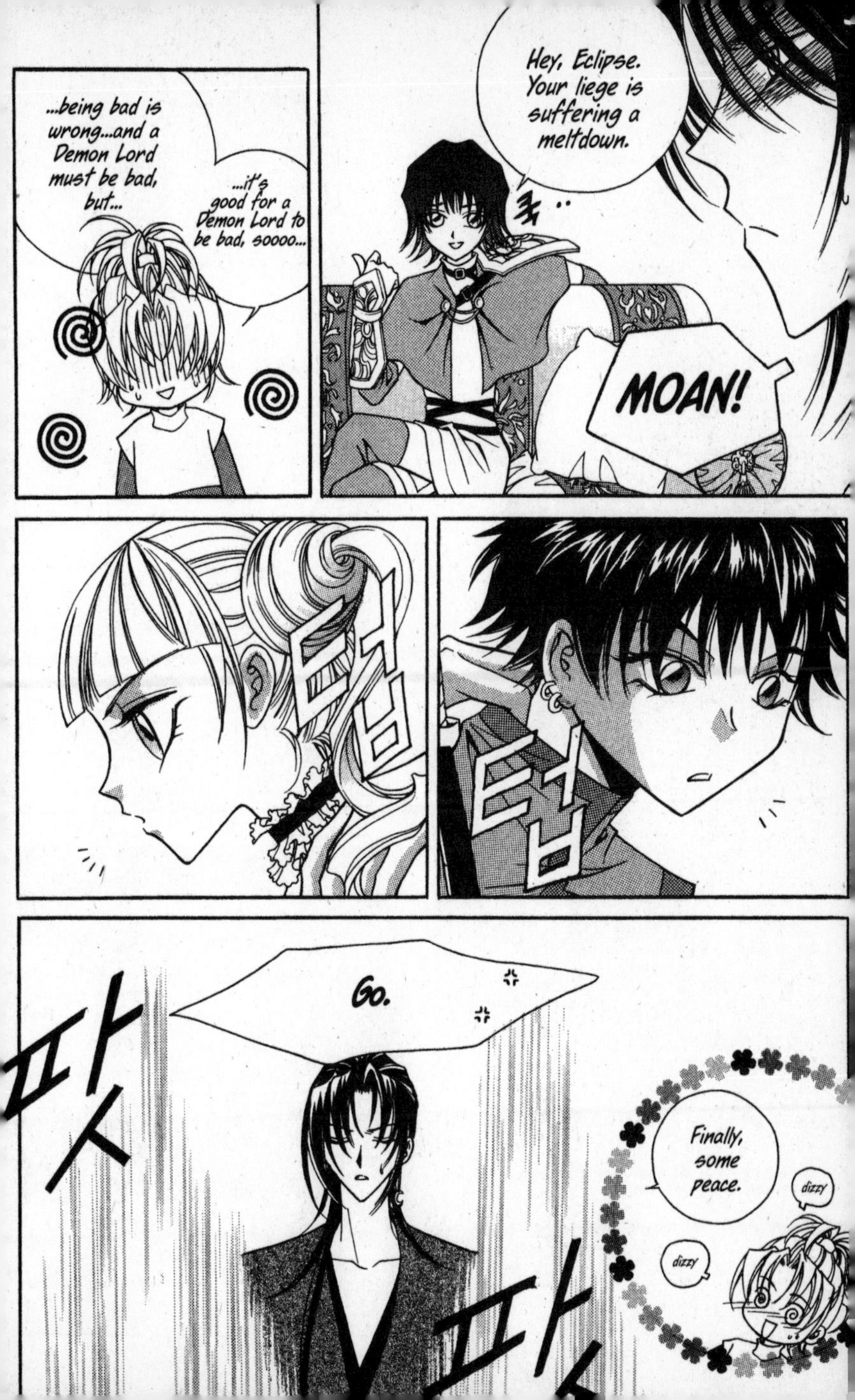
...being bad is wrong...and a Demon Lord must be bad, but...
...it's good for a Demon Lord to be bad, soooo...
Hey, Eclipse. Your liege is suffering a meltdown.
MOAN!
Go.
Finally, some peace.
dizzy
dizzy

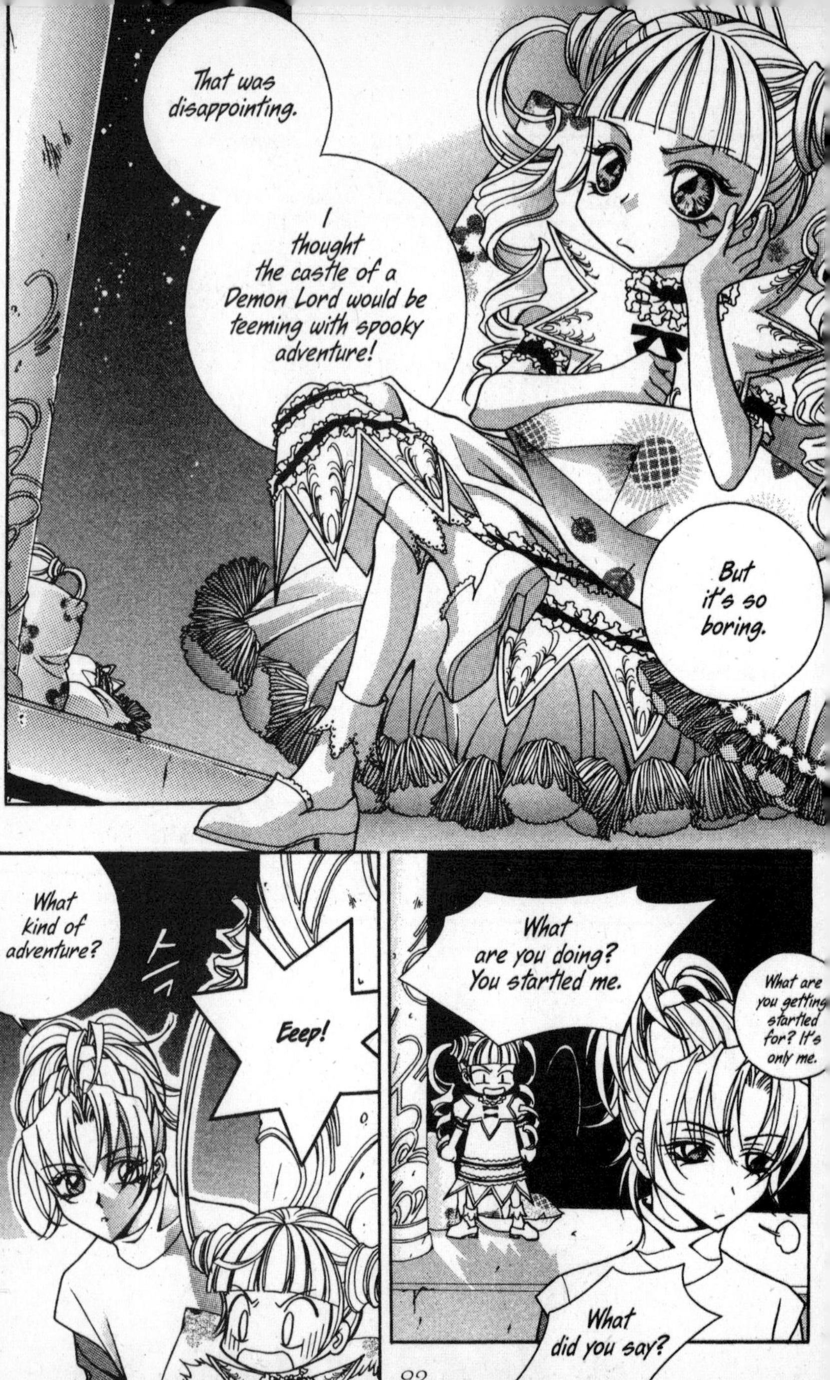
That was disappointing.
I thought the castle of a Demon Lord would be teeming with spooky adventure!
But it's so boring.
What kind of adventure?
Eeep!
What are you doing? You startled me.
What are you getting startled for? It's only me.
What did you say?

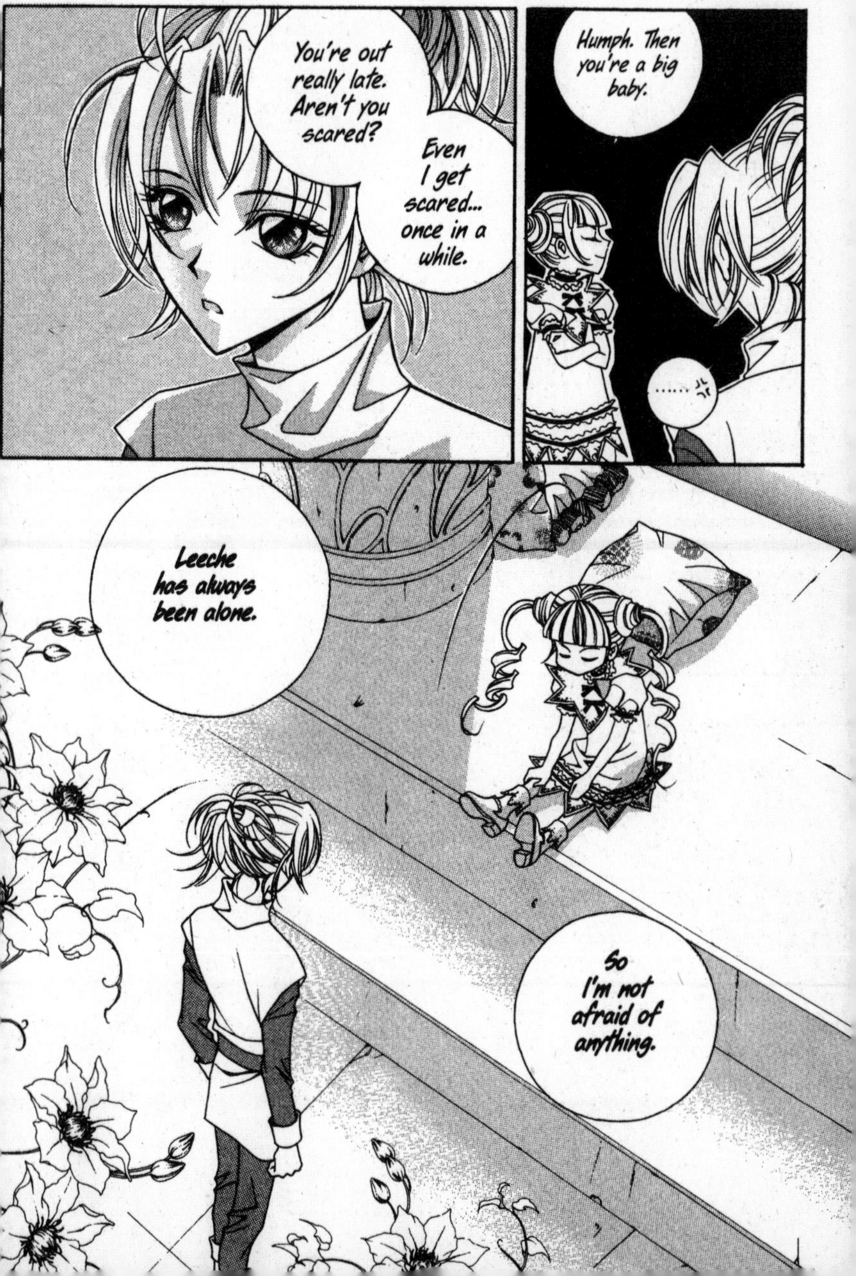
You're out really late. Aren't you scared?
Even I get scared... once in a while.
Humph. Then you're a big baby.
......
Leeche has always been alone.
So I'm not afraid of anything.

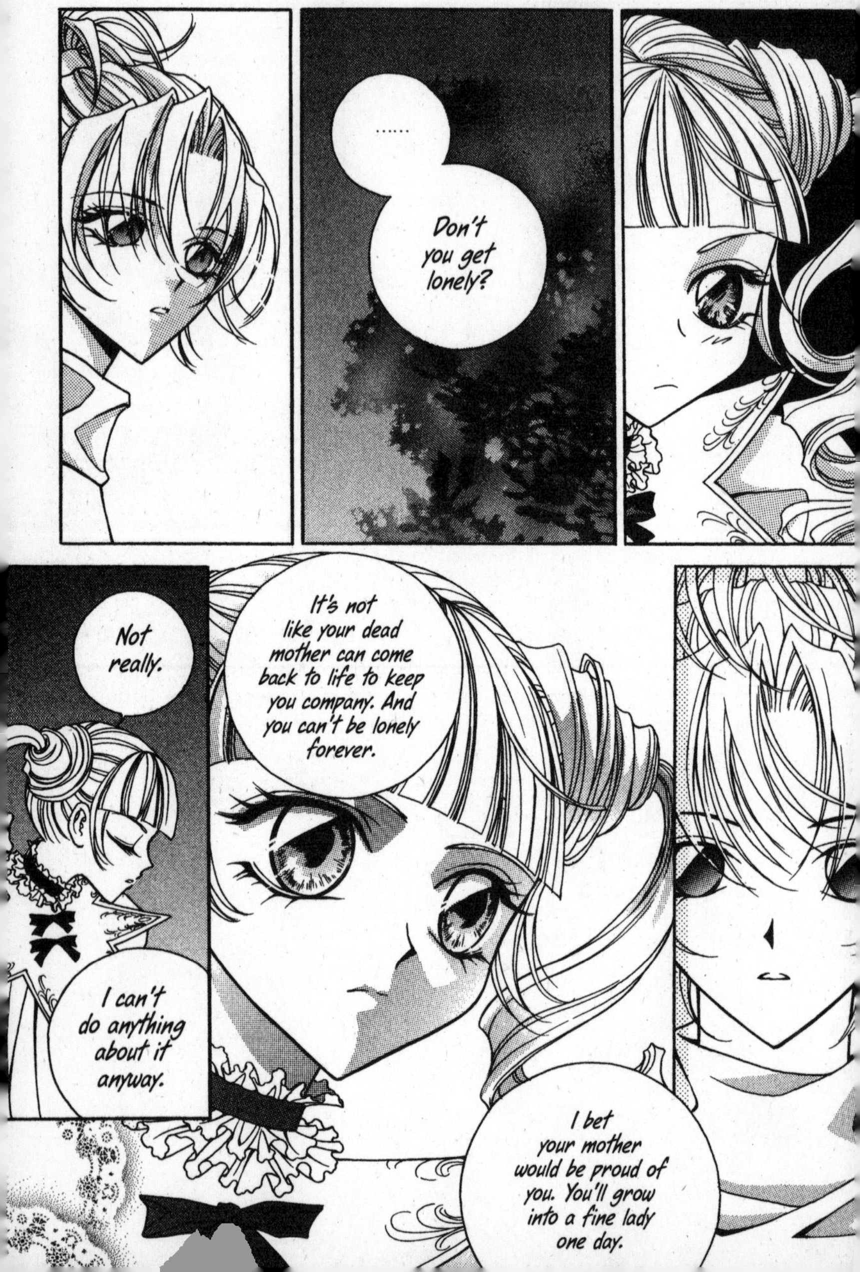
......
Don't you get lonely?
Not really.
It's not like your dead mother can come back to life to keep you company. And you can't be lonely forever.
I can't do anything about it anyway.
I bet your mother would be proud of you. You'll grow into a fine lady one day.

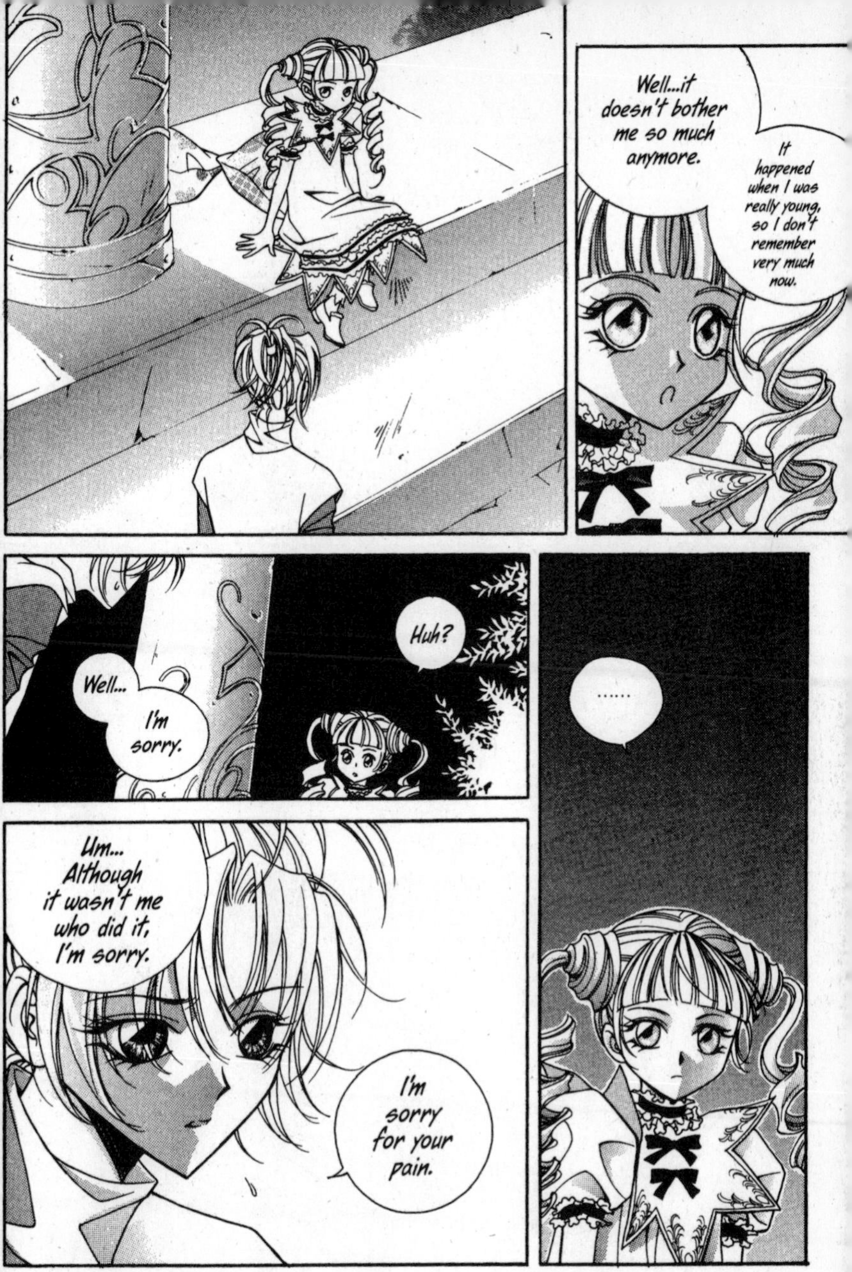
Well...it doesn't bother me so much anymore.
It happened when I was really young, so I don't remember very much now.
Well... I'm sorry.
Huh?
Um... Although it wasn't me who did it, I'm sorry.
I'm sorry for your pain.
......

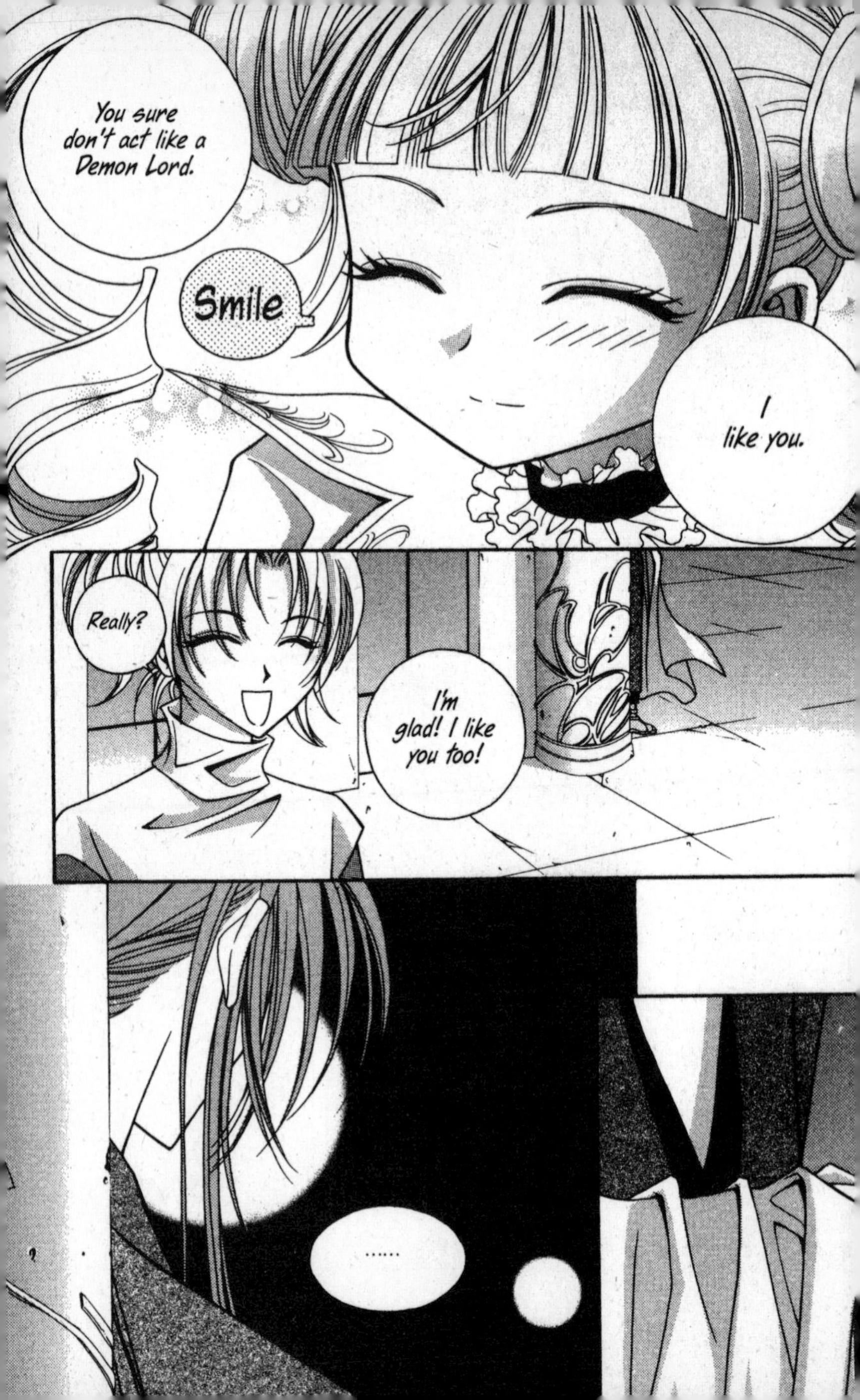
You sure don't act like a Demon Lord.
Smile
I like you.
Really?
I'm glad! I like you too!
......

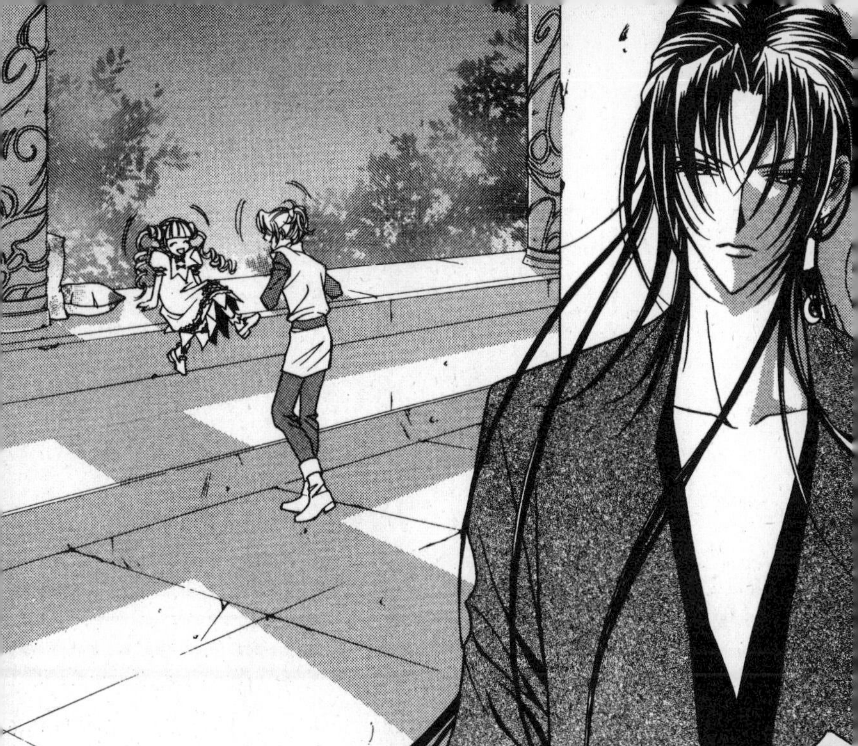

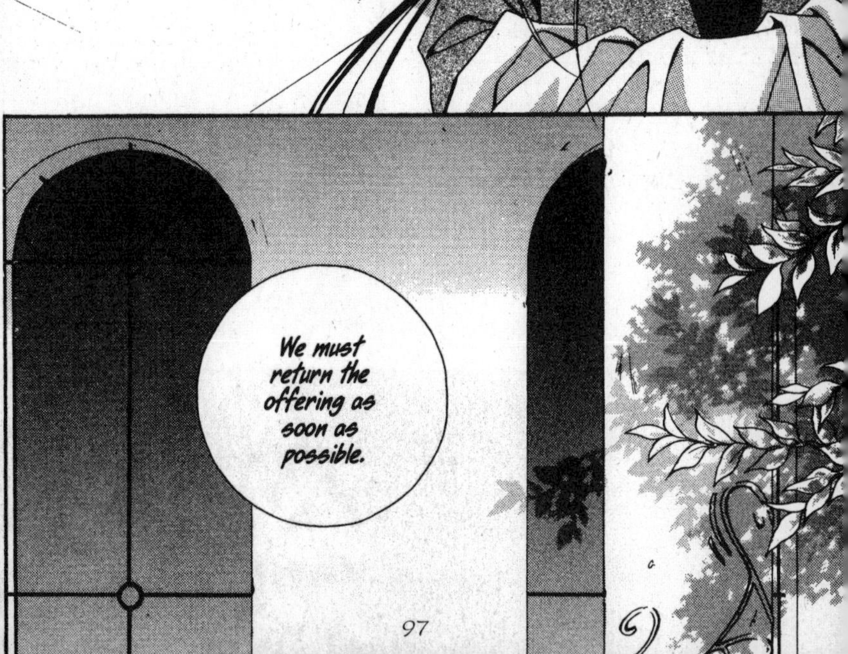
We must return the offering as soon as possible.

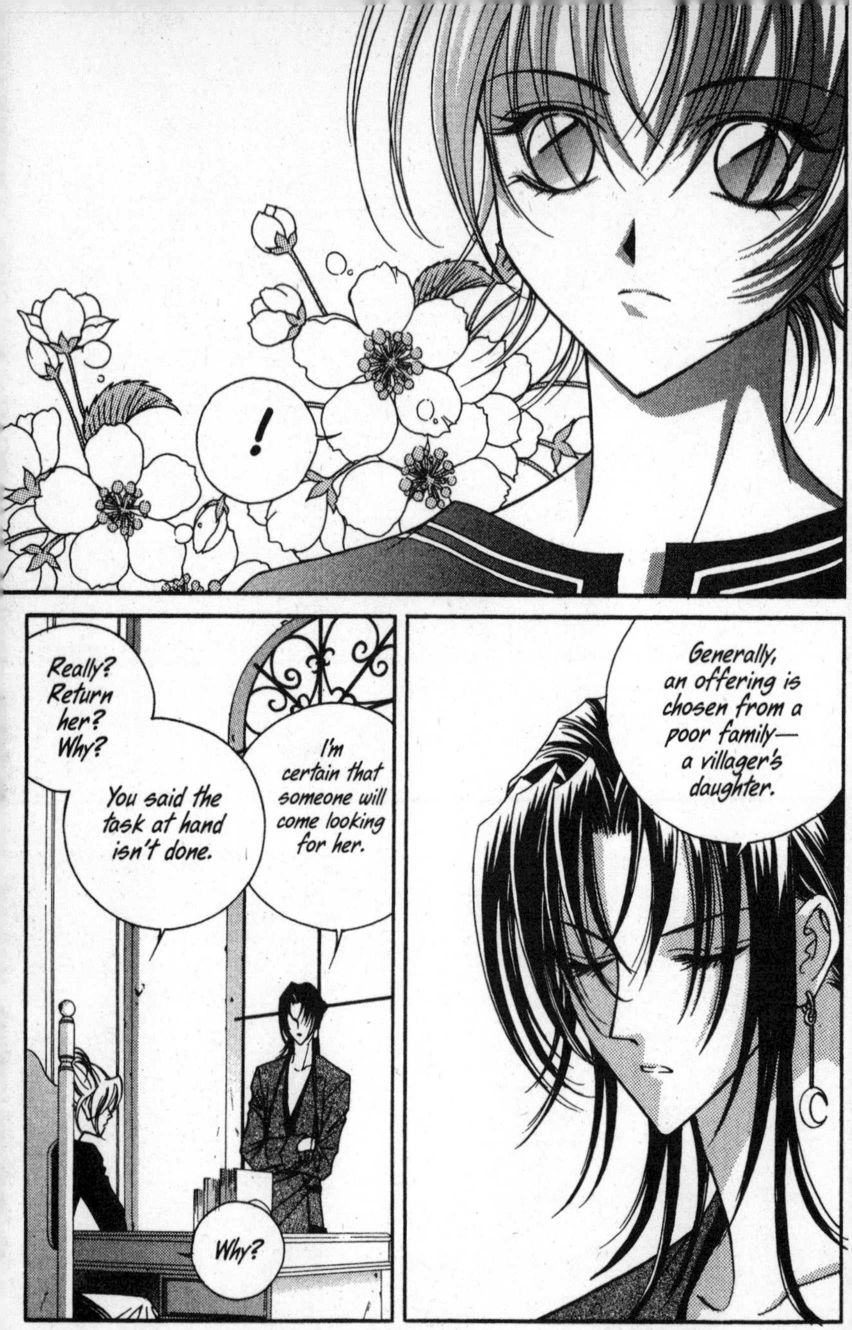
!
Generally, an offering is chosen from a poor family— a villager's daughter.
I'm certain that someone will come looking for her.
Really? Return her? Why?
You said the task at hand isn't done.
Why?

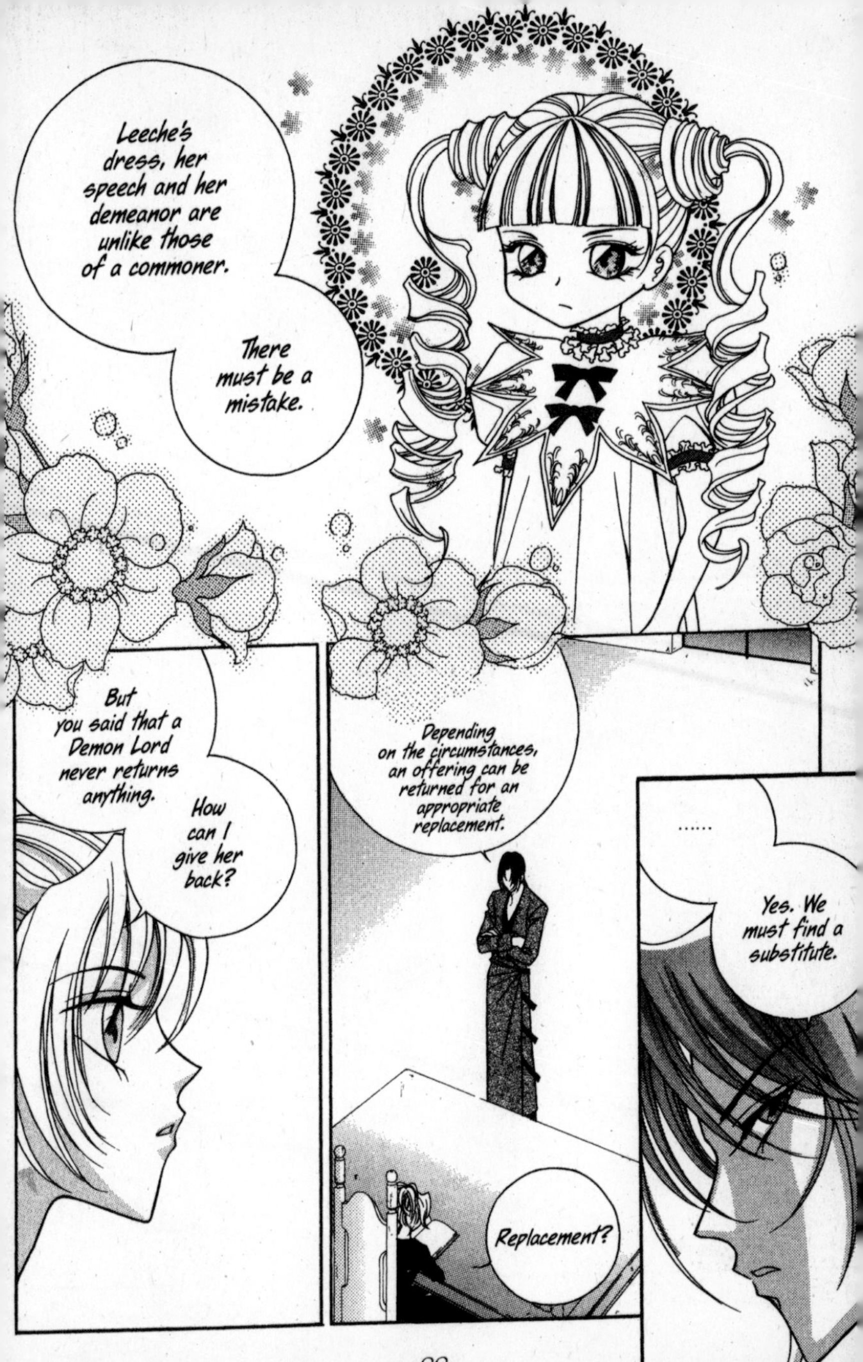

Leeche's dress, her speech and her demeanor are unlike those of a commoner.
There must be a mistake.
But you said that a Demon Lord never returns anything.
How can I give her back?
Depending on the circumstances, an offering can be returned for an appropriate replacement.
Replacement?
......
Yes. We must find a substitute.

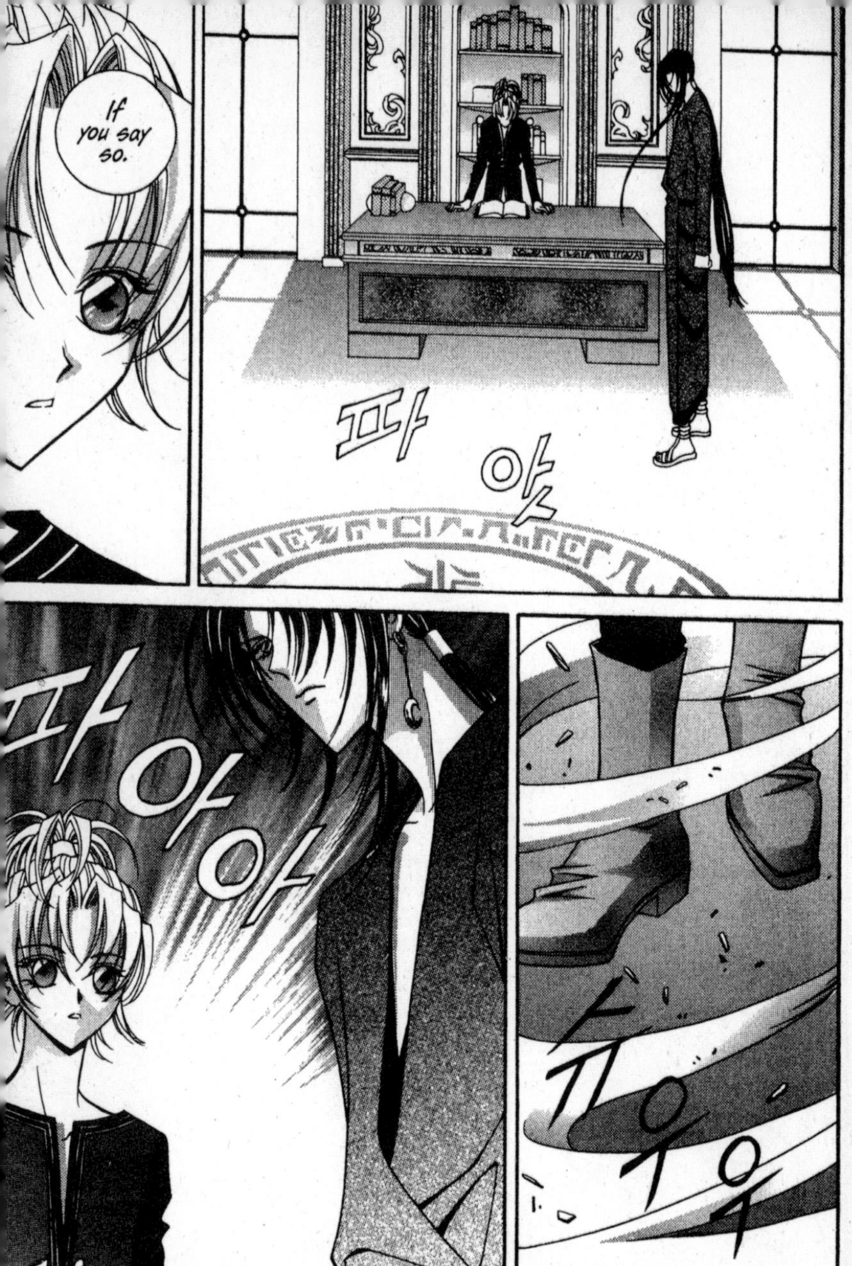
If you say so.
파앗
파아아

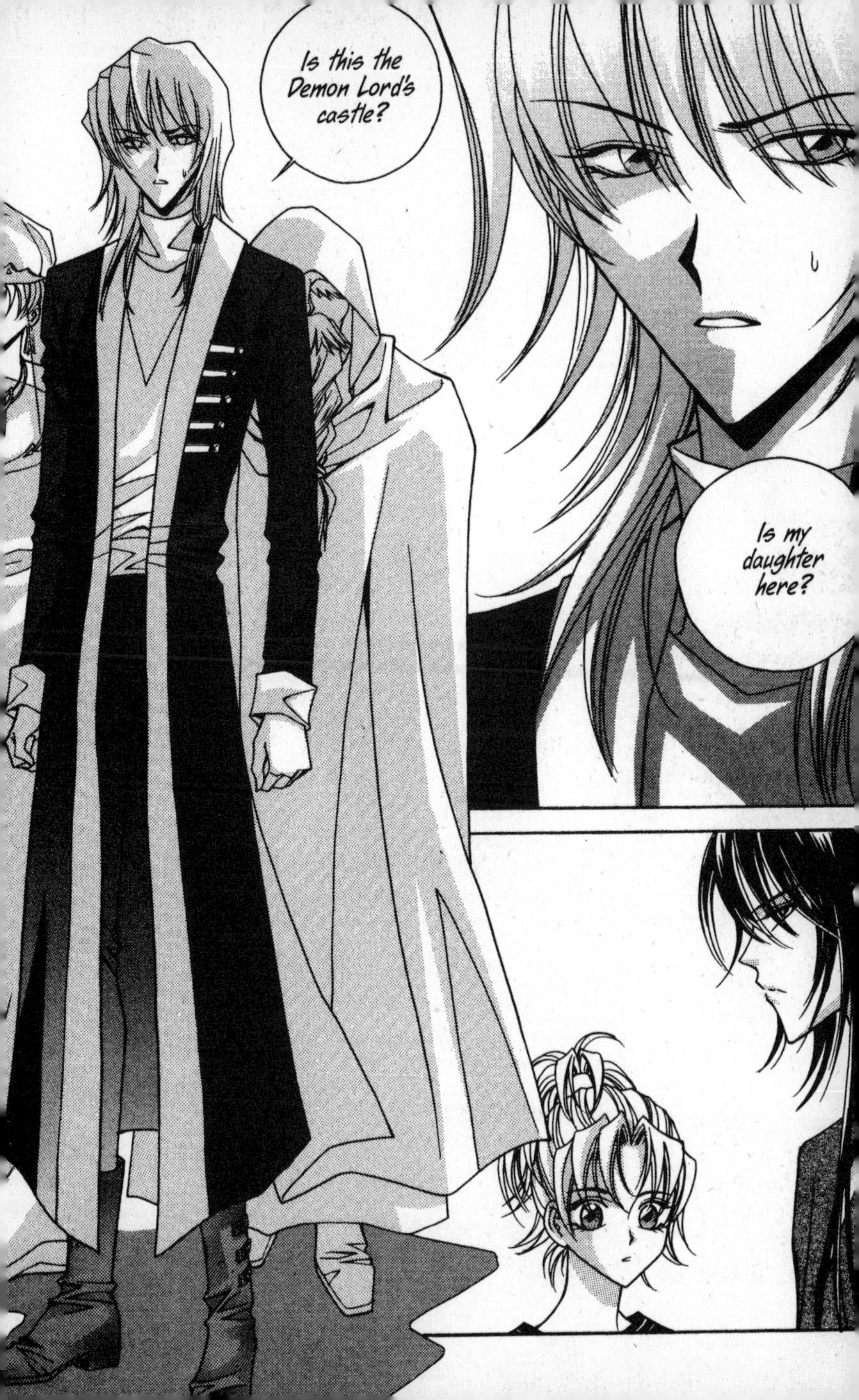
Is this the Demon Lord's castle?
Is my daughter here?

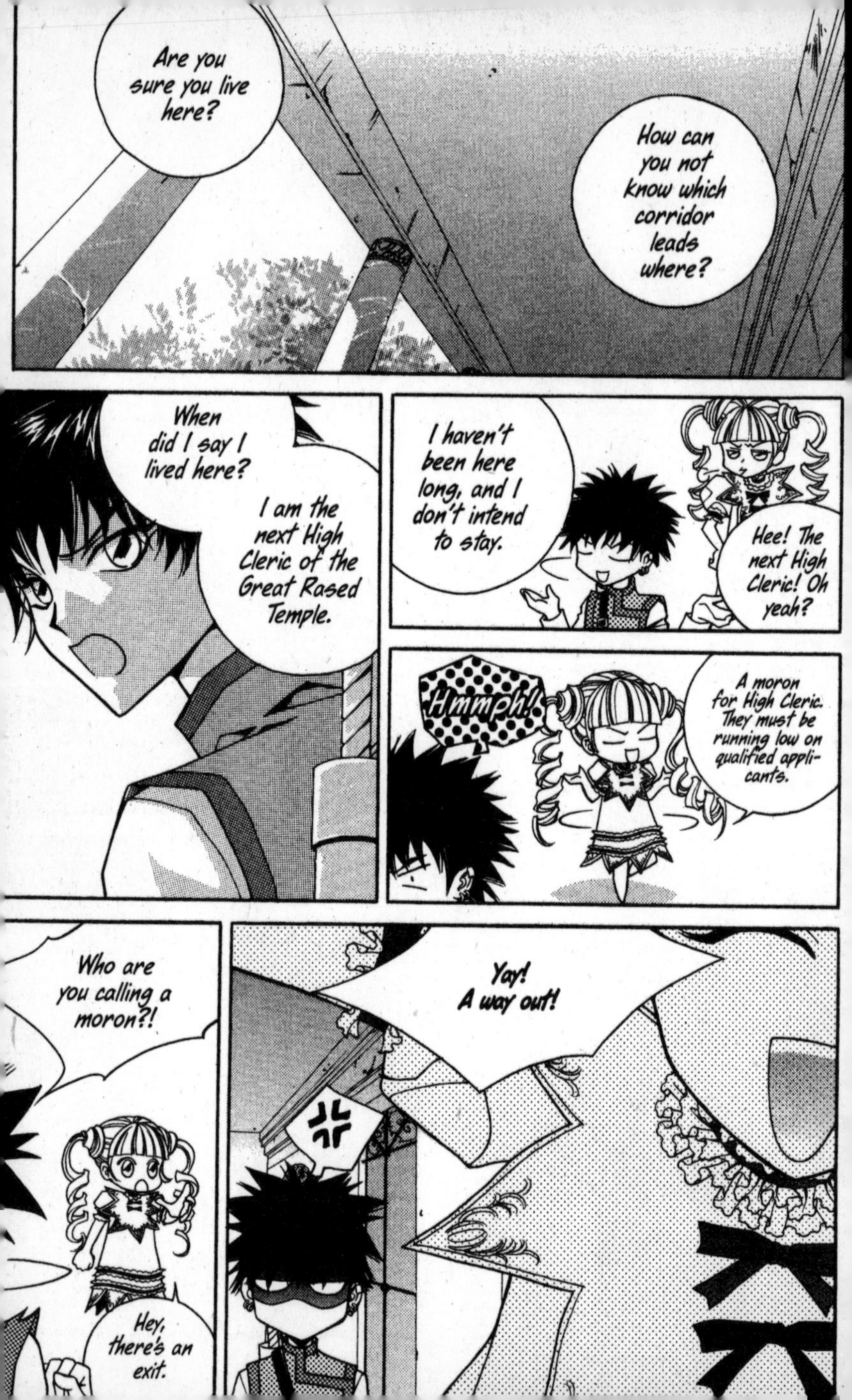
Are you sure you live here?
How can you not know which corridor leads where?
When did I say I lived here?
I am the next High Cleric of the Great Rased Temple.
I haven't been here long, and I don't intend to stay.
Hee! The next High Cleric! Oh yeah?
Hmmph!
A moron for High Cleric. They must be running low on qualified applicants.
Who are you calling a moron?!
Hey, there's an exit.
Yay! A way out!

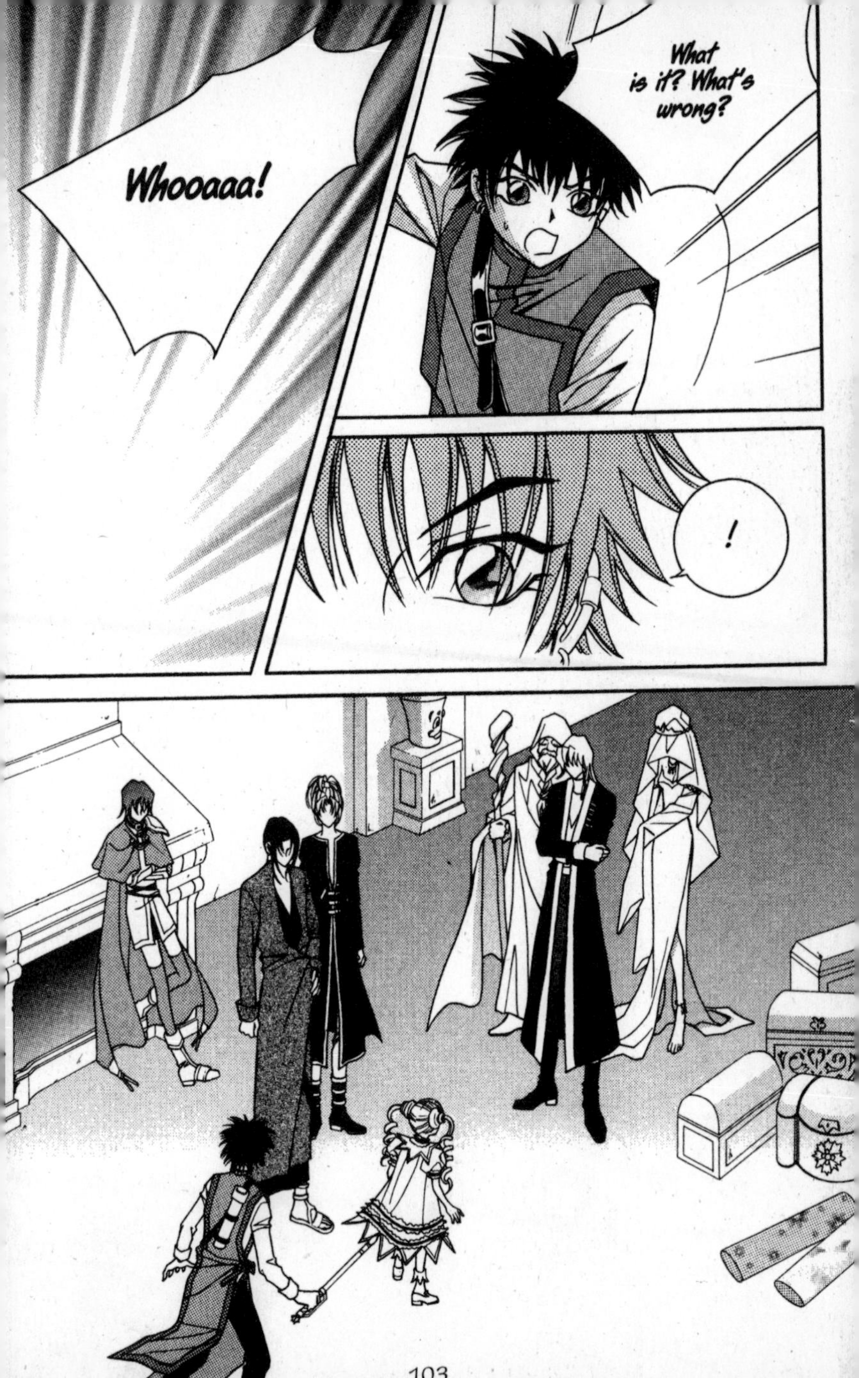
Whooaaa!
What is it? What's wrong?
!

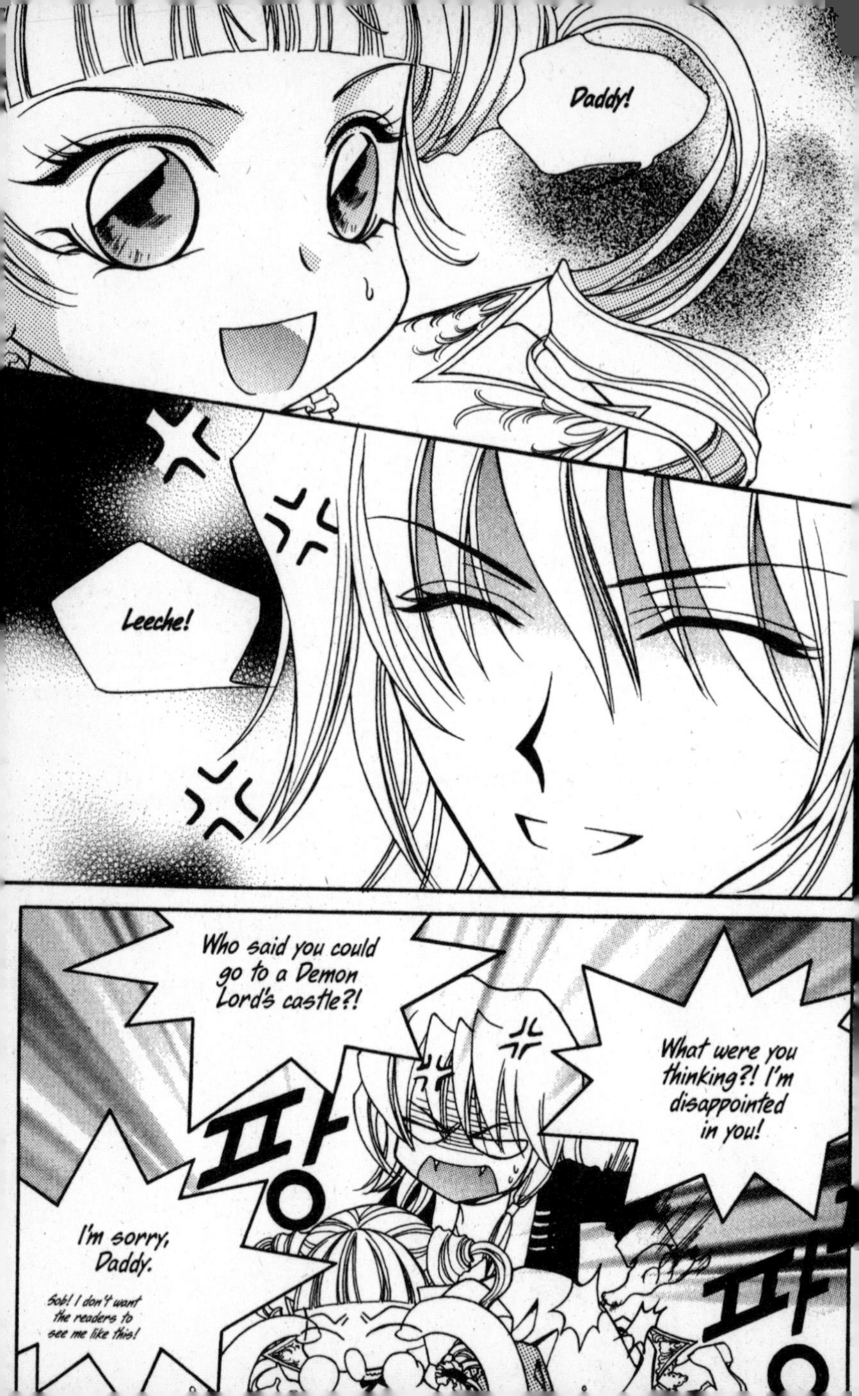
Daddy!
Leeche!
Who said you could go to a Demon Lord's castle?!
What were you thinking?! I'm disappointed in you!
I'm sorry, Daddy.
Sob! I don't want the readers to see me like this!

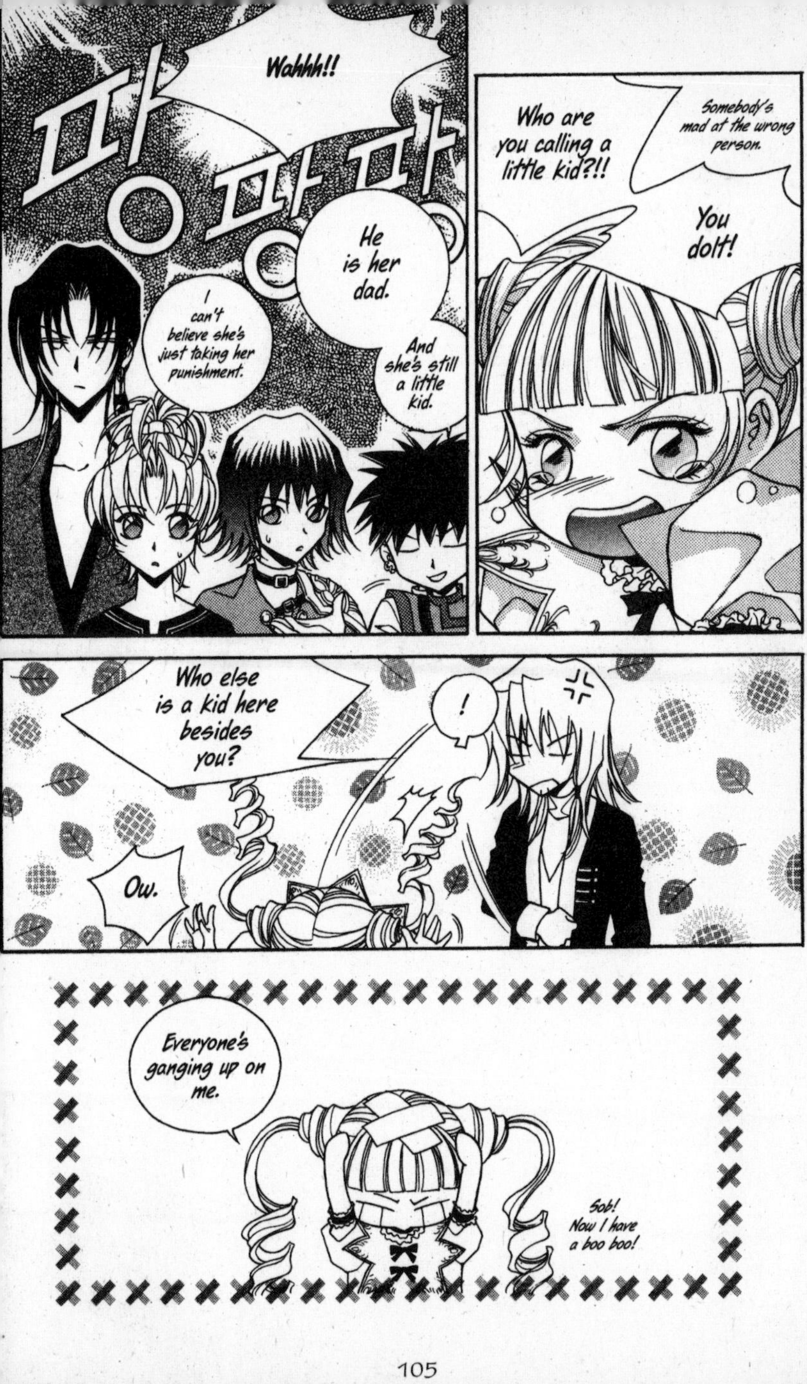
Wahhh!!
I can't believe she's just taking her punishment.
He is her dad.
And she's still a little kid.
Who are you calling a little kid?!!
Somebody's mad at the wrong person.
You dolt!
Who else is a kid here besides you?
!
Ow.
Everyone's ganging up on me.
Sob! Now I have a boo boo!

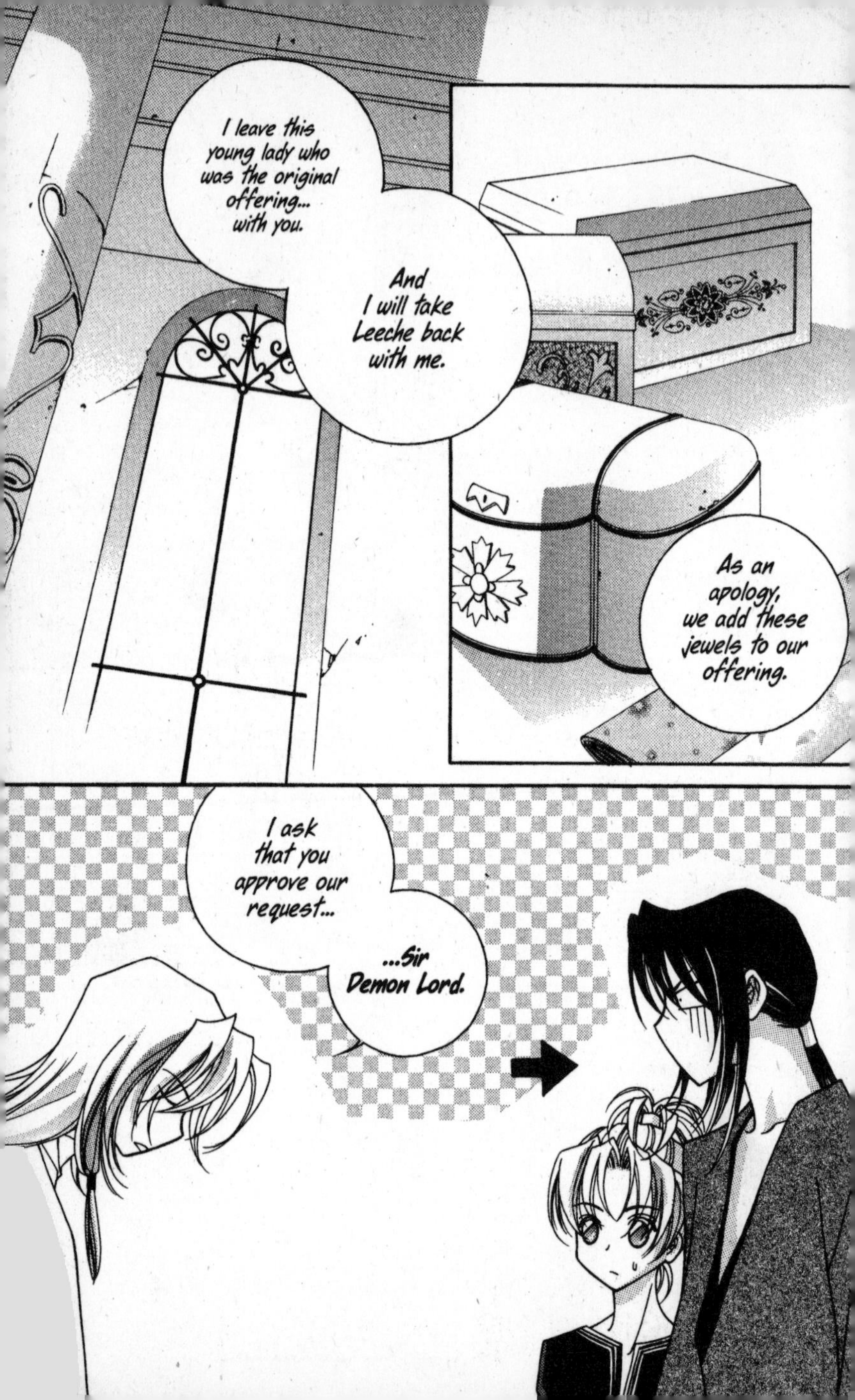
I leave this young lady who was the original offering... with you.
And I will take Leeche back with me.
As an apology, we add these jewels to our offering.
I ask that you approve our request...
...Sir Demon Lord.

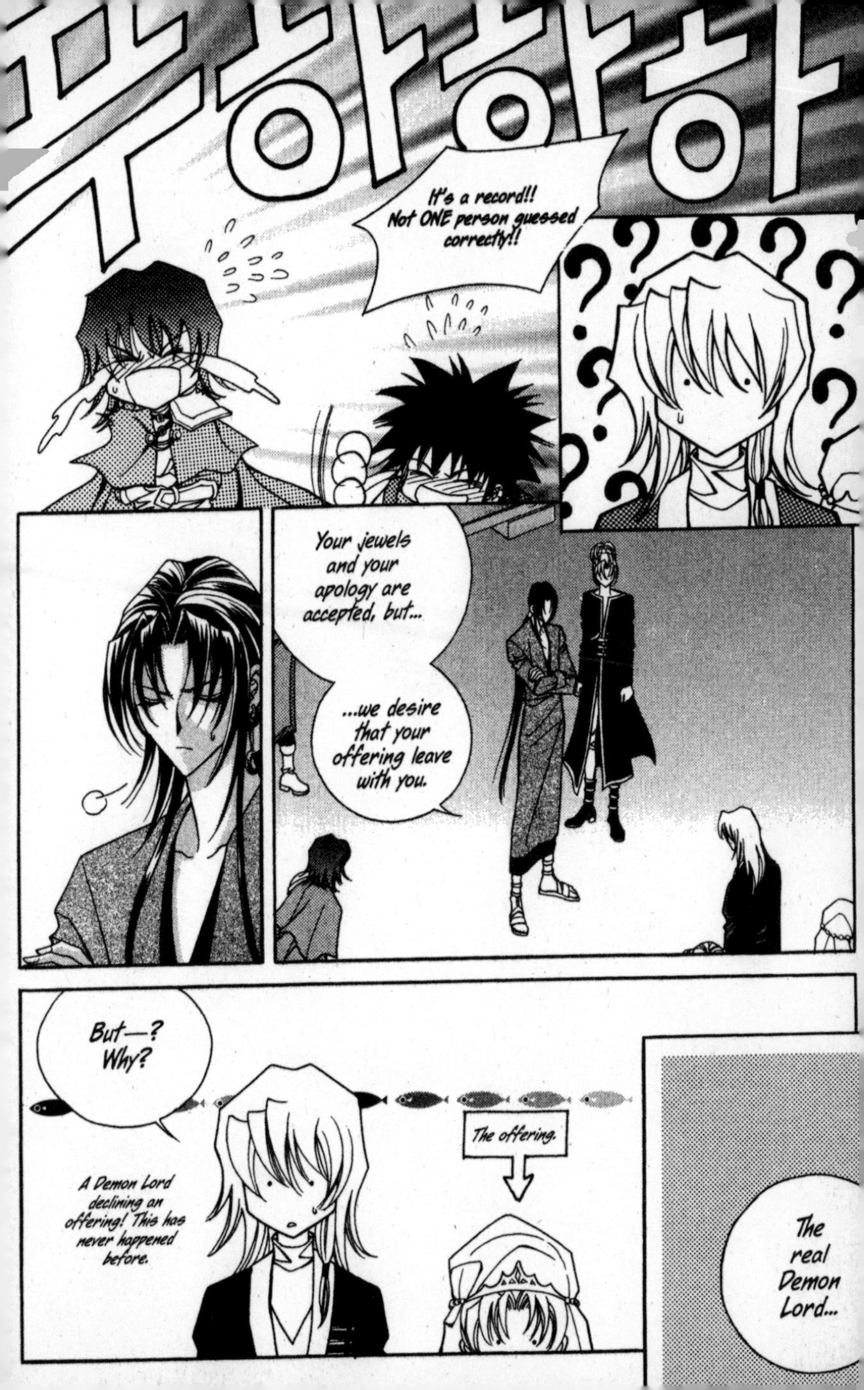
푸하하하
It's a record!! Not ONE person guessed correctly!!
Your jewels and your apology are accepted, but...
...we desire that your offering leave with you.
But—? Why?
A Demon Lord declining an offering! This has never happened before.
The offering.
The real Demon Lord...

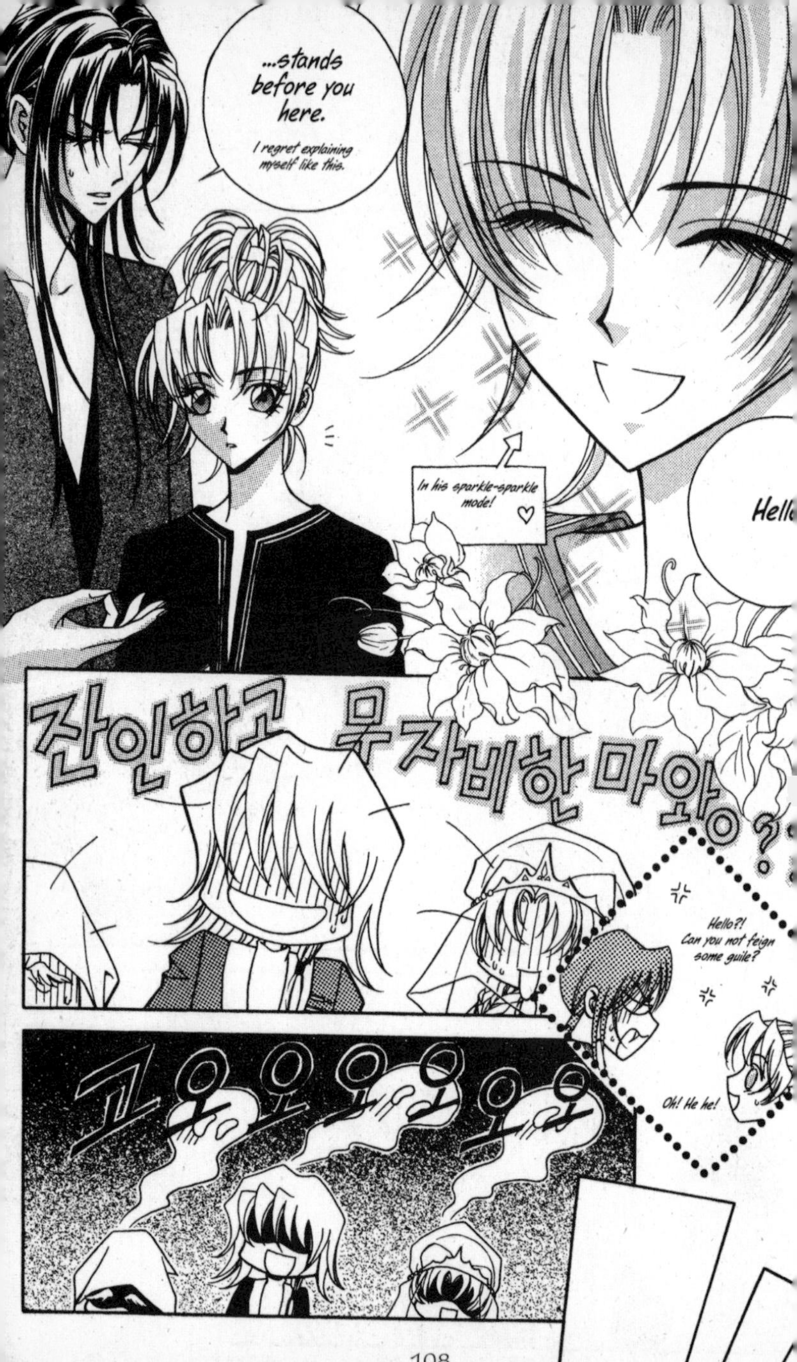
...stands before you here.
I regret explaining myself like this.
In his sparkle-sparkle mode! ♡
잔인하고 무자비한 마왕?!
Hello?! Can you not feign some guile?
Oh! He he!
고오오오오오오

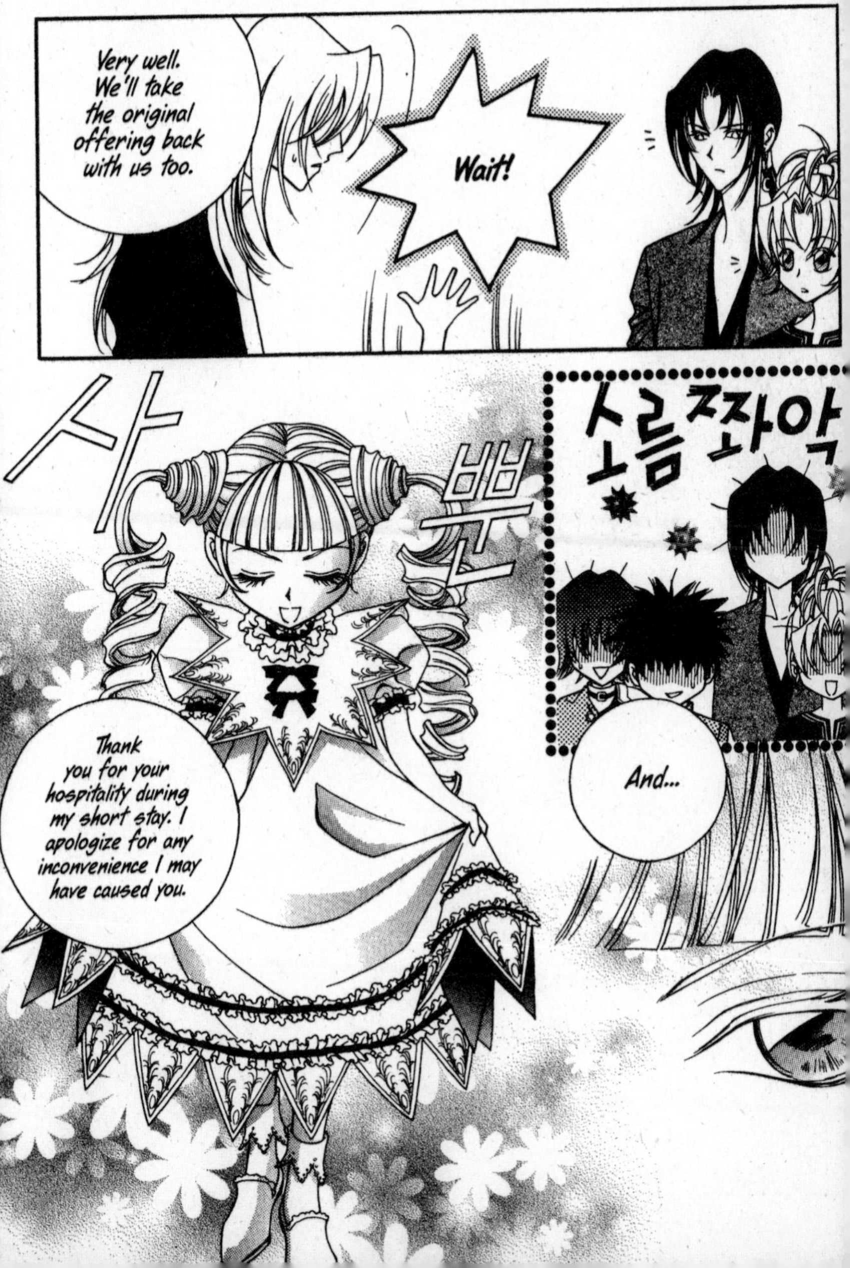
Very well. We'll take the original offering back with us too.
Wait!
사뿐
Thank you for your hospitality during my short stay. I apologize for any inconvenience I may have caused you.
소름 쫘악
And...

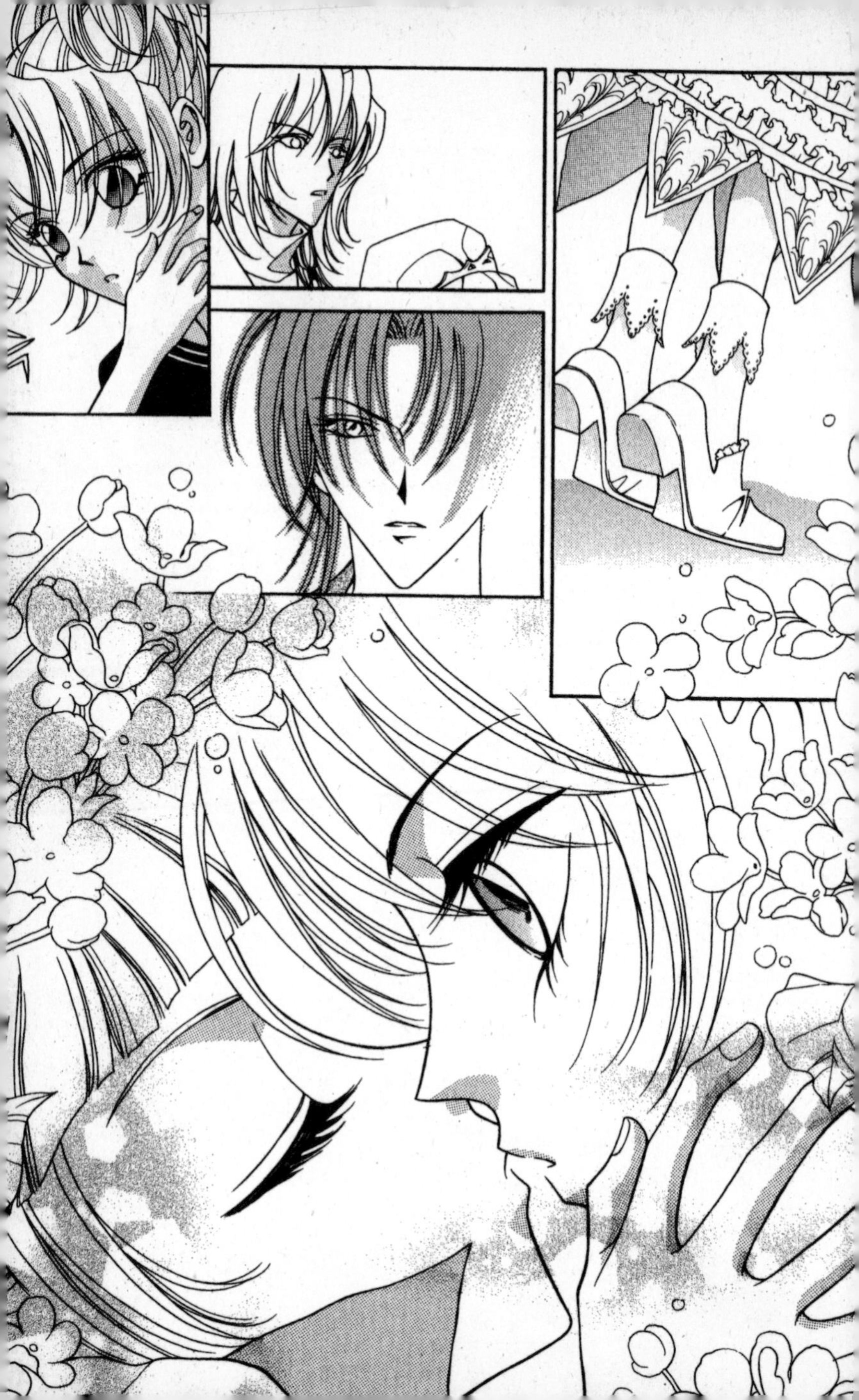

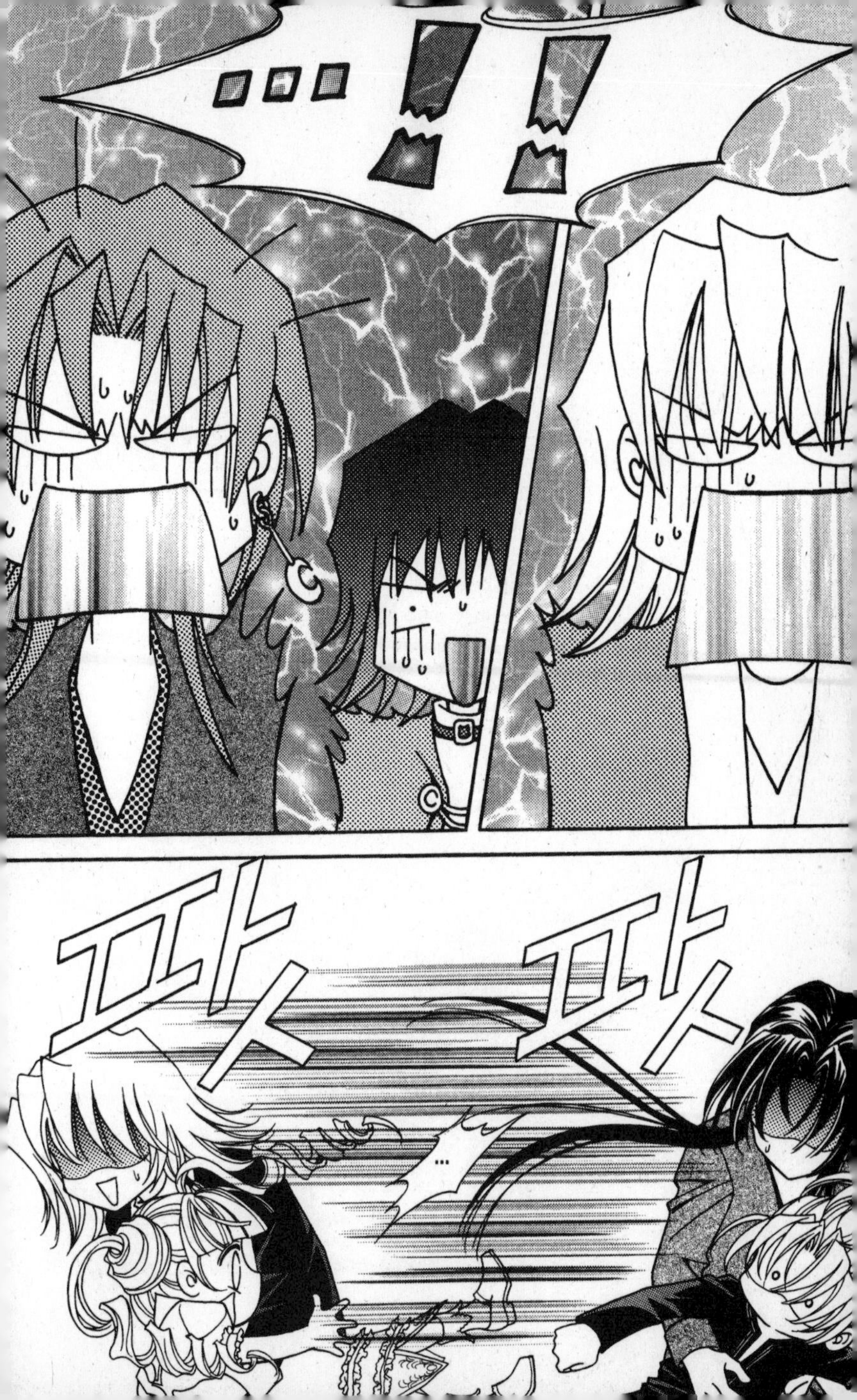
...!!
...

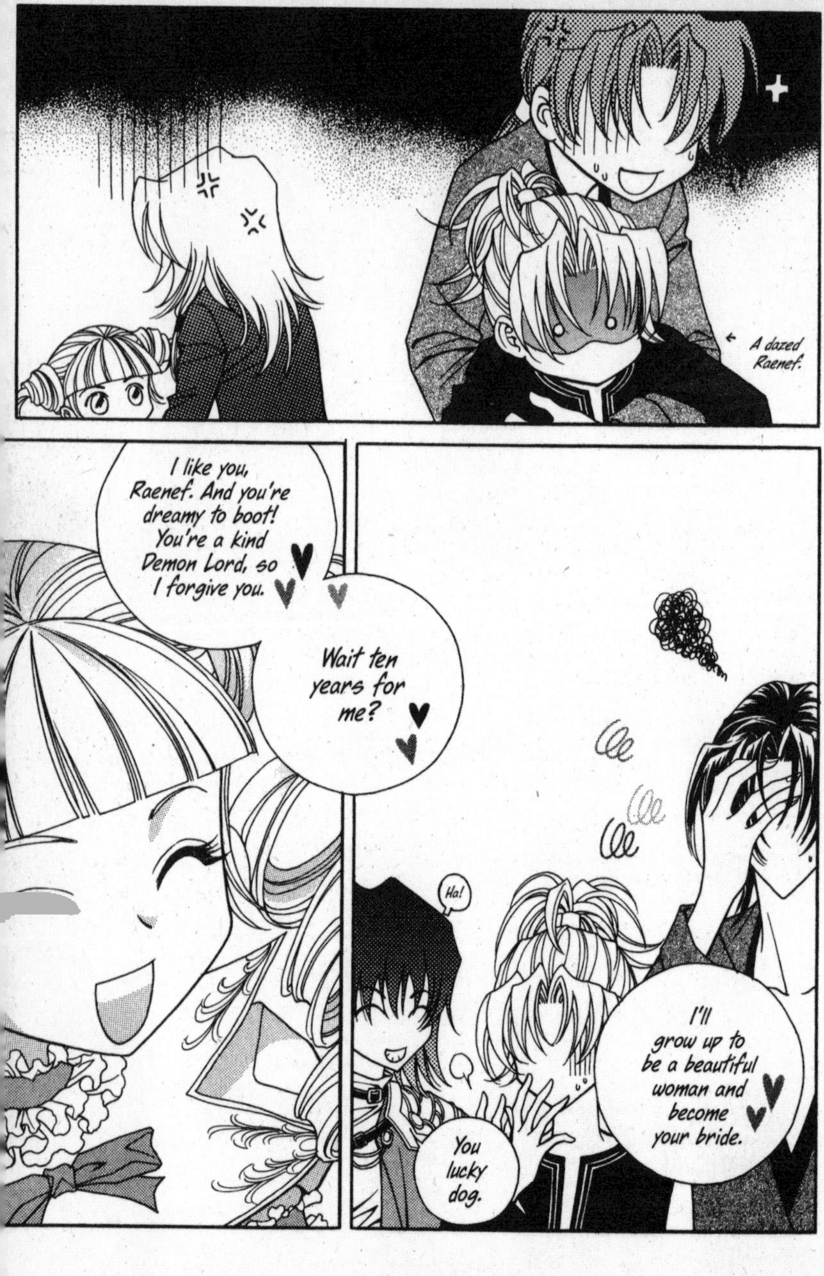

A dazed Raenef.
I like you, Raenef. And you're dreamy to boot! You're a kind Demon Lord, so I forgive you.
Wait ten years for me?
Ha!
I'll grow up to be a beautiful woman and become your bride.
You lucky dog.

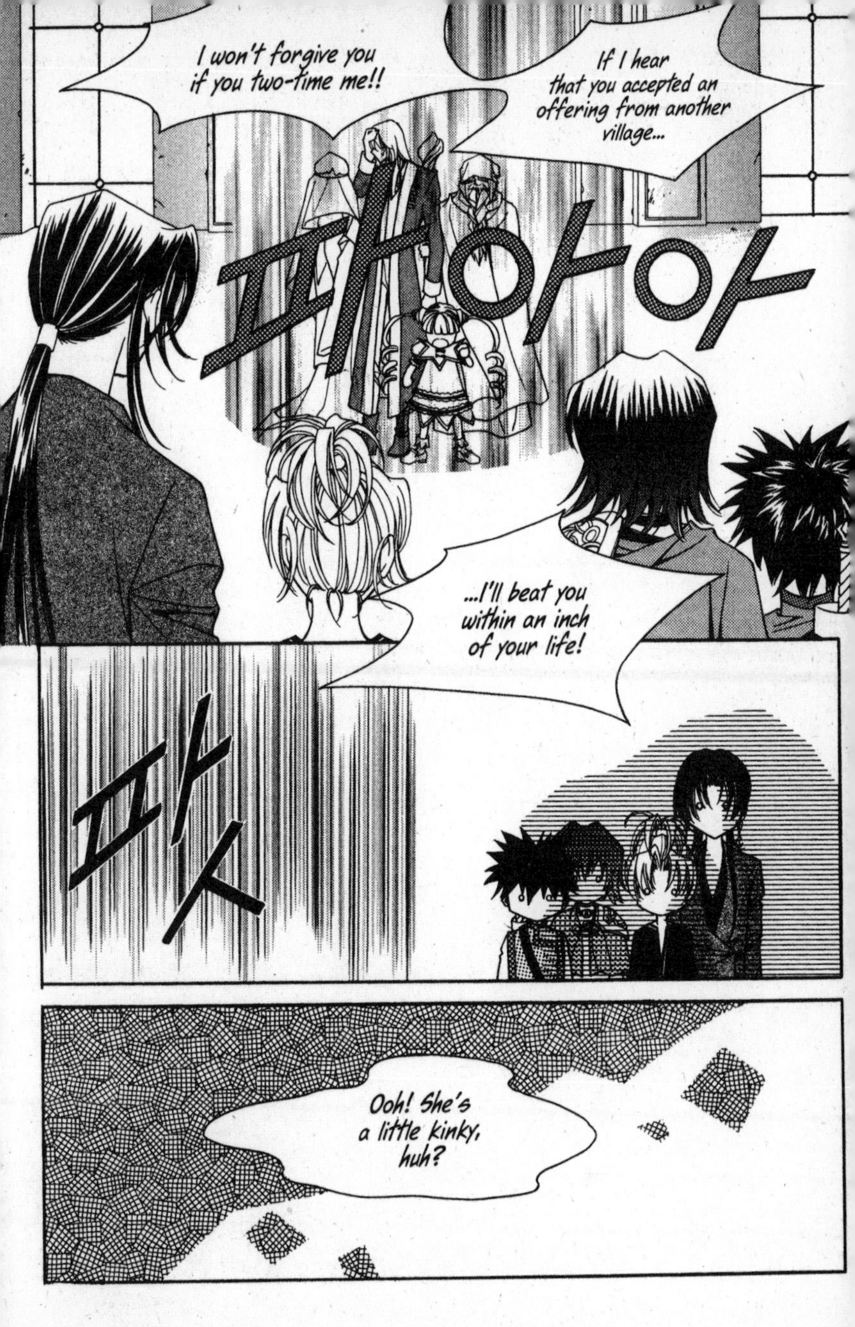
I won't forgive you if you two-time me!!
If I hear that you accepted an offering from another village...
...I'll beat you within an inch of your life!
Ooh! She's a little kinky, huh?

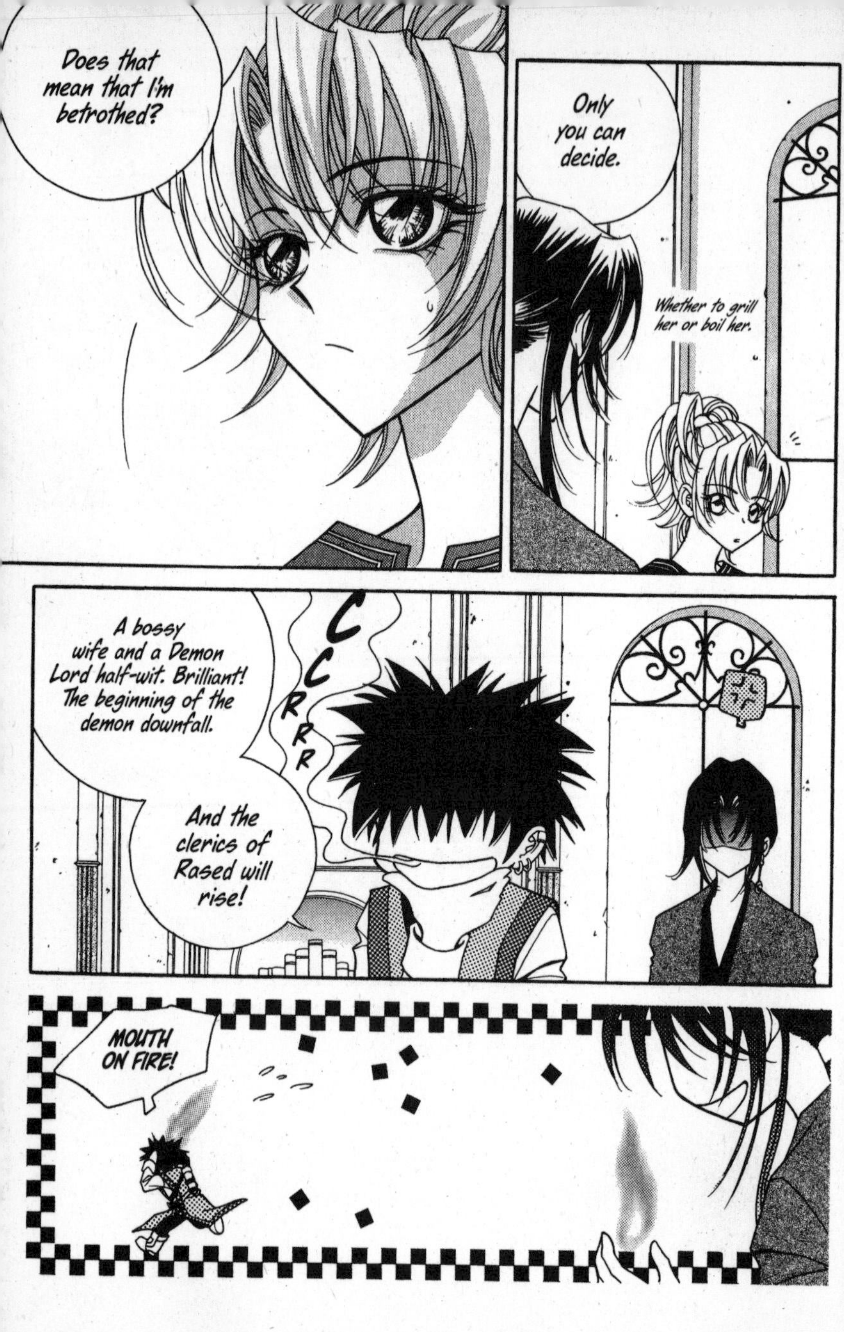

Does that mean that I'm betrothed?
Only you can decide.
Whether to grill her or boil her.
A bossy wife and a Demon Lord half-wit. Brilliant! The beginning of the demon downfall.
CCCRRR
And the clerics of Rased will rise!
MOUTH ON FIRE!

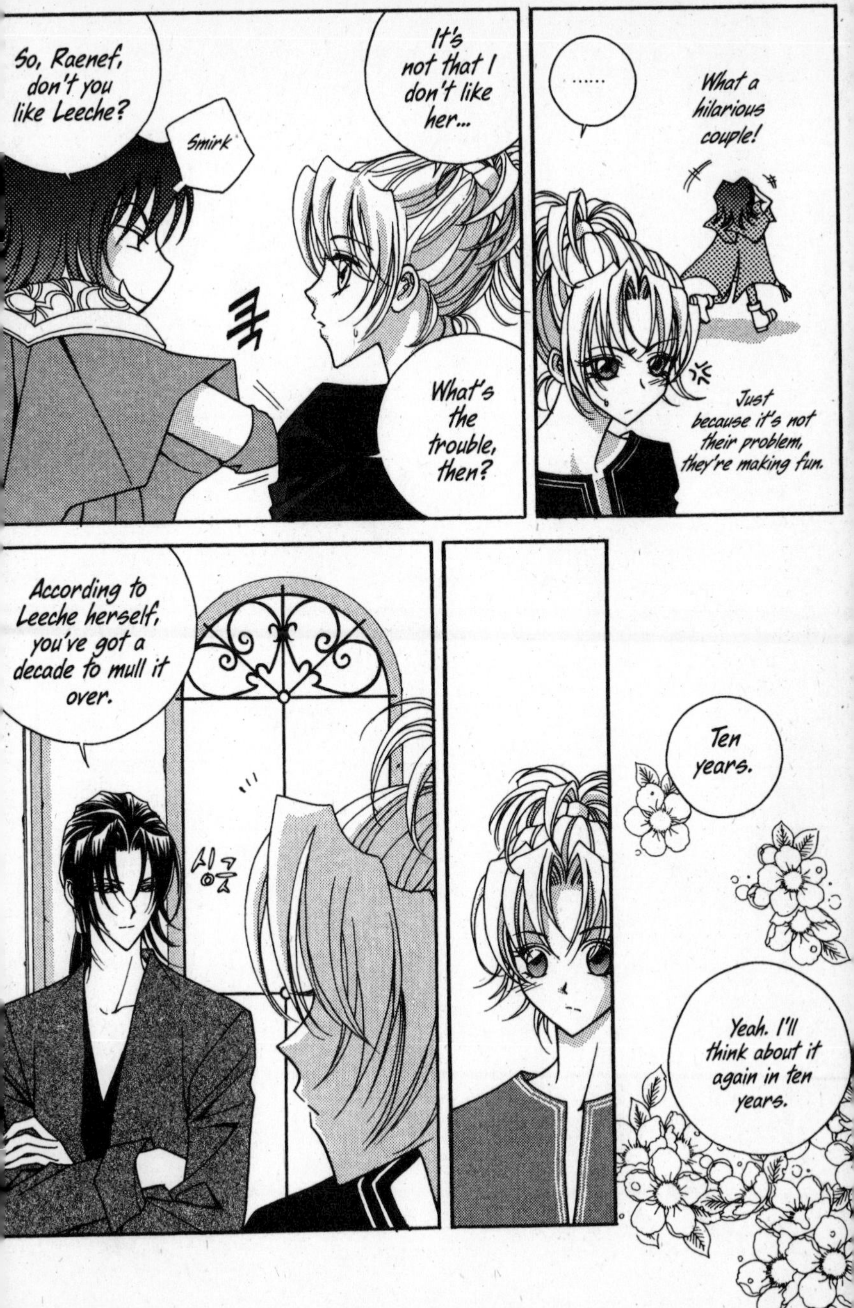

So, Raenef, don't you like Leeche?
Smirk
It's not that I don't like her...
What's the trouble, then?
......
What a hilarious couple!
Just because it's not their problem, they're making fun.
According to Leeche herself, you've got a decade to mull it over.
Ten years.
Yeah. I'll think about it again in ten years.

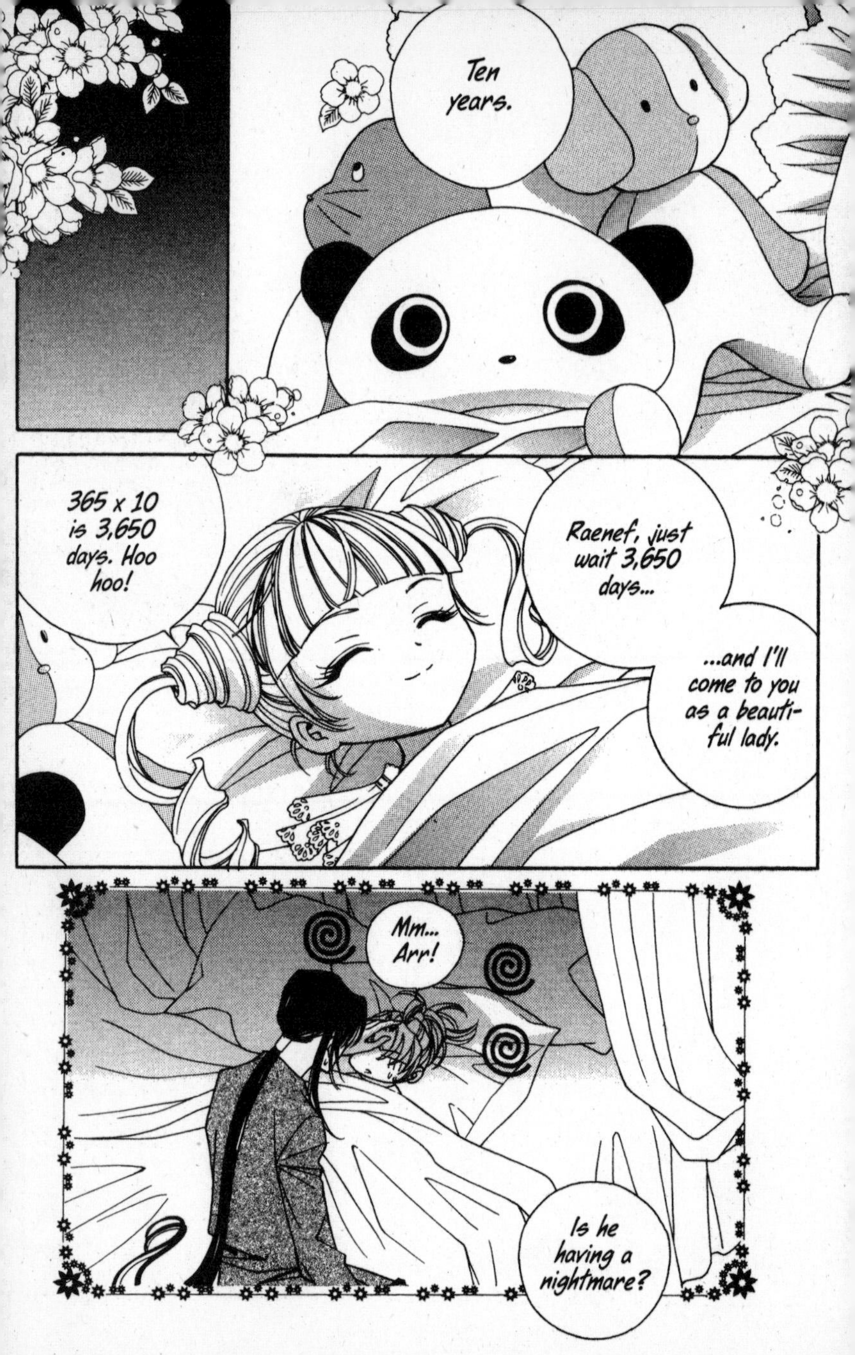
Ten years.
365 x 10 is 3,650 days. Hoo hoo!
Raenef, just wait 3,650 days...
...and I'll come to you as a beautiful lady.
Mm... Arr!
Is he having a nightmare?

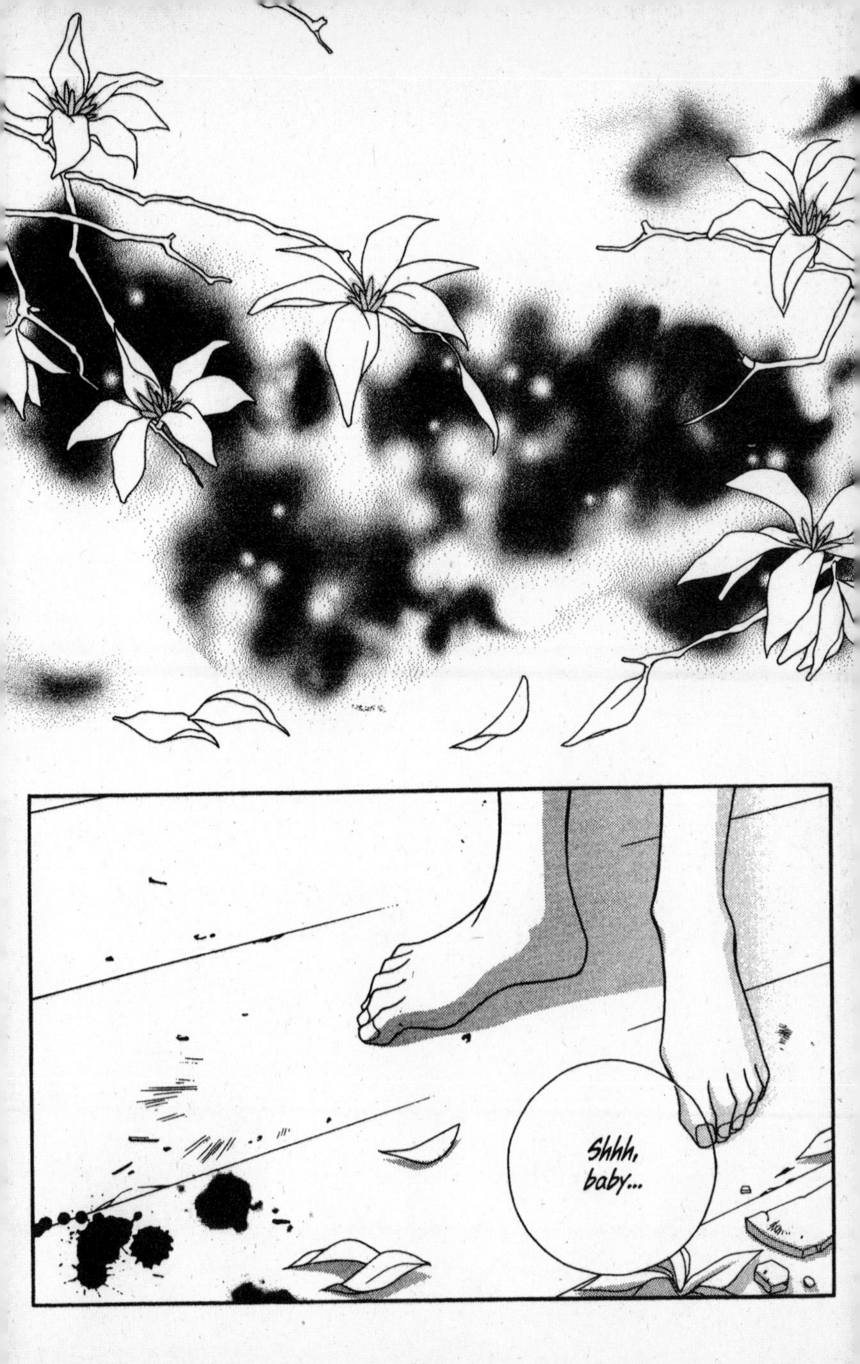
Shhh, baby...

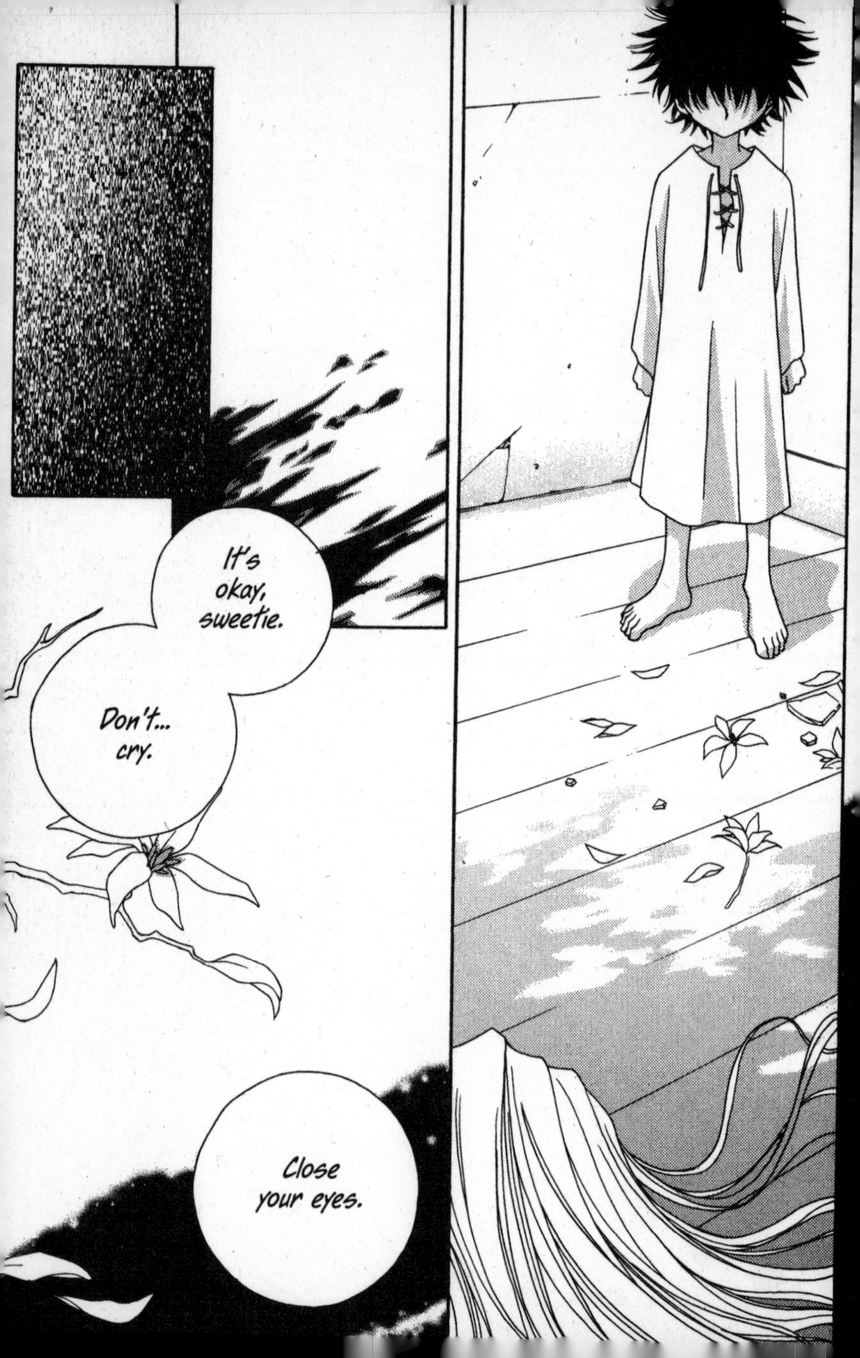
It's okay, sweetie.
Don't... cry.
Close your eyes.

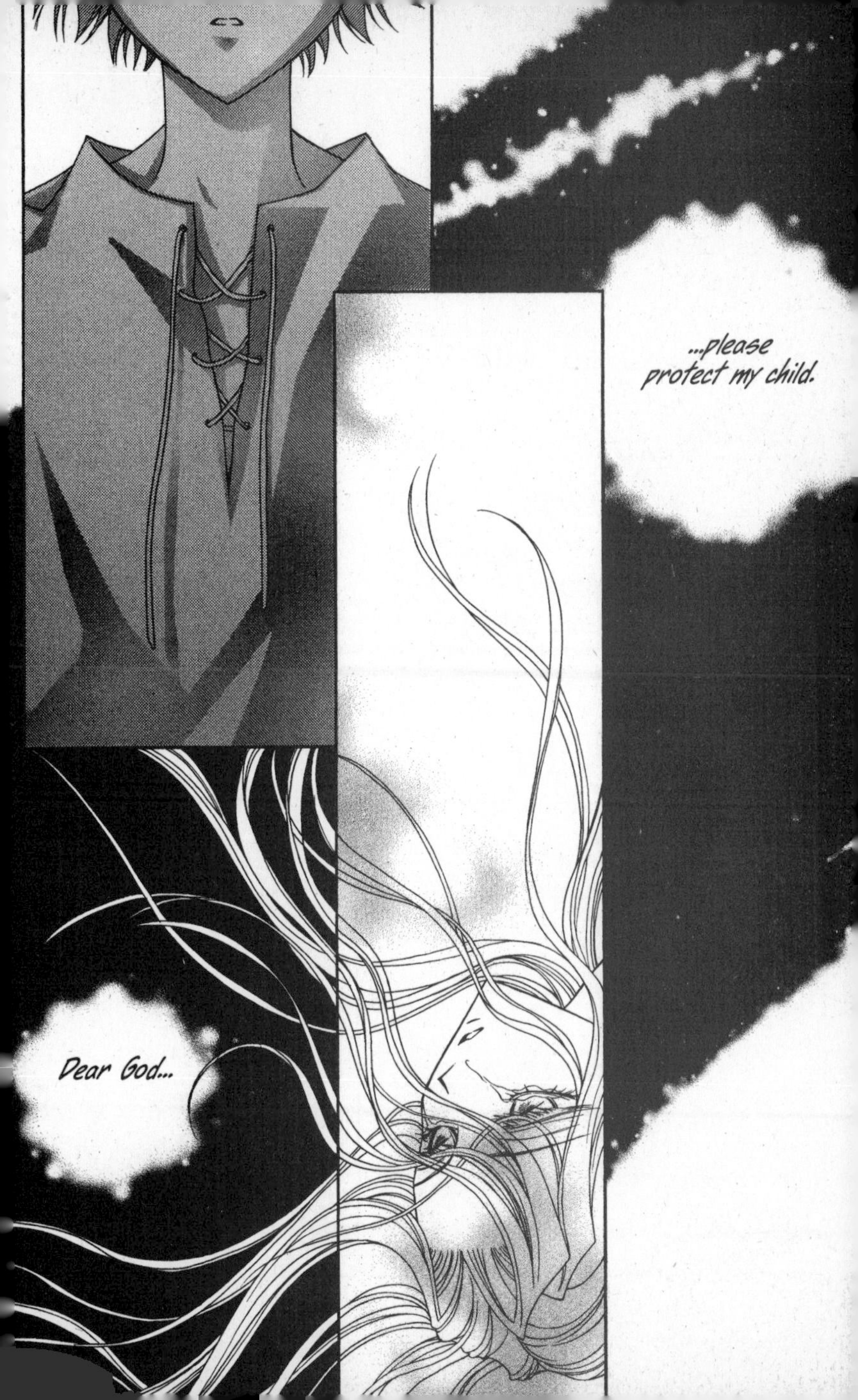
Dear God...
...please protect my child.

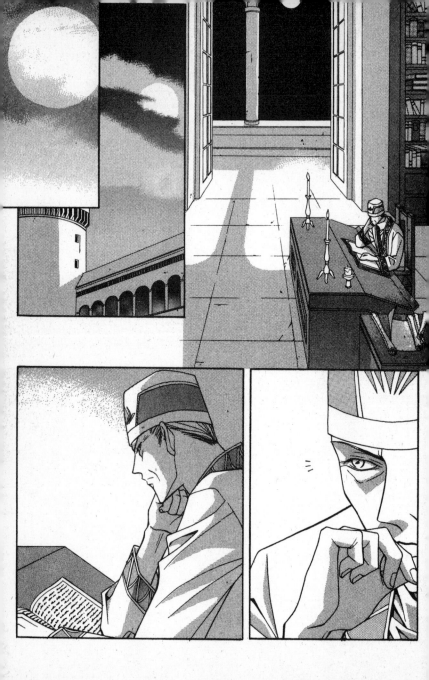

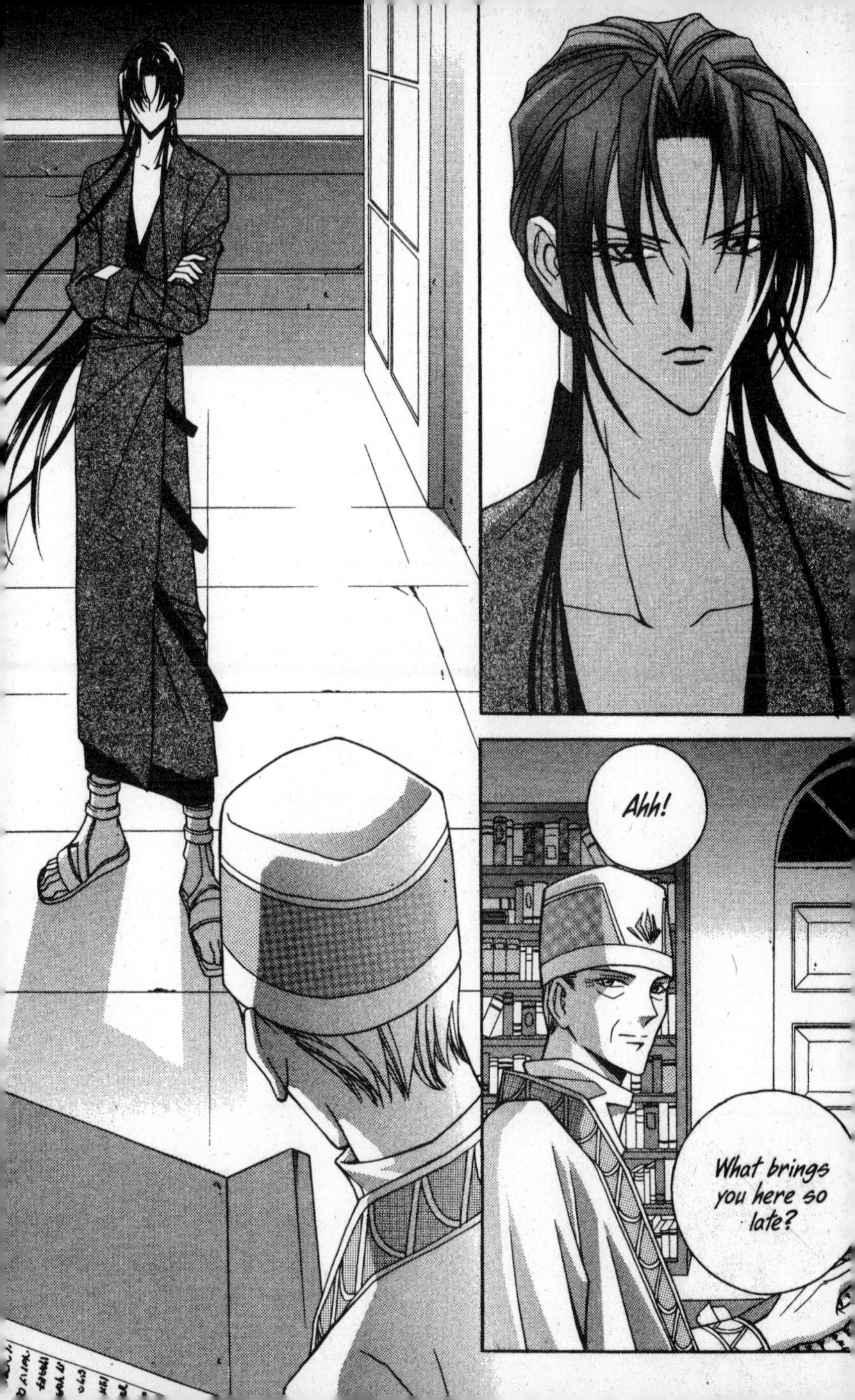
Ahh!
What brings you here so late?

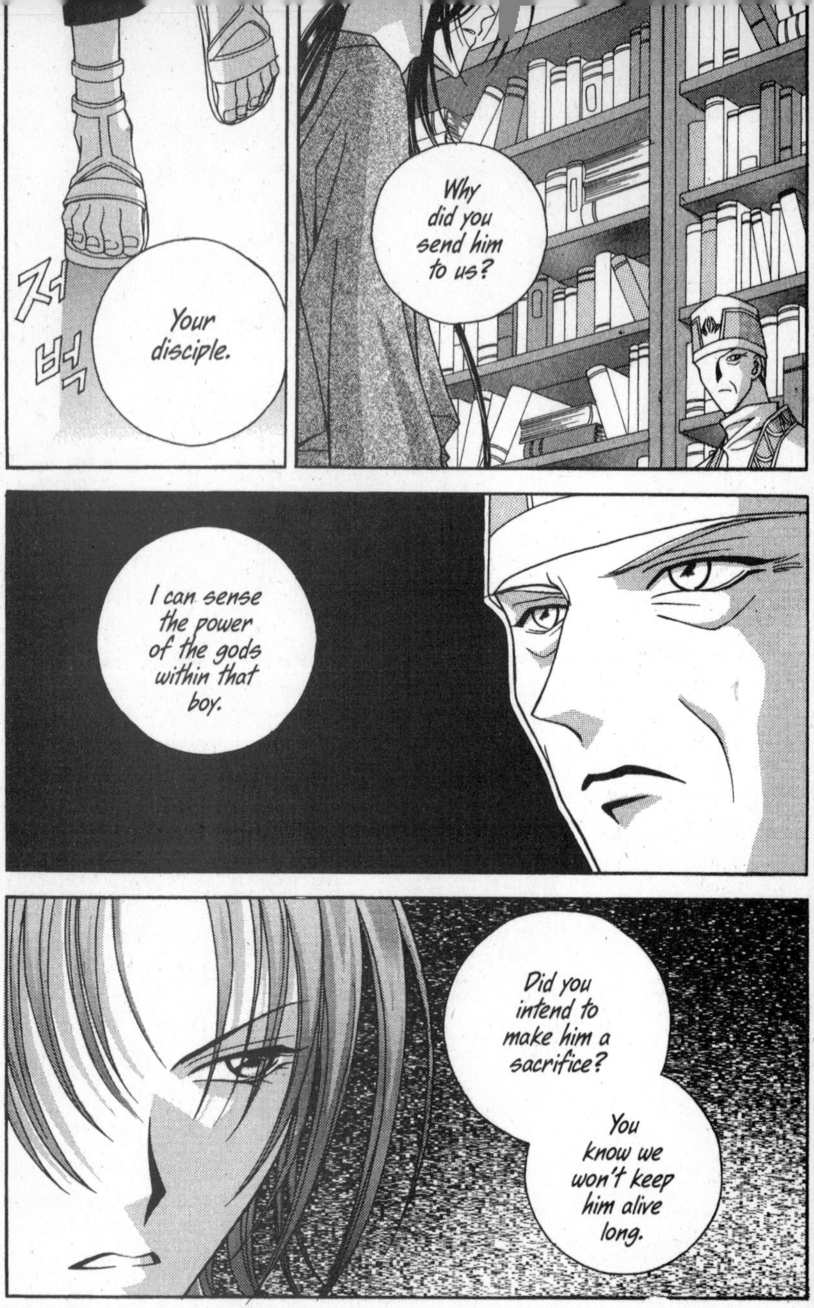
저벅
Your disciple.
Why did you send him to us?
I can sense the power of the gods within that boy.
Did you intend to make him a sacrifice?
You know we won't keep him alive long.

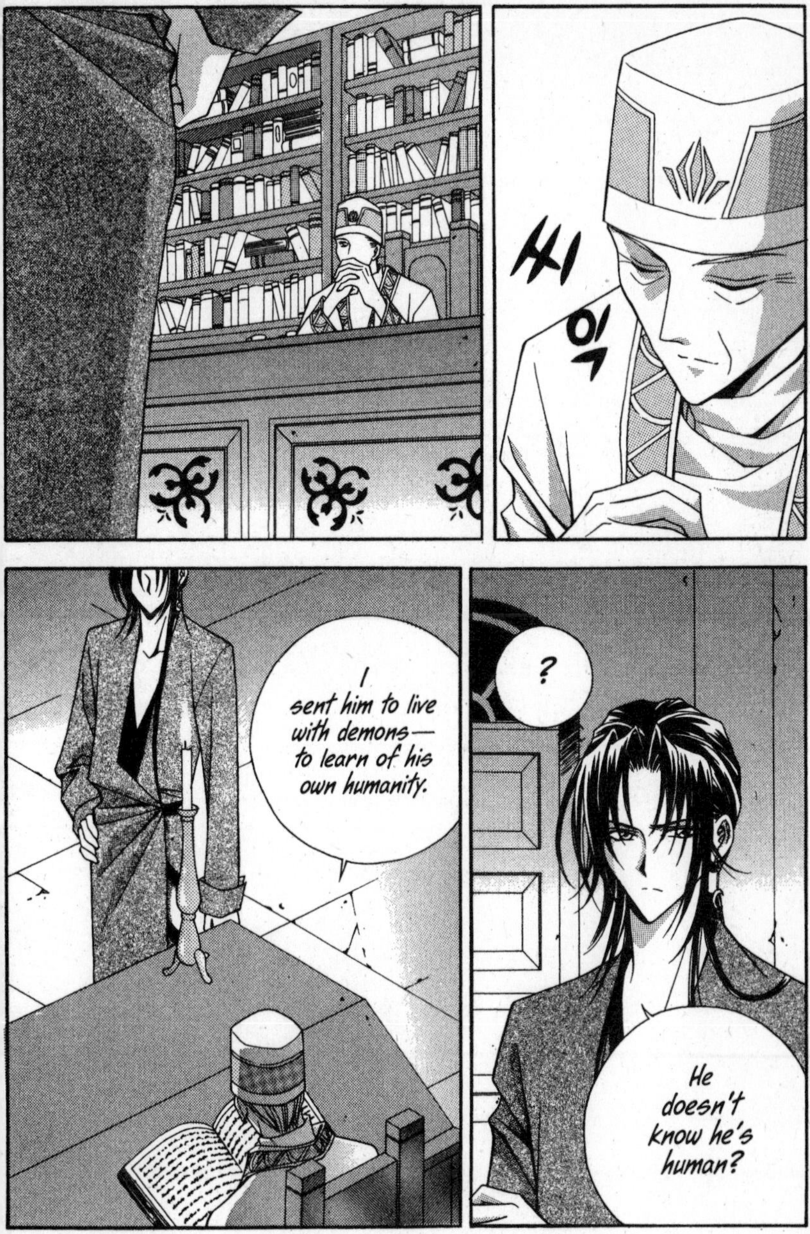
씨익
I sent him to live with demons— to learn of his own humanity.
?
He doesn't know he's human?

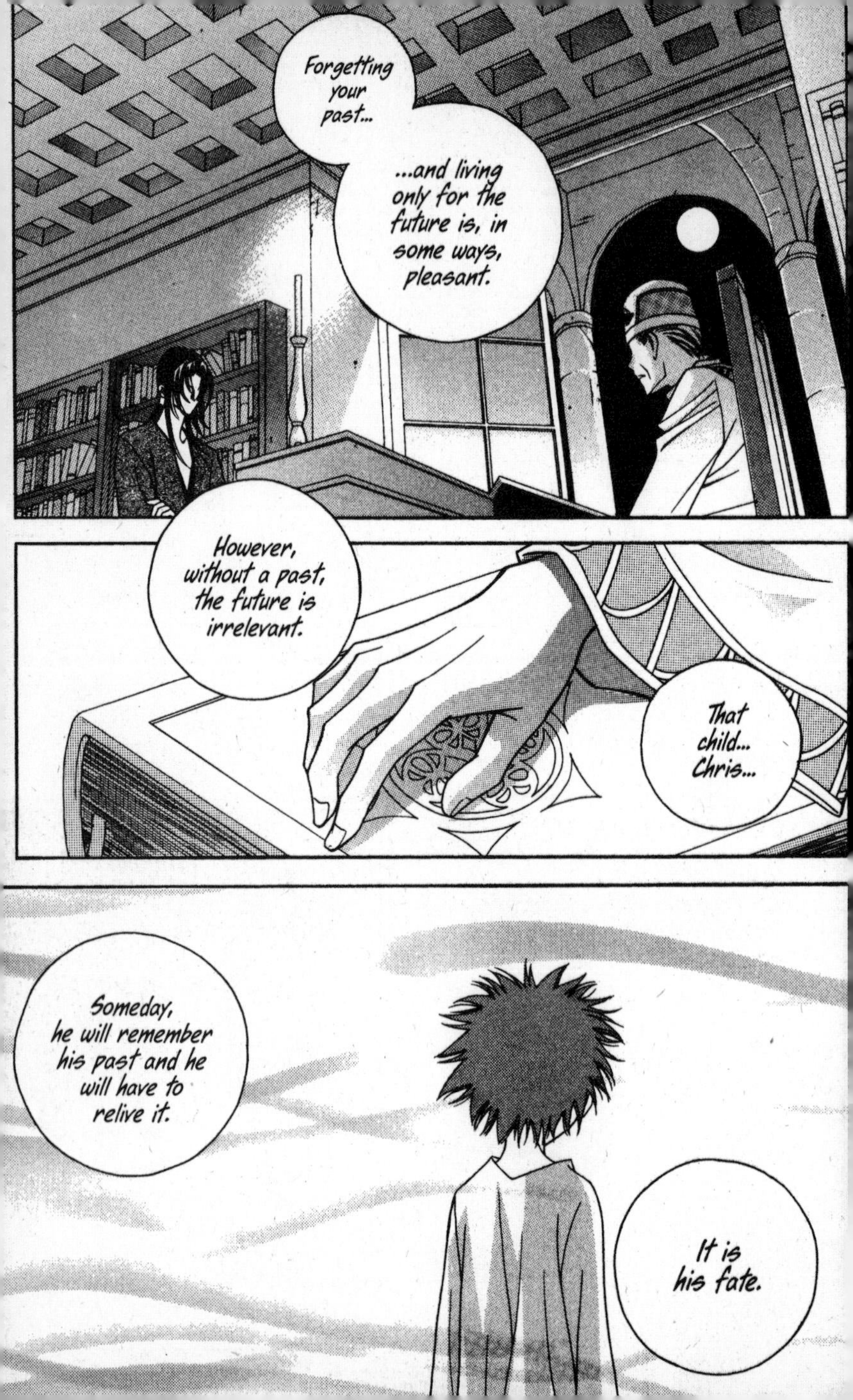

Forgetting your past...
...and living only for the future is, in some ways, pleasant.
However, without a past, the future is irrelevant.
That child... Chris...
Someday, he will remember his past and he will have to relive it.
It is his fate.

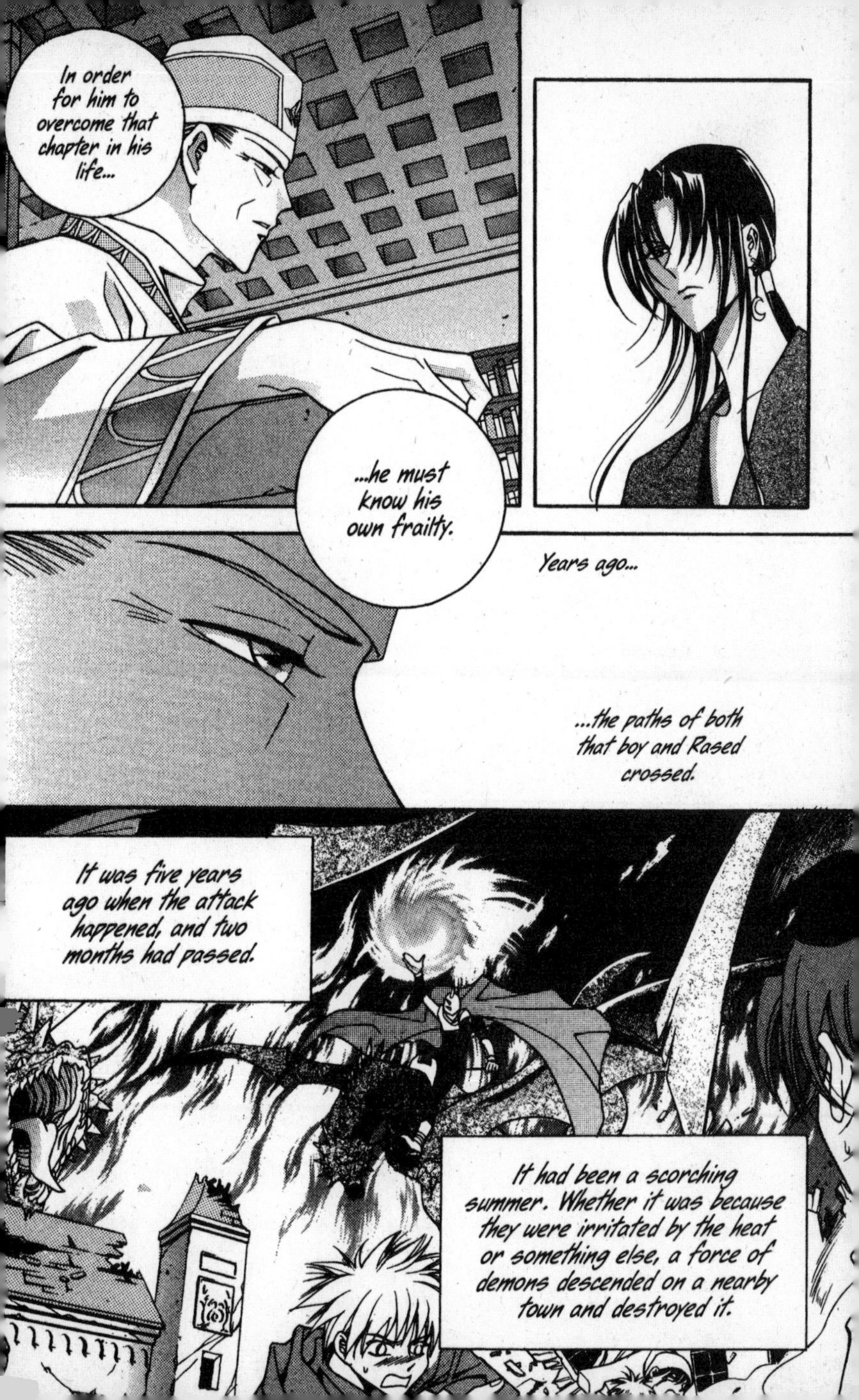
In order for him to overcome that chapter in his life...
...he must know his own frailty.
Years ago...
...the paths of both that boy and Rased crossed.
It was five years ago when the attack happened, and two months had passed.
It had been a scorching summer. Whether it was because they were irritated by the heat or something else, a force of demons descended on a nearby town and destroyed it.

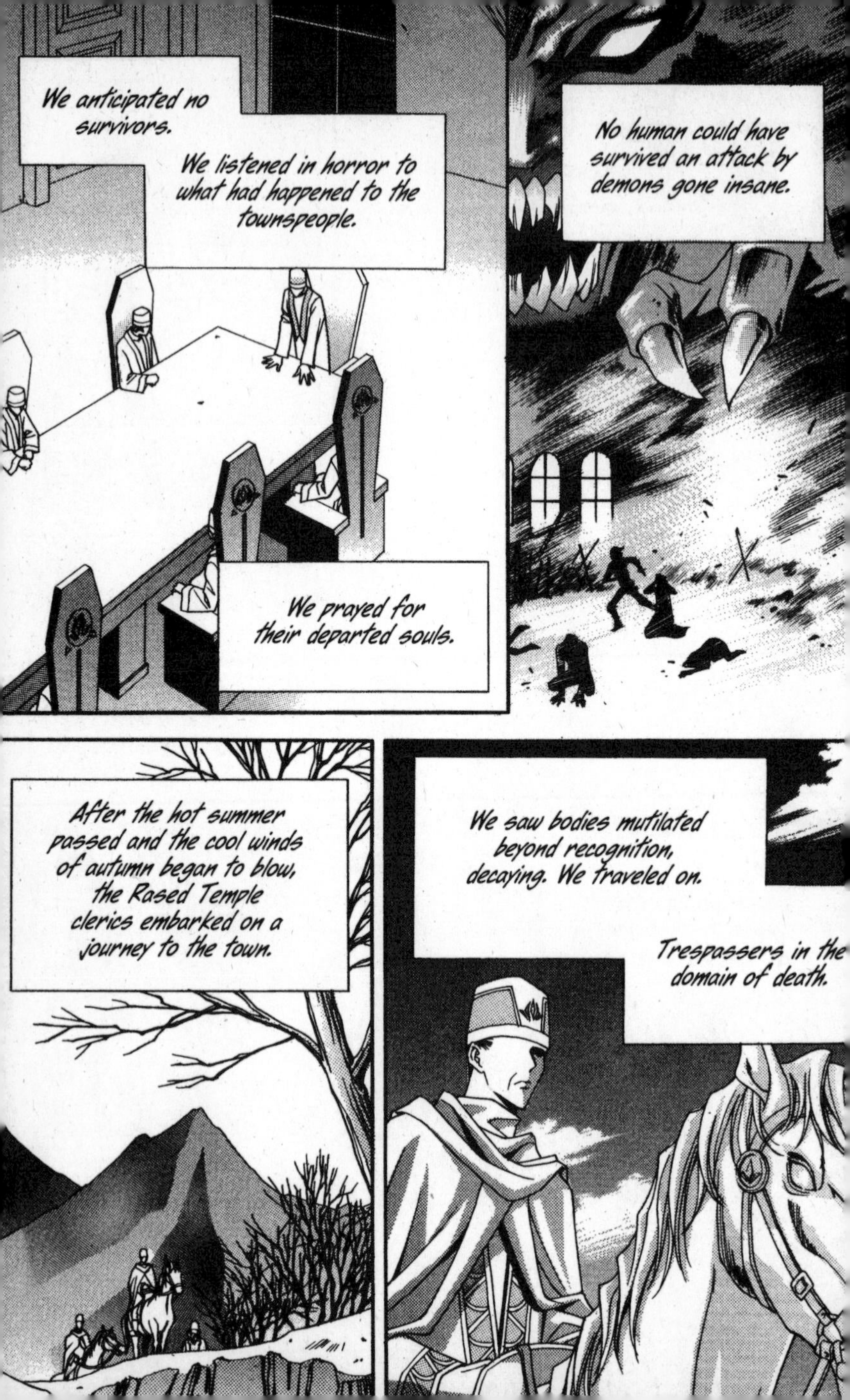
We anticipated no survivors.
We listened in horror to what had happened to the townspeople.
We prayed for their departed souls.
No human could have survived an attack by demons gone insane.
After the hot summer passed and the cool winds of autumn began to blow, the Rased Temple clerics embarked on a journey to the town.
We saw bodies mutilated beyond recognition, decaying. We traveled on.
Trespassers in the domain of death.

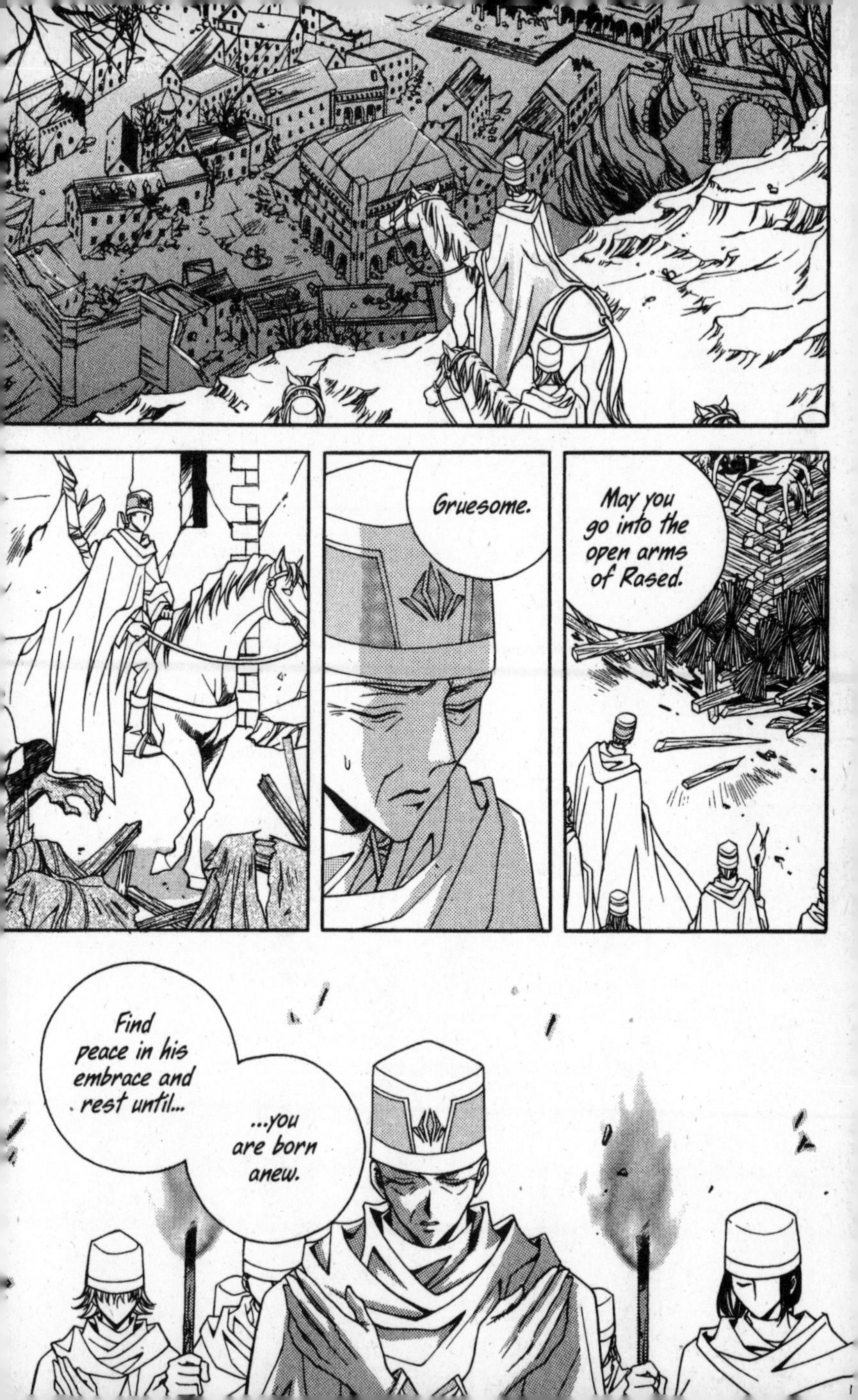
Gruesome.
May you go into the open arms of Rased.
Find peace in his embrace and rest until...
...you are born anew.

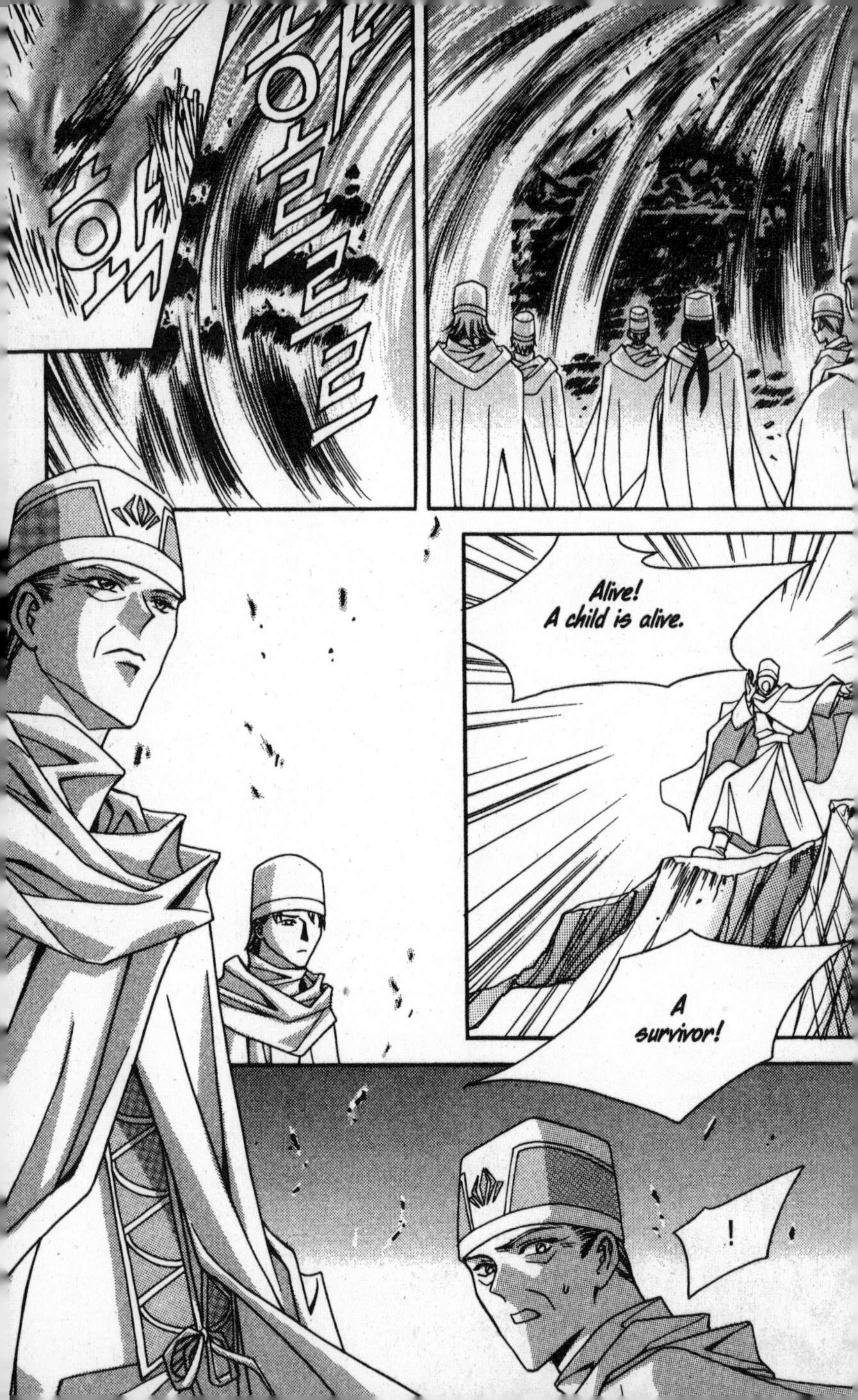
Alive!
A child is alive.
A survivor!
!

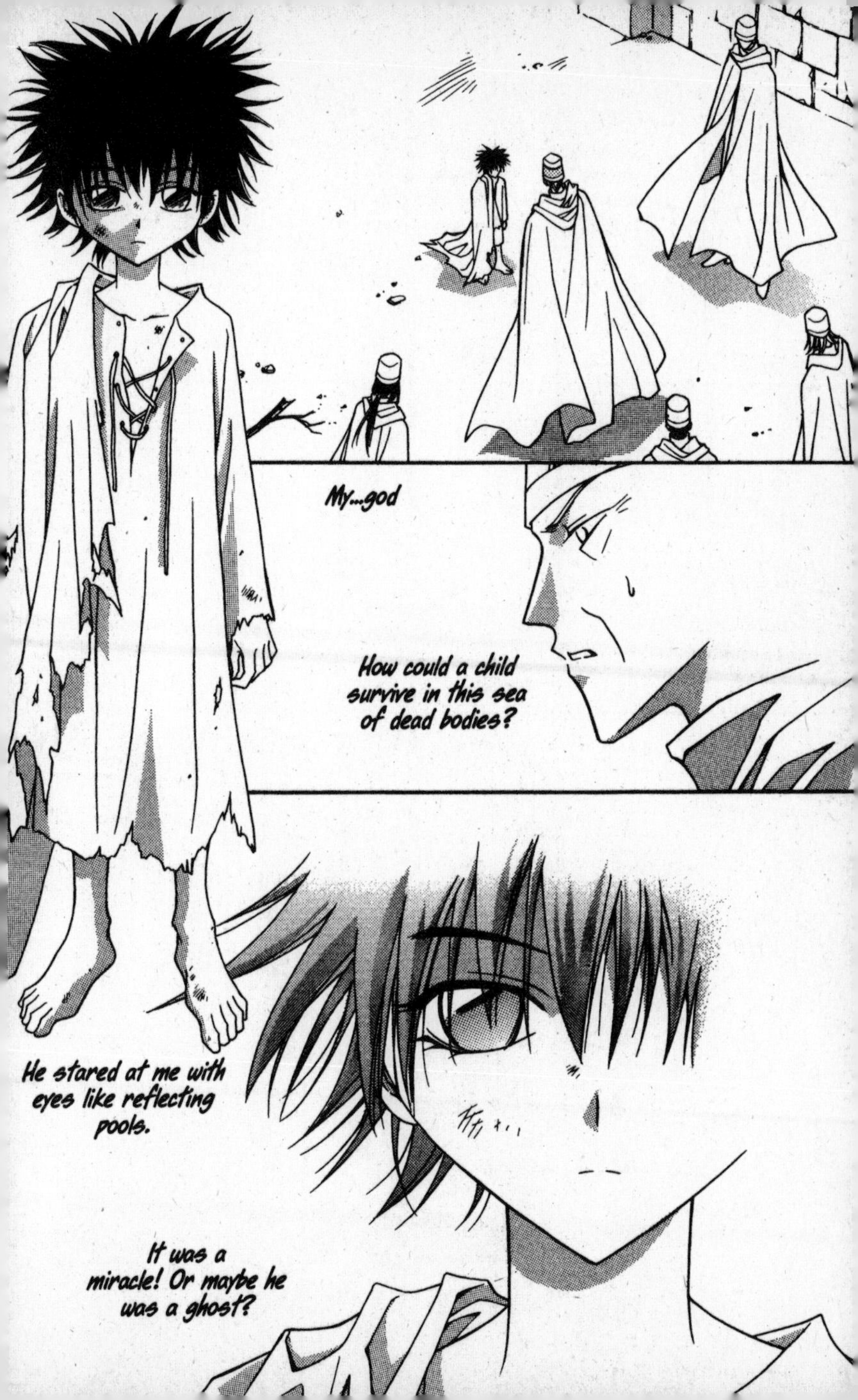
My...god
How could a child survive in this sea of dead bodies?
He stared at me with eyes like reflecting pools.
It was a miracle! Or maybe he was a ghost?

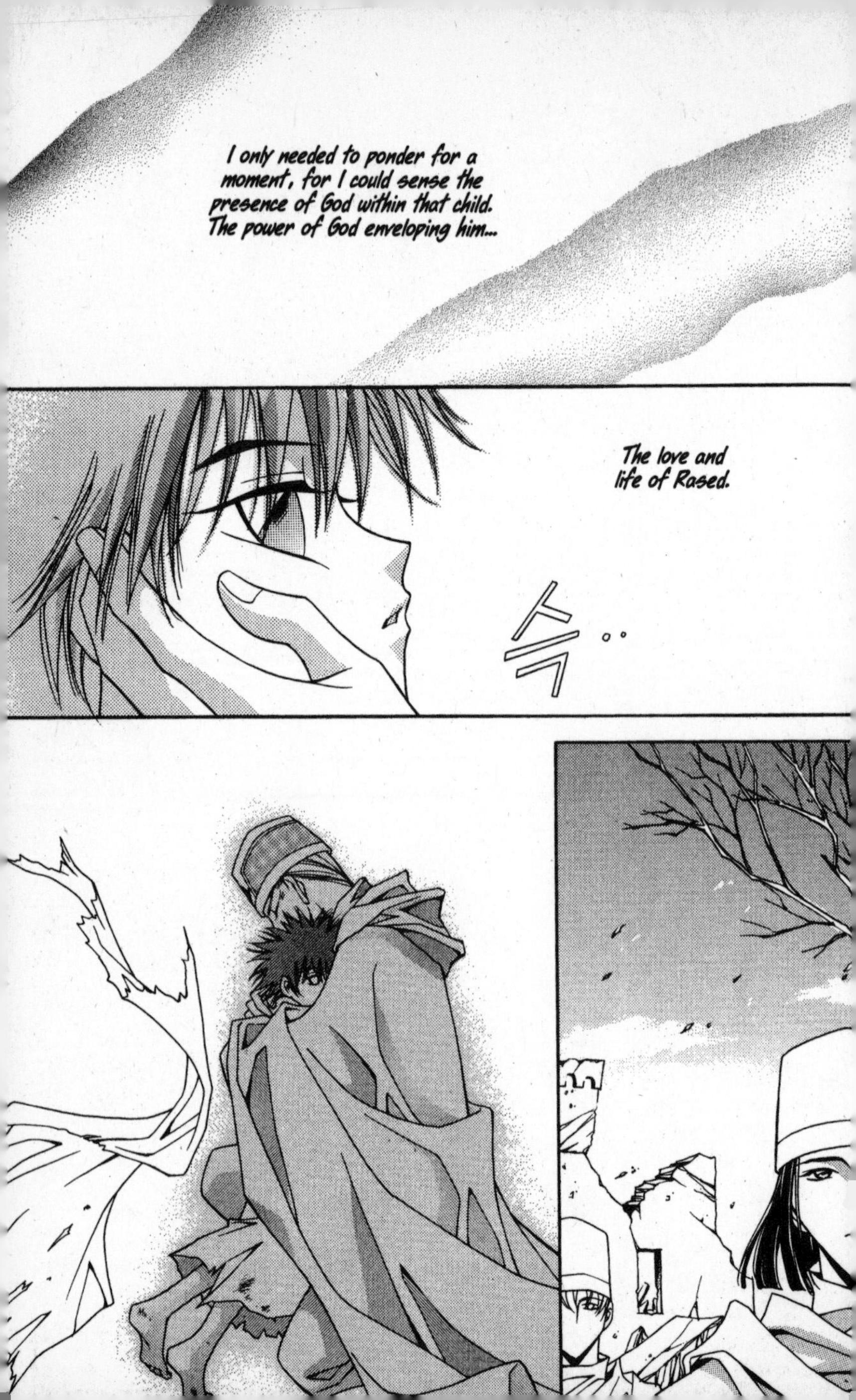
I only needed to ponder for a moment, for I could sense the presence of God within that child. The power of God enveloping him...
The love and life of Rased.

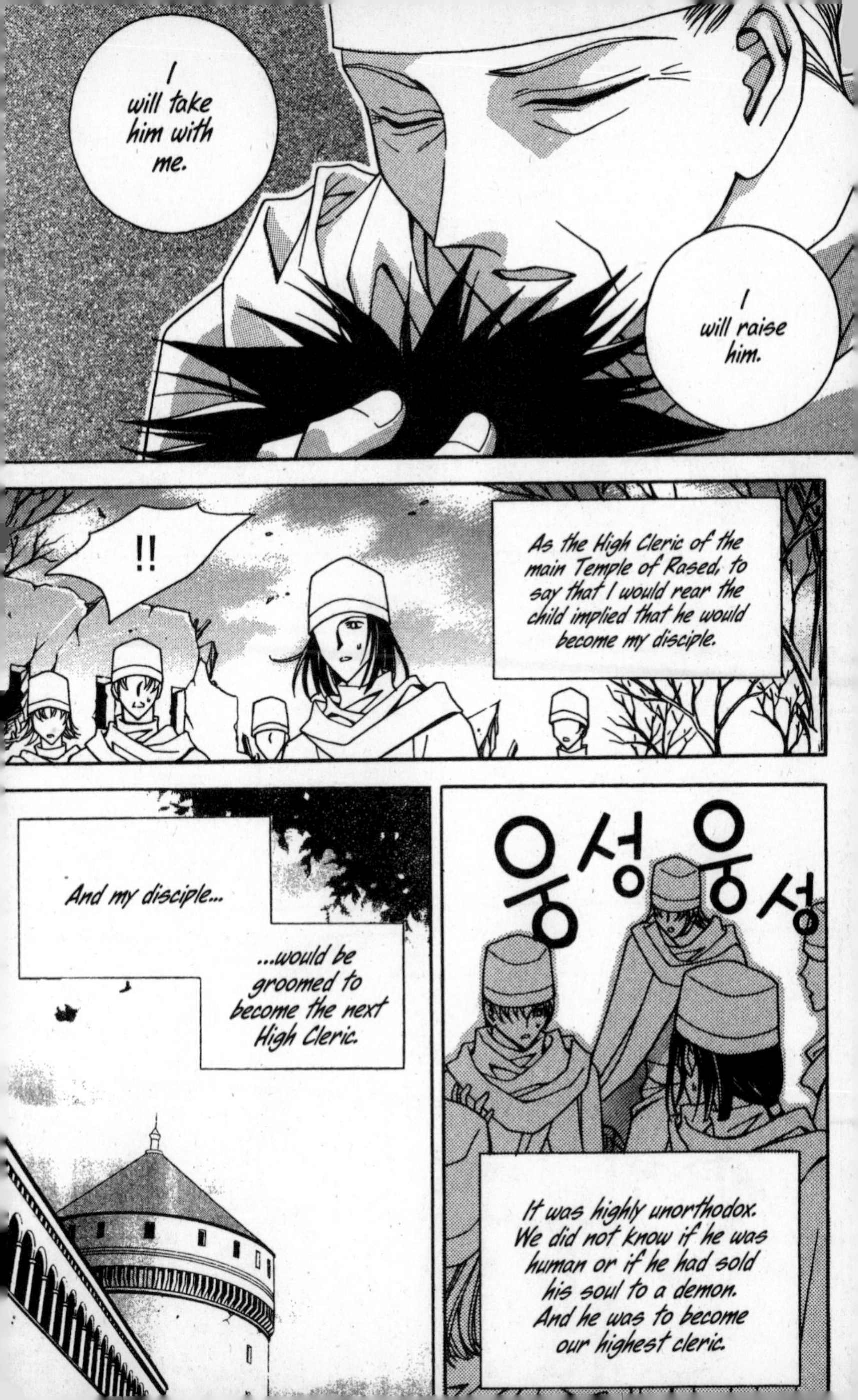
I will take him with me.
I will raise him.
!!
As the High Cleric of the main Temple of Rased, to say that I would rear the child implied that he would become my disciple.
And my disciple...
...would be groomed to become the next High Cleric.
웅성 웅성
It was highly unorthodox. We did not know if he was human or if he had sold his soul to a demon. And he was to become our highest cleric.

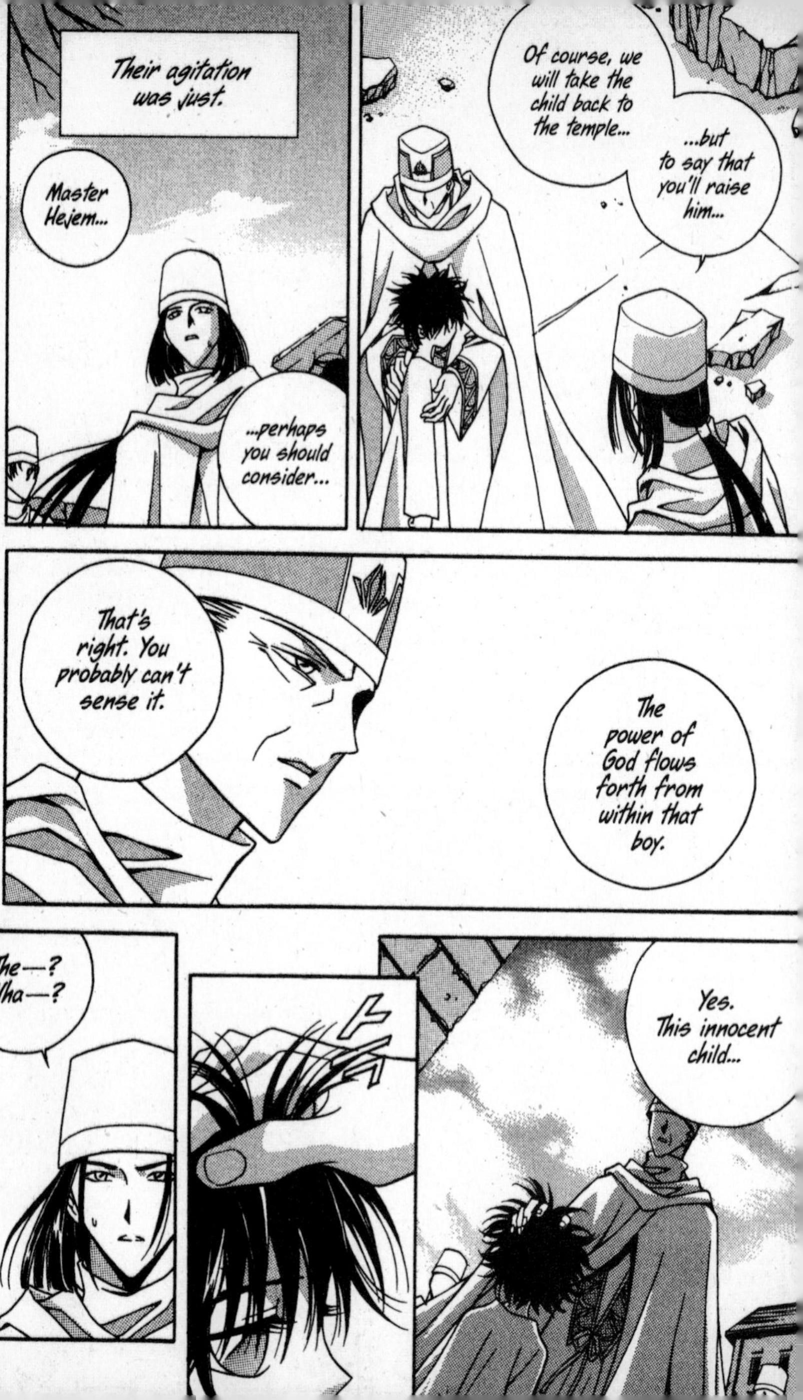
Their agitation was just.
Master Hejem...
...perhaps you should consider...
Of course, we will take the child back to the temple...
...but to say that you'll raise him...
That's right. You probably can't sense it.
The power of God flows forth from within that boy.
The—? Wha—?
Yes. This innocent child...

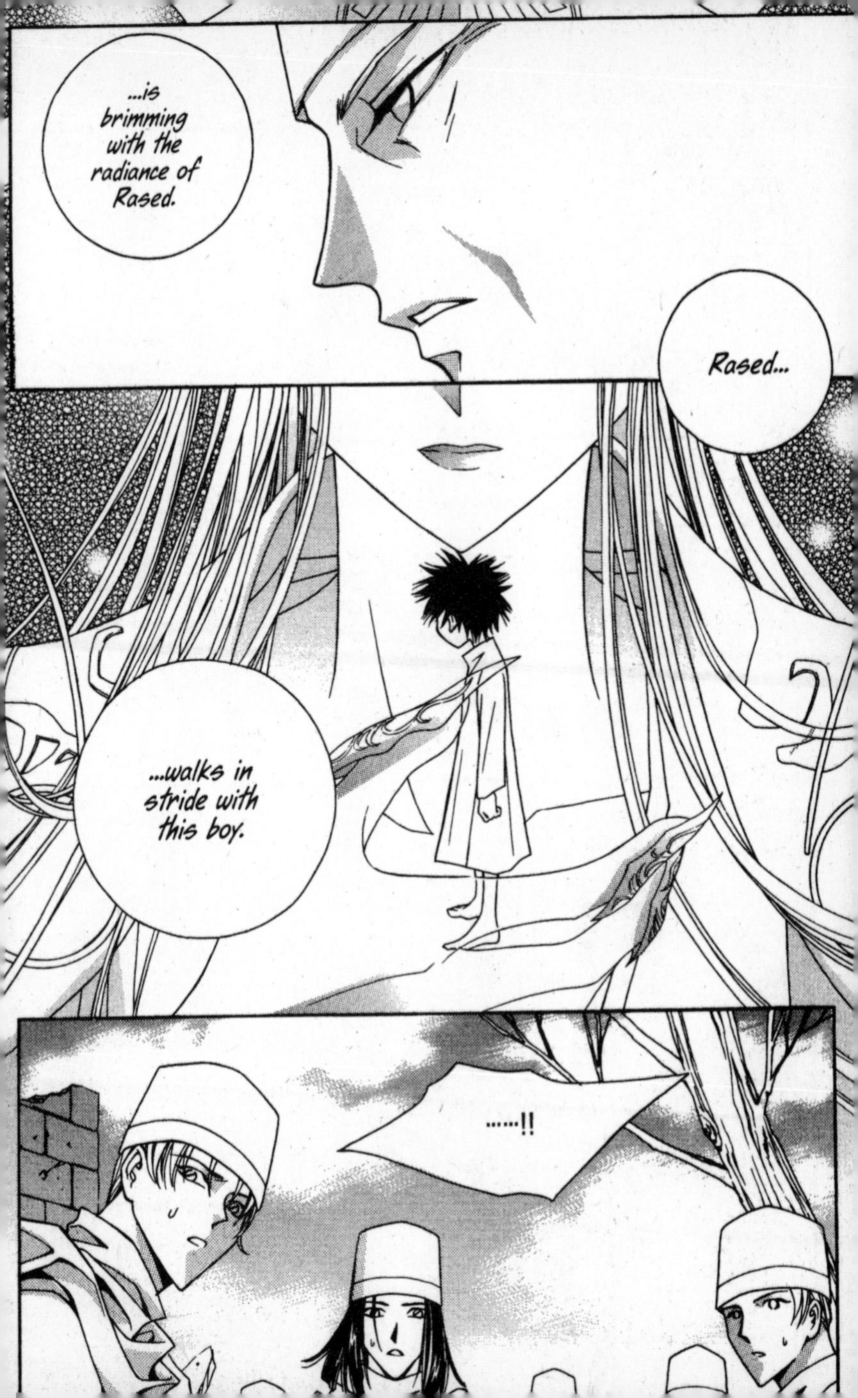
...is brimming with the radiance of Rased.
Rased...
...walks in stride with this boy.
......!!

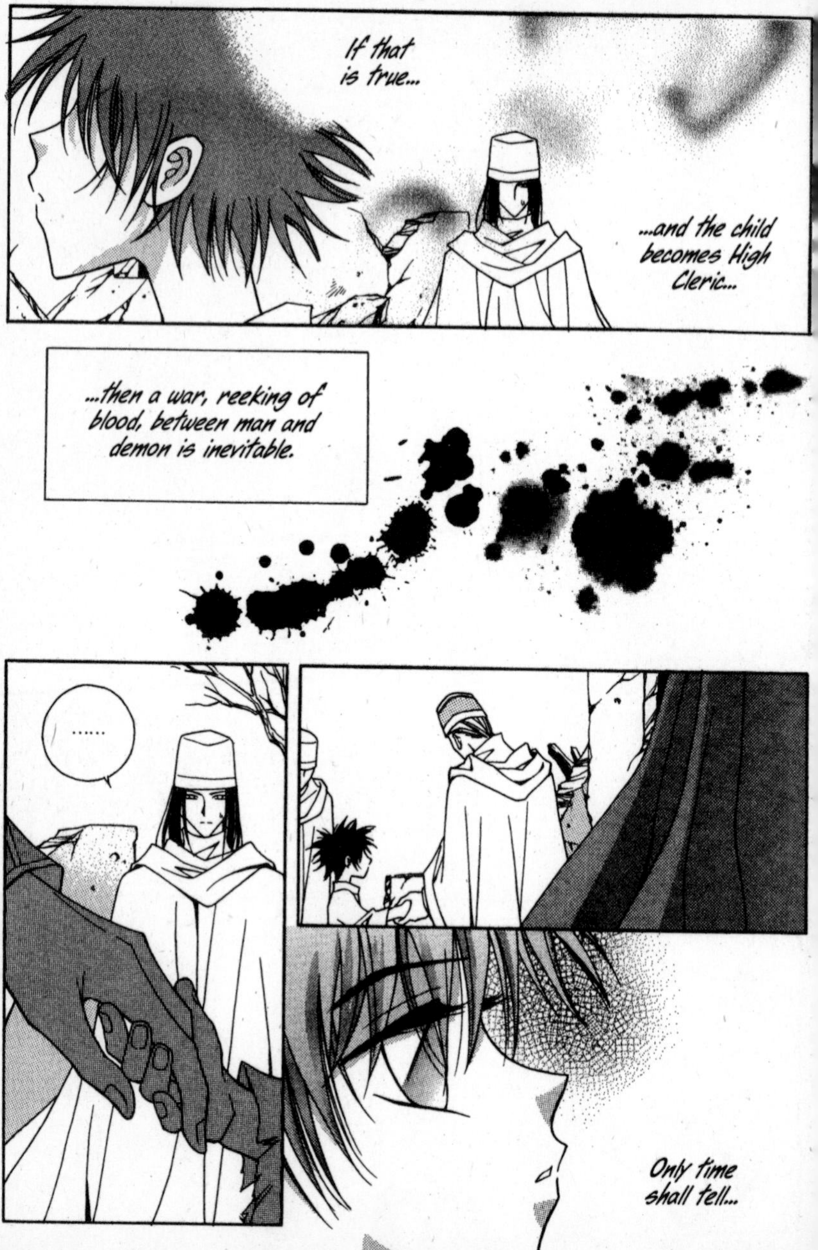
If that is true...
...and the child becomes High Cleric...
...then a war, reeking of blood, between man and demon is inevitable.
......
Only time shall tell...

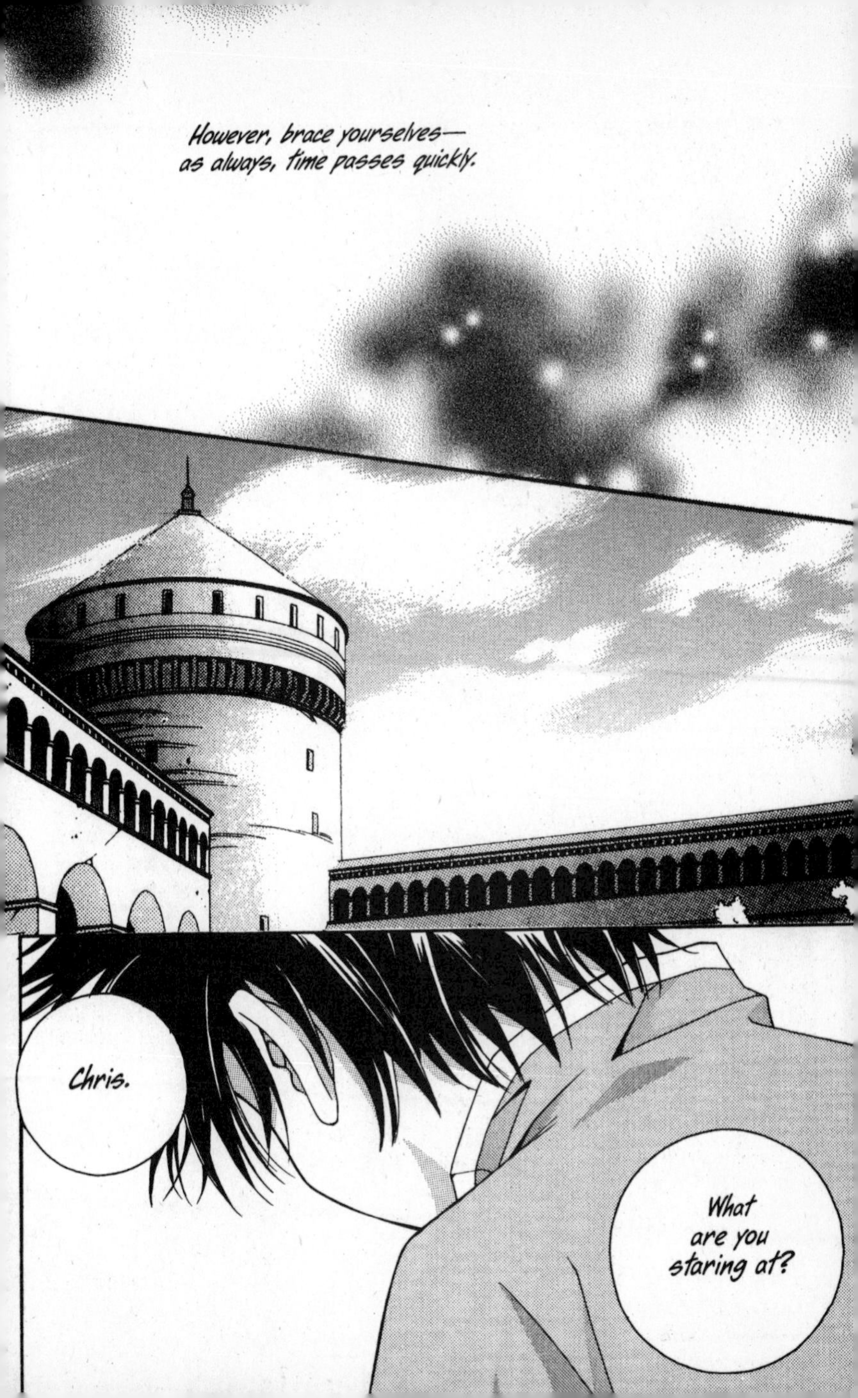
However, brace yourselves—as always, time passes quickly.
Chris.
What are you staring at?

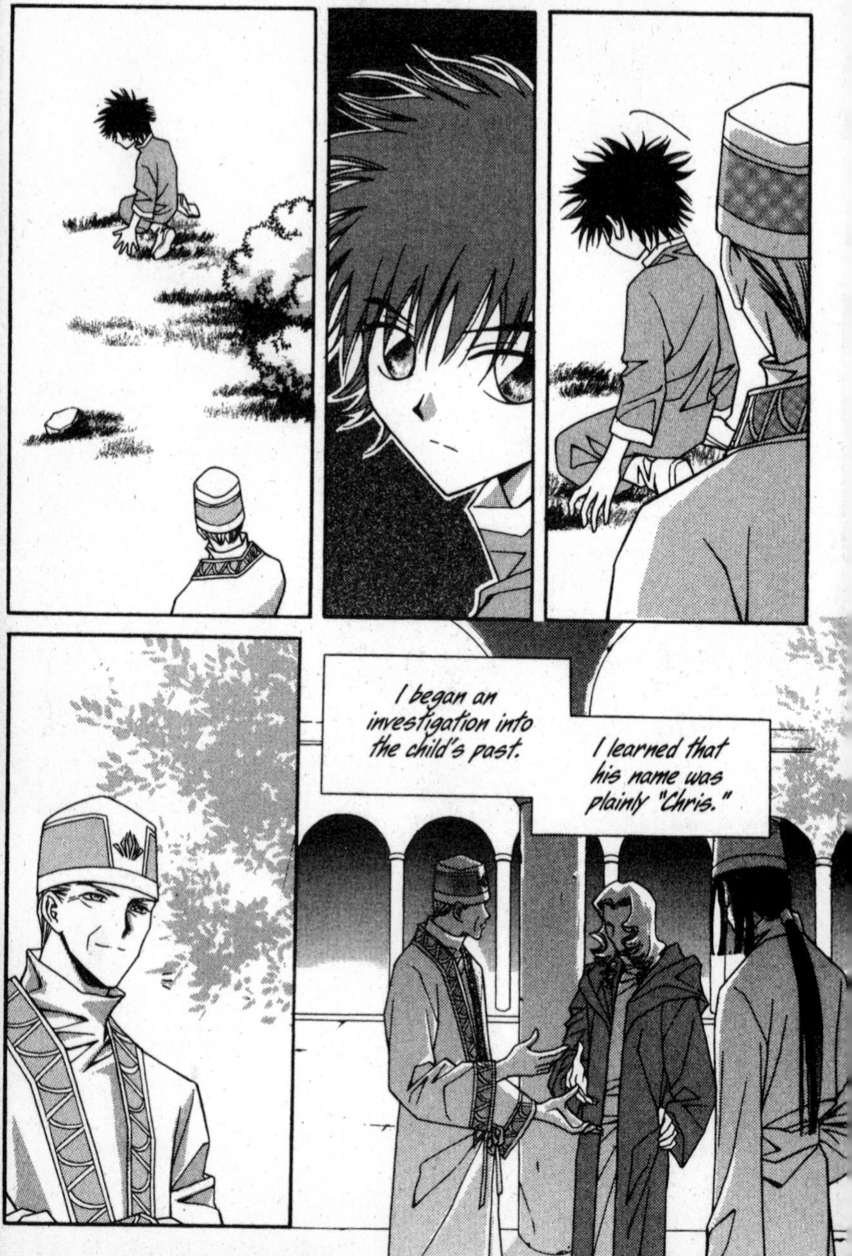
I began an investigation into the child's past.
I learned that his name was plainly "Chris."

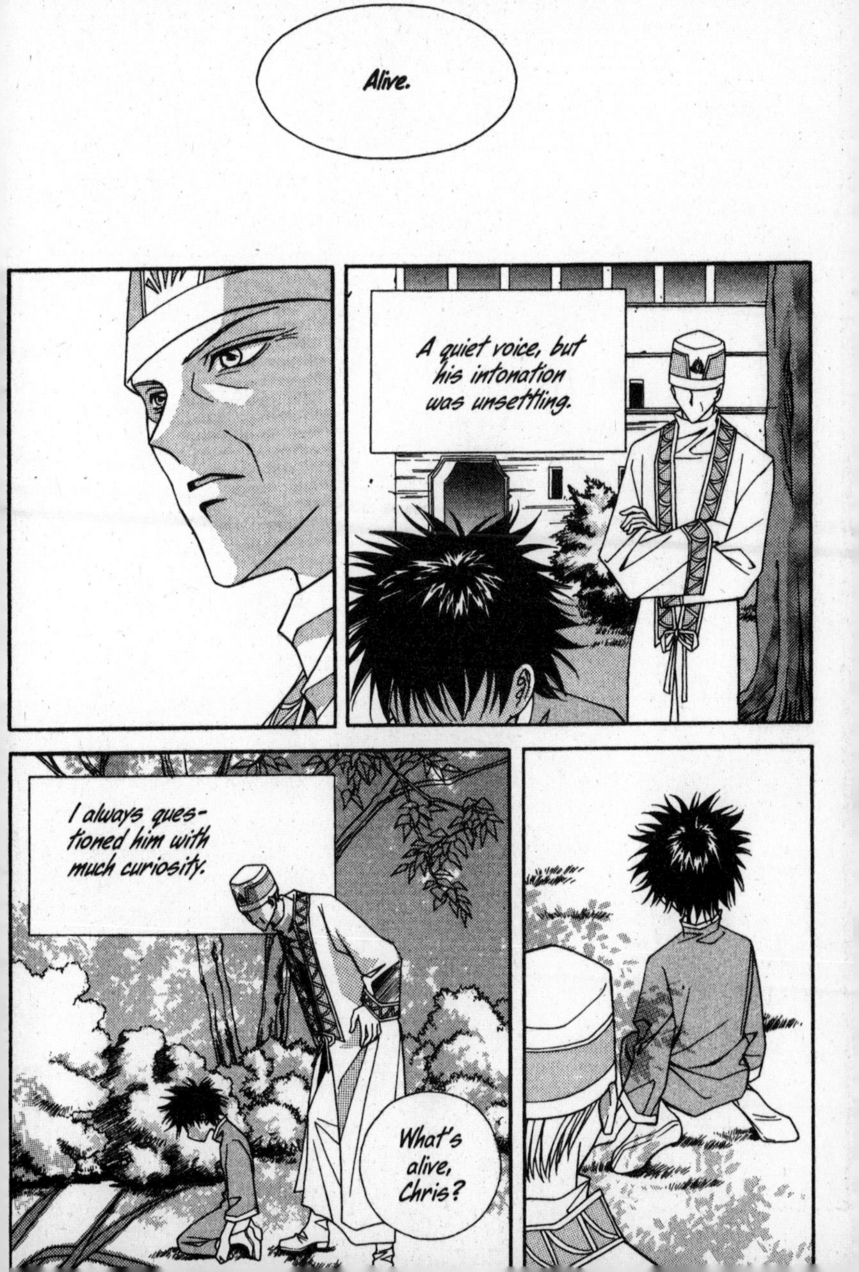
Alive.
A quiet voice, but his intonation was unsettling.
I always questioned him with much curiosity.
What's alive, Chris?

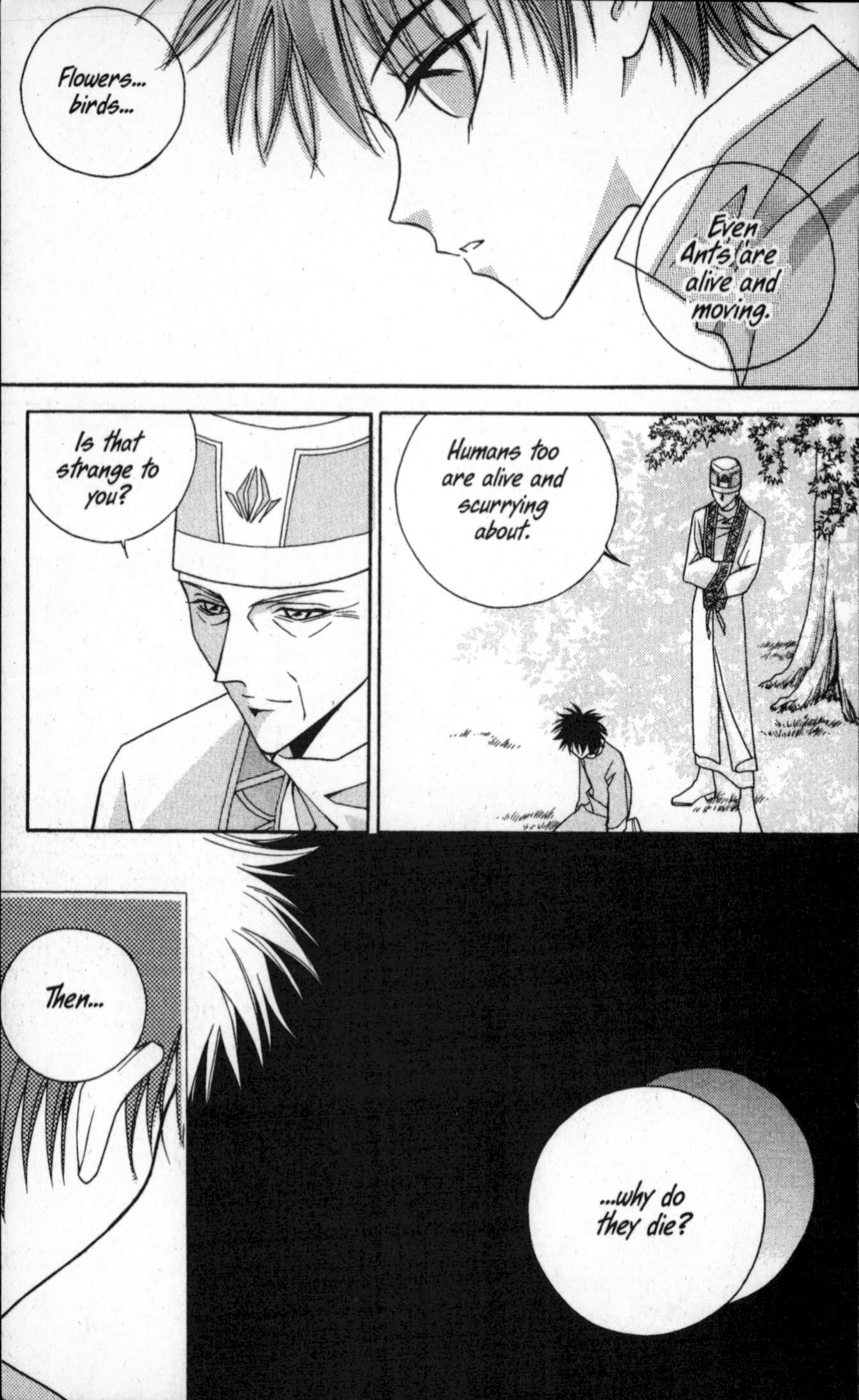
Flowers... birds...
Even Ants are alive and moving.
Is that strange to you?
Humans too are alive and scurrying about.
Then...
...why do they die?

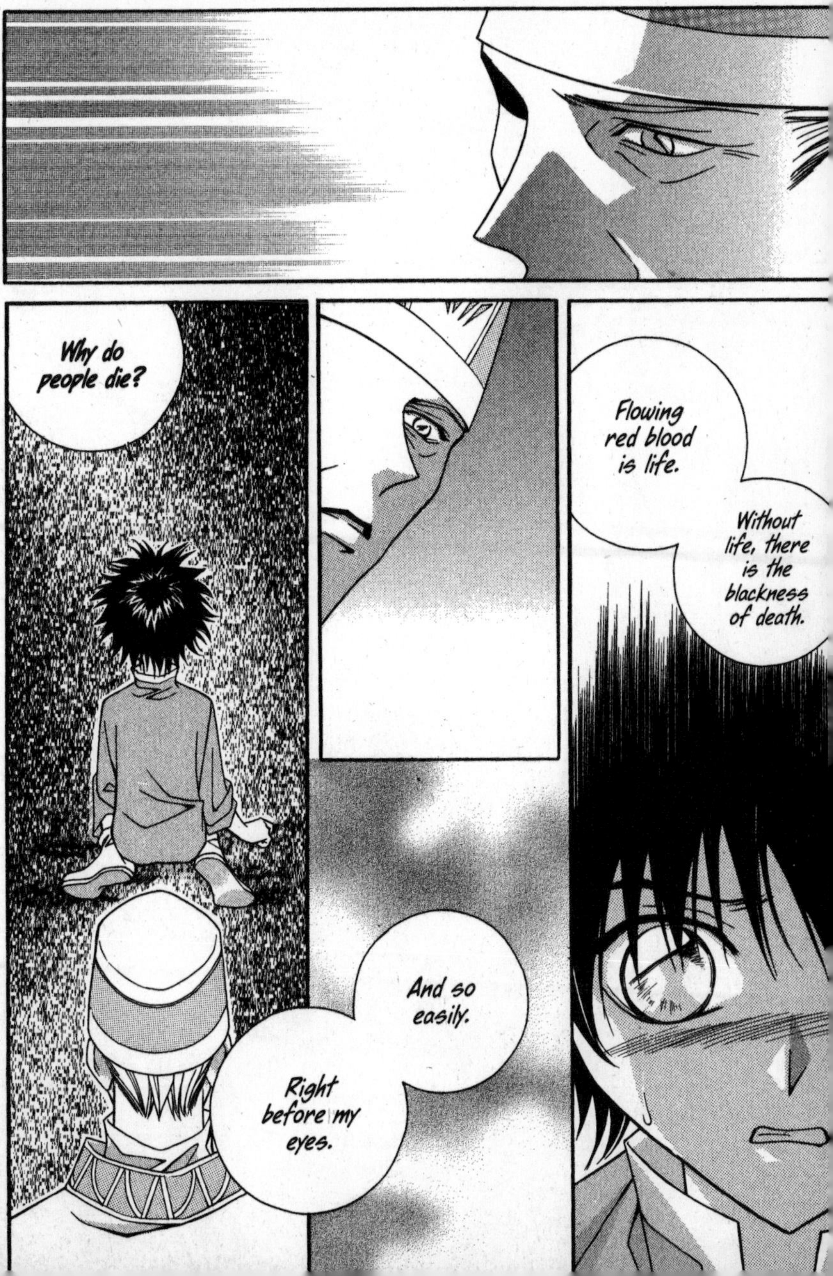
Why do people die?
Right before my eyes.
And so easily.
Flowing red blood is life.
Without life, there is the blackness of death.

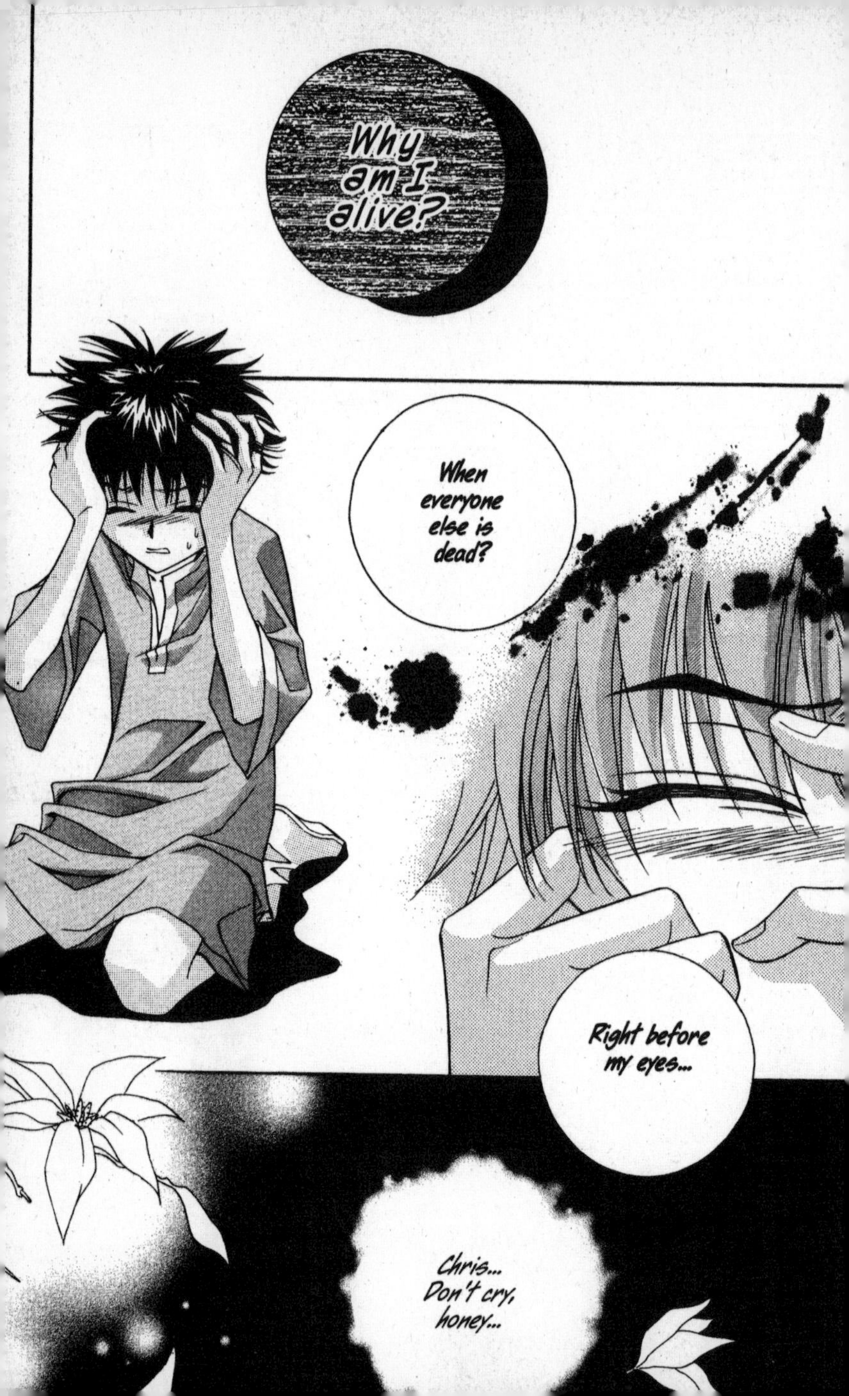
Why am I alive?
When everyone else is dead?
Right before my eyes...
Chris... Don't cry, honey...

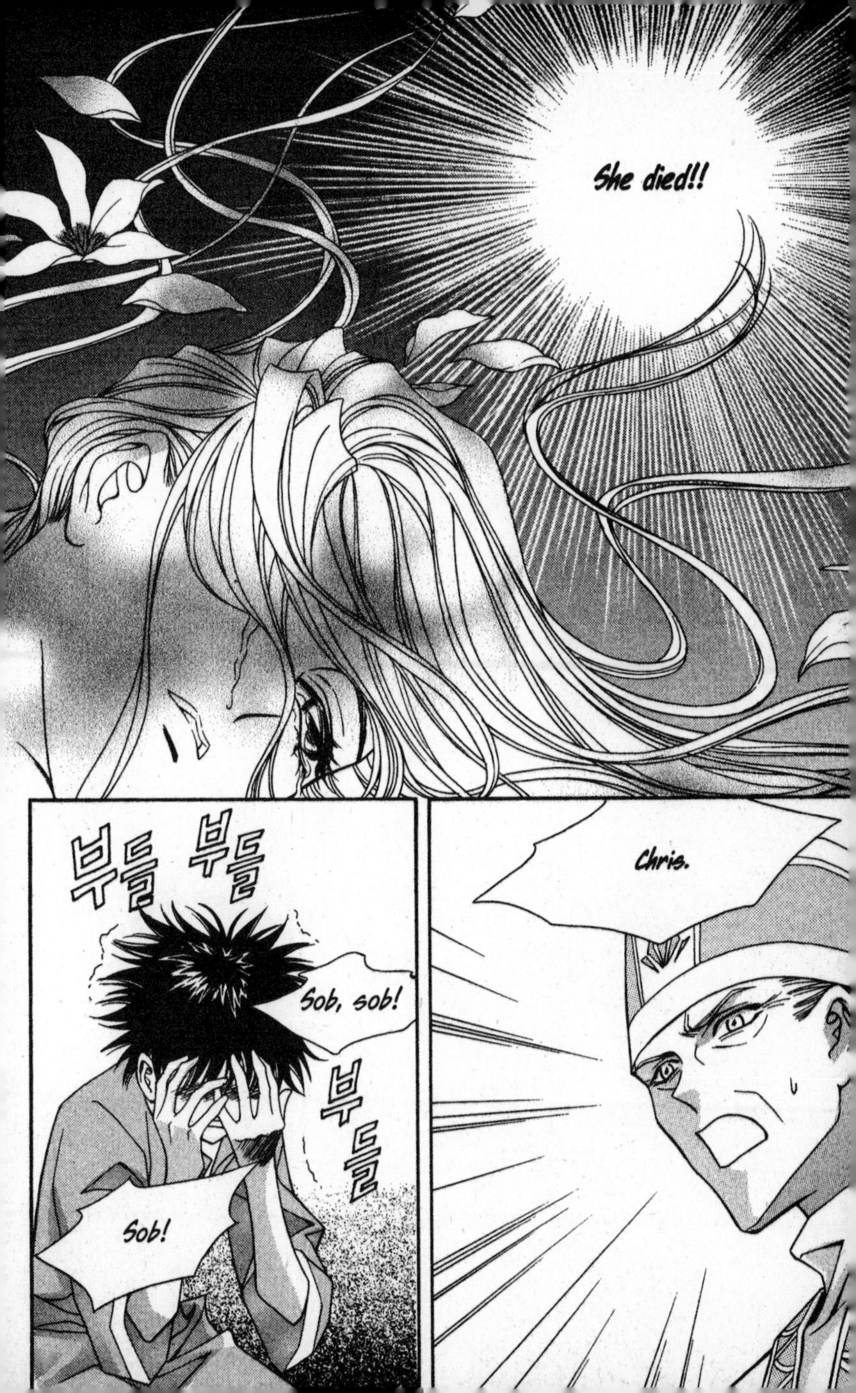
She died!!
부들 부들
Sob, sob!
부들
Sob!
Chris.

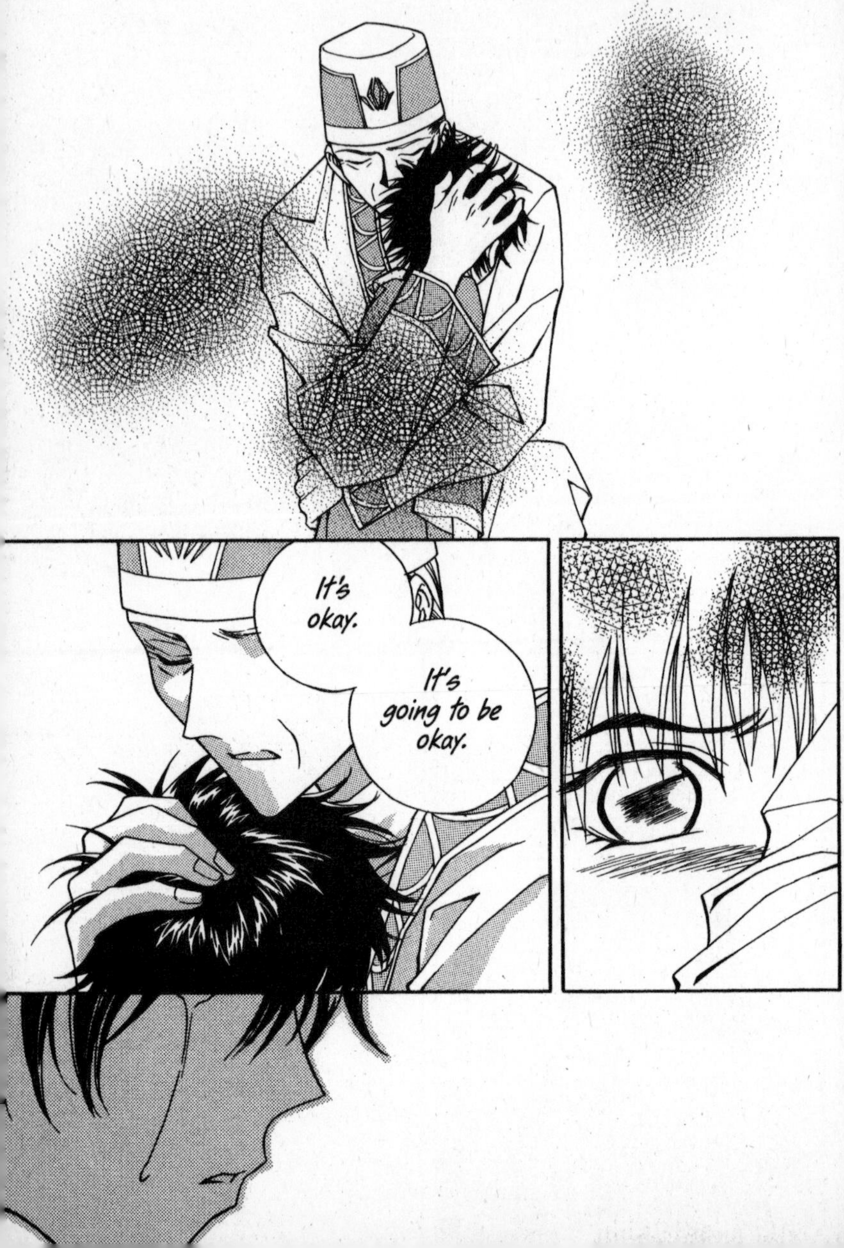
It's okay.
It's going to be okay.

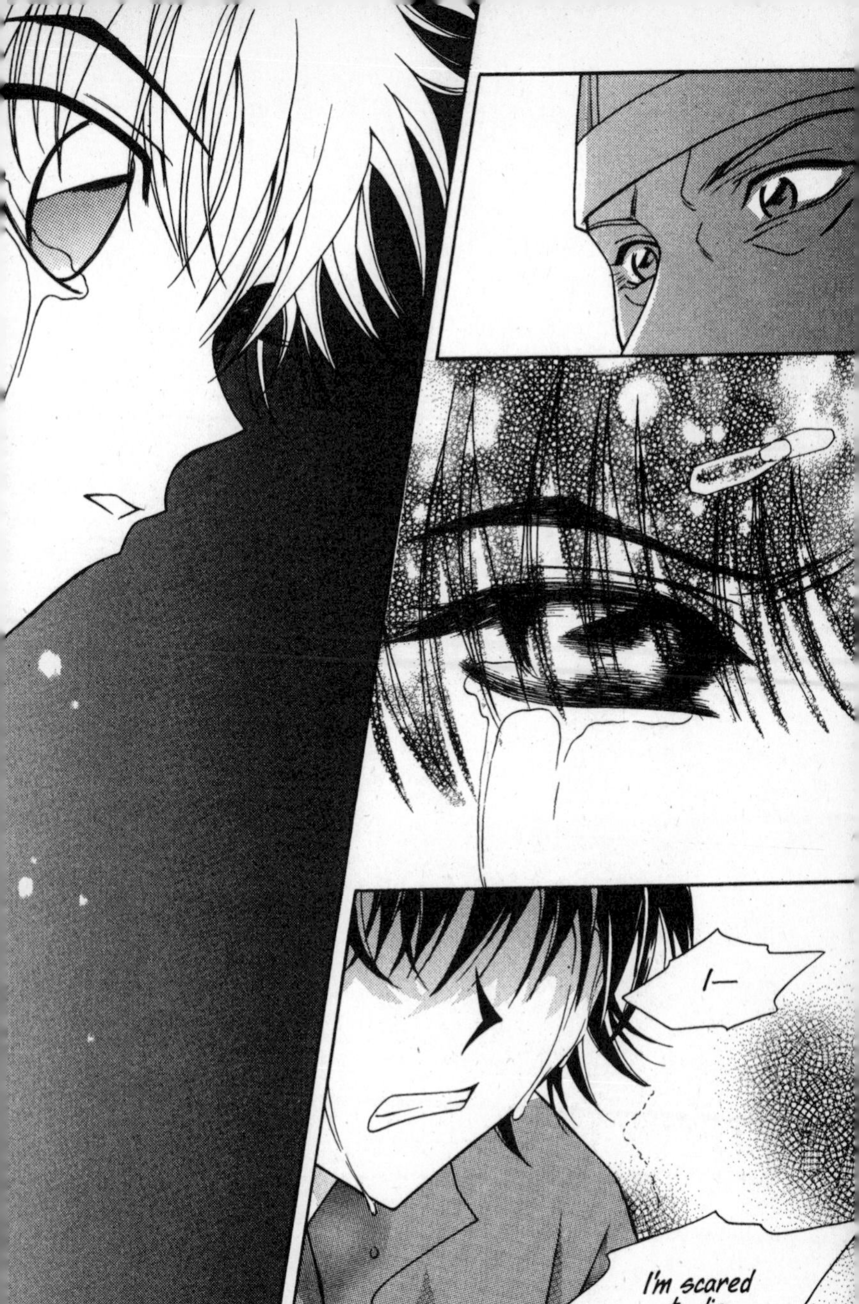
I--
I'm scared to die.

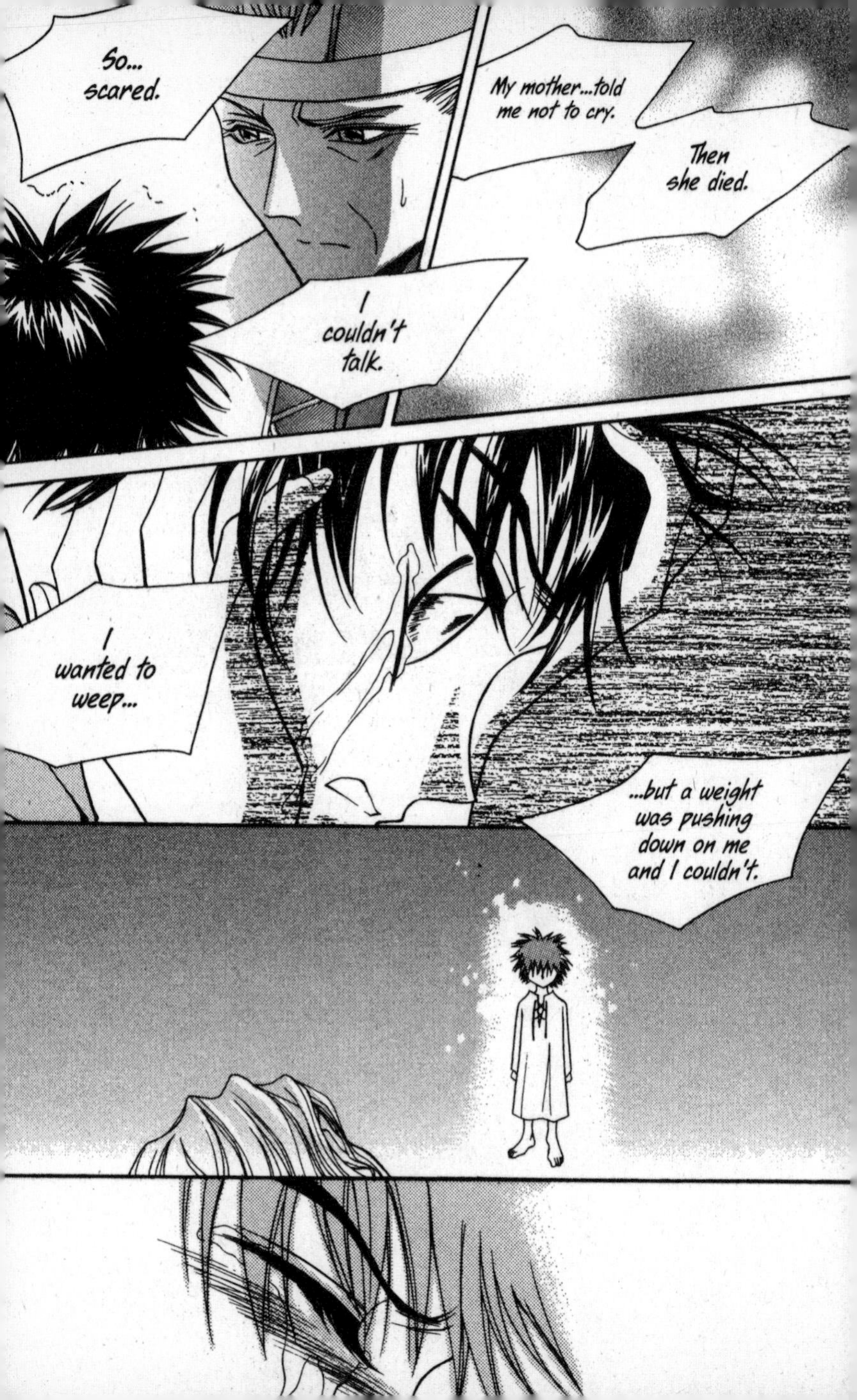
So... scared.
My mother...told me not to cry.
Then she died.
I couldn't talk.
I wanted to weep...
...but a weight was pushing down on me and I couldn't.

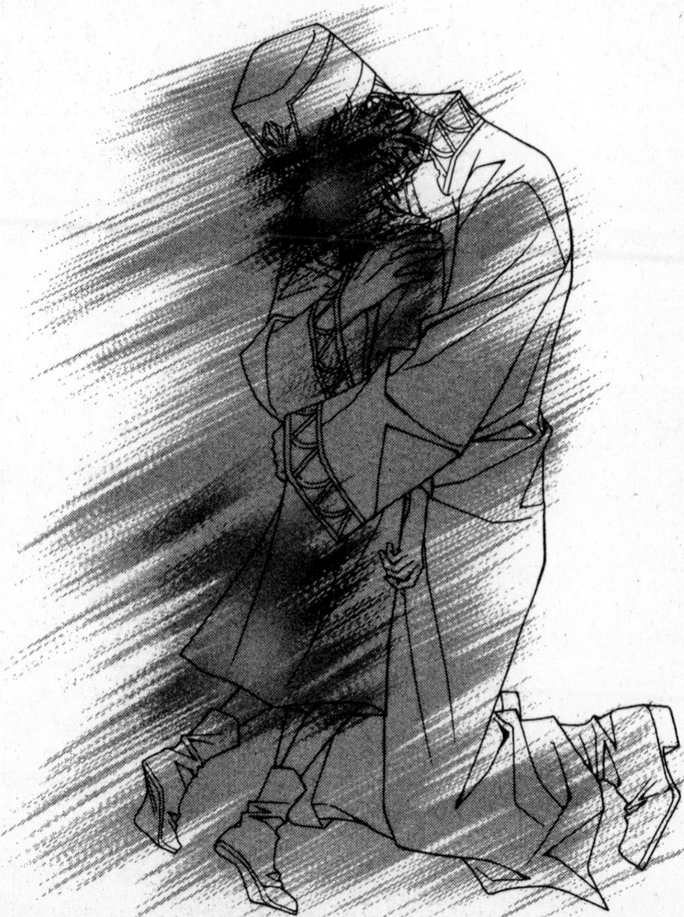

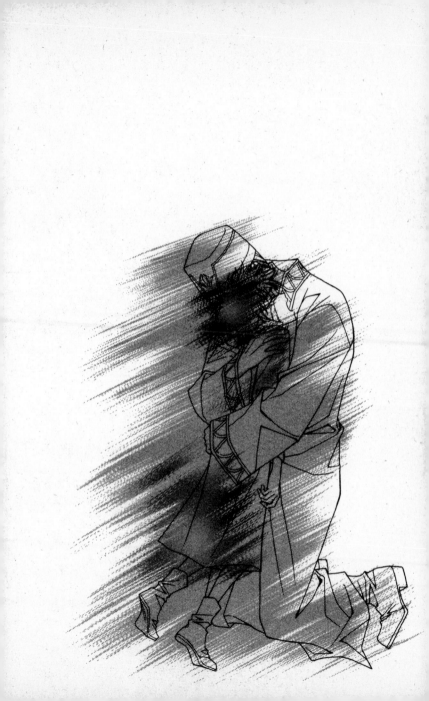

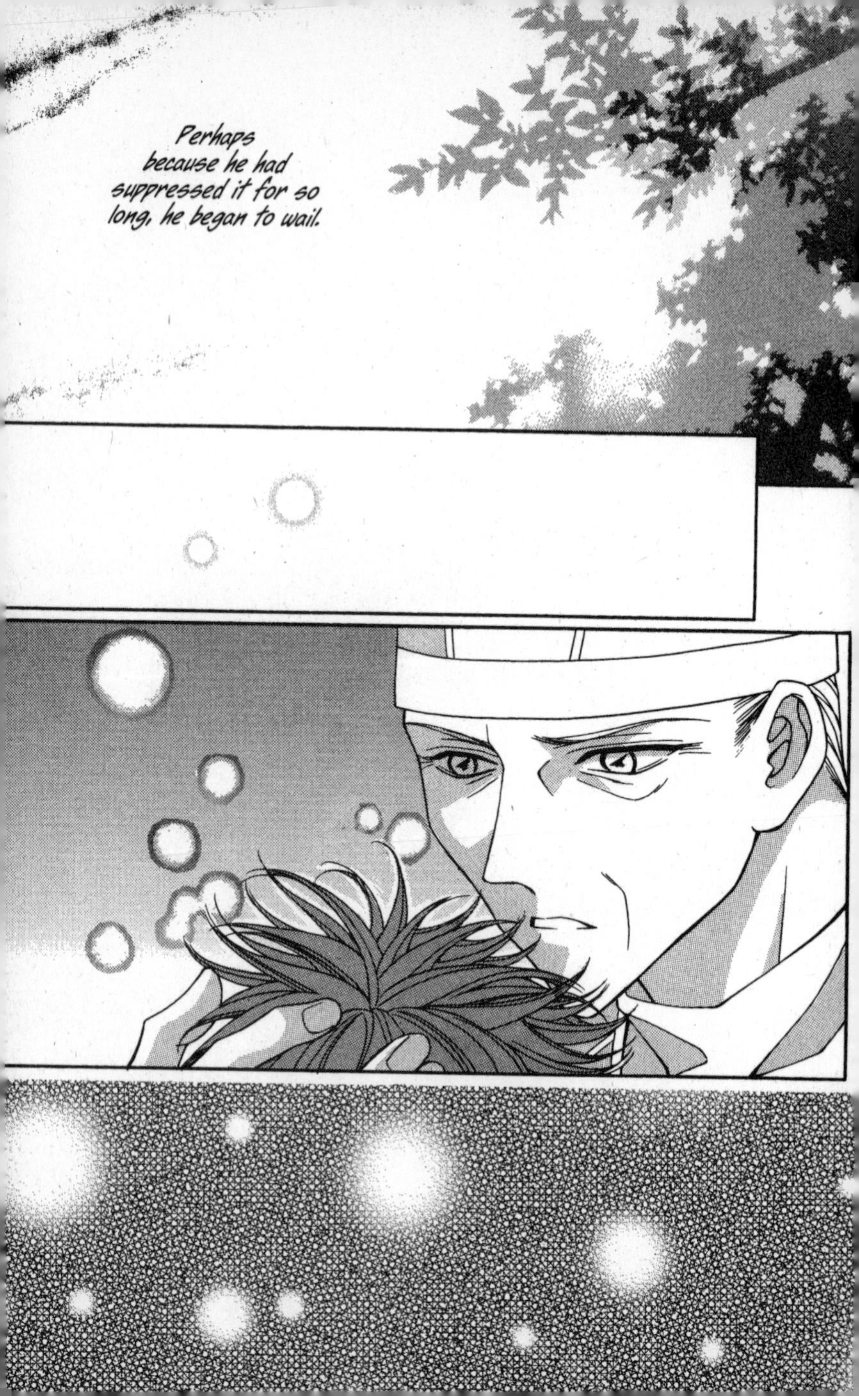
Perhaps because he had suppressed it for so long, he began to wail.

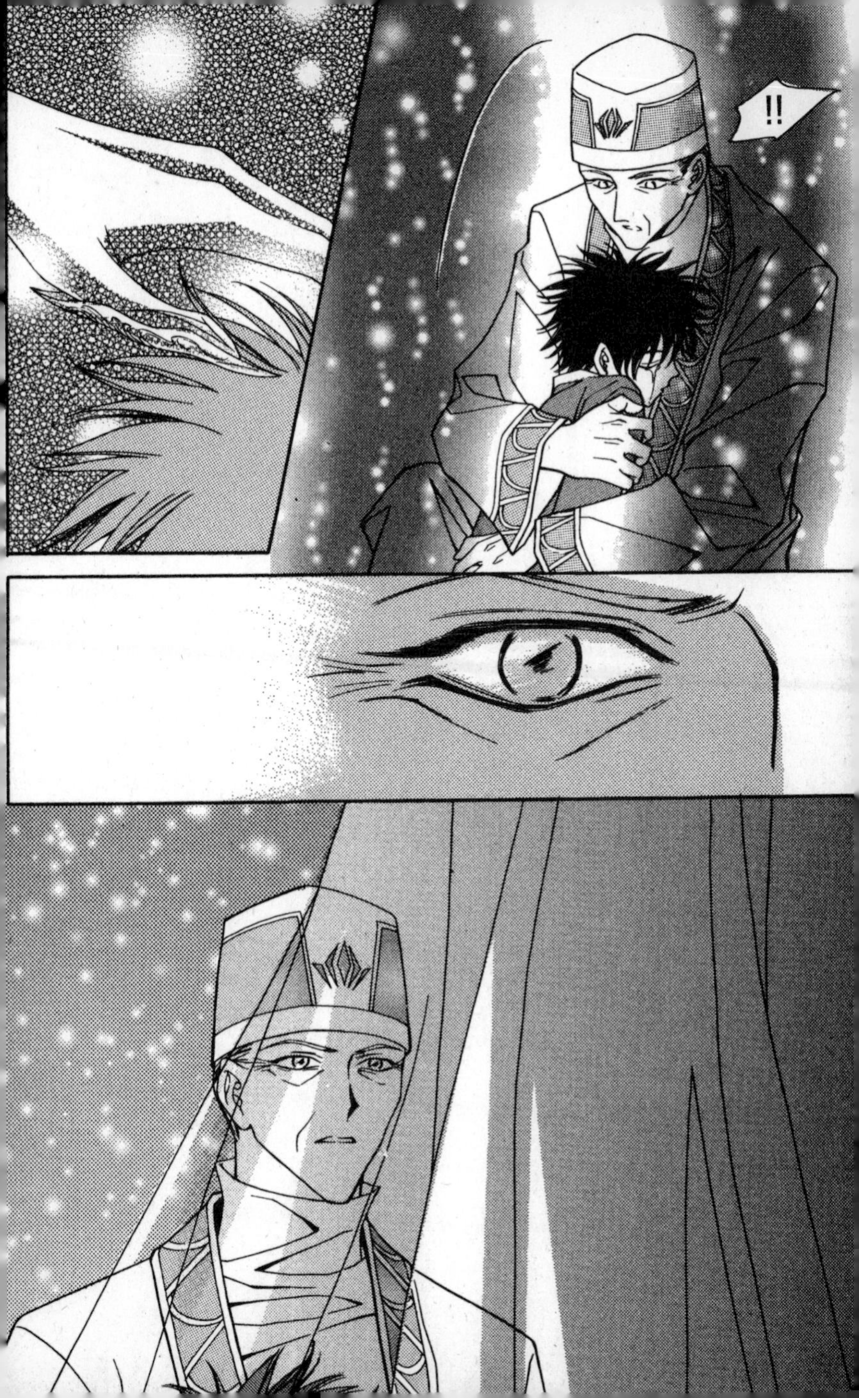
!!

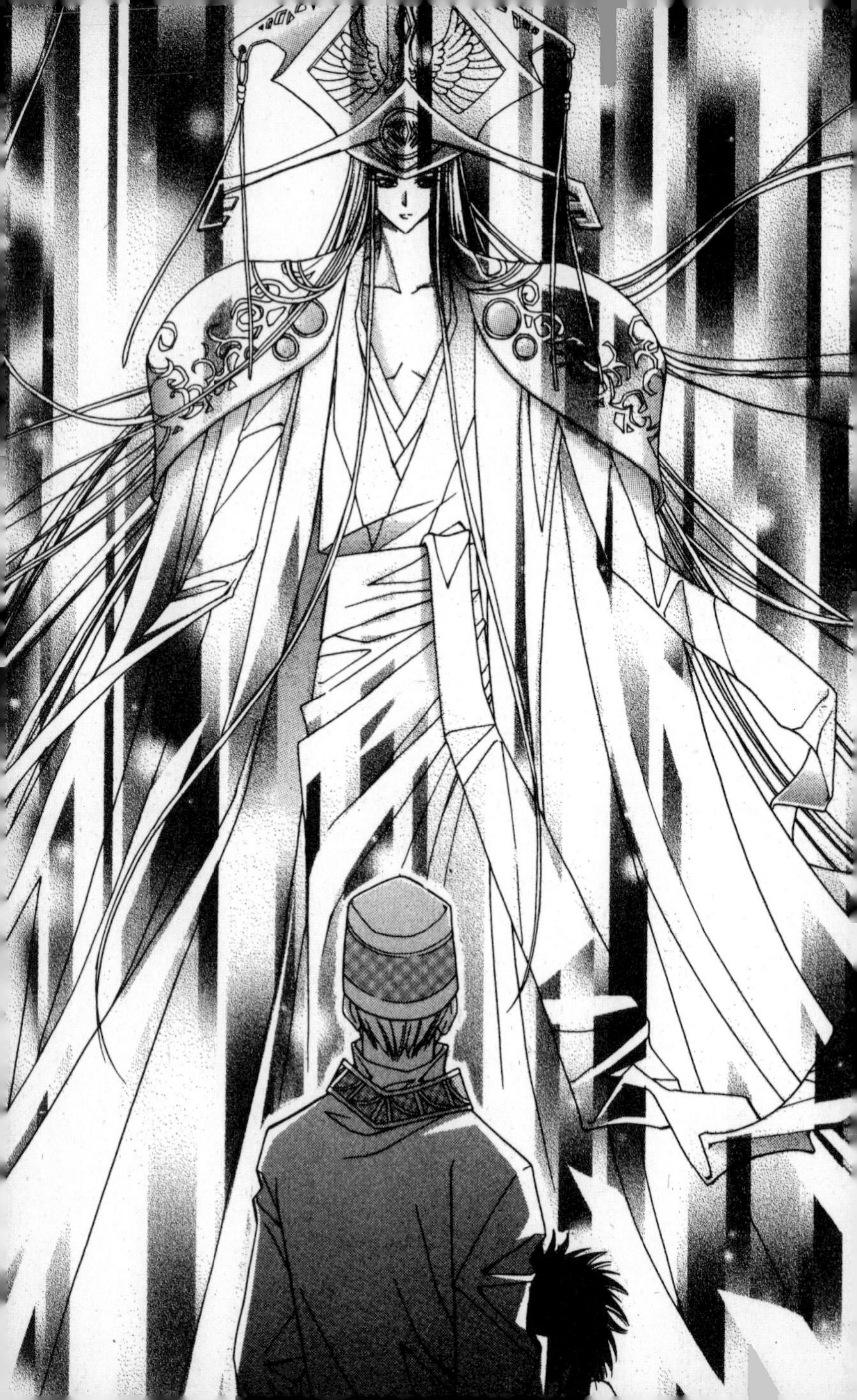

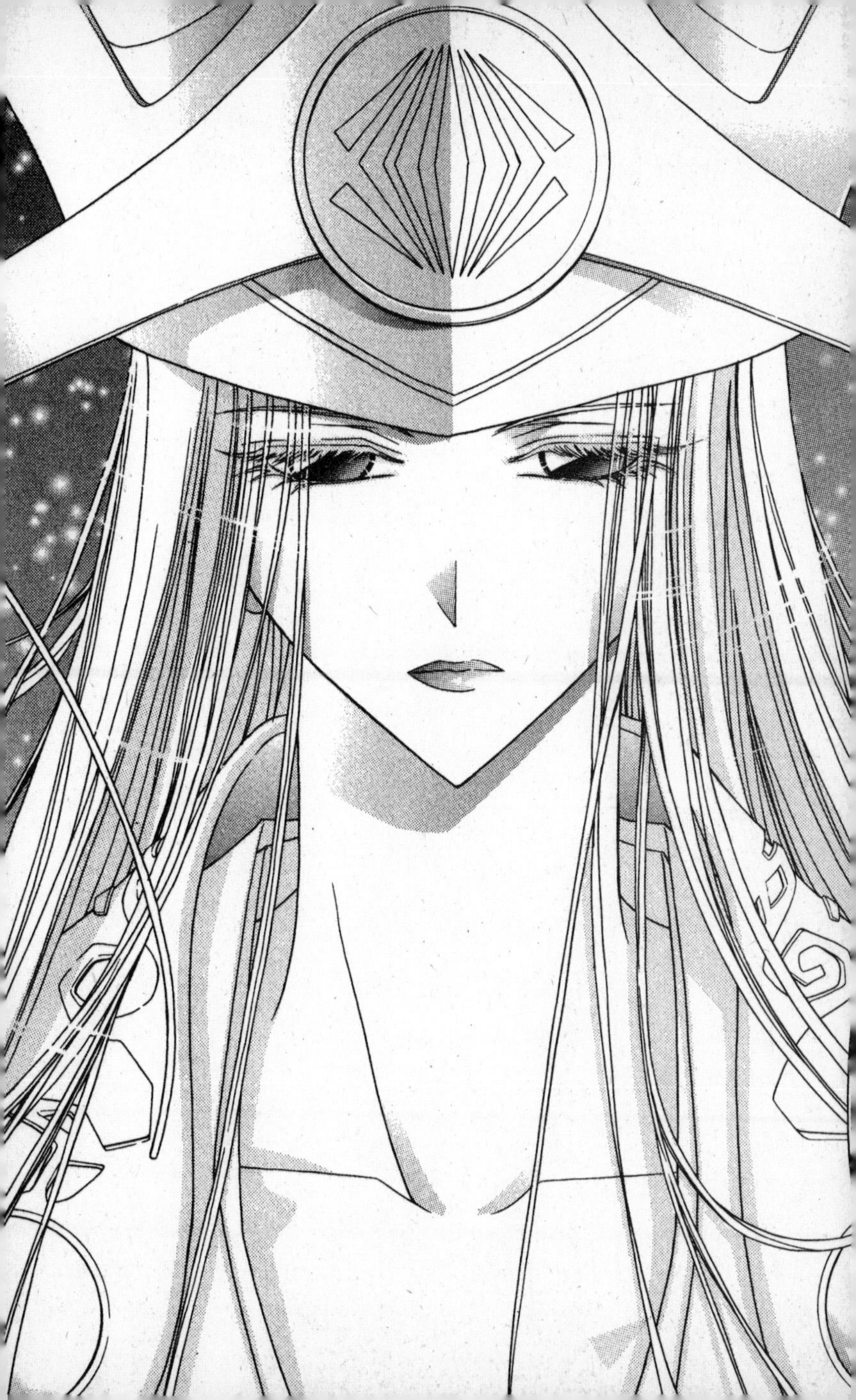

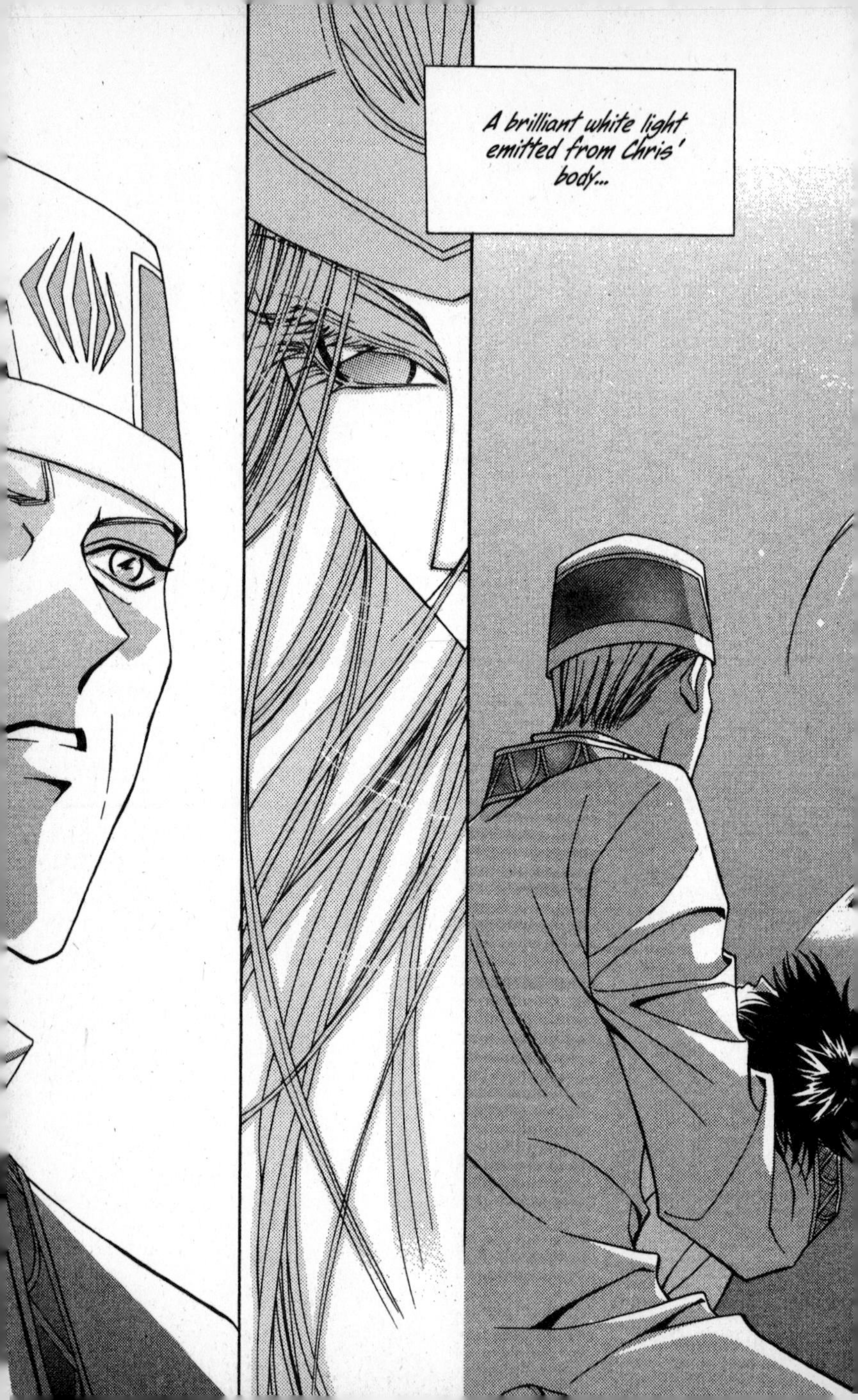
A brilliant white light emitted from Chris' body...

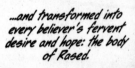

...and transformed into every believer's fervent desire and hope: the body of Rased.

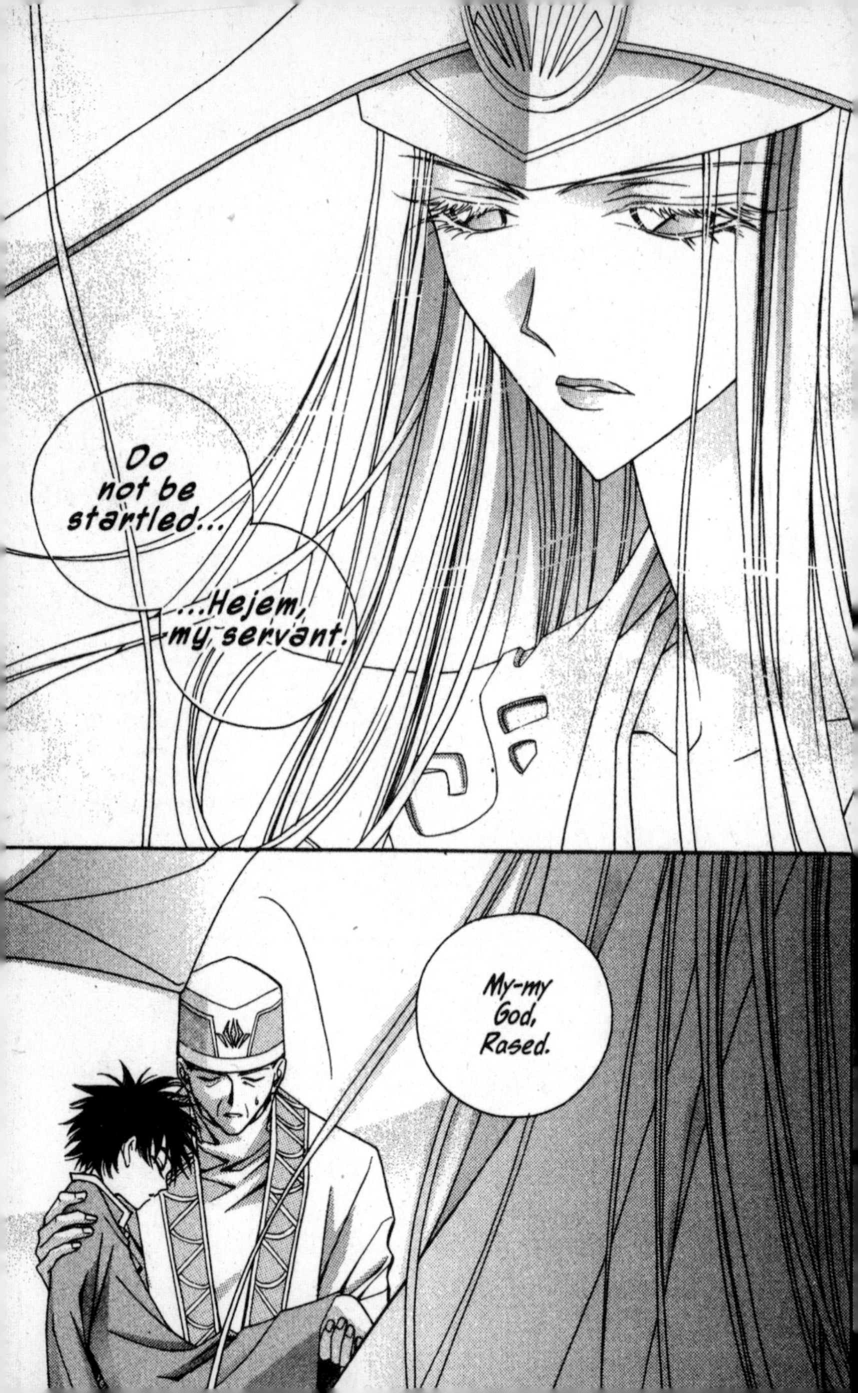
Do not be startled...
...Hejem, my servant.
My-my God, Rased.

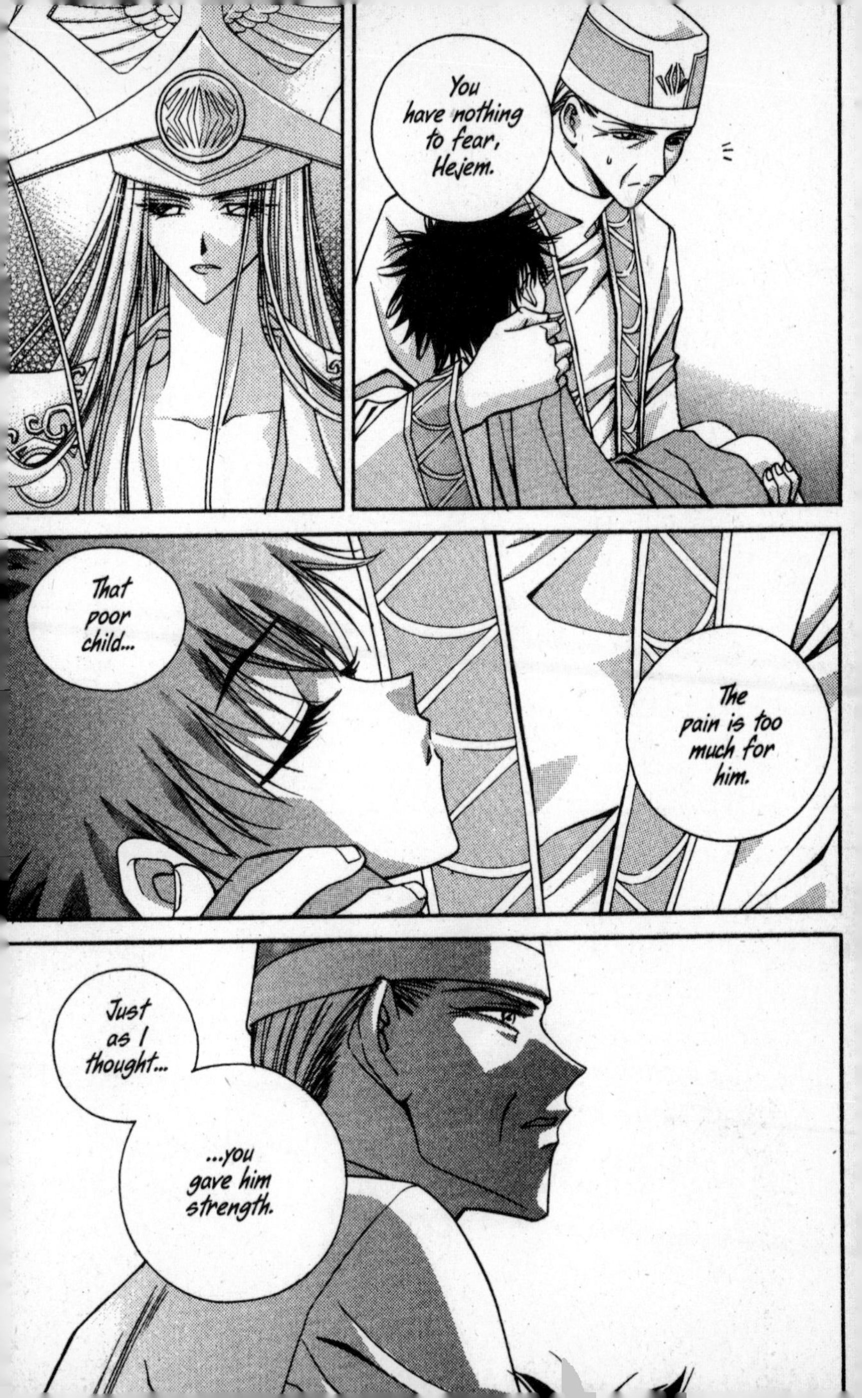
You have nothing to fear, Hejem.
That poor child...
The pain is too much for him.
Just as I thought...
...you gave him strength.

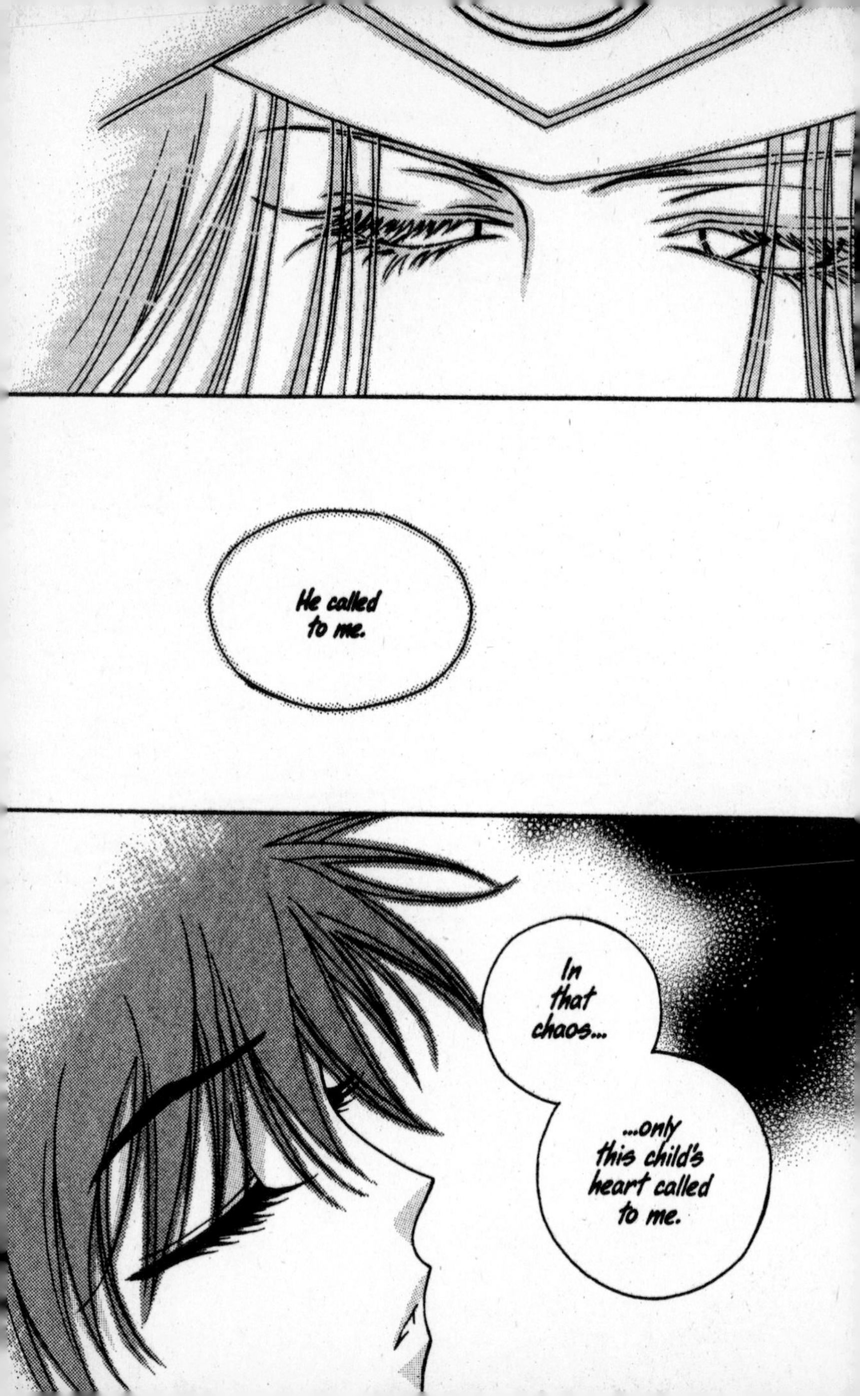
He called to me.
In that chaos...
...only this child's heart called to me.

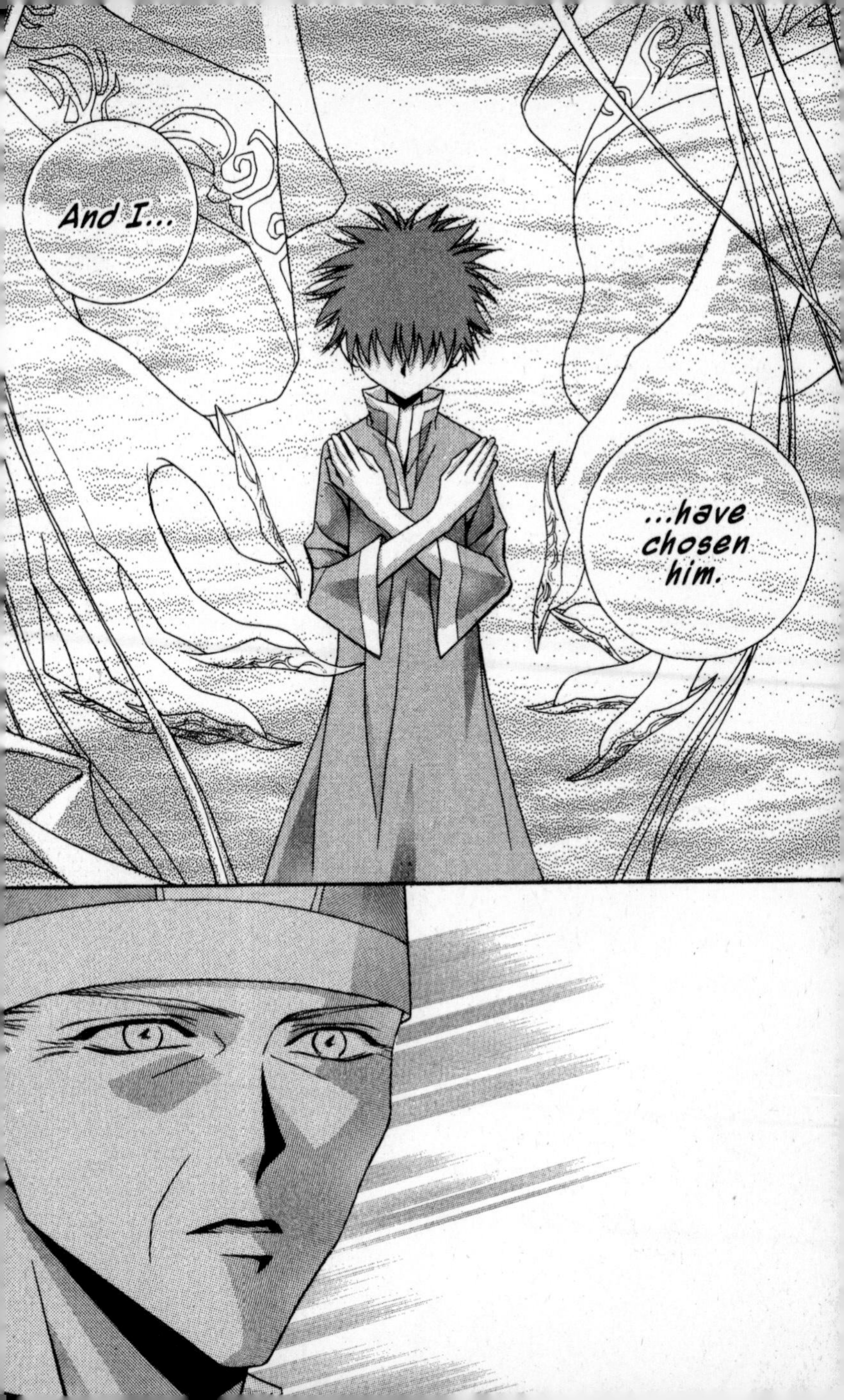
And I...
...have chosen him.

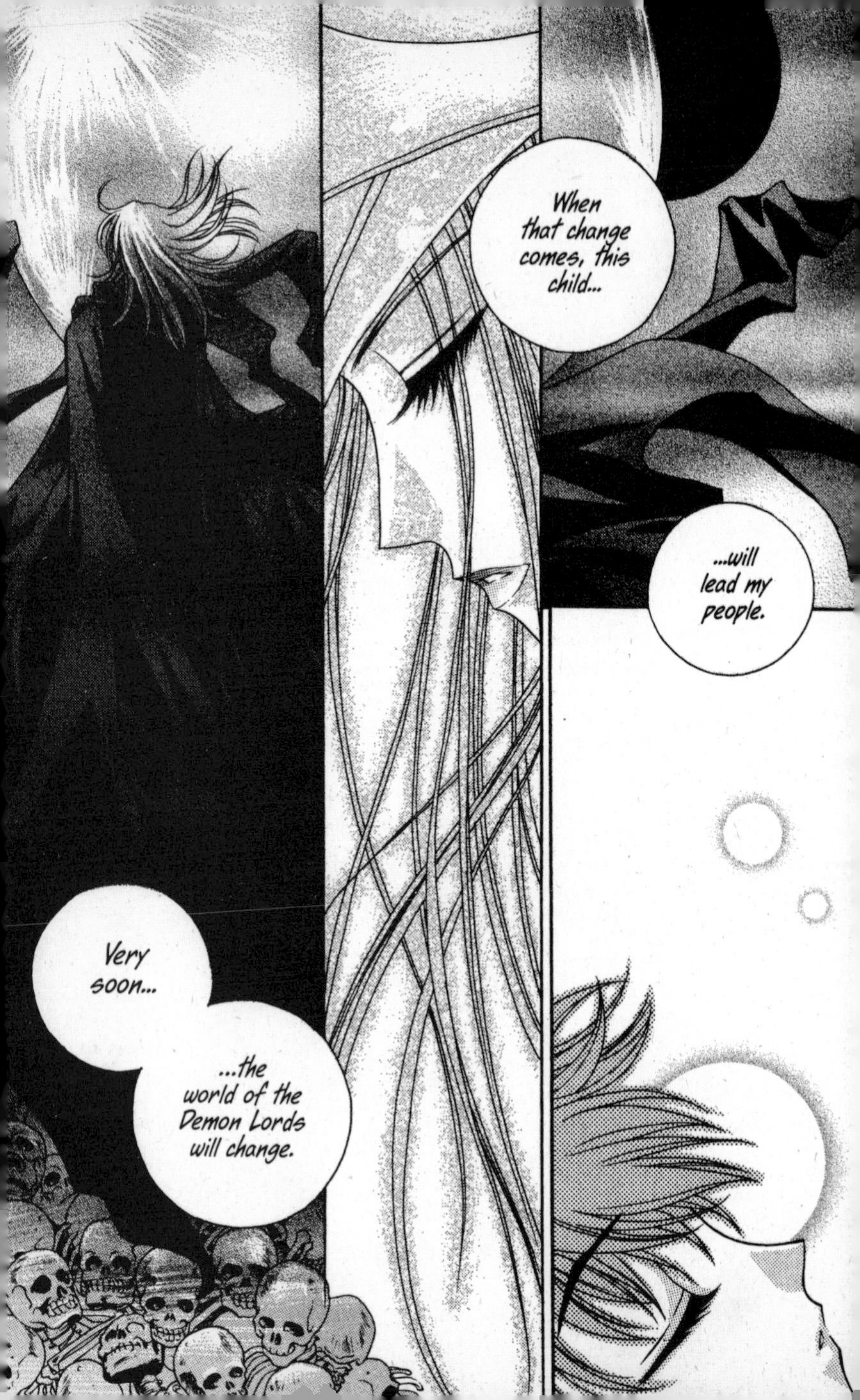
Very soon...
...the world of the Demon Lords will change.
When that change comes, this child...
...will lead my people.

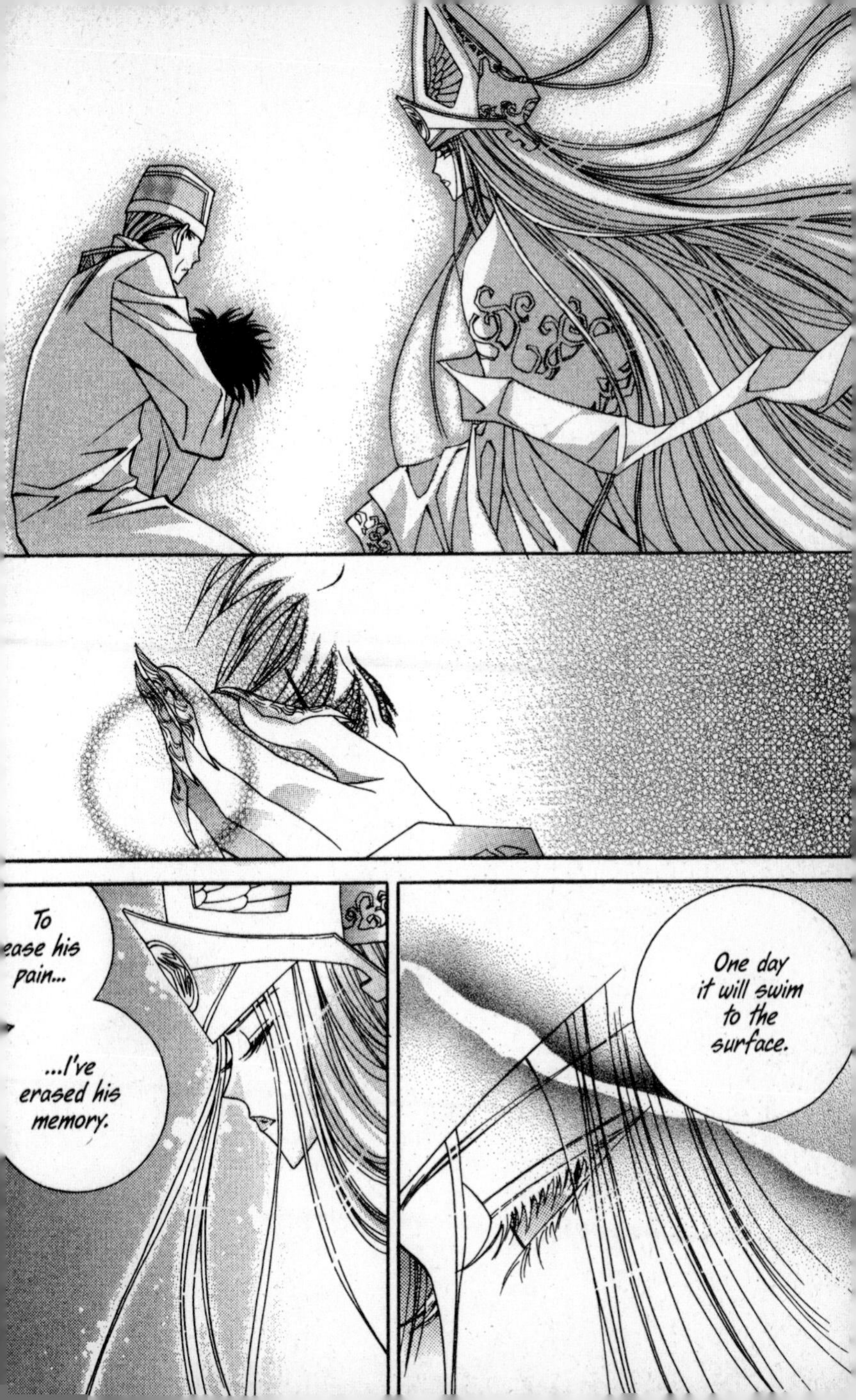
To ease his pain...
...I've erased his memory.
One day it will swim to the surface.

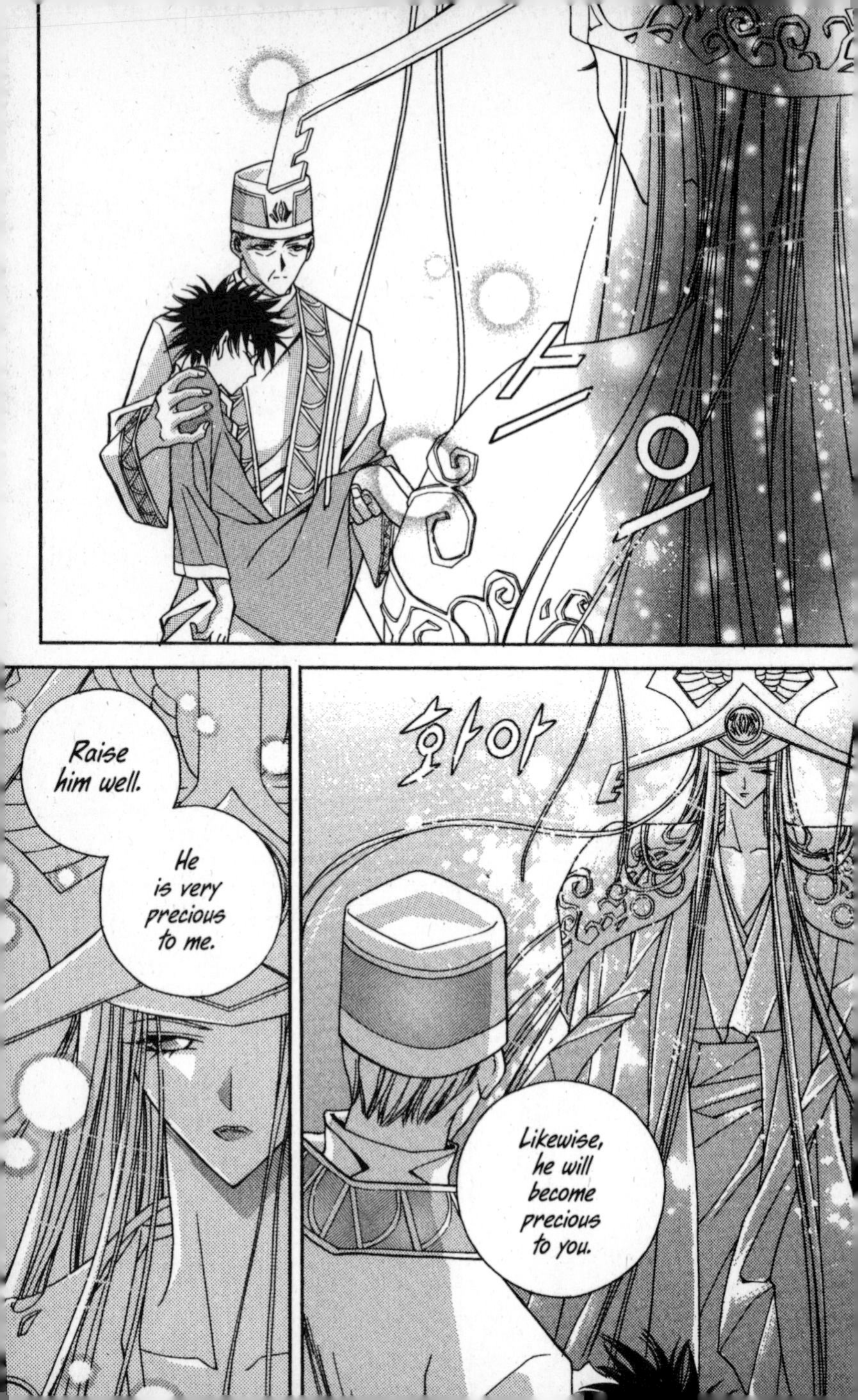
Raise him well.
He is very precious to me.
화아
Likewise, he will become precious to you.

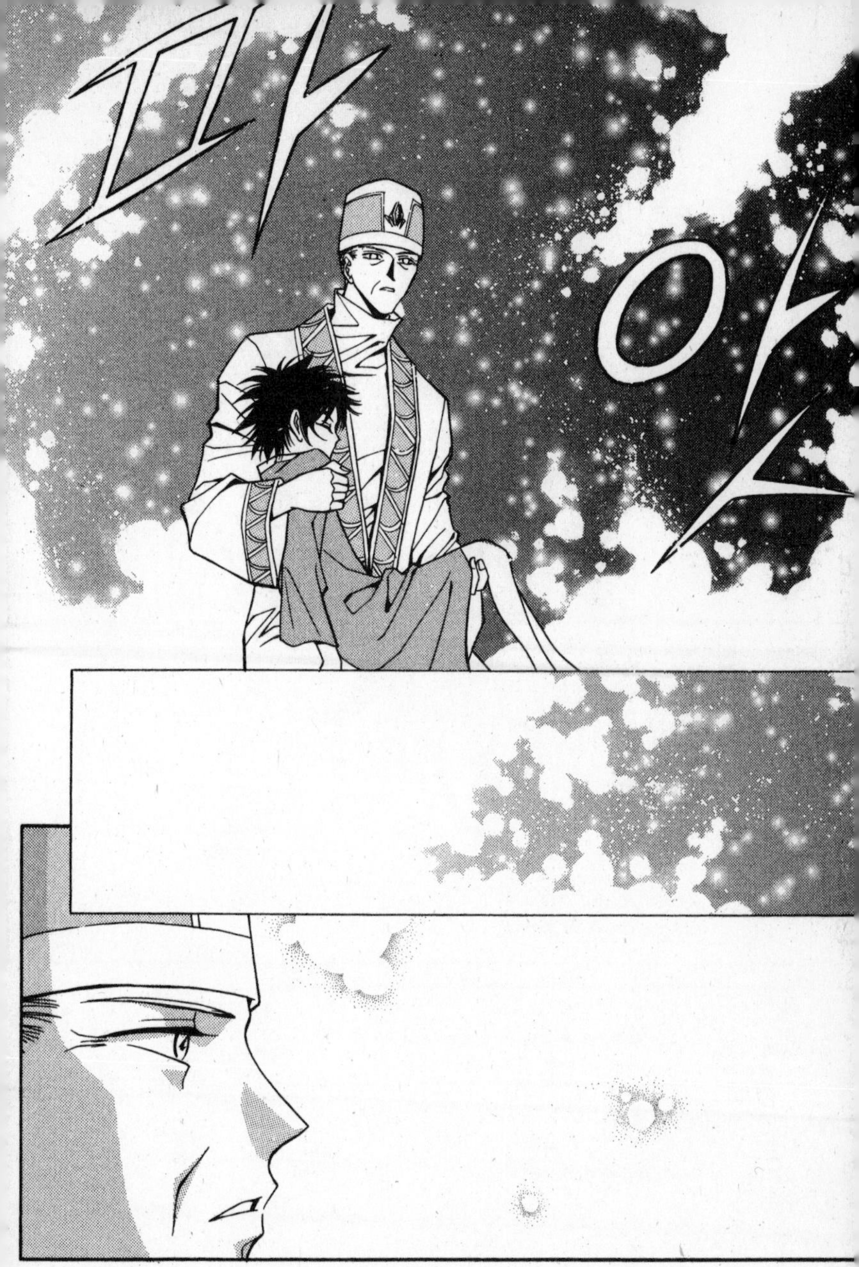
파앗

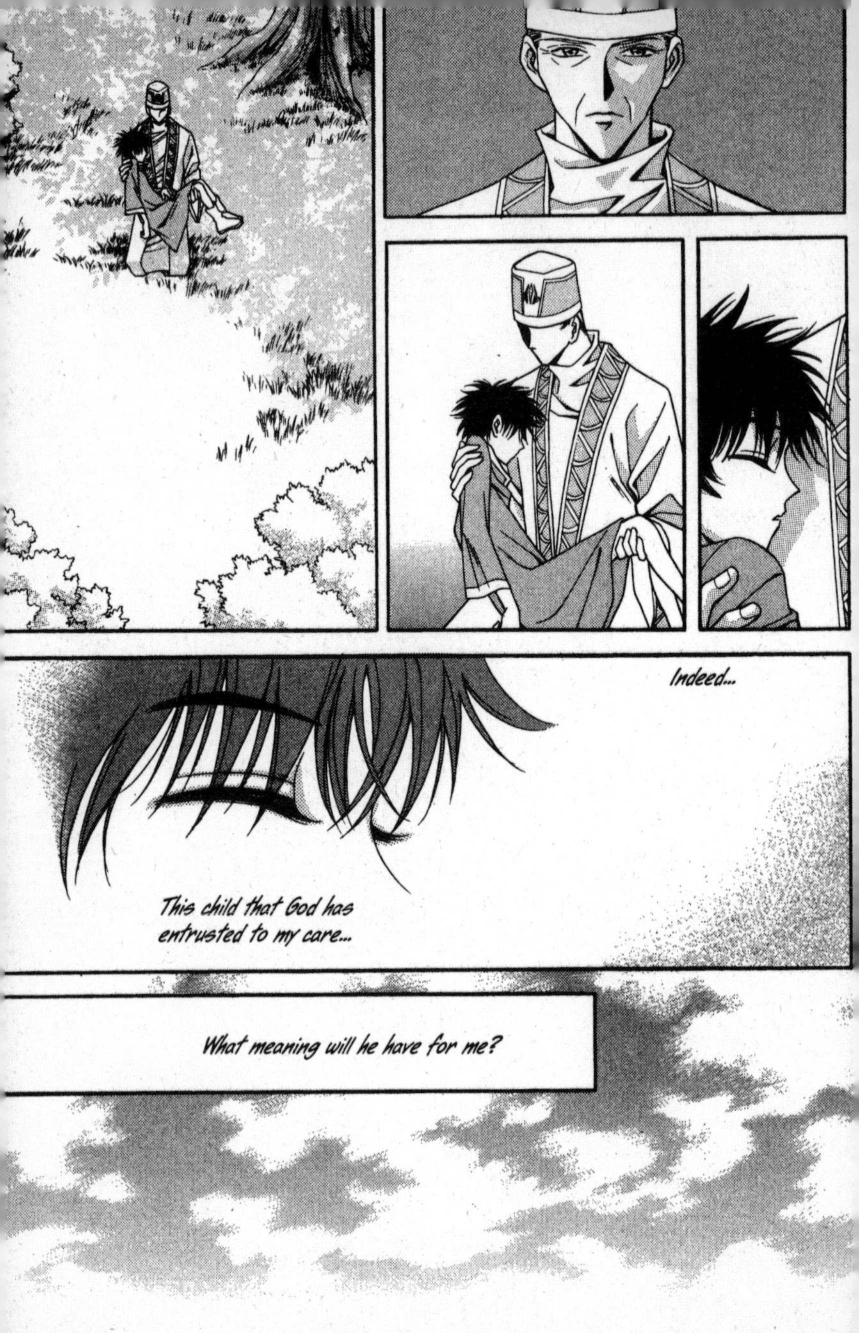
Indeed...
This child that God has entrusted to my care...
What meaning will he have for me?

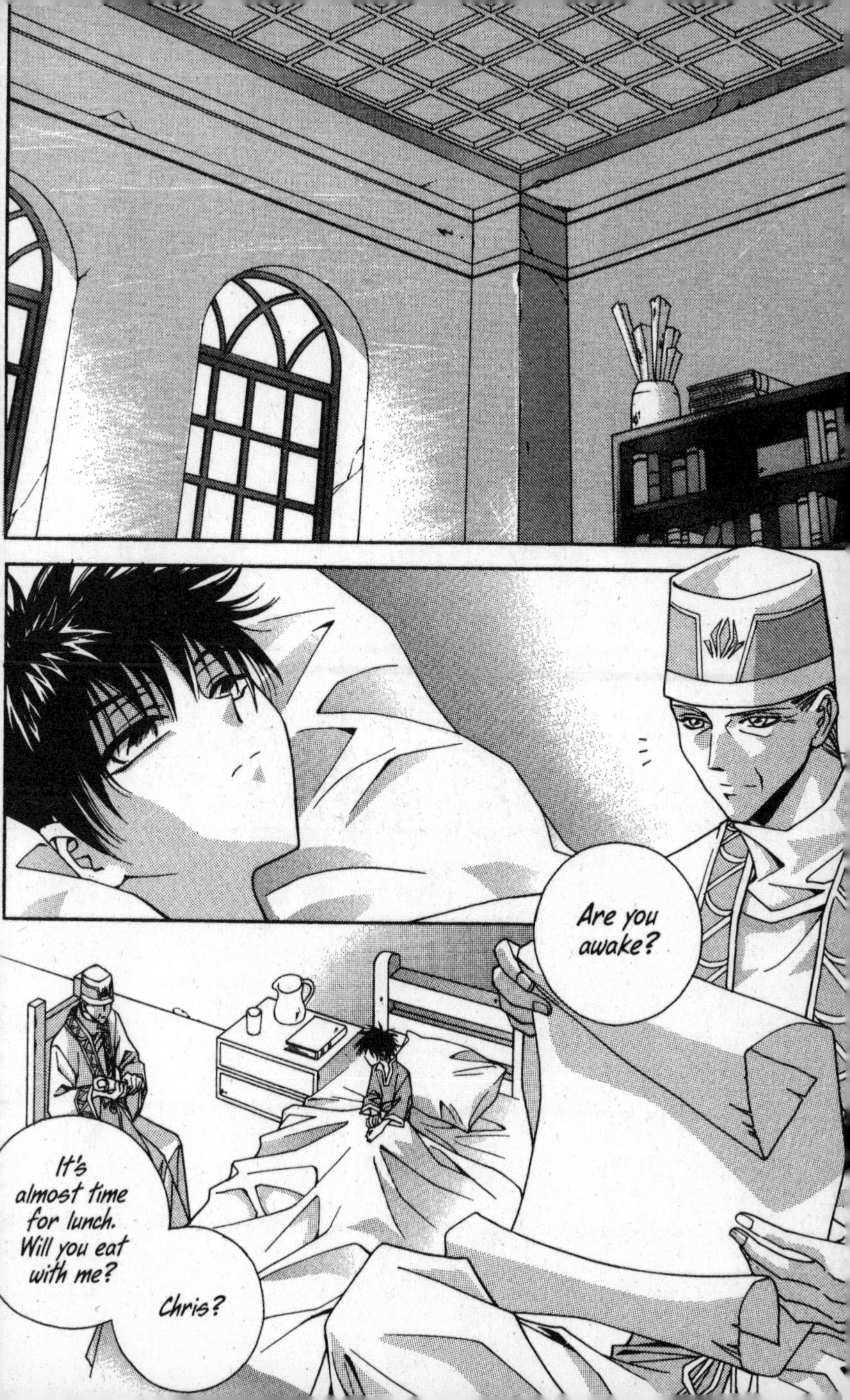
Are you awake?
It's almost time for lunch. Will you eat with me?
Chris?

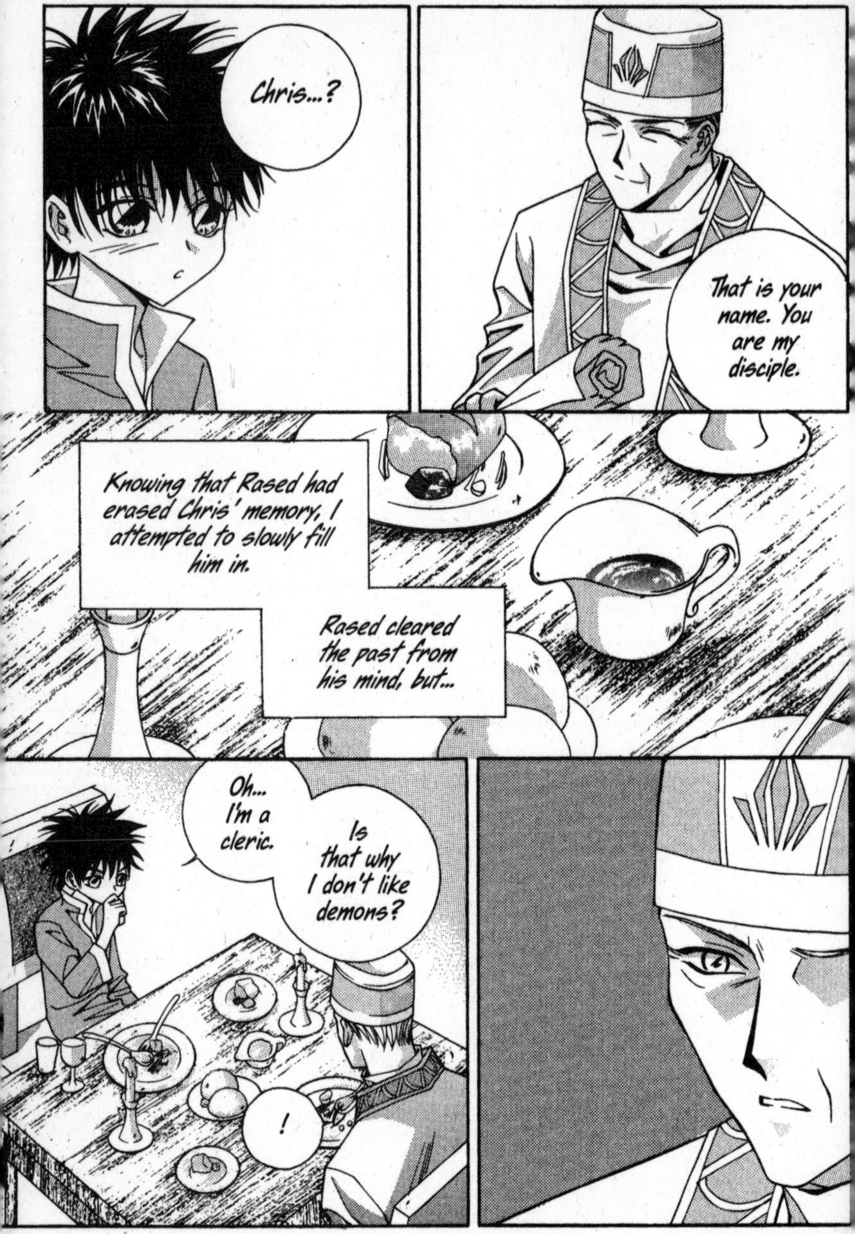

Chris...?
That is your name. You are my disciple.
Knowing that Rased had erased Chris' memory, I attempted to slowly fill him in.
Rased cleared the past from his mind, but...
Oh... I'm a cleric.
Is that why I don't like demons?
!

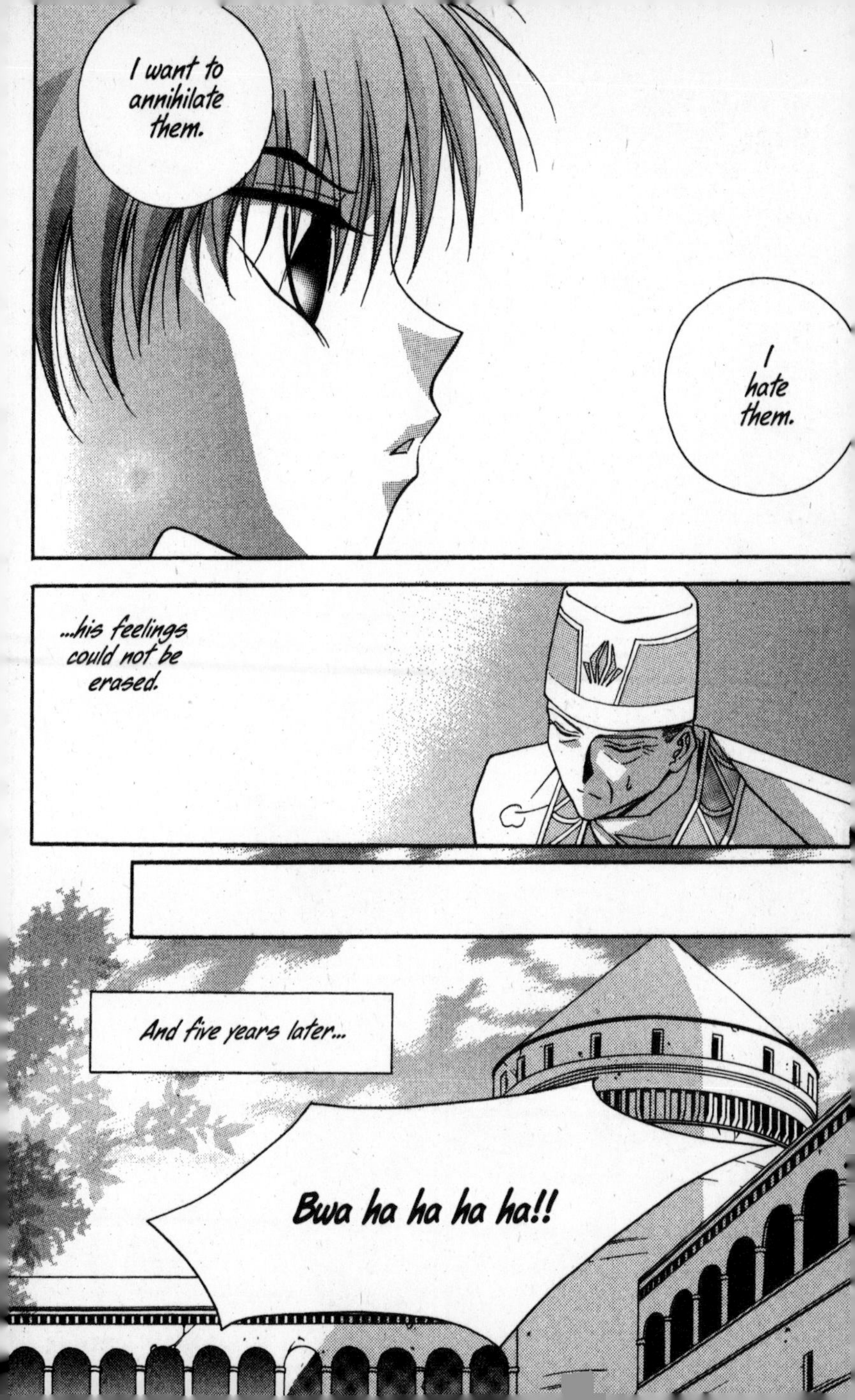
I want to annihilate them.
I hate them.
...his feelings could not be erased.
And five years later...
Bwa ha ha ha ha!!

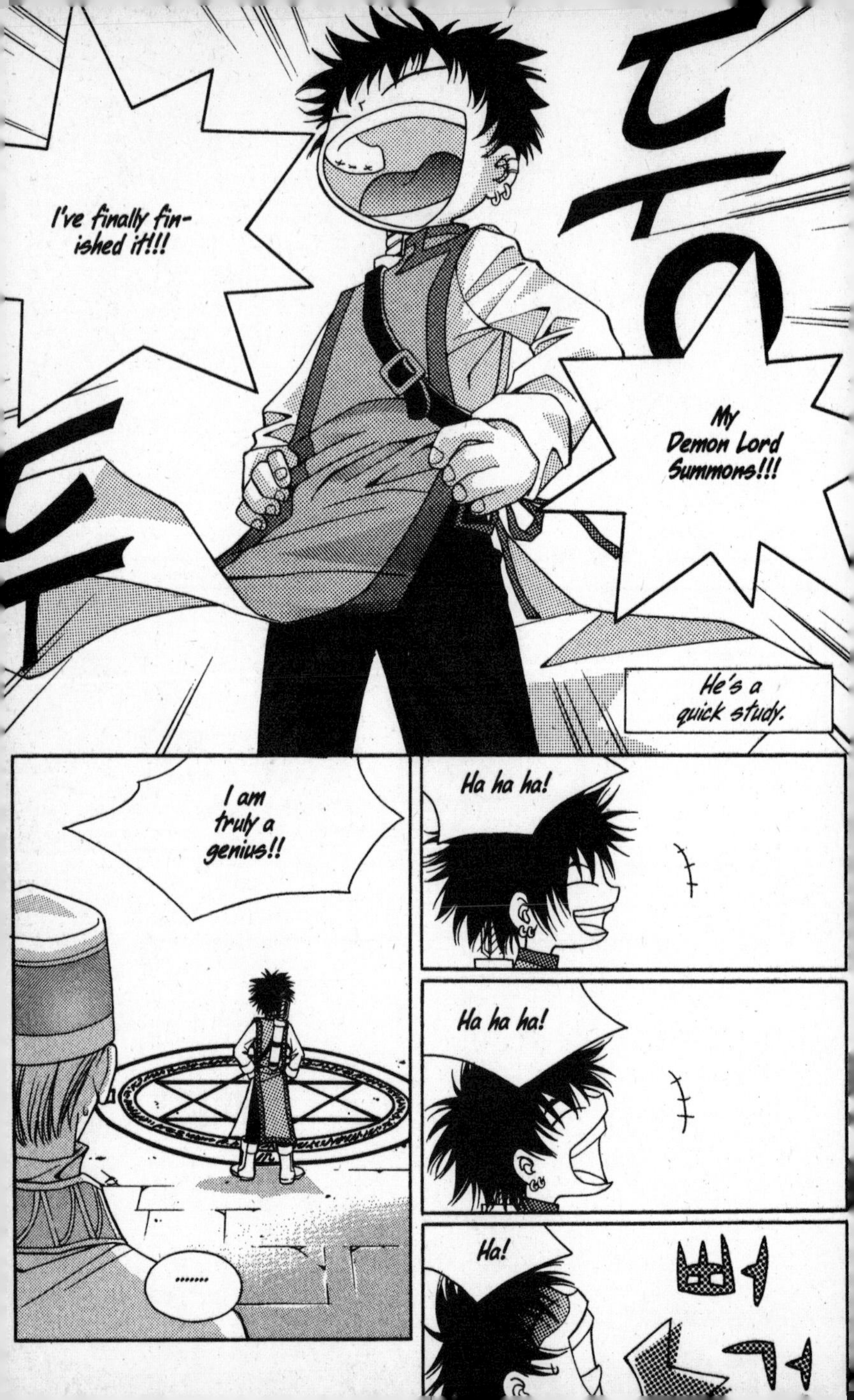
I've finally fin-
ished it!!!
My
Demon Lord
Summons!!!
He's a
quick study.
I am
truly a
genius!!
....
Ha ha ha!
Ha ha ha!
Ha!

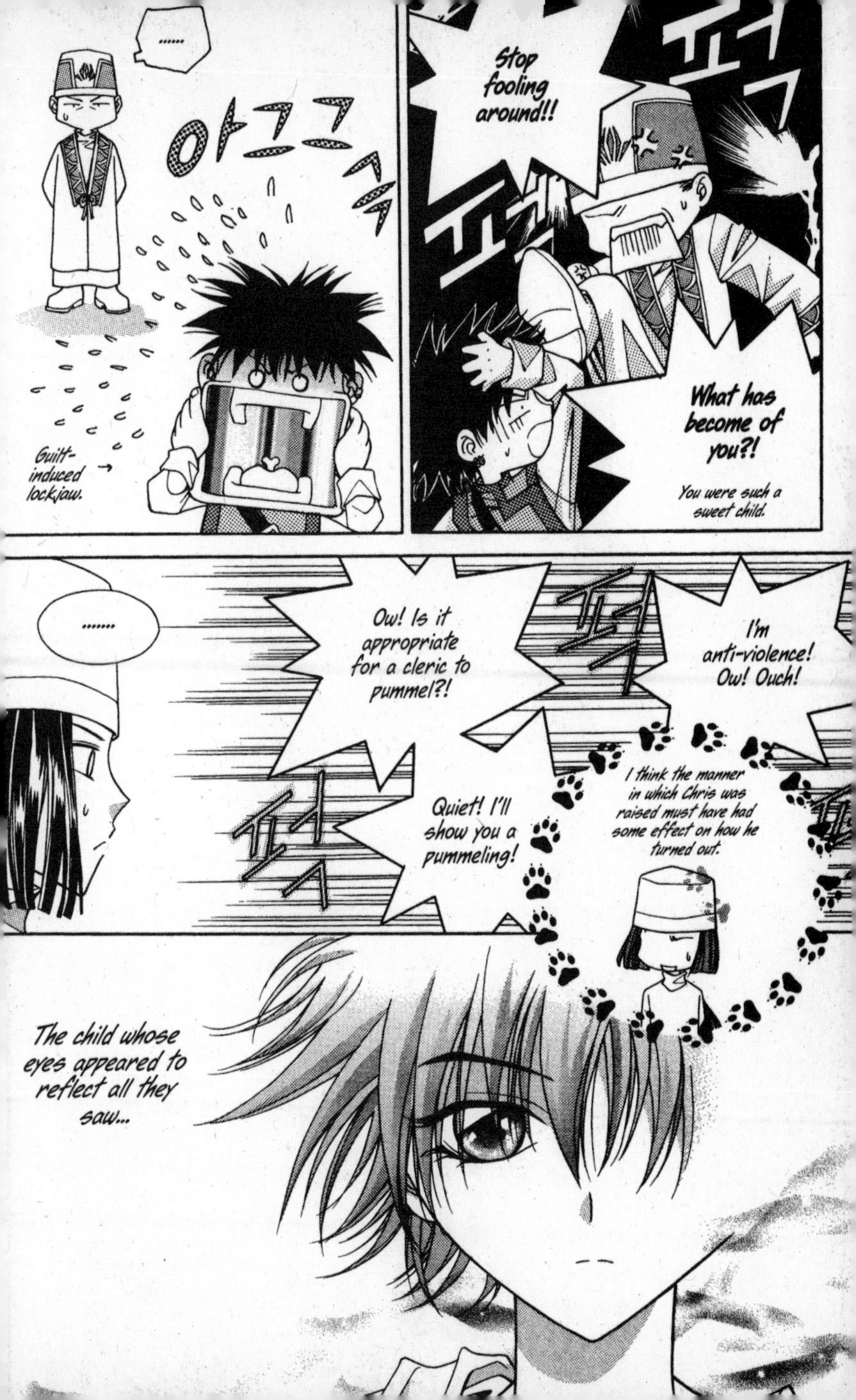
......
Guilt-induced lockjaw.
Stop fooling around!!
What has become of you?!
You were such a sweet child.
......
Ow! Is it appropriate for a cleric to pummel?!
I'm anti-violence! Ow! Ouch!
Quiet! I'll show you a pummeling!
I think the manner in which Chris was raised must have had some effect on how he turned out.
The child whose eyes appeared to reflect all they saw...

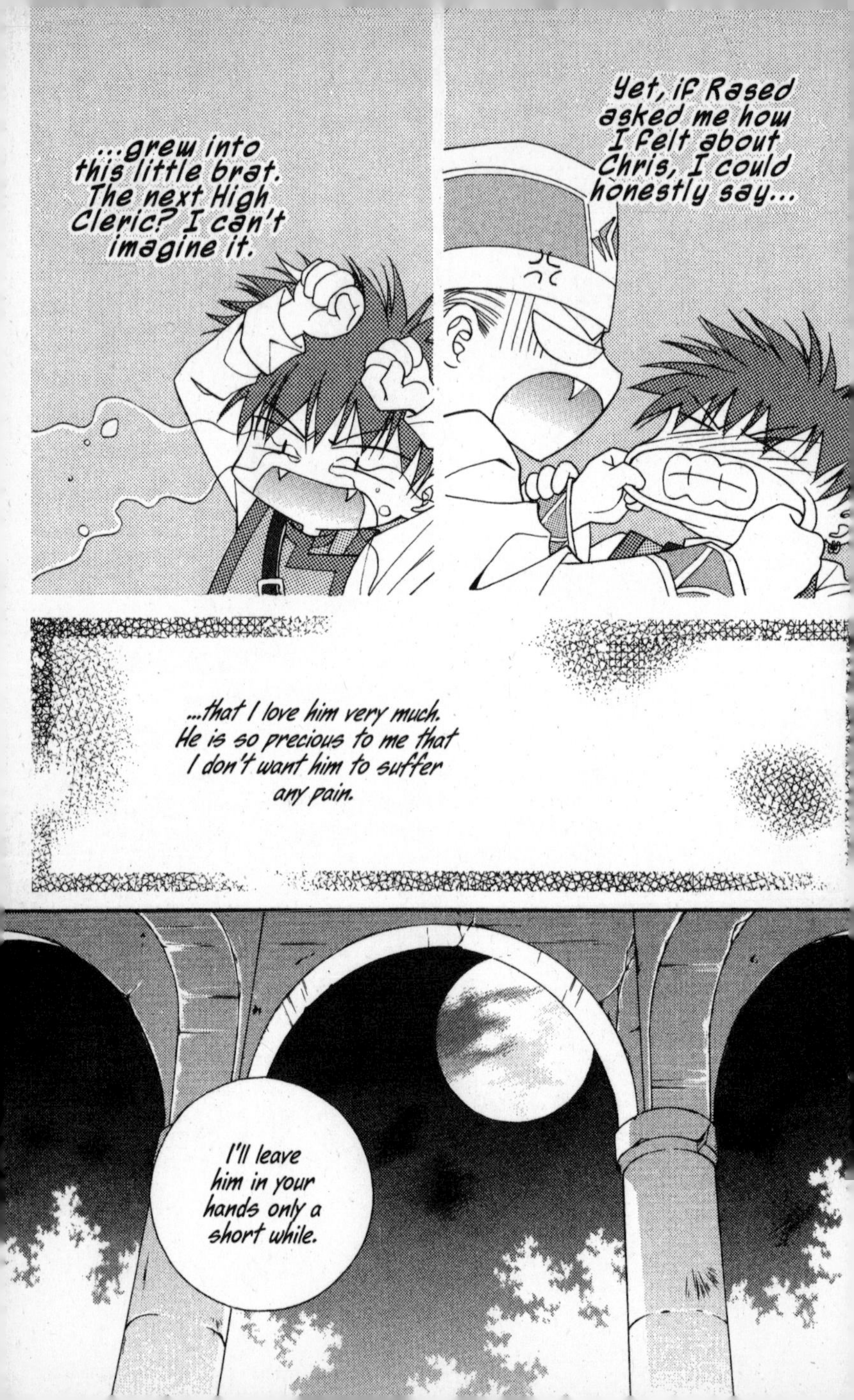
...grew into this little brat. The next High Cleric? I can't imagine it.
Yet, if Rased asked me how I felt about Chris, I could honestly say...
...that I love him very much. He is so precious to me that I don't want him to suffer any pain.
I'll leave him in your hands only a short while.

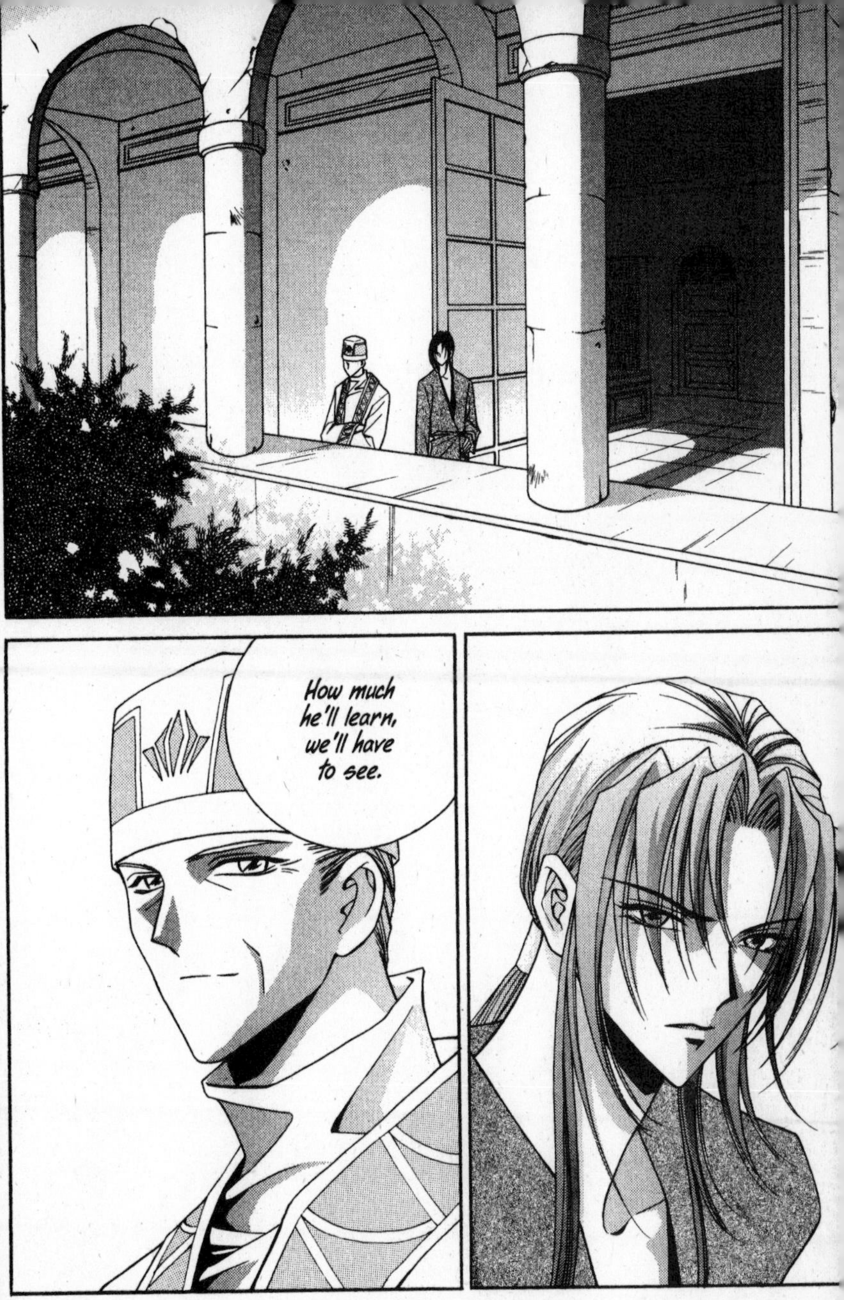
How much he'll learn, we'll have to see.

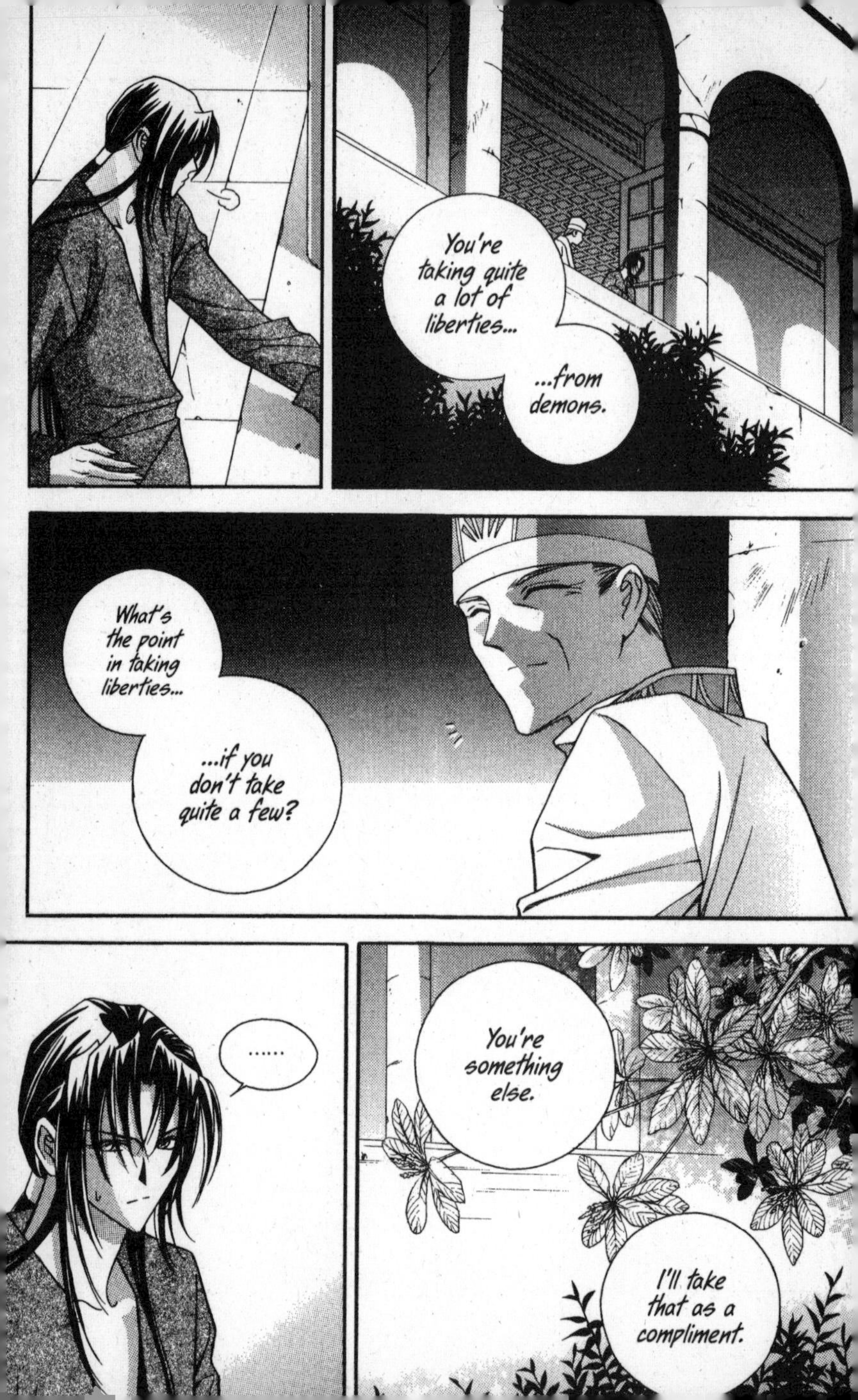
You're taking quite a lot of liberties...
...from demons.
What's the point in taking liberties...
...if you don't take quite a few?
......
You're something else.
I'll take that as a compliment.

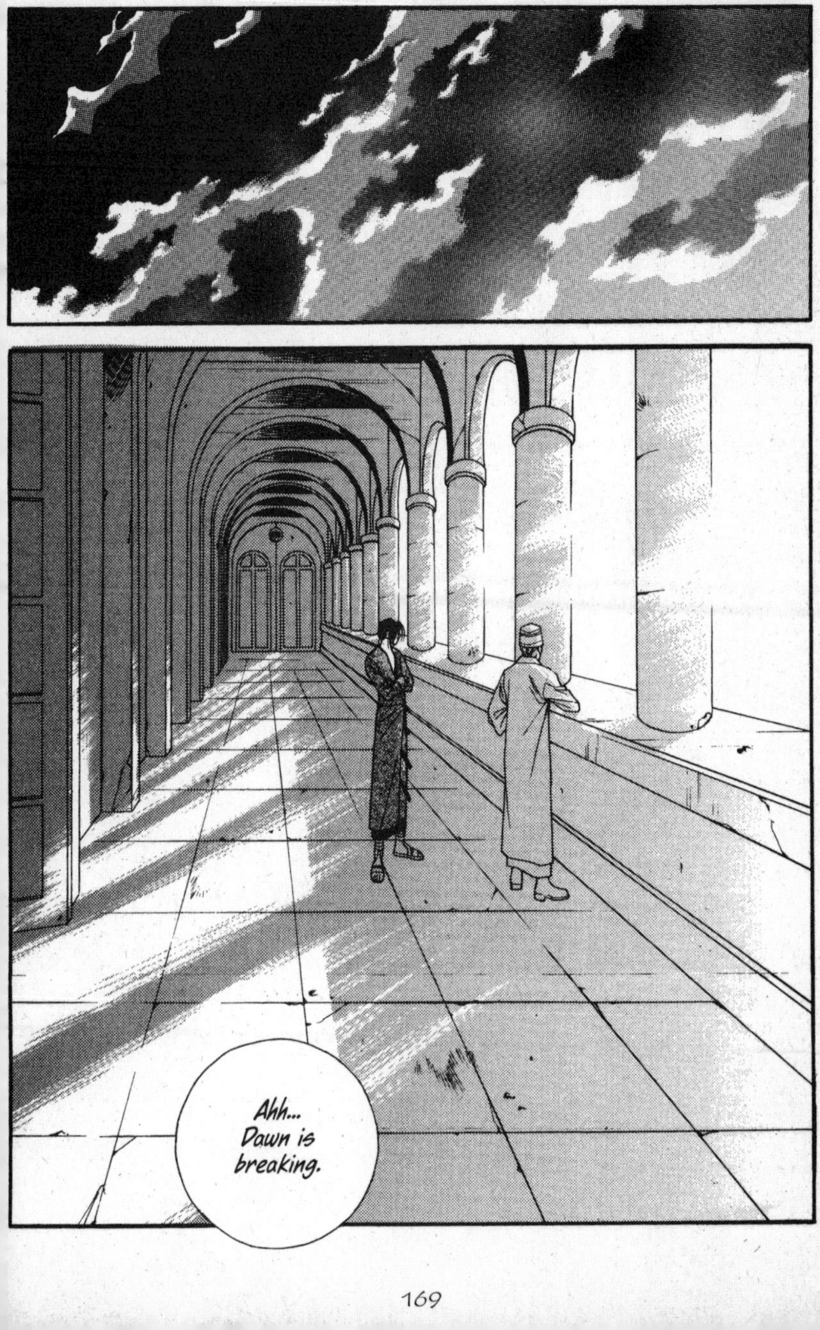
Ahh... Dawn is breaking.

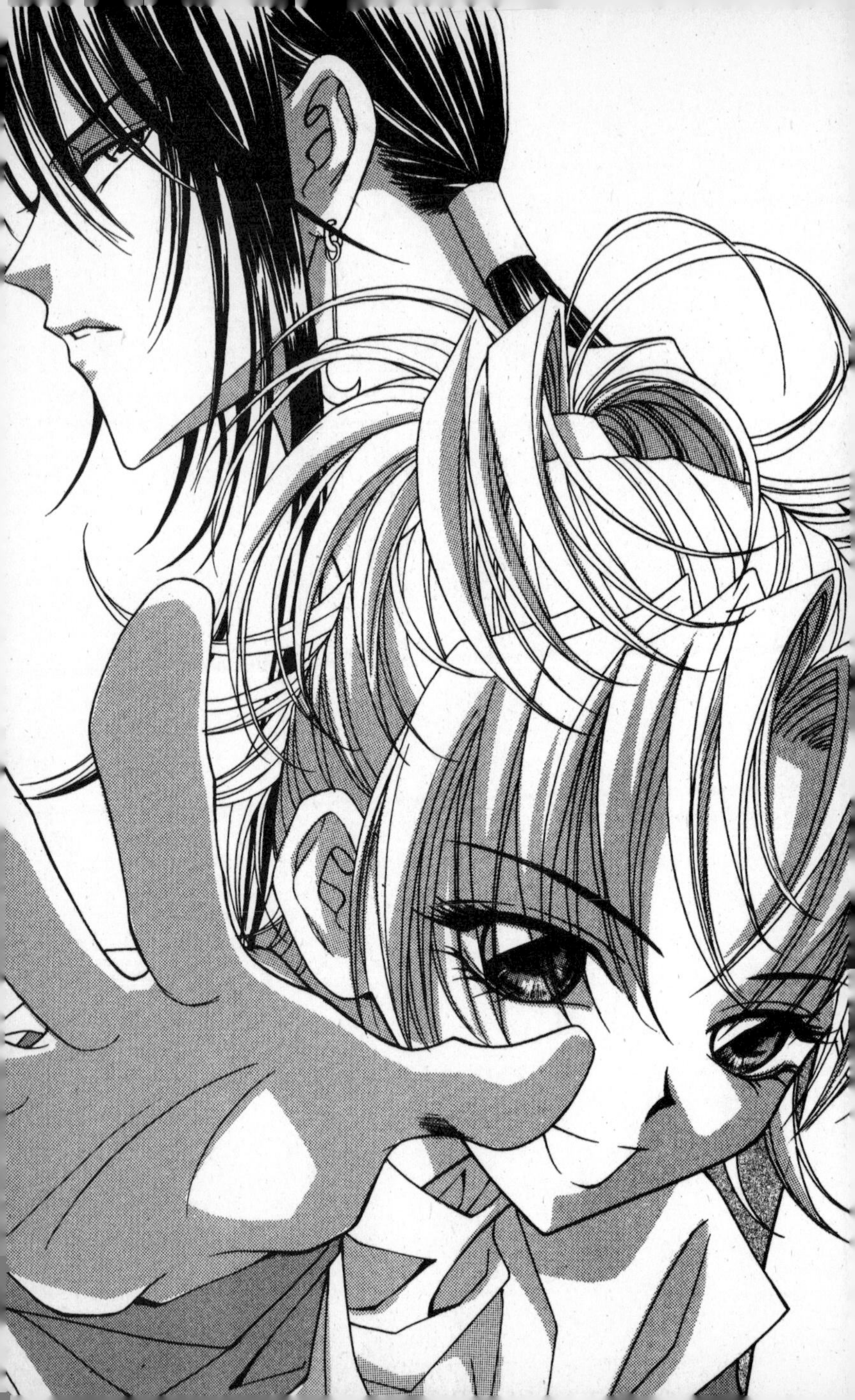

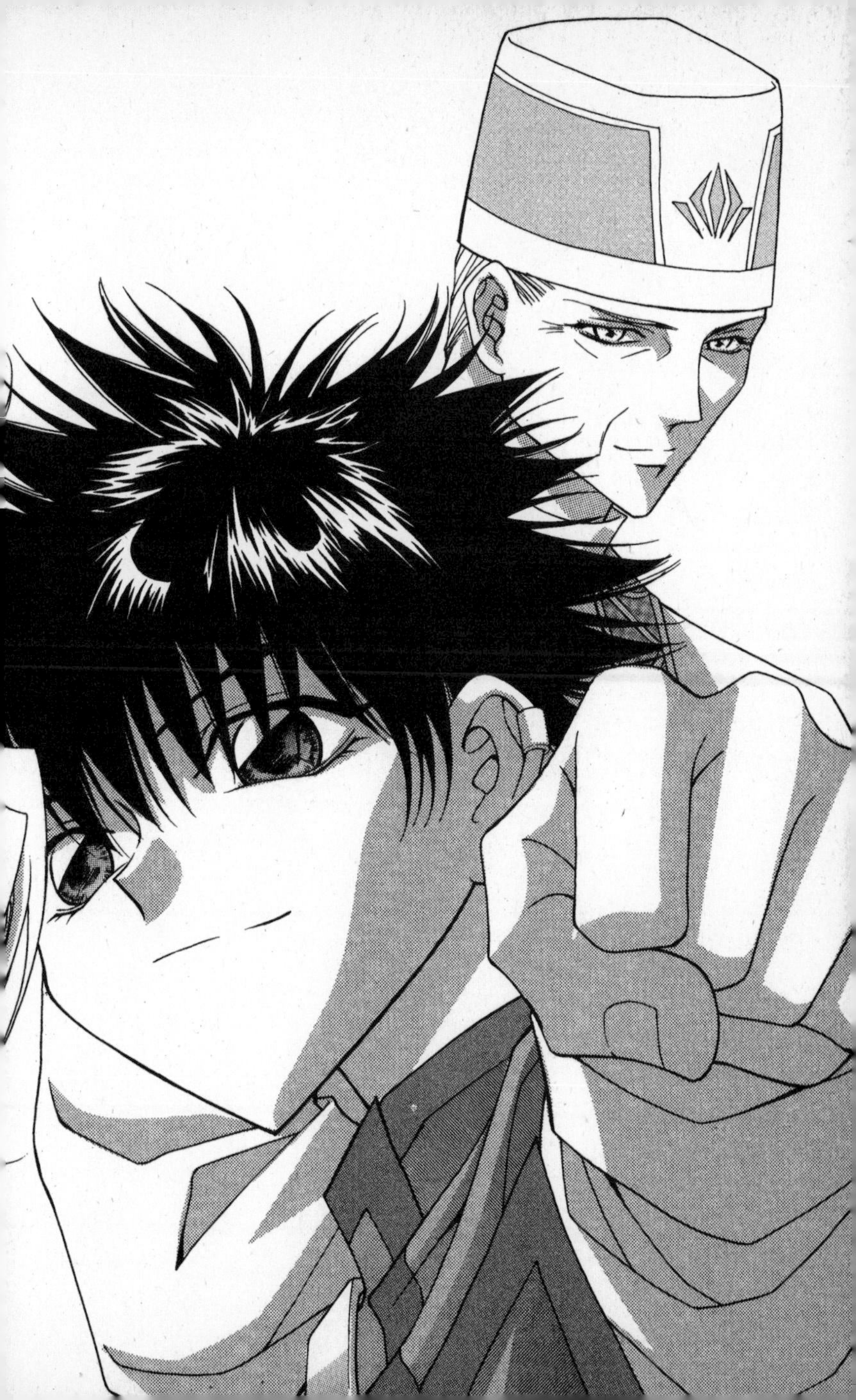

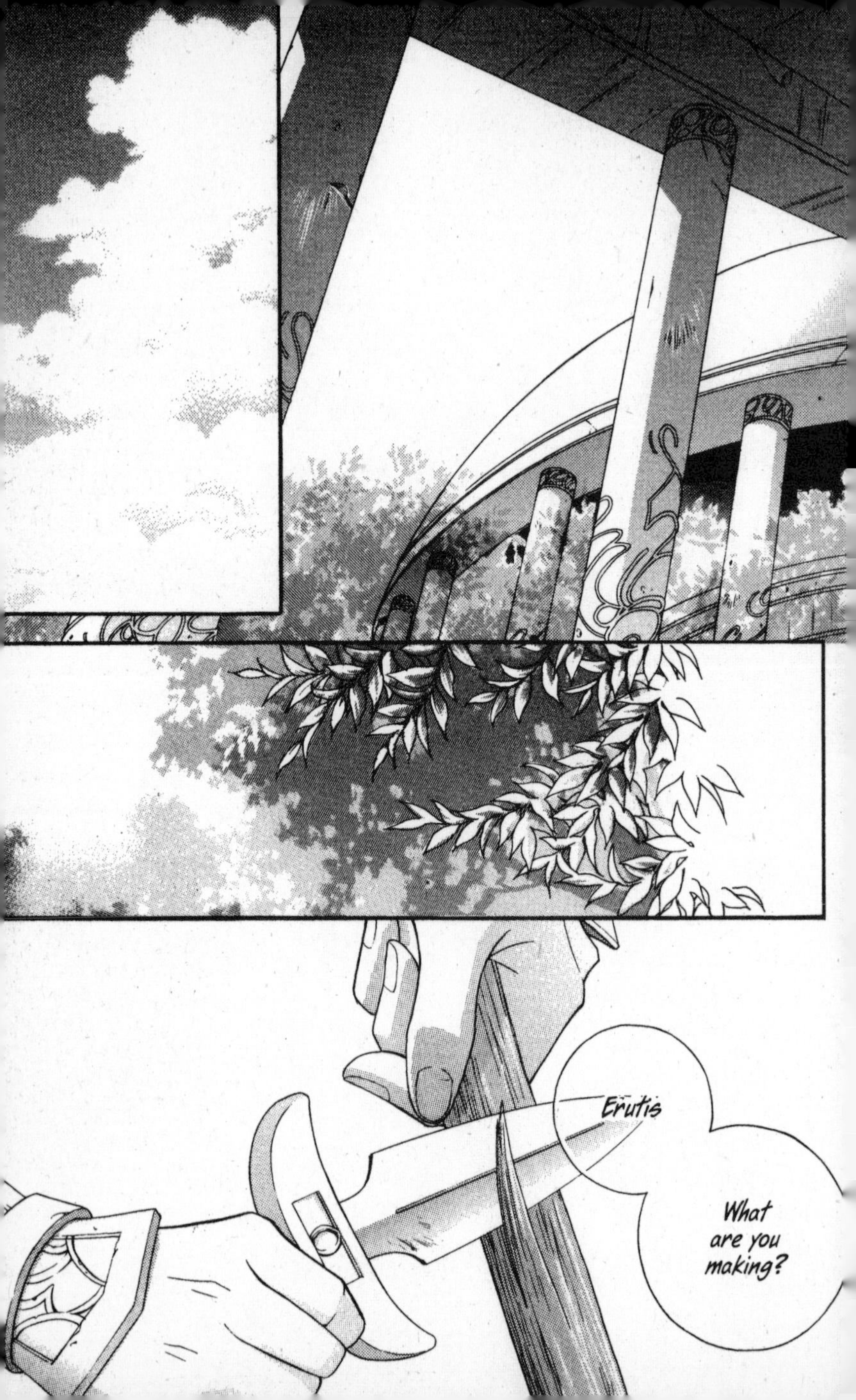
Erutis
What are you making?

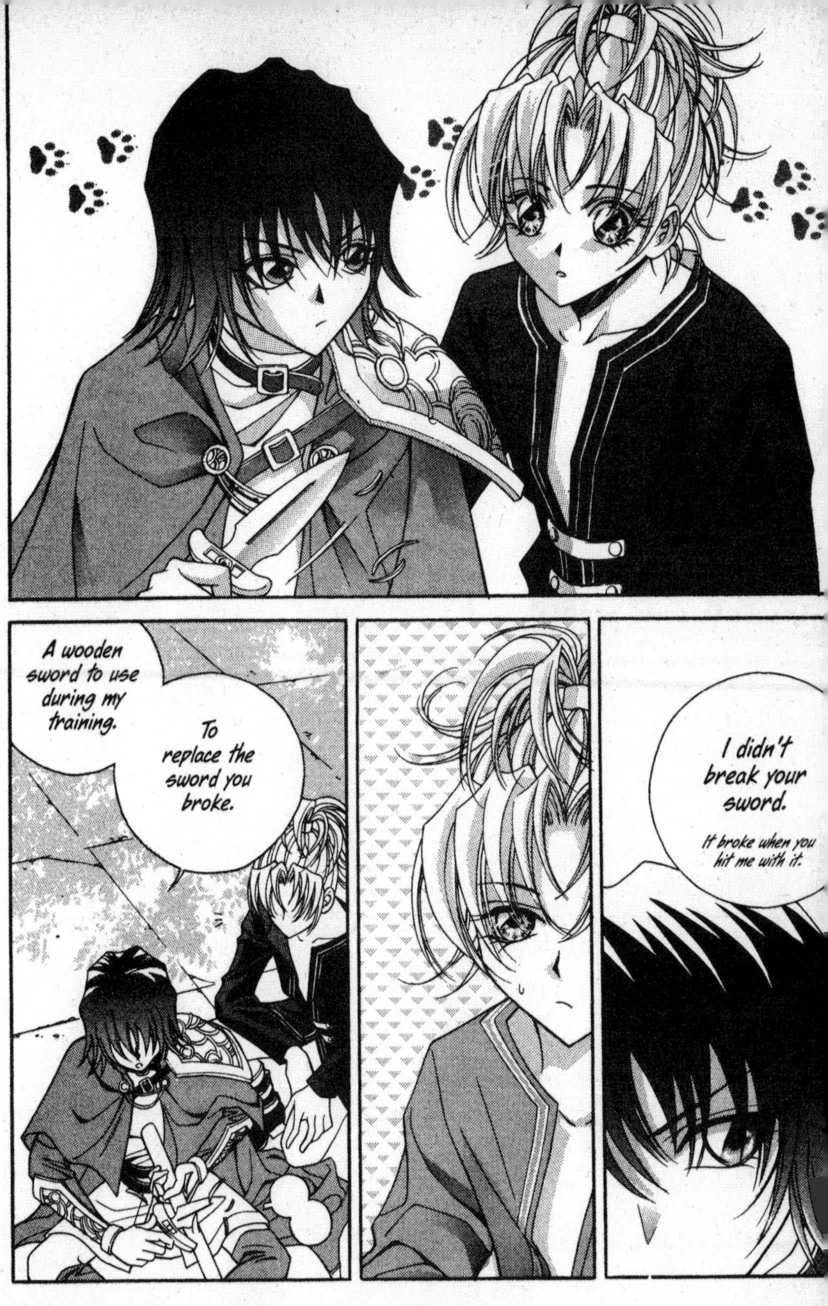
A wooden sword to use during my training.
To replace the sword you broke.
I didn't break your sword.
It broke when you hit me with it.

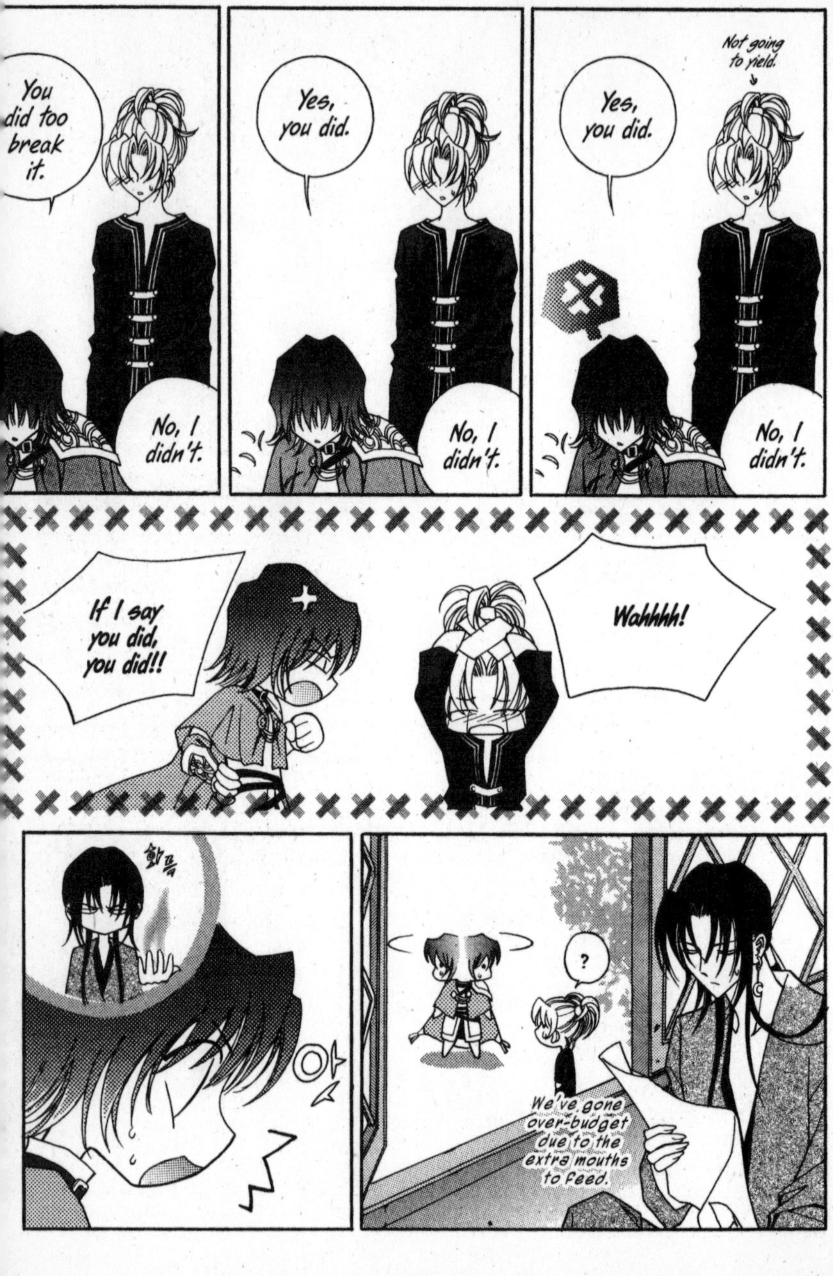
You did too break it.
No, I didn't.
Yes, you did.
No, I didn't.
Not going to yield.
Yes, you did.
No, I didn't.
If I say you did, you did!!
Wahhhh!
?
We've gone over-budget due to the extra mouths to feed.

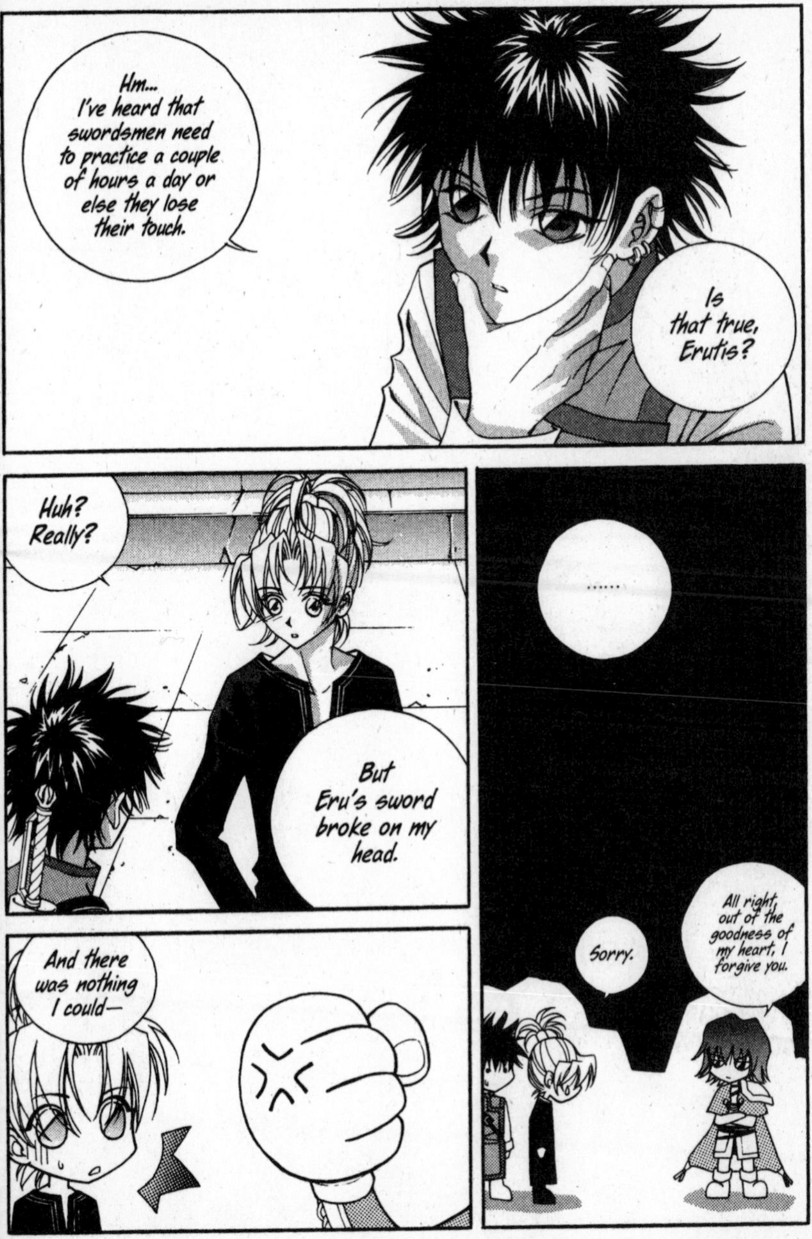
Hm... I've heard that swordsmen need to practice a couple of hours a day or else they lose their touch.
Is that true, Erutis?
Huh? Really?
But Eru's sword broke on my head.
And there was nothing I could—
......
Sorry.
All right, out of the goodness of my heart, I forgive you.

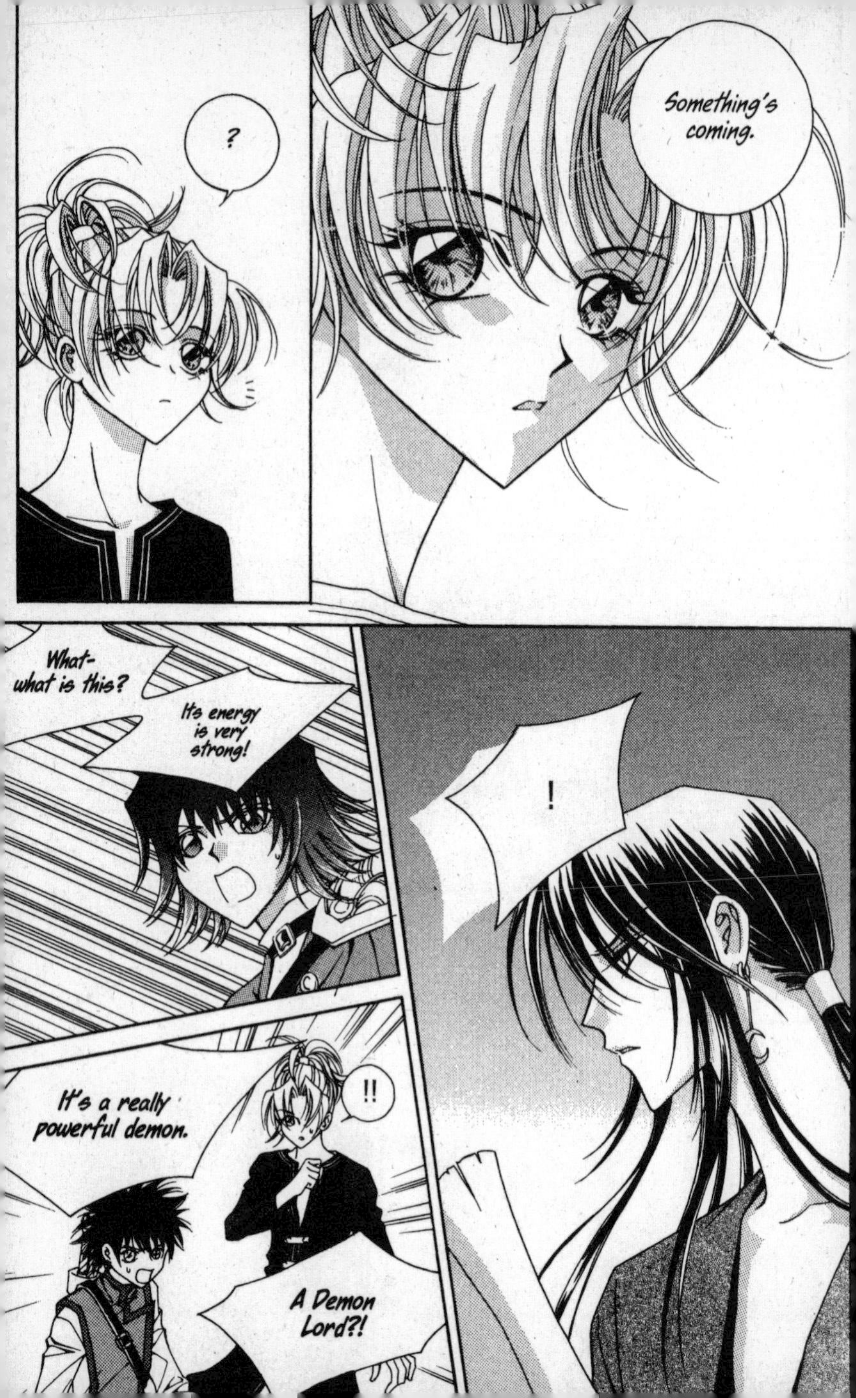
?
Something's coming.
What-what is this?
Its energy is very strong!
It's a really powerful demon.
!!
A Demon Lord?!
!

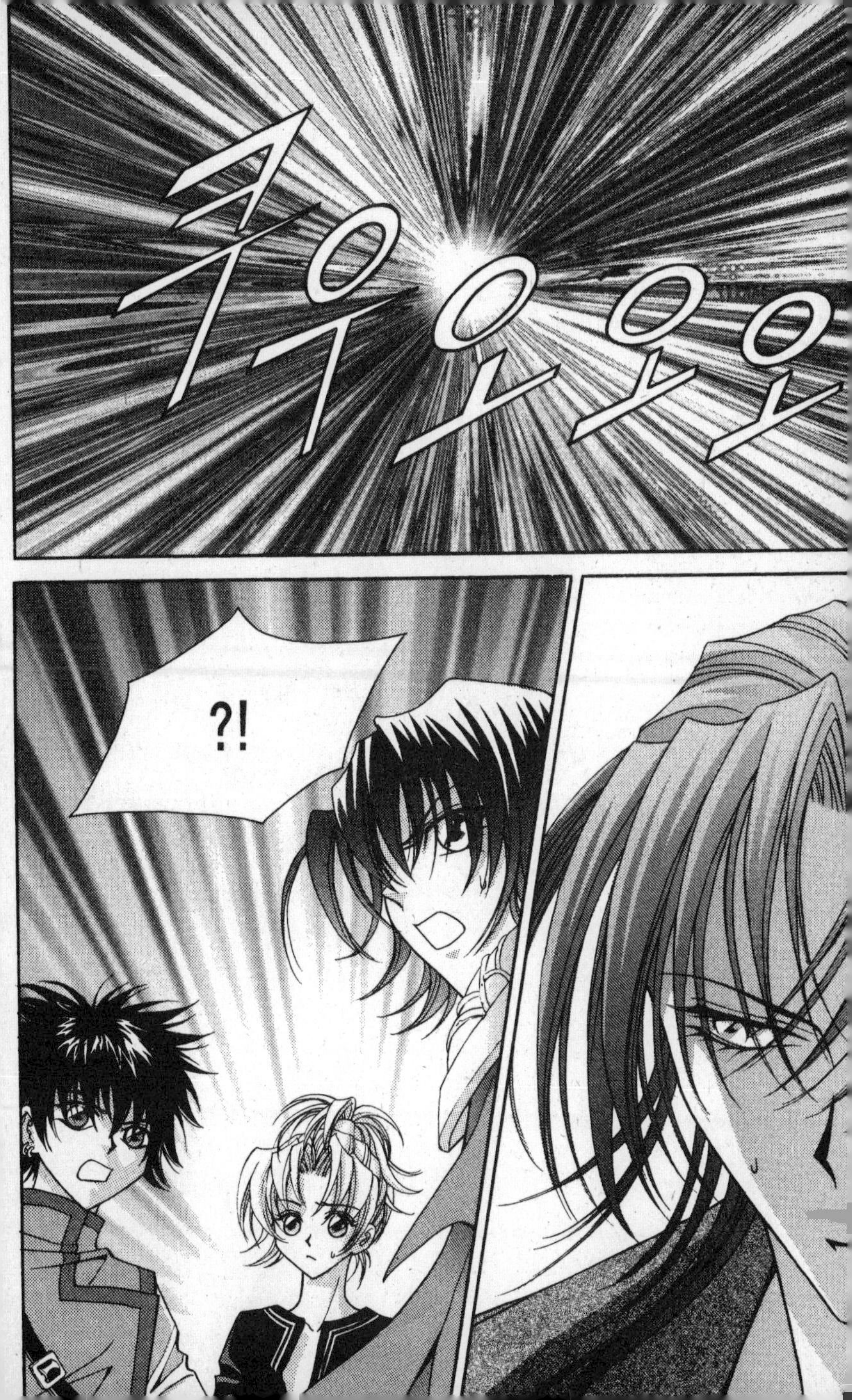
?!

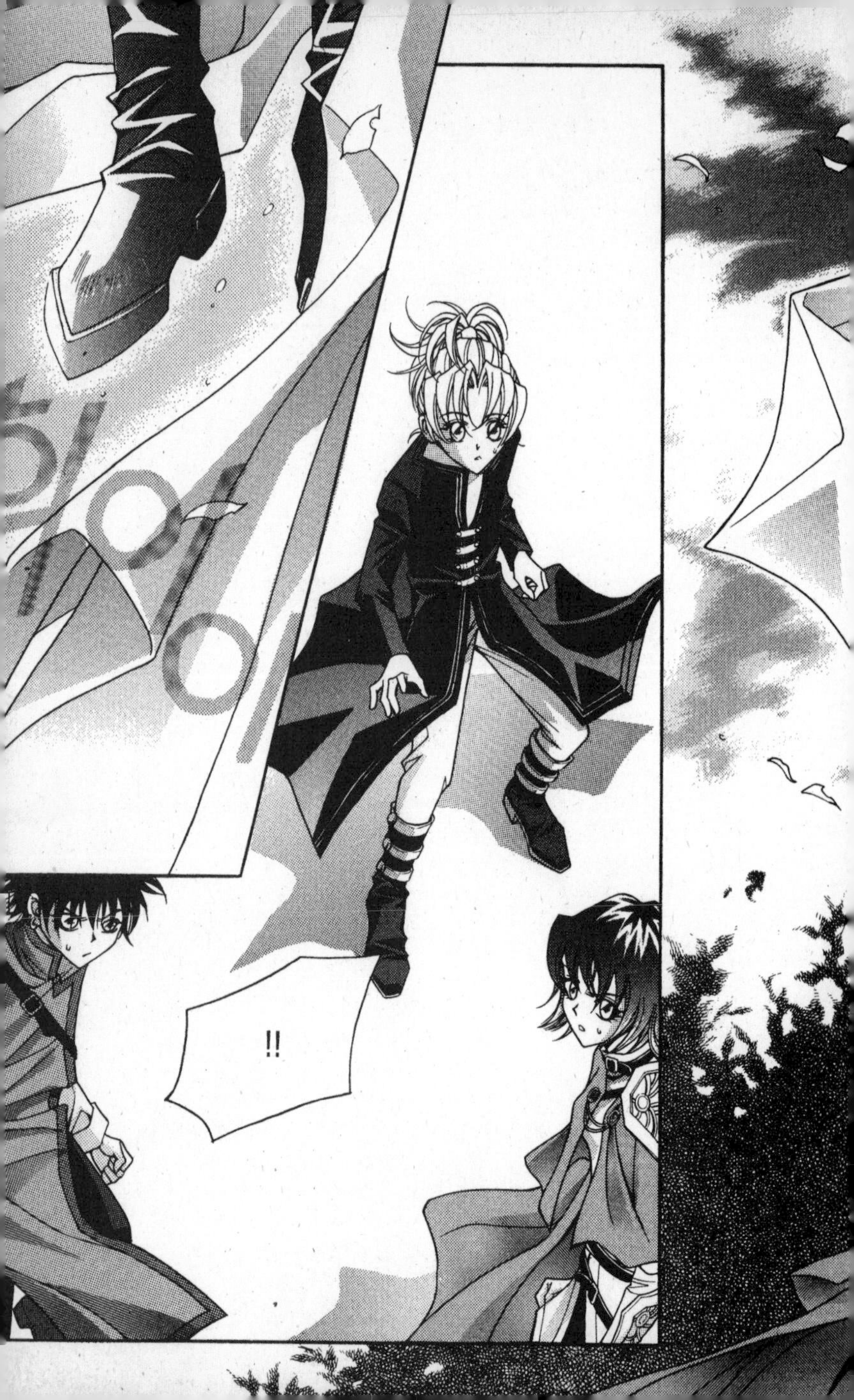
!!

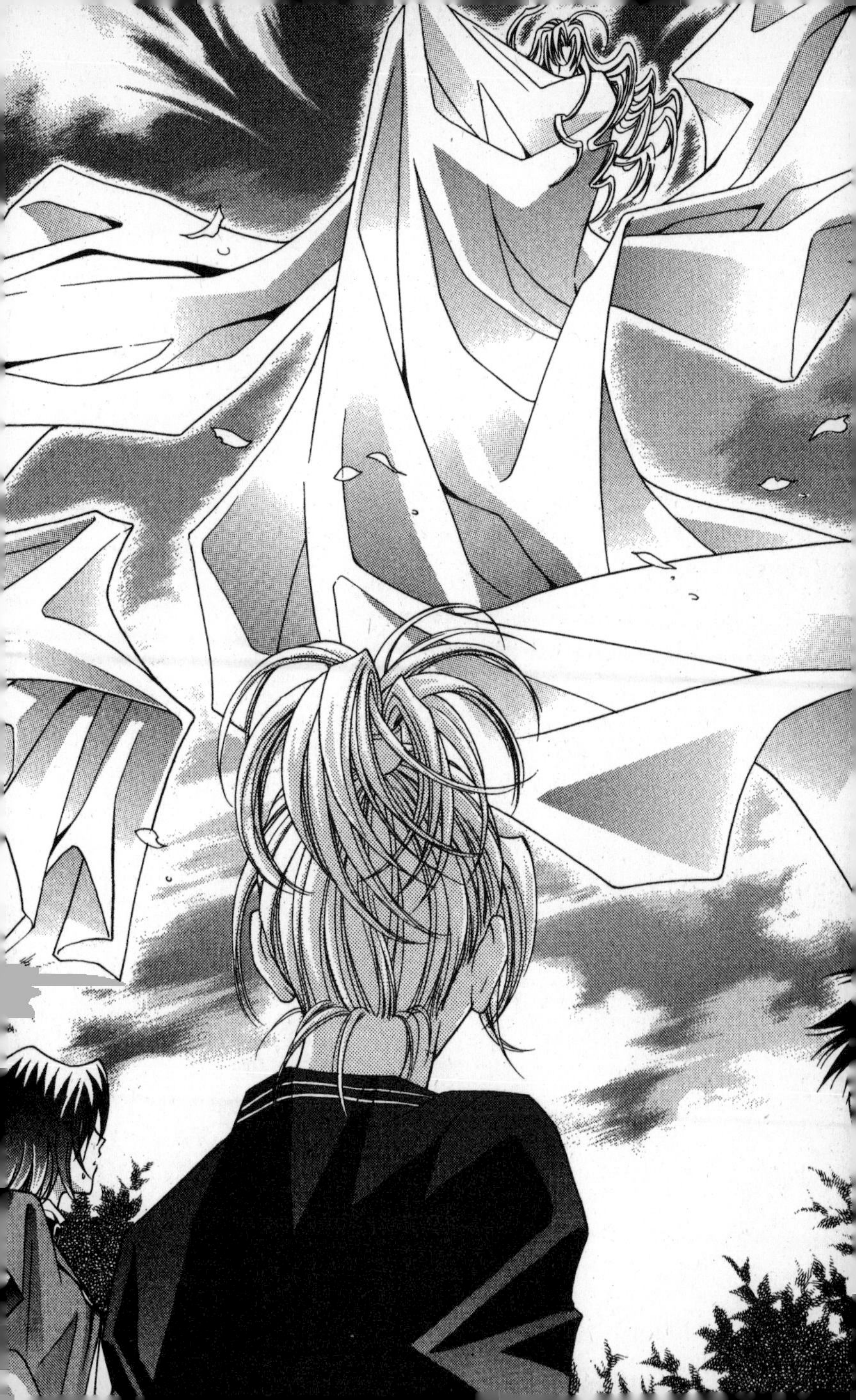

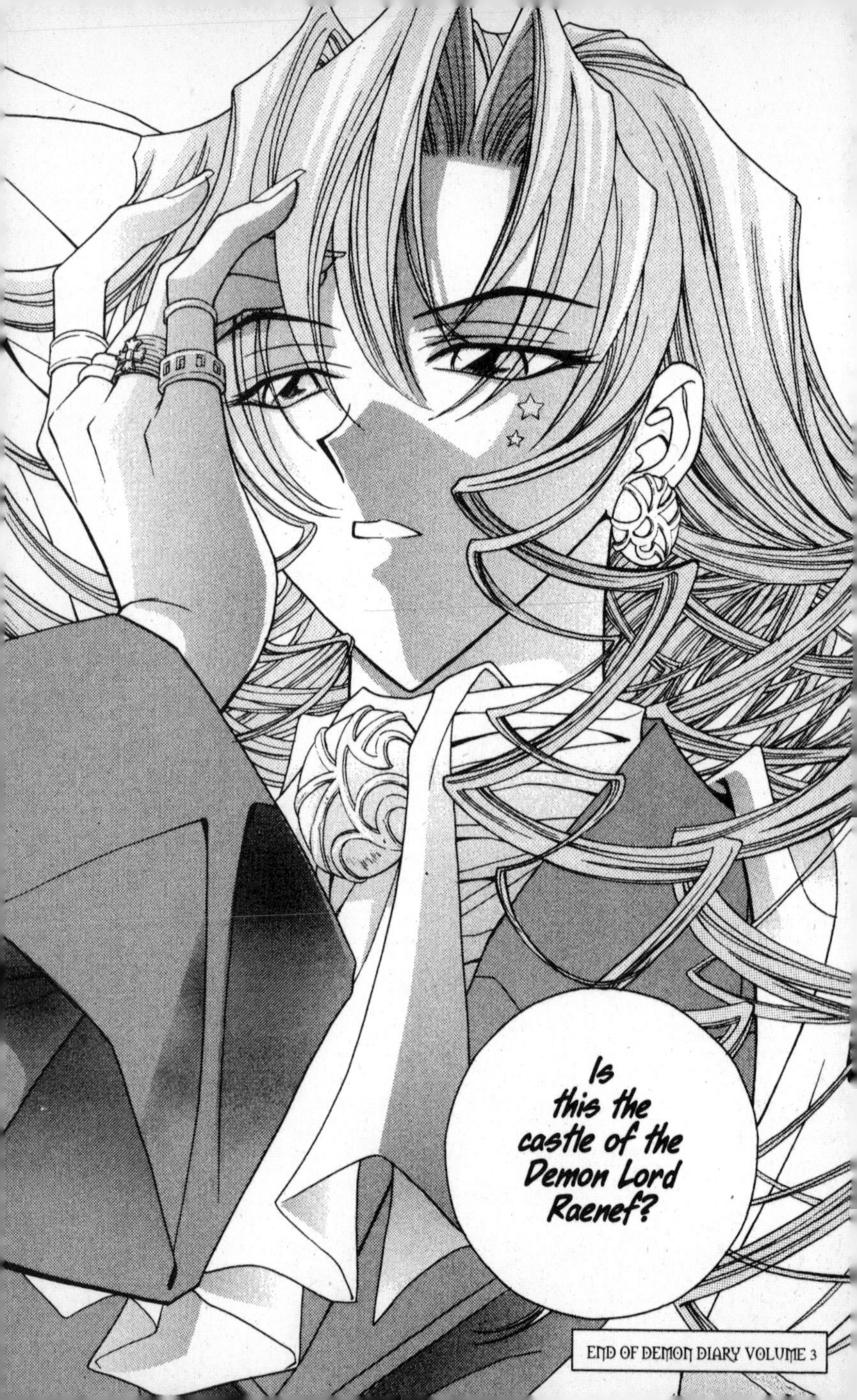
Is this the castle of the Demon Lord Raenef?

END OF DEMON DIARY VOLUME 3

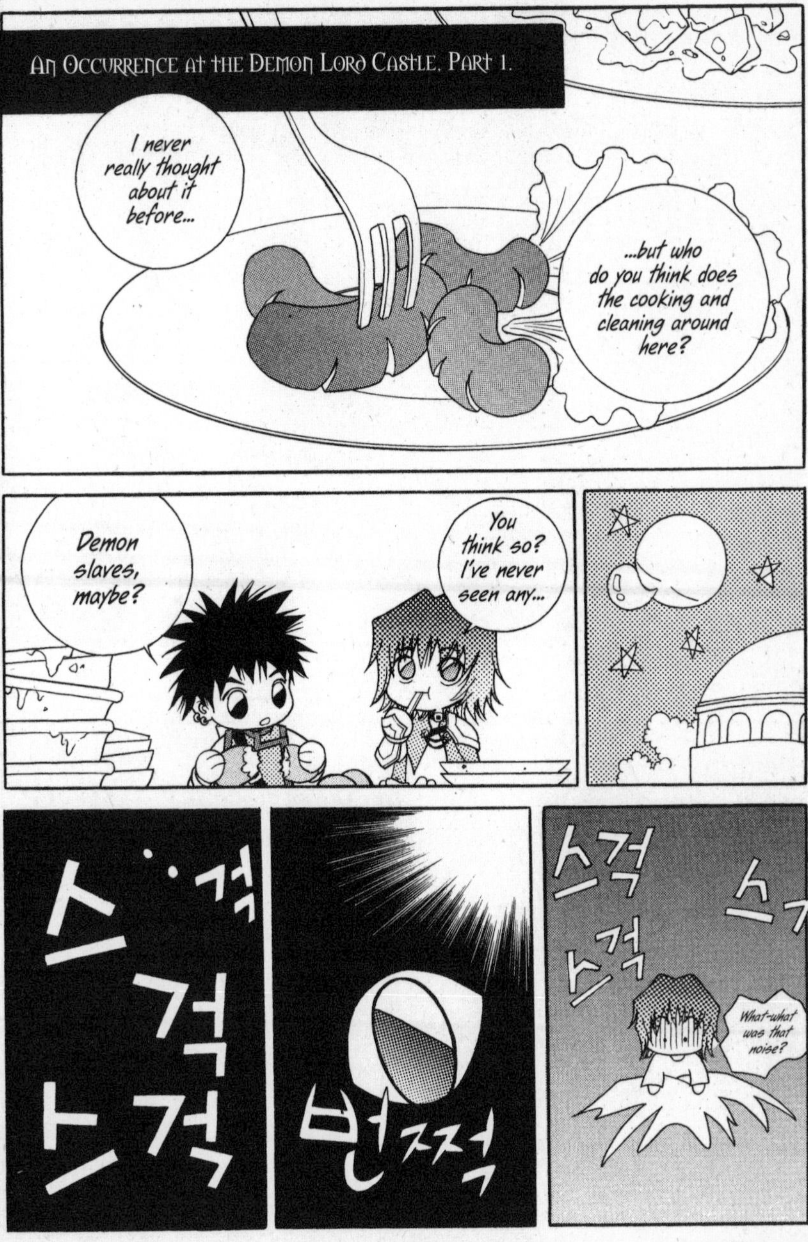
An Occurrence at the Demon Lord Castle, Part 1.
I never really thought about it before...
...but who do you think does the cooking and cleaning around here?
Demon slaves, maybe?
You think so? I've never seen any...
스걱 스걱
번쩍
스걱 스걱 스걱
What-what was that noise?

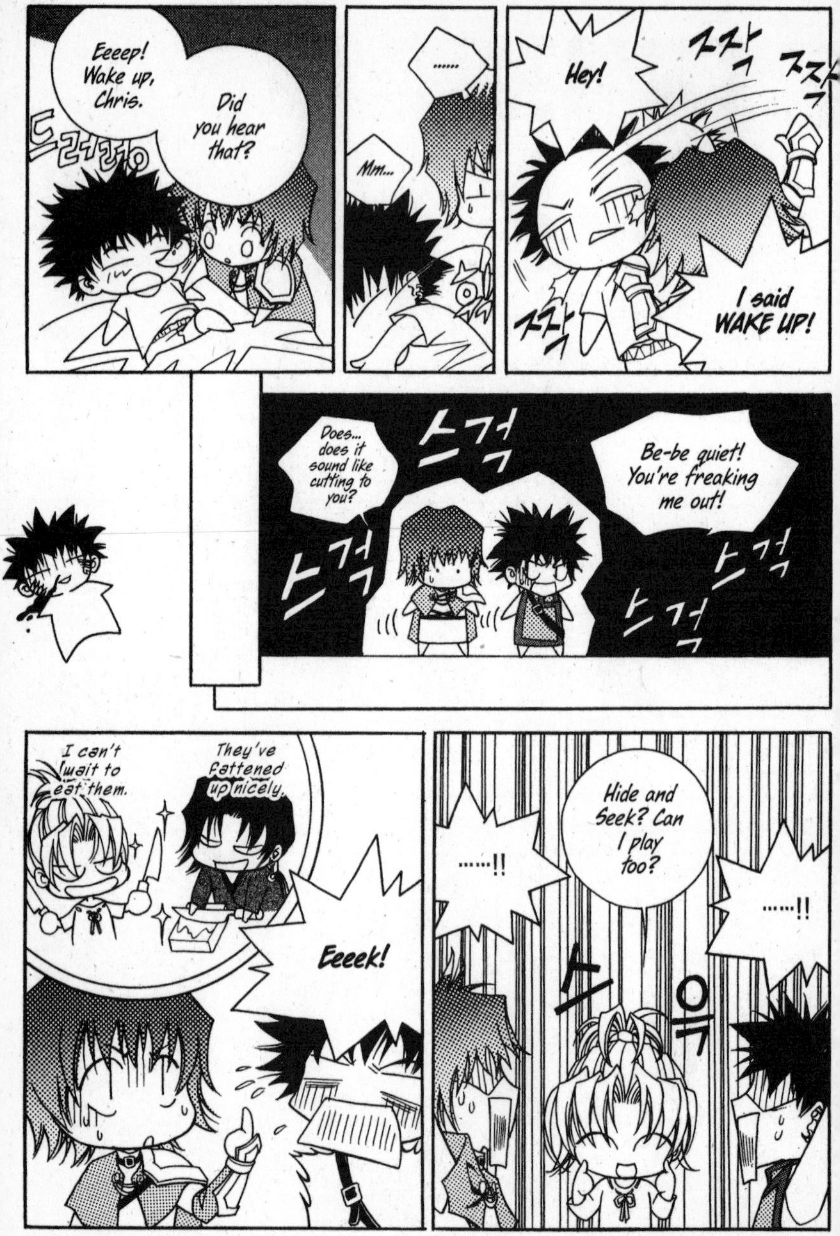
Eeeep! Wake up, Chris.
Did you hear that?
......
Mm...
Hey!
즈작
즈작
즈작
I said WAKE UP!
Does... does it sound like cutting to you?
스걱
Be-be quiet! You're freaking me out!
스걱
스걱
스걱
I can't wait to eat them.
They've fattened up nicely.
Eeeek!
......!!
Hide and Seek? Can I play too?
......!!
스윽

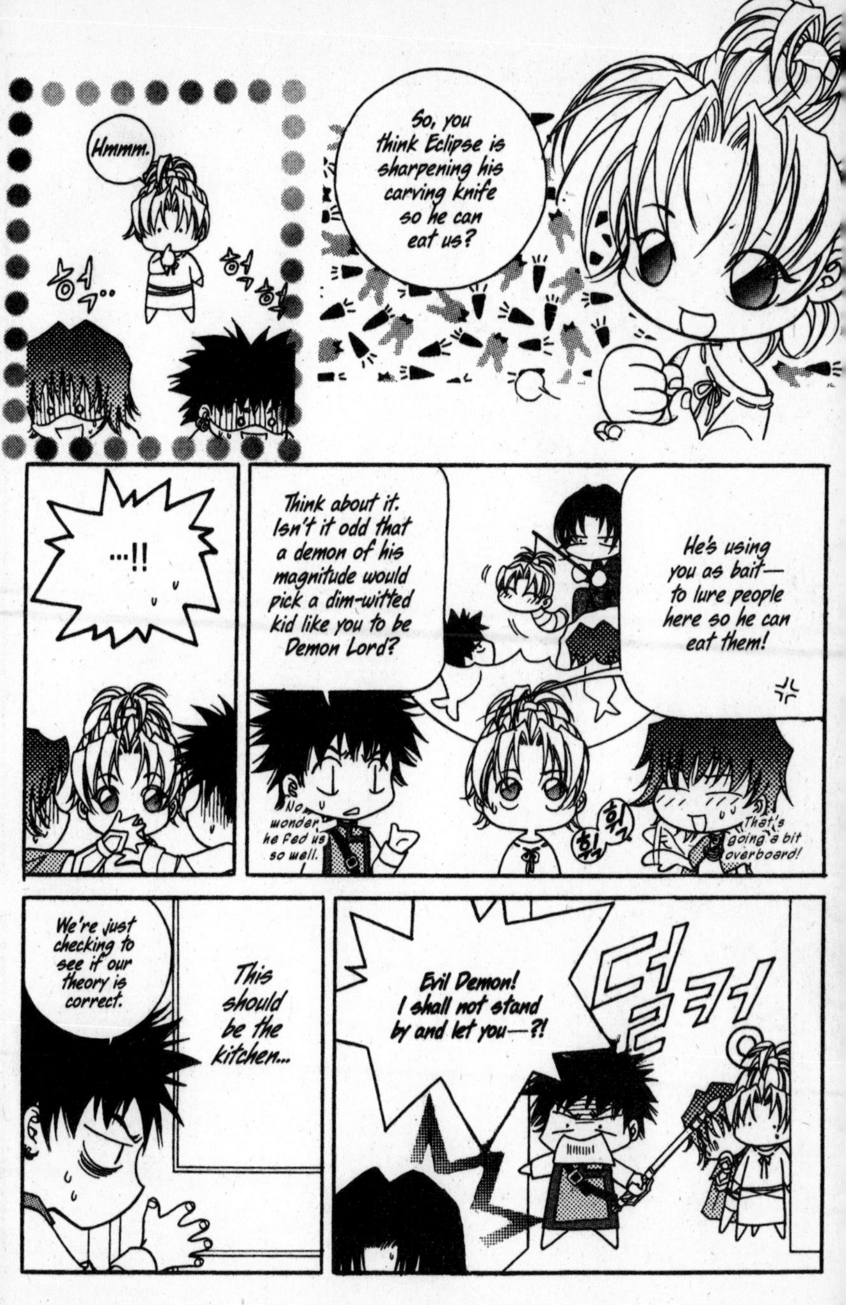
Hmmm.
So, you think Eclipse is sharpening his carving knife so he can eat us?
...!!
Think about it. Isn't it odd that a demon of his magnitude would pick a dim-witted kid like you to be Demon Lord?
He's using you as bait—to lure people here so he can eat them!
No wonder he fed us so well.
That's going a bit overboard!
We're just checking to see if our theory is correct.
This should be the kitchen...
Evil Demon! I shall not stand by and let you—?!

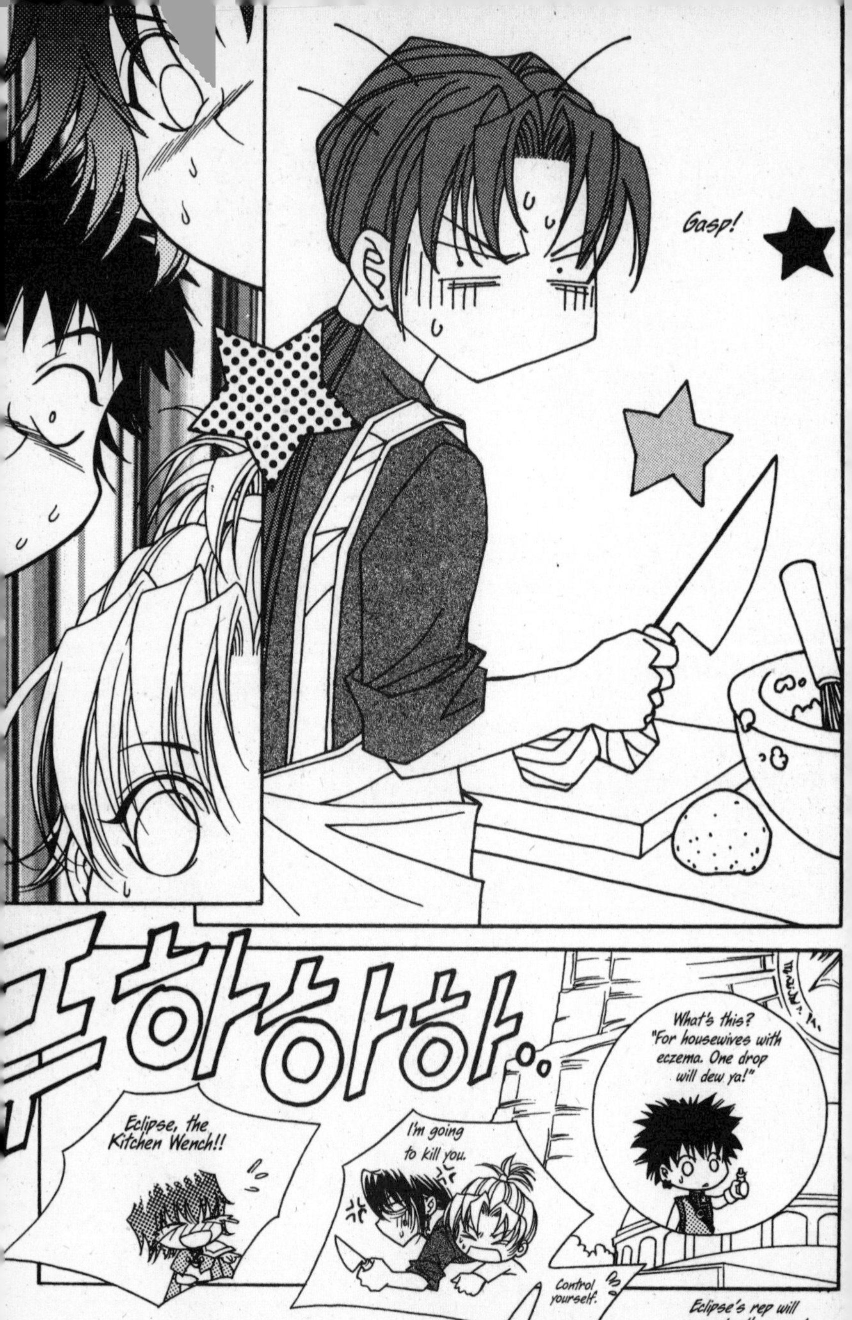
Gasp!
하하하하。。
Eclipse, the Kitchen Wench!!
I'm going to kill you.
Control yourself.
What's this? "For housewives with eczema. One drop will dew ya!"
Eclipse's rep will never be the same!

An Occurrence at the Demon Lord Castle, Part 2

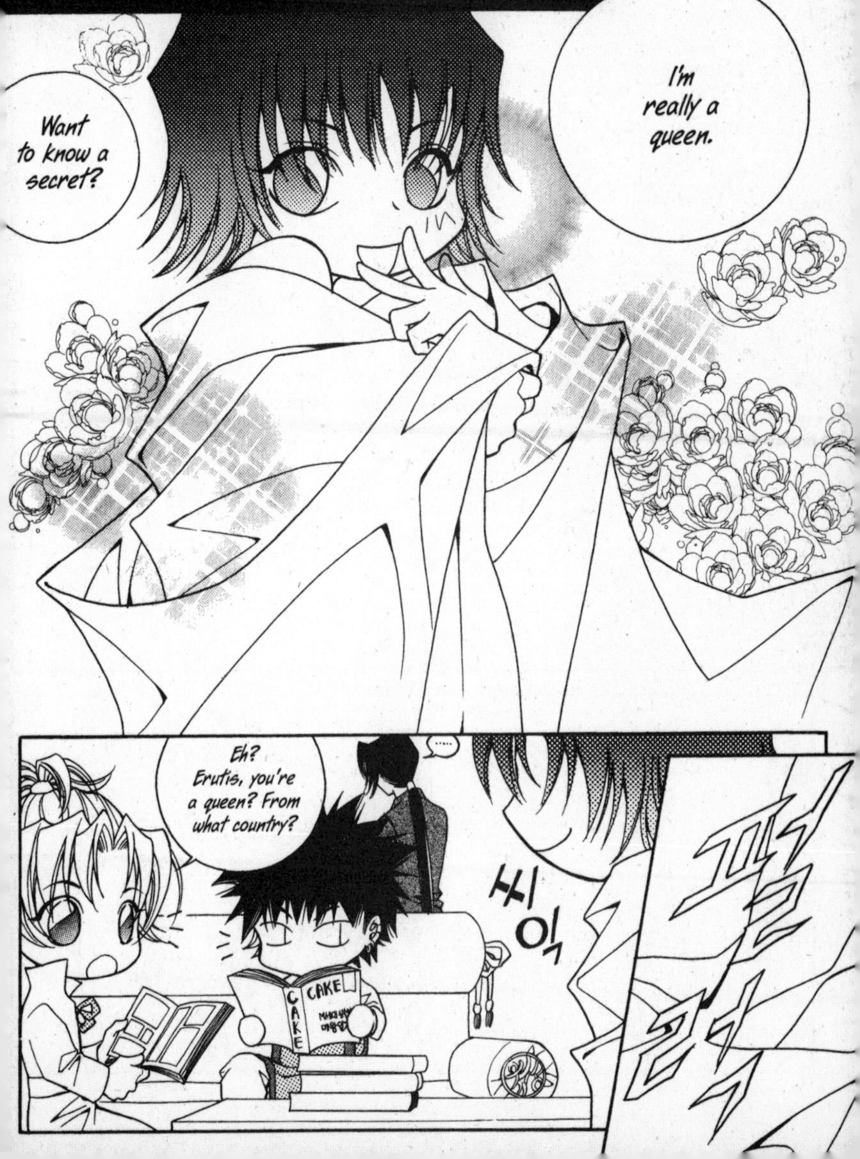
Want to know a secret?
I'm really a queen.
Eh? Erutis, you're a queen? From what country?
.....
CAKE

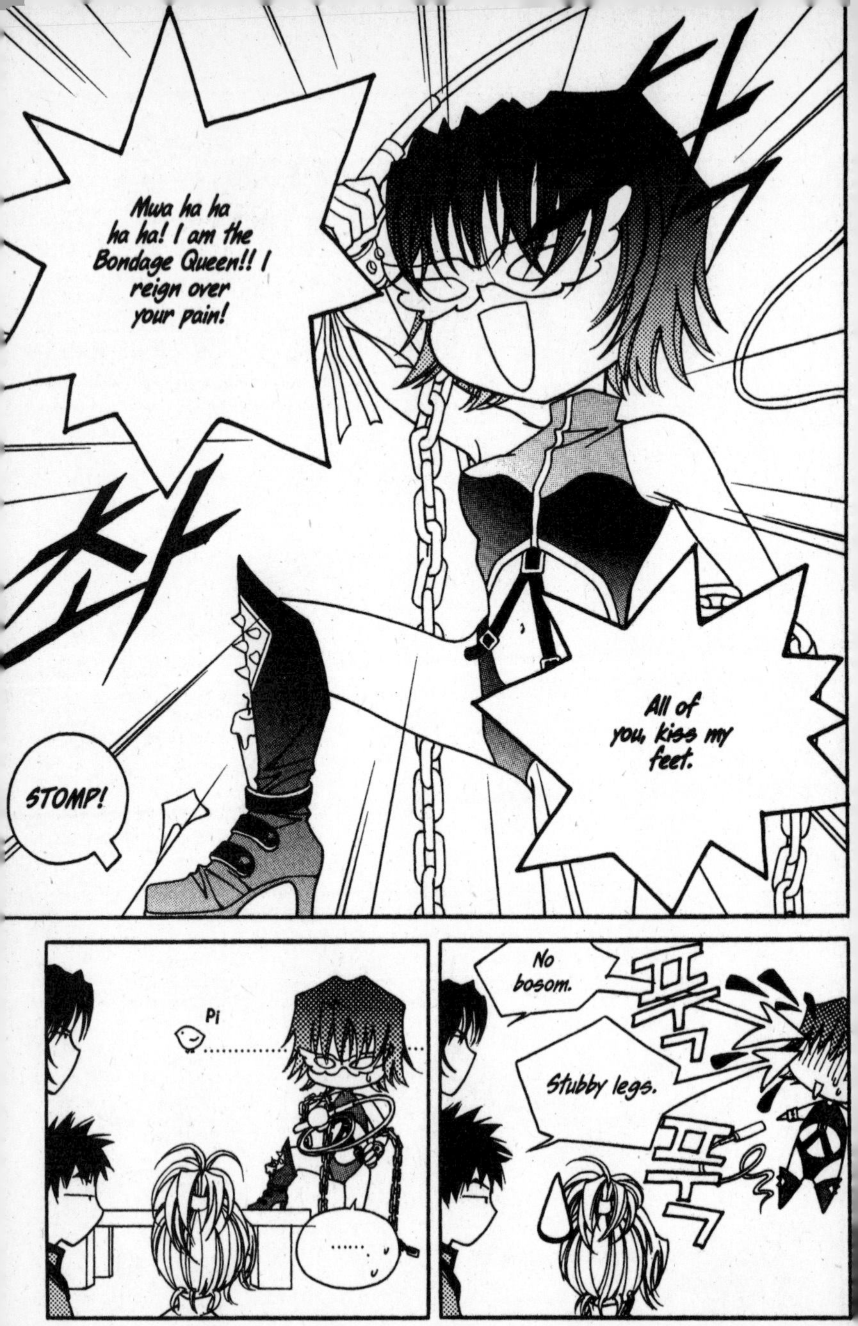
Mwa ha ha ha ha! I am the Bondage Queen!! I reign over your pain!
All of you, kiss my feet.
STOMP!
Pi
......
No bosom.
Stubby legs.

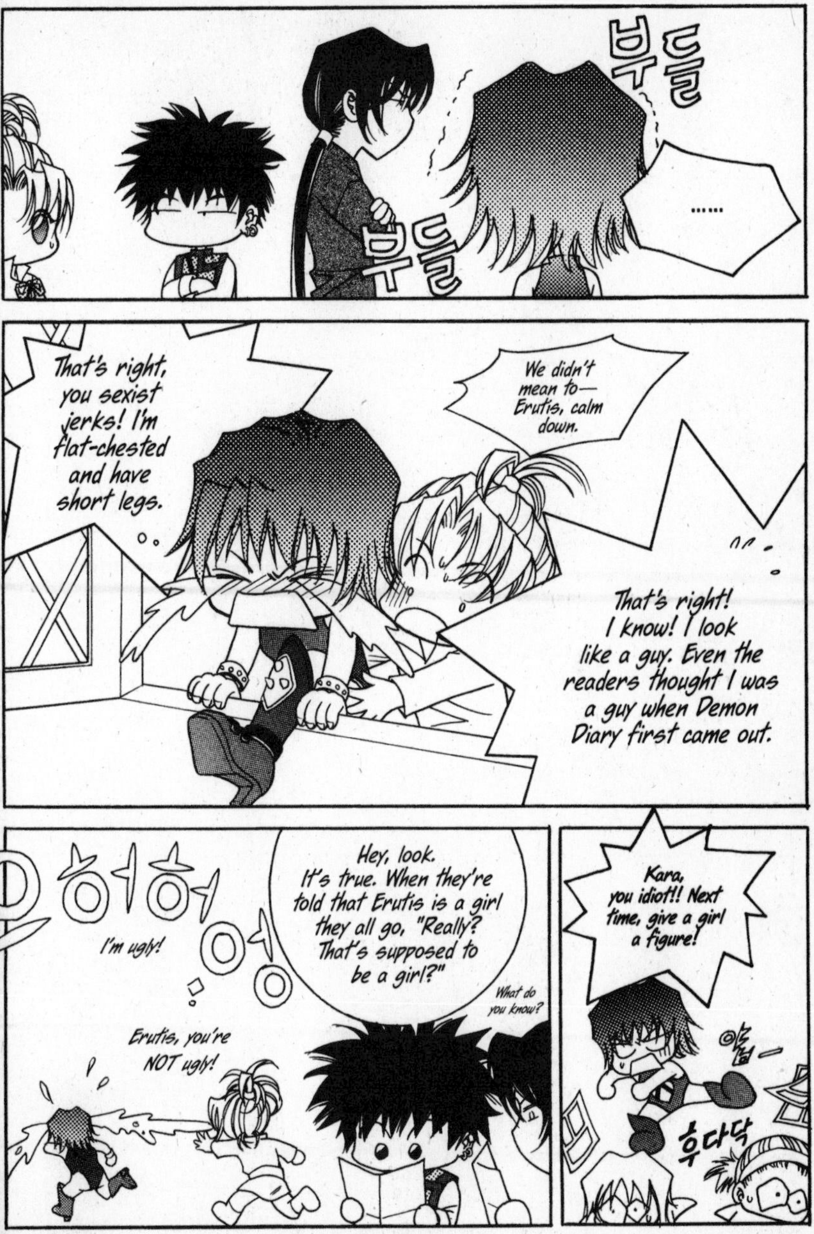
부들
......
부들
That's right, you sexist jerks! I'm flat-chested and have short legs.
We didn't mean to— Erutis, calm down.
That's right! I know! I look like a guy. Even the readers thought I was a guy when Demon Diary first came out.
으허허어
I'm ugly!
Hey, look. It's true. When they're told that Erutis is a girl they all go, "Really? That's supposed to be a girl?"
What do you know?
Erutis, you're NOT ugly!
Kara, you idiot!! Next time, give a girl a figure!
얍—
후다닥

Preview for Volume 4

The powerful and imposing Krayon, one of the five oldest demons, appears in the Demon Lord's castle with a dangerous challenge—he wants to see if young Raenef truly is a worthy heir to demon royalty. When Chris senses tremendous power coming from Krayon, who has a long, mysterious history with Eclipse, it is apparent that Krayon's real motives might not be entirely genuine. When Eclipse is confronted with the question of loyalty, which master will he choose to serve? And will Raenef, Erutis, and Chris be able to fight the good fight?

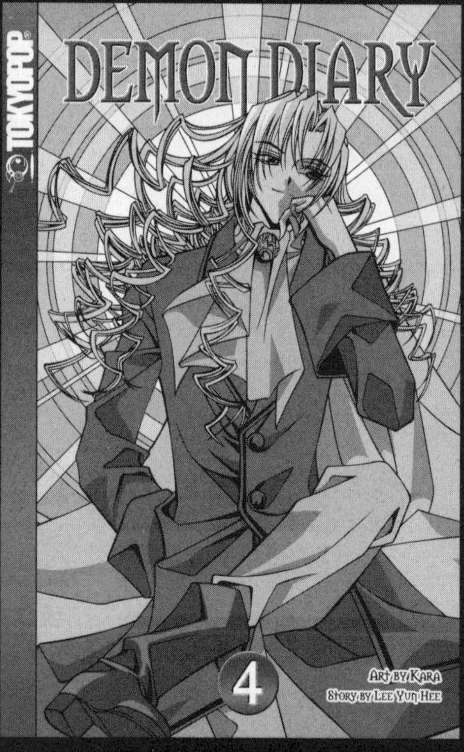
TOKYOPOP
DEMON DIARY
4
ART BY KARA
STORY BY LEE YUN HEE

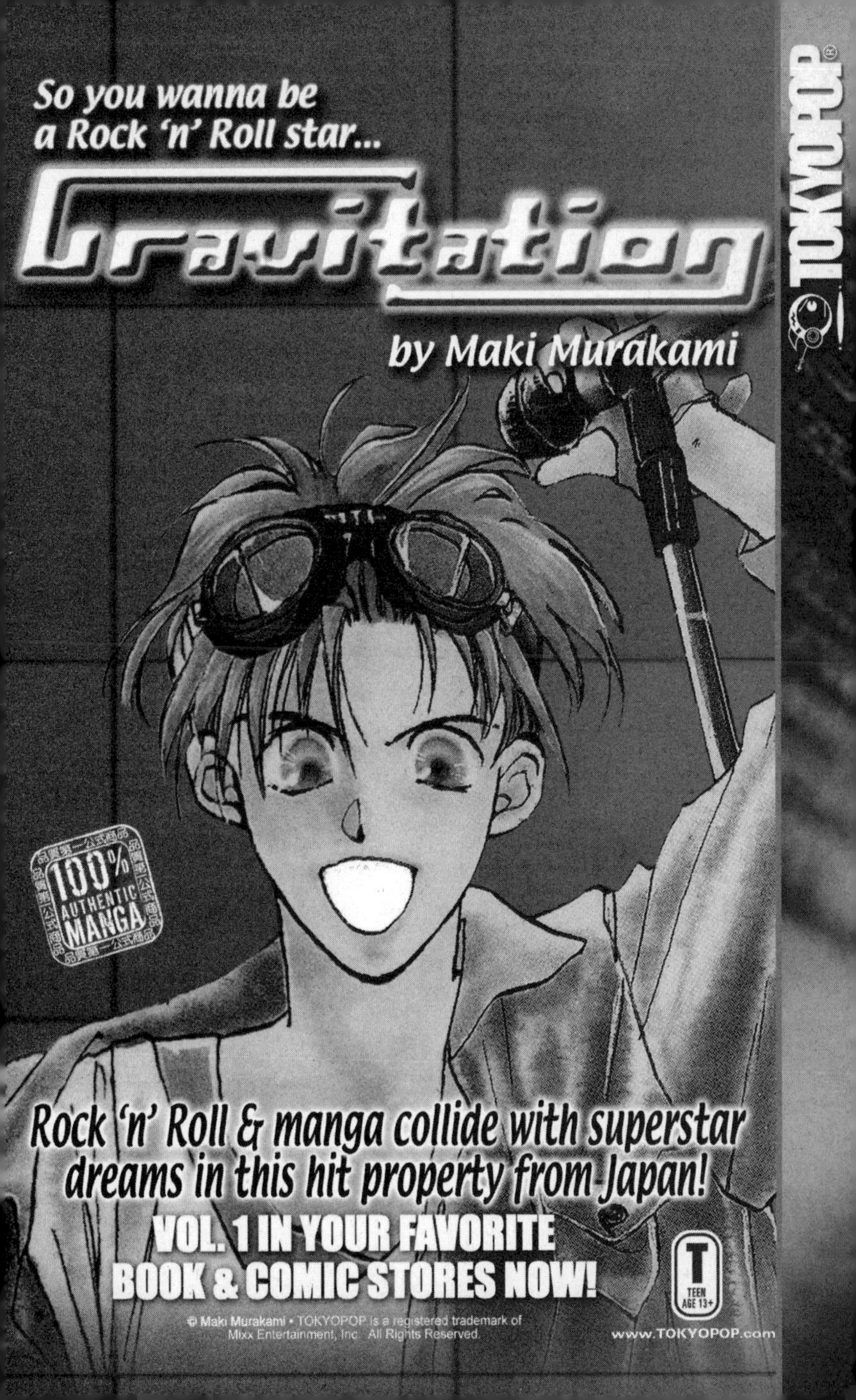

TOKYOPOP®
So you wanna be a Rock 'n' Roll star...
Gravitation
by Maki Murakami
100% AUTHENTIC MANGA
Rock 'n' Roll & manga collide with superstar dreams in this hit property from Japan!
VOL. 1 IN YOUR FAVORITE BOOK & COMIC STORES NOW!
T TEEN AGE 13+
© Maki Murakami • TOKYOPOP is a registered trademark of Mixx Entertainment, Inc. All Rights Reserved.
www.TOKYOPOP.com

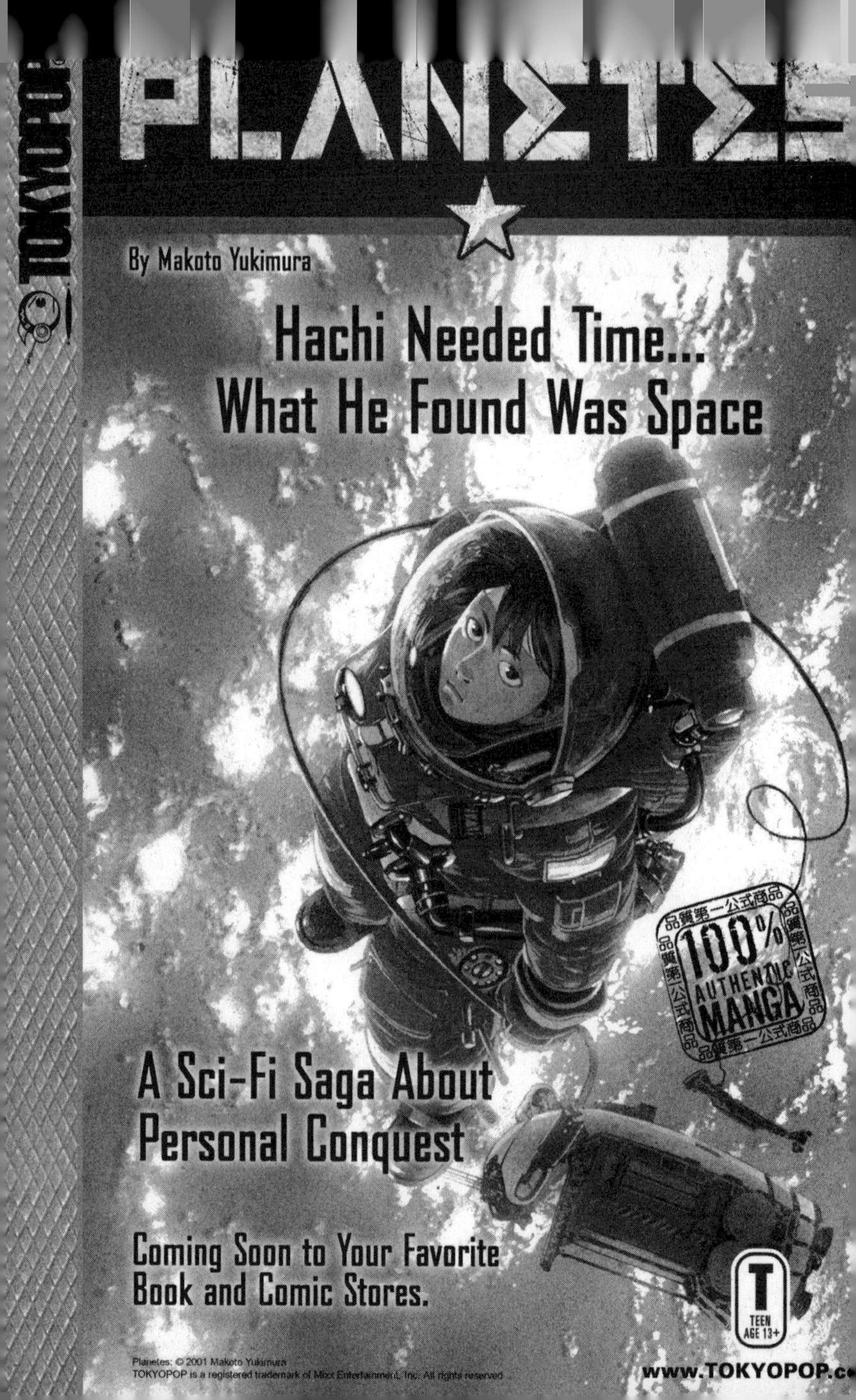
TOKYOPOP
PLANETES
By Makoto Yukimura
Hachi Needed Time...
What He Found Was Space
品質第一公式商品
100%
AUTHENTIC
MANGA
A Sci-Fi Saga About
Personal Conquest
Coming Soon to Your Favorite
Book and Comic Stores.
T
TEEN
AGE 13+
Planetes: © 2001 Makoto Yukimura
TOKYOPOP is a registered trademark of Mixx Entertainment, Inc. All rights reserved
www.TOKYOPOP.co